Murder State

MURDER STATE

California's
Native
American
Genocide,
1846–1873

Brendan C. Lindsay

University of Nebraska Press
Lincoln and London

Library of Congress Cataloging-in-Publication Data

Lindsay, Brendan C.
Murder state: California's native American genocide,
1846–1873 / Brendan C. Lindsay.
    p. cm.
Includes bibliographical references and index.
    ISBN 978-0-8032-2480-3 (cloth: alk. paper)
    ISBN 978-0-8032-6966-8 (paper: alk. paper)
1. Indians of North America—California—History—
19th century. 2. Indians of North America—Crimes
against—California. 3. Indians of North America
—California—Government relations. 4. Genocide—
California—History—19th century. 5. California—
Race relations. 6. California—History—19th century.
I. Title.
E78.C15L56 2012   979.4'04—dc23   2011044313

Set in Adobe Caslon Pro by Bob Reitz.
Designed by A Shahan.

Contents

List of Tables   viii

Preface   ix

Acknowledgments   xiii

Introduction: Defining Genocide   1

PART 1. IMAGINING GENOCIDE
Introduction   35

1. The Core Values of Genocide   43
2. Emigrant Guides   70
3. The Overland Trail Experience   109

PART 2. PERPETRATING GENOCIDE
Introduction   127

4. The Economics of Genocide in Southern California   135
5. Democratic Death Squads of Northern California   179

PART 3. SUPPORTING GENOCIDE
Introduction   225

6. The Murder State   231
7. Federal Bystanders to and Agents of Genocide   271
8. Advertising Genocide   313
   Conclusion: At a Crossroads in the Genocide   335
   Epilogue: Forgetting and Remembering Genocide   349

Notes   361

Bibliography   407

Index   427

Tables

1. Population Estimates for California, 1848–1910   128
2. Native Children Living in Non-Native Households   267

Preface

This book was inspired in part by my experiences in academia over the past seven years, including time as a university lecturer and graduate student. As I studied and taught about the history of California and the United States, I encountered many students, colleagues, and faculty unwilling to accept the argument that genocide had been committed upon Native Americans in California and the United States during the nineteenth century. Some suggested that the tremendous loss of lives was instead an unintended consequence or even a necessary evil of the advance of Western civilization or national progress. A common sentiment was that the democracy of the United States in the nineteenth century bore little resemblance to the Holocaust of the twentieth century. The urge to compare, I believe, is not uncommon; many people cannot conceive of any study of genocide without making such a comparison. I am sympathetic to the reasons why one might find it an inescapable comparison to attempt. The Holocaust is so monstrous, so recent, and so well documented (by the perpetrators, in particular) that it often overshadows all else in genocide studies. But my reason for pursuing this study does not rest upon a desire to make a comparison of genocides or measure atrocity against atrocity. Rather the motive for this book rests upon a very practical foundation.

Native Americans in California today are making inroads in matters of health, cultural renewal, sovereignty, and the reclaiming of lost lands and other rights. California voters, teachers, courts, and lawmakers thus continue to face choices that affect Native American people in the state. If my personal experience serves as any indicator of the perceptions of many of these decision makers, it is vital that people should be made fully aware that the present is a product of the past as regards Native American peoples in California, their history, present numbers, and state of affairs. A key to understanding the relationship between Native Americans and non-Natives in California is to recognize that our shared past contains a genocide of monstrous character and proportions, perpetrated by democratic, freedom-loving U.S. citizens in the name of democracy, but really to secure great wealth in the form of land against Indians cast as savage, uncivilized, alien enemies. This seems the key point to be made about how California came to exist in its present form, especially as the land we occupy today is the very same ground on which these terrible crimes took place. We Californians are the beneficiaries of genocide. I suspect few Californians today contextualize their homes as sitting upon stolen land or land gained by bloody force or artful deceits, nor do they likely consider the social and political questions of present-day Native American affairs in this light. Californians have to make informed choices in voting, educating children, and judging the remarks and policies of our political leadership where Native American affairs are concerned. I hope this study can provide such background information for making informed, intelligent decisions today.

Moreover it would not hurt for most of us to be reminded that the rhetoric of freedom, liberty, and democracy has been put to terrible use in the past, and can be so again. In nineteenth-century California many settlers needed only hubris and self-interest to make a start on genocide. For them, centralized government and its accoutrements cost too much money and took too much time to deliver on their demands; average white citizens in California could dispose of Native American people on their own and simply send the bill to the government for reimbursement. Self-described hard-working, self-sufficient, entrepreneurial citizens claimed they were doing their pragmatic best to bring peace, law, and order in the name of democracy, progress, and the fulfillment of Manifest Destiny by killing or relocating uncivilized savages in California. Indeed democracy as a political system served as a genocidal mechanism. The will of the white majority, enshrined as the sacred will of the people, drove the democratic process of creating a multifaceted campaign of genocide in California, in which Native people were starved to death, worked to death, shot to death, or so badly broken by poverty, exposure, and malnutrition as to waste away from diseases at an alarming rate. Representatives were elected, laws enacted, meetings held, and companies of volunteers empowered, all in the name of *legally* removing or exterminating Native peoples in the state. What one might describe as an appalling crime today was in the nineteenth century typically legal or at least not illegal enough to bring widespread censure or prosecution for the perpetrators. How could it, when the majority of white settlers in California promoted and supported, directly by participation or indirectly by apathy, the horrendous campaign and its outcomes?

Many tens of thousands of Native Americans perished in this genocide, but the tenacity of California's Indigenous population outlasted attempts to exterminate them, which has now allowed a recent revitalization. My hope is that this work will convince people to aid in the continued restoration of Native lands and tribal sovereignty.

Acknowledgments

The life of this book began as my doctoral dissertation at the University of California, Riverside. All told, it has been more than seven years in the making. In this time I have accumulated many debts of gratitude. I would like to thank my mentors, colleagues, friends, and family for their encouragement and support during this long and sometimes arduous process. Without their assistance this book would not have been possible.

I owe thanks to several organizations for their generous financial support, some extending back as early as the dissertation phase of this project. The American Philosophical Society supported this research with a Philips Fund Grant for Native American Studies, allowing me to travel and engage in research at several locations in northern California. The Office of the President of the University of California made me a dissertation-year fellow and allowed me the money and time to research and write without having to worry about other obligations during the final year of the dissertation process. At the University of California, Riverside, the Graduate Dean's Office provided a Dissertation Research Grant and the College of Humanities awarded a Graduate Student Humanities Research Grant, both of which made several research trips possible. The History Department and Graduate Division also provided fellowships, covering all of my time in graduate school, making my dream an affordable reality. Thank you to all of these organizations for their generosity and kind assistance. In the process of expanding my dissertation into this book I have received generous support from the California Center for Native Nations and the Rupert Costo Chair in American Indian Affairs, both located at the University of California, Riverside.

I would also like to thank the staffs of the Tomás Rivera Library at uc Riverside, the California State Archives, the California State Library, the Bancroft Library at uc Berkeley, the Meriam Library at csu Chico, the John M. Pfau Library at csu San Bernardino, the Tehama County Library, the California Military Museum, the Seaver Center for Western History Research at the Natural History Museum of Los Angeles County, the Rupert Costo Library of the American Indian at uc Riverside, and the U.S. National Archives and Records Administration, Pacific Branches (Laguna Niguel and San Bruno), for their help retrieving, viewing, and copying manuscript and microfilm collections. The Tomás Rivera Library Interlibrary Loan Department provided indispensible support in obtaining microfilms, articles, and books from libraries and collections all over the United States.

Although I have offered general thanks to all concerned, I would be remiss if I did not mention some individuals who played particularly important roles. I have many excellent colleagues and mentors in the California State University system who have helped either directly or indirectly in this process. I appreciate their support, encouragement, good humor, and the collegial atmosphere they have helped build and maintain. In particular I would like to thank Richard Johnson, John Moore, Anthony Brundage, Mahmood Ibrahim, Daniel K. Lewis, Amanda Podany, John Lloyd, John Pohlmann, Michael Smith, and Gayle Savarese at the California State Polytechnic University, Pomona, and at the California State University, San Bernardino, Pedro Santoni, Tim Pytell, Tom Long, James Fenelon, and Pam Crosson.

I have also had a chance to speak about my work in public several times, where I met other scholars and received helpful feedback. One occasion stands out. At the twenty-third annual California Indian Conference in 2008 I had the pleasure to be part of a panel on genocide that included Jack Norton, whom I had not previously met but had greatly admired for his foundational work on genocide in California. I would like to thank him for his graciousness and his enthusiasm and encouragement of my work, and also for the great work he has done, which inspired me well before I met him.

I would like to thank Matthew Bokovoy, Sara Springsteen, Cara Pesek,

Mikah Tacha, and Elisabeth Chretien at the University of Nebraska Press for their help and support. My profound thanks to Judith Hoover, whose superb copyediting on behalf of the press made the book better. I appreciate the crucial role each played in bringing this book to publication.

Clifford Trafzer, the chairperson of my dissertation committee, my friend and mentor, treated me like a scholar of equal standing from the first day of our relationship and has made me feel like a member of his family since. Though he would deny it, I owe Cliff a great debt. I intend to pay part of it by emulating his fine example as a teacher and a scholar.

Cliff and my other dissertation committee members, Michelle Raheja and Monte Kugel, helped bring my dissertation into being with their guidance and support. Sharon Salinger, my MA advisor, and Roger Ransom, whom I vainly attempt to emulate in my approach to teaching, joined the members of my dissertation committee as part of my PhD oral committee, collectively offering many valuable critiques of my project in its earliest stages. Their mentorship helped bring this book to life. I deeply appreciate their time and devotion to students, despite the demands of busy lives, research, and schedules of their own. I would also like to extend my thanks to the anonymous reviewers who critiqued my manuscript for the University of Nebraska Press. Their comments, corrections, and criticisms helped me refine my arguments, correct errors of fact, and improve my manuscript markedly. The time and energy of these named and unnamed scholars contributed to making this work better, and I fully admit that any remaining weaknesses are mine alone.

Above all I have to thank my family and friends. The Zetlmaier, Gerard, Marikian, Davoren, McSweeney, Longanbach, Dubiak, De Sagun, Dela Cruz, Arthur, and Stewart families have all made my life richer by our friendships. My late father, Charles Lindsay, my mother, Patricia Lindsay-Kieffer, my brother, Richard Lindsay, and my sisters, Erin Lindsay and Ellen Holt, all influenced who I am and what I have been able to accomplish. I can only hope I have done them justice. My wife, Anne, is the most important person in my life. Without her this book could never have happened. Words cannot express my gratitude and love.

Murder State

Introduction
Defining Genocide

Now sir I have purchased of the State of California Eden Valley with School Land Warrants. I have by the laws of this State the right of possession—I demand protection from the State. . . . I am attacked by Indians in front and the tax collector in the rear. . . . I did hope that at least our State Government could afford to investigate the grievances which I have laid before your Excellency, If thought advisable to send some Gentlemen to Eden + Round Valleys. To make such an investigation I will be happy to afford here any facilities—I may be found at Benicia.

Serranus C. Hastings to Governor John B. Weller, May 4, 1859

Judge Serranus C. Hastings was an important man in 1859, when he wrote his indignant cry for aid to the governor of California, John B. Weller. As the former first chief justice of the California State Supreme Court and the third attorney general, Hastings commanded a great deal of respect because of his office and his place as a founder of California law and order. And so on his past merits alone one could expect that the governor would take note of such a letter. But his influence did not stop there. Indeed by the time he wrote this letter, Hastings had left the bench and the prosecutor's seat, but he arguably exercised greater public influence in pursuit of his interests in private life. As Hastings admitted in the excerpt above, he came to own all of Eden Valley, which was only part of his vast real estate holdings. He also owned hundreds of head of cattle and horses and was one of the wealthiest men in the state, and so was influential in another way. His wealth lasted him the remainder of his life and allowed him to make an endowment to create the Hastings School of Law in San Francisco, which continues to operate and bear his name today. Hastings's role as a jurist of the highest order and the endower of a prestigious law school are ironic distinctions given the injustices he helped perpetrate.

Despite his wealth and notoriety, Hastings is emblematic of many of his fellow migrants to antebellum California. His indignant tone and demand for due representation and protection was not unique and can be detected in numerous letters, petitions, reports, and newspaper articles written by myriad whites from the United States emigrating to and settling in California. Indeed Hastings and many others used the democratic process and the structures of republican government to call for and execute a massive genocide of "Indians" during the second half of the nineteenth century.[1] Hastings and his fellows committed, directly and indirectly, some of the foulest depredations that men have committed against their fellow men in human history, and they did so openly and under the color of authority, legally, and in the name of freedom and democracy, with the countenance of the silent majority of the non-Indigenous population acting as interested but apathetic bystanders. In fact the landed interests of men like Hastings formed the central motive for genocide in California. The overlay of Euro-American culture, in particular its democratic institutions, made freedom, happiness, and property holding for California Indian peoples nearly an impossibility, as Euro-Americans devised a system that legally treated all Indians more like animals than people—indeed often with less respect than animals—and allowed for their legal mistreatment. Mostly this was done to achieve the goal of getting lands owned by the Indigenous peoples of California into the hands of Euro-American settlers.

It is the openly arrived at and executed genocide of Native peoples in order to secure property with which I am concerned in this study. The years 1846 to 1873 saw the creation, through the democratic processes and institutions of the people of the United States, of a culture organized around the dispossession and murder of California Indians.

This paradoxical, democratically imposed system naturalized atrocity against Indian peoples and led to their near eradication by 1900, an extinction avoided in large part by Native Americans' own strategies of resistance and noncooperation. The history of the motives and mechanisms for the genocide of California's Indigenous peoples, however, is one only slowly making itself part of the mainstream narratives of California and U.S. history. Compared to other topics in state and national history articles on and book-length treatments of the California genocide are a relative rarity. Yet important works do exist, and they informed my thinking on the subject.

Scholars have advanced important research on a variety of aspects of Native American history in California during the nineteenth century, including some that relates to the topic of genocide. Although I cannot cover all of them here, some mention of those most relevant to this study beyond the citations in the notes and bibliography are in order. Especially since the 1940s scholars have created a valuable body of research illuminating aspects of Native American genocide following the U.S. conquest of California.[2] The chief pioneer in such history is undoubtedly Sherburne F. Cook. Although not a historian by training—something not uncommon among scholars of California's Native American history—Cook nonetheless began the first serious investigations into the history of Indian-white relations in nineteenth-century California in the 1940s.[3] His demographic study of population and loss exposed the massive death rates among California Native Americans in the period of Euro-American contact and invasion and led to obvious questions about the sources of decline. Cook shone the spotlight of inquiry on the coming of European and Euro-American settlers, soldiers, and missionaries beginning in 1769. Although elements of his work have been disputed by some later scholars, his broad conclusions regarding the negative demographic consequences of white settlement for Native American peoples in California are generally accurate.[4] Other pioneering researchers followed Cook, including Jack D. Forbes and Robert F. Heizer, whose investigations into California's brutal history established the patterns and direction of inquiries, inaugurated themes to explore, and paved the way for later researchers.

Jack Forbes argued that the murder and dispossession of California's Native population was driven by the popular will of white settlers. This was an influential idea for later scholars in thinking about responsibility for genocide. As I note later in this work, thousands carried out the direct, bloody genocide. Were they the only parties guilty? In *Native Americans of California and Nevada* (1969), Forbes suggested that the crime was committed not by a relative few, but rather by the white population at large as an extension of their popular will.[5] This I too believe to be the case, a case that massive amounts of evidence bear out.

My beginning forays into these massive amounts of evidence began with the work of Robert Heizer, who documented the atrocities against Native Americans by Euro-American settlers in California in several books. In works such as *"They Were Only Diggers"* (1974) and *The Destruction of California Indians* (1974) he presented primary source evidence detailing the terrible history of Indian-white relations in the state, sometimes with powerful editorial remarks and sometimes without comment or interpretation.[6] His coverage ranged from material on Indian reservations to child stealing and treaty making and breaking. Though he did not make explicit arguments about genocide and often left the reader to contextualize much of the material, his work has been of great benefit to anyone interested in studying California's genocidal past, as has been that of Cook, Forbes, and others.

By the 1970s the work of these pioneers helped inspire a new generation of important scholarship on a variety of aspects of the California Native American experience. George Harwood Phillips's *Chiefs and Challengers* (1975) was the first of several books he wrote over a thirty-year period, exploring themes as diverse as Native American resistance and agency, the formation of reservations in California, the attitudes and actions of Indian agents, and the consequences of non-Native presence in California for Native peoples.[7] Phillips in particular provided the definitive research on the history of early California Indian reservations during this time, and I rely heavily on him for my understanding of the complex history of this subject.

Published the same year, Chad L. Hoopes's *Domesticate or Exterminate* (1975) detailed the consequences of the eighteen unratified federal treaties made with California's Native populations. Hoopes's monograph serves as the foundation of my understanding of the treaties made with a portion of Native Americans in California and then discarded by the U.S. Senate.

In 1977 William Coffer's essay "Genocide of the California Indians" appeared in *Indian Historian*; it represents what appears to be the first concise scholarly attempt to connect the term "genocide" to the history of Native Americans in California after Euro-American invasion. Beginning with Spanish conquest, Coffer argued, "nearly every method of extermination was attempted during the early days of Indian-white contact, with physical genocide as the goal."[8] Although quite brief, the essay began a scholarly conversation that has never quite faded away.

The earliest extended, detailed discussion of California Indian genocide was Jack Norton's *When Our Worlds Cried* (1979), still one of the few books with California Indian genocide as its central topic. Norton made strong, interpretive arguments using the ubiquitous evidence of genocide extant from the nineteenth century. He employed the 1948 United Nations Convention on the Prevention and Punishment of the Crime of Genocide as his investigative lens, demonstrating the genocidal character of white settlers' and miners' activities in northwestern California lands of the Hupa people, using the Convention as an unbiased, third-party model of genocide and its defining characteristics; subsequent scholars of Native American genocide, including myself, use the Convention as our model as well.[9] In this and later work Norton also questioned the role of democracy in these atrocities, a question I have taken to heart in the work that follows by fully developing arguments and evidence of the negative role played by democratic forms.[10]

Not long after Norton, Estle Beard and Lynwood Carranco's *Genocide and Vendetta* (1981) explored the so-called Indian wars of the Round Valley region of northern California.[11] Their findings suggest that Norton's example of the Hoopa Reservation was not a unique experience confined to the Hupa alone. In fact Beard and Carranco's microhistory re-exposed perhaps the most well-documented genocide (at the time, by the perpetrators, press, and government) committed against Native Americans over an extended period of time. The archives of the state and federal government and the region yielded up hundreds of newspaper articles, claims, petitions, and other documentary evidence of genocide against the Yuki and other Native peoples around Round Valley. Indeed the evidence was voluminous to the point that Beard and Carranco could not employ it all.

Years later scholars such as Benjamin Madley and Frank H. Baumgardner continued to add depth and detail to the story of Round Valley. In his microhistory, *Killing for Land in Early California*, Baumgardner augmented the story of Round Valley with much new evidence, formerly available but not previously utilized by Beard and Carranco. Although Baumgardner is not arguing that a genocide occurred in Round Valley, his work nonetheless examines the Euro-American goal of obtaining Native American lands and helps shed light on events and ideas that, in my view, are clearly genocidal.[12] In his 2008 essay, "California's Yuki Indians: Defining Genocide in Native American History," Madley used the Yuki of Round Valley as a case study of genocide. Building on the groundwork laid by Baumgardner and Carranco and Beard in assembling the narrative of events in Round Valley, and like Norton applying the UN Convention, Madley presents the events of the 1860s in Round Valley as a clear example of genocide.

James J. Rawls's *Indians of California* (1984) looked at California Native American history over a broader spectrum of time and within the boundaries of the state of California. Rawls argued that Euro-American settlers' changing perceptions of Indians were a reflection of their self-interested designs. He suggested that three major changes in perception took place in the nineteenth century because of the uses that settlers had for California's Native American population. First, Euro-Americans alleged that Indians were oppressed peoples in order to make their invasion and occupation of Mexican California look like a noble endeavor to free enslaved Indians from Mexican tyranny. Second, after obtaining California by treaty with Mexico, settlers wished to harness the labor of Indians, much as the Spanish and Mexicans had done previously, and so treated them as primitives in need of white help to organize and civilize them through labor for whites. Third, after 1870, when the demand for Native American labor evaporated, California's Indigenous peoples became obstacles to progress who needed to be relocated to reservations or exterminated. In terms of the study at hand, Rawls helps one understand some of the changing motives within the population committing genocide over time.

Albert Hurtado too has examined several aspects of the nineteenth-century California Native American experience, most prominently the labor relations of Natives and non-Natives. His seminal work, *Indian Survival on the California Frontier* (1988), examined the survival strategies employed by California's Native peoples of various regions confronted by white settlement.[13] Hurtado argues that Indigenous peoples, despite inundation by settlers, adapted and survived through accommodation, assimilation, and resistance during the Spanish, Mexican, and American periods of California history—although his work focuses primarily upon American settlement, from 1846 into the 1860s. Hurtado's work on labor relations between settlers and Native Americans was particularly valuable for me as I considered the motives behind the actions of many settlers and lawmakers in early American California.

In a style reminiscent of Heizer's earlier efforts, Clifford Trafzer and Joel Hyer published an edited collection documenting California's Native American genocide, *Exterminate Them!* (1999). Focusing on southern California during the era of the California Gold Rush, the book assembled many of the written accounts of atrocity openly available for public consumption in the 1850s and 1860s, offering present-day readers incontrovertible evidence of genocidal intent. Trafzer and Hyer's book was particularly important because of its regional focus, as most work on Native American genocide has focused on the central and northern portions of the state. *Exterminate Them!* filled an important niche and also provided revealing looks into the potential resources available to a study hoping to include southern California as an integral part. It also provided a treasure trove of starting evidence for southern California, in the same manner as Heizer's work provided for northern California.

Scholars focused on topics other than California Indians have also played an important part in my study. The controversial scholar Ward Churchill, perhaps the best-known scholar researching Native American genocide in North America, used California for evidence and examples of genocide.[14] Laurence Hauptman, usually identified with his work on the Iroquois, has also looked to California when considering the issue of Native American genocide.[15] Indeed academics in a variety of fields, particularly sociology, have employed the case of California Indians in the growing field of genocide studies. Key among these are Frank Chalk, Kurt Jonassohn, Daniel Chirot, Clark McCauley, and Bruce Wilshire, whose work has been crucial to my understanding of genocide theory, especially the roles played by various parties in genocide.[16]

The work of these scholars, as well as those cited in the notes throughout this book, are crucial to this study. Without their previous work a study of this scope and scale would truly be impossible. And it is in its scope and scale, among other reasons, that I hope this book will be of use and interest to general readers and scholars alike. I expect the book can help correct some of the historical silence heretofore prevalent in discussing genocide in California. In researching the historiography on California's Native American genocide and topics related to it, I found no study of the genocide on a statewide scale. Similarly I found no monographs examining the way a democracy behaved in a genocidal atmosphere, whether it resisted genocidal impulses or, conversely, helped to express them. I also discovered but few works examining the role played by the average white Californian in the genocide, finding that most studies focused only on those hired or volunteering to commit the actual physical acts of murder. For these reasons I believe this study may prove useful to academics.

In mainstream U.S. history texts and courses experienced by most students in primary and secondary education, the first thirty years of California history under the aegis of the United States is often approached as only slightly tarnished by the neglect of Native Americans and other nonwhite peoples living in the state during conquest or joining the influx of people during and after the Gold Rush. Sadly sometimes this history is covered as little more than the rip-roaring good times of gold miners or the triumphal joining of east and west via the Transcontinental Railroad. Better treatments have gone as far as to discuss the land dispossessions of Native Americans, but most works ignore the outright violence, punitive murders, rapes, and legalized slavery at the time. Given these silences, particularly outside of academia, many Americans today are hesitant to accept that our state or our nation has a genocidal past. Such claims run contrary to the narrow, often saccharine versions of U.S. or Californian history we have been taught. Given such conditioning, it is not surprising that a person without any detailed knowledge on the subject of Native American genocide would refuse to accept such a conclusion from a scholar having studied the matter for many years. Such are the pitfalls when dealing with a silenced history, problems I wish for this study to help solve by recasting part of the state and national narrative for mainstream readers.

Given these goals and circumstances, I examine the formative years of the state of California with a focus on proving that the genocidal neglect, abuse, and murder of California's Native American population were commonly known to Euro-Americans and their various levels of government in California, which supported genocide by apathy, if not by open participation and active public support. In short, I will argue that most property-holding, adult white male U.S. citizens in California—in other words, the electorate—at the very least tacitly supported the system of atrocities attempting to circumscribe or eliminate Native Americans in the state. Thousands of white men certainly went so far as to participate directly in genocide by murdering thousands of Indian men, women, and children. But perhaps the more important story to share is that of the hundreds of thousands of white citizens who, through apathy, inaction, or tacit support, allowed the extermination to proceed directly by violence or indirectly through genocidal policies of cultural extermination and planned neglect.

I will cover a broad span of time and work within the boundaries of what became the state of California in 1850. Beginning with the invasion and settlement of California by overland settlers from the United States in the 1840s, the study will extend into the 1870s. While the 1873 end date of the title may seem a bit arbitrary, I selected this periodization to present the era when genocide was most directly physical and observable and committed mainly by the citizenry.[17] Also by 1873, with the advent of the Modoc War in northeastern California, a grim transition of sorts had begun in earnest. In the 1870s and 1880s a shift away from direct, overt genocide to genocide perpetrated through neglect and cultural assault was in motion. The shift being a massive and complex topic on its own, here readers will find an extended conclusion and epilogue briefly providing an overview rather than engaging in a full exploration of this different incarnation of genocide, an exploration I hope to soon undertake as another project. In terms of physical location, much of California and the overland routes into it along the Santa Fe Trail and the Oregon-California Trail will be discussed. Whenever possible I have avoided including evidence that draws upon issues related to the territories nearby to California, in particular Oregon, New Mexico, Nevada, and Arizona, so as to not confuse the case.

Methodologically I employ genocide theory, especially as conceived by sociologists, and historical investigation to make a sustained case for the charge of genocide at the statewide level and at the hands of ordinary white citizens using genocide as a tool to effect a change in property ownership or to protect property already held. It is one of my purposes to ask readers to recognize the pervasiveness of hate and atrocity toward Native Americans in the history of the United States, and to recognize that even those with reservations or objections did little substantively to stop such horrors, and thus by their apathy were actually tacit supporters of genocide. It is not my intent to suggest that white settlers living in California and perpetrating genocide thought what they were doing, directly or indirectly, was wrong. In fact I would suggest that they felt much the opposite. However, they were nonetheless involved in a case of genocide by virtue of their intent and its consequences. Indeed both the feeling of rightness and the genocidal nature of these intentions and their consequences were not unique to California in the nineteenth century.

Of course the violent interactions of settlers from the United States and Native Americans began long before the American conquest of California in 1846. For most white settlers coming to California, it began with their experiences of Indigenous peoples elsewhere in the United States. One must keep in mind, however, that these interactions were not necessarily born of the reality of firsthand experience. In many instances emigrants to California previously lived where no Indians lived any longer. They had grown up in an atmosphere of imagined Indians. They knew Indians only through the memories of parents or grandparents or other relatives, or through stories told or printed of the frontier as it had been before or currently stood. These imagined experiences of Indians were powerful. Thousands of Americans going west hated and feared Indians without ever seeing or interacting with an Indian.[18] This hateful core value was the seed of destruction planted in California by Euro-Americans, nourished with greed and blood and brought to a stunted but satisfactory fruition for the planters by the near destruction of California's Native peoples. This hatred and fear of Indians and greed for the lands they occupied made genocide palatable and possible. The answers as to why hold great meaning, not just historically but for our contemporary world too.

The elements of various historical genocides, according to many genocide scholars today, have much in common even across a broad spectrum of time, whether one considers an example from the nine-teenth century or the twenty-first. The earliest writings specifically on genocide flowed from the pen of Raphael Lemkin in 1944. Lemkin was a Polish lawyer who had been working in the field of international law for well over a decade, with an emphasis on conflict and violence. He was the man in fact who coined the term "genocide." He described it as a crime "old in practice" that had continued its development in the world he now lived in.[19] In making this distinction he introduced a key point: in defining genocide he was not engaged in an imaginative enterprise, describing some new phenomenon. Genocide had been going on for centuries, and Lemkin was only connecting a term to this horrendous crime. In creating a typology to detect, identify, and even prevent future instances of genocide, he reviewed the clearest evidence available to him.

The case at hand for Lemkin was the extermination of Jews, Gypsies, communists, and homosexuals, to name several of the groups targeted for destruction by the Nazi Third Reich. In looking into this case Lemkin was looking back at evidence and analyzing it for patterns. This is a key distinction, as many people, including some scholars, have come to identify genocide as unique to the Holocaust. Scholars calling the Holocaust unique, and the singular yardstick to measure all other cases of mass murder, would do well to remember that the term as originally intended did not hold the Holocaust to be the singular example of genocide, but rather the most immediate. Not only did Lemkin broaden his thinking about genocide beyond the Nazis, but he was careful to mention earlier examples of genocide, referring back to the Ancient world and the premodern era. Indeed Lemkin connected the process of civilization in the modern era with a move away from genocidal warfare.[20]

Lemkin defined genocide as the mass murder of ethnic or national groups, past or present.[21] Unfortunately, because of a contemporary wealth of evidence related to his work in connection with the aftermath of the Holocaust, conceptions of genocide that have flowed out of his initial investigations have been applied by others as specific to the Holocaust. Rather than forming an example of genocide, it has become *the* example or *the* definition of genocide, and in the process perhaps discouraged many scholars from investigating instances of possible genocide, let alone actually referring to them as genocides. Debates over *a* holocaust versus *the* Holocaust persist. As Irving Horowitz observed, a macabre debate exists as to who is worthy of the distinction of holocaust survivor in "a bizarre struggle over language [that] remains a grim reminder of how easy it is for victims to challenge each other, and how difficult it is to forge common links against victimizers."[22]

Despite this misapplication of Lemkin's original intentions, Lemkin himself was careful to expand on the many varieties of genocide, both subtle and obvious.[23]

Lemkin carefully explained the many nuances that "the destruction of a nation or ethnic group" entailed. He made it clear that destruction need not mean physical death for all the members of a given group. Attacks on social and cultural structures, such as language and religion, or on national identity or economic vitality could be construed as genocidal as long as the end goal was the "destruction of the essential foundations of the life of national groups" for the purpose of destroying the group.[24] For the purposes of this study, practices in California by Euro-Americans such as indentures, apprenticeships, legal marginalization, and relocation will be analyzed as genocidal practices. Clearly the goal of practices such as these was an end to Indianness by negation of group identity, replacing it with Euro-American language, customs, and culture. In other words, nineteenth-century whites from the United States controlling California intended genocide in the same manner that Lemkin codified it in his definition of genocide.

Moreover Lemkin noted that immediacy in time or space was not necessarily a key feature in attaining a genocidal goal. Genocide might be committed in a very short period of time, or it might be carried out over an extended period of time. It might be subtle, through education or political negation, or obvious, by means such as removal or mass murder. Lemkin detailed many techniques of genocide that oppressor groups might apply in order to destroy a group over time. Political, social, cultural, economic, biological, physical, religious, and moral "debasements" might all serve to destroy the sinews of group cohesiveness. This process would be aimed at either the literal destruction or complete removal of a group, or its complete sublimation into the oppressor group, or a combination of these.[25]

A point of departure between Lemkin's and my research—and where I differ with many other scholars writing on genocide—concerns the central coordination of genocide. Lemkin clearly envisioned a centralized authority at the heart of the genocidal process; given the examples he chose, such as the Roman Empire and Nazi Germany, this is not surprising. Each had strong, centrally organized programs of genocide.[26] In nineteenth-century California, however, one finds genocide organized from the periphery, with the general public serving as the force pushing for Indians to be exterminated.

The genocide of Native people in California was openly executed by the white population of the state. Because this definition differs from Lemkin's and that of most other mainstream scholars of genocide, a discussion of the definition and the systematic methods of analysis that will be applied to the evidence presented here is necessary. In order to make a clear and concise argument that a genocide was perpetrated—knowingly and with the motive of obtaining land and other wealth—in the second half of the nineteenth century, I utilize the definitions and methods employed by two sets of contemporary scholars, in addition to many of the foundations set down by Lemkin.

First, the Lemkin-inspired 1948 United Nations Convention on genocide, used by the Hupa scholar Jack Norton in *When Our Worlds Cried*, offers an unbiased structure to consider the evidence. The 1948 Convention takes a broadly conceived, inclusive approach to examining and defining genocide.[27] Unlike Lemkin, it does not focus on a central authority and allows both states and individuals to be held accountable for the organization and commission of genocide. Adopted as Resolution 260 (III) A of the General Assembly on December 9, 1948, the Convention on the Prevention and Punishment of the Crime of Genocide consisted of a preamble and eight articles designed to codify the original condemnation of genocide as an abhorrent international crime by an earlier resolution of the United Nations in 1946.[28] Following the example set by Lemkin in his recognition of genocide as a crime with a long history, the 1948 Convention opened with the admission "that at all periods of history genocide has inflicted great losses on humanity."[29] As such the General Assembly resolved to stamp out the crime by codifying its parameters into international law so that nations might cooperate to bring violators to justice or, better still, prevent future occurrences.

While many of the nineteen articles help one to establish an intellectual framework for approaching the study of a potentially genocidal conflict, some are more important than others for the purposes of this study. In particular, Articles 2, 3, and 4 are key because of their definitional clarity as to what constitutes genocide, what acts related to crimes of genocide are punishable, and who is answerable for the commission of genocide, respectively.

Article 2 established that the intent to commit genocide rather than a successful genocidal outcome was the decisive factor in determining if genocide had or had not been committed:

ART. 2. In the present [1948] Convention, genocide means any of the following acts committed with intent to destroy, in whole or in part, a national, ethnical, racial or religious group, as such:
  (a) Killing members of the group;
  (b) Causing serious bodily or mental harm to members of the group;
  (c) Deliberately inflicting on the group conditions of life calculated to bring about its physical destruction in whole or in part;
  (d) Imposing measures intended to prevent births within the group;
  (e) Forcibly transferring children of the group to another group.

This is the broadly conceived definition of genocide in its most important form. It includes not just physical genocide through murder of a group, be it some or all members, but also elements of cultural genocide, psychological genocide, and economic genocide that might also be perpetrated upon people, and as much as an actual murder contribute to the death of a culture. Many of the nuances of genocide listed above coincide with the strategies employed by Euro-Americans in California in the second half of the nineteenth century. Murder, the kidnapping of children, rape, the drop in birthrates due to malnutrition and diseases introduced or exacerbated by Euro-Americans, and the mental and physical stress and anguish of having their homes destroyed and finding themselves hunted or forcibly relocated onto reservations all contributed to the near eradication of Native Americans in California between 1846 and 1873. Euro-Americans of the era, however, would argue that their attempts to eradicate savage Indians were legal and in self-defense, typically of property as opposed to life. And they would be right in the context of nineteenth-century local, state, and federal laws. In nineteenth-century American California, killing Indians was essentially legal, based on the unwillingness of prosecutors, lawmen, and courts to bring killers of Native Americans to justice. But as with other cases of genocide, justice should not be left in the hands of the murderers—something even Euro-Americans of the nineteenth century would have agreed with, as long it was not justice for Native Americans or other nonwhite groups being sought.

In Article 3 the General Assembly then defined the variations of genocide, again incorporating the idea that the intent to commit the act was enough to find one guilty:

> ART. 3. The following acts shall be punishable:
>   (a) Genocide;
>   (b) Conspiracy to commit genocide;
>   (c) Direct and public incitement to commit genocide;
>   (d) Attempt to commit genocide;
>   (e) Complicity in genocide.

Whether one actually committed genocidal acts or intended to commit such acts, or even only aided or abetted genocide, directly or indirectly, one was considered criminal and a perpetrator of genocide. The Convention goes on to state in Article 4 that "persons committing genocide or any of the other acts enumerated in Article 3 shall be punished, whether they are constitutionally responsible rulers, public officials or private individuals."

While the 1948 Convention is the basis for international laws concerning genocide today, it is not an exercise in presentism to employ the Convention as a model in a study of genocide for a period well before its creation or, for that matter, genocide being coined as a term.[30] As Lemkin did, one can look back to find the roots of genocide. Settlers from the United States in California, despite this temporal gap, conceived of what they called "extermination" in exactly the same way that many conceive of genocide today. Kidnapping children, creating conditions that promoted or exacerbated famine, creation of a slave labor system, commission of outright murder, and "education for extinction" were conceived of as ways of exterminating recalcitrant Indians or at least Indianness, the same as the United Nations Convention regards it as genocide today.[31] As there is no statute of limitations on the crime of genocide, a look back is a particularly useful exercise in the legal sense of the case presented.

The work of the genocide scholars Daniel Chirot and Clark McCauley, especially their collaboration *Why Not Kill Them All?*, provides another important framework for examining the motivations of those who commit genocide or allow it to proceed unabated, as well as some of the latest scholarship in genocide studies. An important focus inspired by their research is to recognize that while any case of genocide is an atrocity born of the hatred, fears, and desires of the perpetrators and bystanders, it is often exacerbated to new levels of terror by the agency and resistance of their intended victims. This is a key to understanding the multiplicity of motives caught up in the vortex of genocide. While all men did not share Serranus Hastings's motives of securing large property holdings, most of them shared a democratic ideology and a prejudiced view of savage Indians that let their motives coexist with his, and thus allowed the genocide to continue. Moreover as California's Native Americans were pushed into mountainous terrain, deprived of traditional food sources, and hunted, they responded by raiding livestock and attacking settlers, miners, and emigrants to keep what little they had left. Rather than recognizing these actions as resistance to their own actions, Euro-Americans perceived them as wanton, unprovoked savagery and became that much more determined to exterminate the barbarous Indians. Chirot and McCauley's examination of justifications for genocide is instructive in looking at the evidence related to the conflict between California Indians and American citizens.

Chirot and McCauley assign four main motives behind genocide: "convenience," "revenge," "simple fear," and "fear of pollution."[32] By asking one's sources how convenience, fear, or revenge figured into the actions of Americans in California, one finds their motives consistent with other perpetrators of genocide. Because I apply them in the following chapters, some background explanation of Chirot and McCauley's categories of justification is in order.

Convenience is the most common justification for carrying out genocide. In starkest terms, killing is perceived as easier and cheaper than accommodation or compensation. The weaker group stands in the way of the ambitions of the stronger group, and genocide flows out of callous pragmatism. What is more, as the lesser group puts up a resistance to the goals of the stronger, the cost of nonviolence increases and killing is seen as even more justified. Chirot and McCauley argue that more than just a financial cost needs to be considered. The moral costs are also important. Many people will see beyond the obvious material benefits of this quick achievement of goals through violence. As such it becomes necessary to justify what one might otherwise see as immoral actions. By using the example of the Cherokee Removal, Chirot and McCauley point out that Euro-Americans assuaged their consciences by pointing to the legal decisions leading to the removal, allowing them to equate law with justice and morality, and also by referring to racial differences to claim a right of superiority in their actions. Additionally Euro-Americans claimed that the removals were acts of humanity: feckless Indians could not live long in the presence of whites, and their only hope of survival was to be relocated. The deaths attendant with the removals, then, became the cost of a correct and moral decision, and certainly a much lower cost than had whites not taken such proactive steps.[33]

Revenge can be in part a strategy to show a lesser group the extreme costs of disobedience to the stronger group's whishes, in other words, to show them the price of resistance. It can also be associated with wounds to pride, honor, or self-image. Revenge can in fact defy considerations of cost or material benefits, and instead be ascribed to "anger at the thought of injured honor [which] becomes a primary motive in itself."[34] Chirot and McCauley suggest:

> When individuals feel that a wrong has been committed against them, they seek justice. Despite many efforts to separate justice from revenge, the distinction frequently gets lost. Justice easily becomes a matter of honor. And revenge pursued for reasons of honor and justice against a collective entity, be it a family, a village, a clan, a tribe, or a whole nation removes whatever moral scruples the avenger may have against massacring the supposed offenders. These offenders may have been simply defending themselves against greedy interlopers, or they may have been aggressors themselves. It no longer matters once the stronger party claims that justice is on its side.[35]

Past wrongs or injuries too, not even suffered by the present involved parties but between them in the past, can serve as motivation in extracting revenge upon a group.[36] In this way the actions of unrelated Native American peoples, present and past, informed the hatred of many Euro-Americans living in California.

Related to this sense of real and imagined wrongs is "simple fear," which is fear of one's own extermination at the hands of another, even weaker group. This can be the trigger for what Chirot and McCauley call the "genocidal impulse." People kill without reference to combatant or noncombatant out of fear of the revenge of those not dealt with immediately.[37] Women and children left alive might offer a threat in the future. In the story of California's Native American genocide, women and children—even infants—were murdered, perhaps in reference to such reasoning.

Finally, a "fear of pollution" often infects stronger groups, who sometimes kill or deport groups out of fear of contamination by that group. Included in this category are perceived threats to the purity of one group by contact with another. This can be associated with ideas about race, class, or religion.[38] Euro-Americans, including those in California, looked down upon Indians as animals, according to some a type of pre-historic aberration still present among fully developed humanity. These ideas, informed by the Social Darwinism and pseudoscience rampant in the second half of the nineteenth century, were the foundation of Euro-American thinking about relationships between whites and Indians. In California Native Americans were often treated as if they were a contagious disease, to be eradicated lest the contagion threaten whites.

These categories are not exclusive or even "mutually exclusive."[39] However, they do represent categorical justifications found in many examples of genocide. Whatever the category, one must also recognize the myopia of the Euro-Americans seized by the "genocidal impulse" in California. As white settlers pushed Native populations, Native Americans pushed back, fighting to maintain their lands, cultures, and sovereignty. Euro-Americans, however, described Indians as aggressors, recalcitrant savages unwilling to see the light of superior culture and religion, or as animals to be killed or run off because they were driven by instincts to commit depredations upon whites, despite the fact that many settlers and government officials understood their own complicity in bringing about the violent agency of Native peoples. This is of first importance in understanding the motivations of and roles played by bystanders during California's Native American genocide.

As the scholar Arne Vetlesen recently remarked, "The moral issues raised by genocide, taken as the illegal act *par excellence*, are not confined to the nexus of agent and victim. Those directly involved in a given instance of genocide will always form a minority, so to speak. The majority to the event will be formed by contemporary bystanders."[40] This idea is a common underlying principle of genocides. As Vetlesen points out, genocides are conducted typically by small groups, but with the tacit authority granted to them by the majority of their society. These bystanders are aware of the genocide and usually do nothing to stop it.⁴¹ However, they may be converted into agents themselves, either for or against the victimized group, based on the events that transpire in the course of the genocide.⁴² In the genocide under study here, the events typically converted bystanders into active agents against Native Americans. Angered or frightened by Native American responses to Euro-American action, bystanders' conversion to active genocidal agency and complicity was demonstrated by their votes, petitions, and sometimes active enrollment in murderous volunteer companies. Others, like newspaper publishers and editors, acted in more subtle ways as opinion makers and biased filters of information. At the same time a few members of the growing Euro-American population in California acted as agents in support of Native peoples, to give voice to the wrongs being committed all across the state. In particular members of the literary community, such as Helen Hunt Jackson, wrote public denouncements of the actions of Americans in California, although at a time when the greatest damage had already been done. Less vociferous but still countenancing a change in policy were newspapers published in places where Indians had effectively ceased to live, such as San Francisco and New York. In spite of these clear objections, the wealth of published accounts makes it apparent that there was a clear understanding among Euro-Americans in California that extinction was the destiny of all Indians. And judging by the overwhelming support for policies designed to bring this destiny to quick fruition, it is obvious that Euro-American bystanders lent the silent support of a democratic majority to the slaughter and neglect that devastated the Native American population. Government agents can be analyzed in a similar fashion.

Vetlesen also introduces an interesting category he calls "bystanders by formal appointment."⁴³ He cites the twentieth-century example of UN peacekeepers stationed in Bosnia, where, despite the standing UN Convention on Genocide, genocide was committed. One can discern some limited similarities to federal Indian agents and U.S. Army officers on the scene in nineteenth-century California.⁴⁴ These Indian agents and soldiers, despite their objections to the actions of white

settlers against Indigenous peoples, acted almost as third-party observers in the conflict. Restrained by state and federal laws and, for
the soldiers, orders and codes of honor, they seldom raised a hand
against a countryman, despite the obvious wrongs being committed
upon Native Americans supposedly under their charge. Ultimately,
however, the comparison cannot hold up, because these federal officers did eventually act against Indian peoples, sometimes as violently
and inhumanely as civilians did, whenever they were presented with
evidence of Indian offenses against American citizens. While some
agents and officers showed restraint, mainly these federal officials were
called upon to do their duty to the people of the United States at the
command of leaders democratically elected and empowered, and thus
were complicit in genocide as well.[45]

Employing the methodologies gleaned from Lemkin, the 1948
United Nations Convention, Chirot and McCauley, and others, I
systematically analyze primary evidence and arrive at the conclusion
that in this case, rather than a government orchestrating a population
to bring about the genocide of a group, the population orchestrated
a government to destroy a group. The evidence of genocidal intent
seems unequivocal in the main. Those Euro-Americans in California
who did not want Indians exterminated wanted them reeducated or
removed. Still others wanted access or continued access to their labor. By the definitions offered by Lemkin and the United Nations,
genocide was the clear intent of Euro-Americans in California. They
organized around central ideas prevalent at the time: Manifest Destiny and the known savagery of Indians. Rather than an all-powerful
central leader supported by a coterie of like-minded men controlling
the government, one finds that individual Americans possessed of notions of democracy, ultra-individualism, and the pioneer spirit wanted
to engage democracy to bring about their collective will to eliminate
Native Americans as obstacles to landholding and general conceptions
of wealth and security. Using petitions and letters to their representatives, votes in elections, and the long-established American tradition
of militia and volunteer companies, average white citizens called for

the extermination of Indians through nearly all of the genocidal means described by Lemkin, the 1948 United Nations Convention, and Chirot and McCauley.

In very simple terms, if genocide had existed as a term in the nineteenth century, Euro-Americans might have used it as a way to describe their campaign to exterminate Indians. While few people today would want to hear that our nation's history includes genocide, the evidence shows this as the inescapable conclusion. The California story is only one example of the Native American genocide lasting for centuries. Indeed the genocide is still ongoing if one concedes that its suppression, its silencing in mainstream U.S. history indicates complicity across time and space. While California's is but one example of Native American genocide, the fulsome evidence of it provides a firm pathway to exploring other examples in the history of the United States and the Americas.

This study is divided into three parts. In part 1, "Imagining Genocide," I discuss the historical and cultural foundations of Native American genocide by examining the way Euro-Americans imagined Indians, as well as the motives of emigrants from the United States to California during the era just prior to the war with Mexico and into the Gold Rush era. The ideas and aspirations of these thousands of would-be settlers and miners are key to understanding how Euro-Americans conceived of California, Native Americans, and Manifest Destiny as they arrived and commenced upon genocide. In a broad sense I seek to understand the foundational thinking of Euro-American emigrants: How did unthinkable acts, such as the purposeful murder of infants, become thinkable, thinkable in fact to people who valued freedom, had deep faith, loved their own children, and sought to make better lives for themselves and their families? How could otherwise good people commit such heinous atrocities, and indeed honor and celebrate those atrocities?

The answers lie in what the evidence makes abundantly clear. Many of the Euro-Americans flooding into California in these years came with existing fear, hatred, and racism directed at Indians. An important piece of evidence in examining Euro-American perceptions of Native peoples and the preconceived strategies suggested for dealing with them is printed trail guides and emigrant guides, which played upon fears of Indian savagery already present in the Euro-American consciousness. Although many emigrants on the westward trails had never met a Native American person and hailed from places that had long ago exterminated or removed their local Indigenous populations, most had clear ideas of what Indians were: dangerous savages to be feared and never trusted. Trail guides advised travel in large parties bearing plentiful weapons and ammunition ready to hand. A policy of shoot first and ask questions later was typically advised, a practice that would continue among the volunteer companies that massacred Native Americans in California. Despite these latent fears and vivid warnings, according to a recent definitive study of hundreds of trail narratives, violence was actually quite rare between Euro-Americans and Native Americans on the overland trail during the 1840s and 1850s.[46] My own research coincides with this conclusion as well.

In the more than two dozen trail narratives and diaries I examined for this study, Indian difficulties were much feared and discussed as threats to life and limb, but never encountered. It was this fear, though, that is key to our understanding of Euro-American sentiments about violence committed against Native Americans in California during the nineteenth century. Despite the lack of evidence of hostilities between emigrants and Native Americans, sensationalized accounts of Indian violence and savagery obtained by rumor or in print were vivid in the minds of many emigrants. This was apparent in their recording of fearful rumors heard along the trail. Given these rumors, emigrants were convinced by the prescriptive oral and written literature of trail and emigrant guides that it was their vigilance and strength of arms that kept Indians at bay on the trail, and not the will of Native American peoples to trade or to allow emigrants to pass unmolested. As such upon reaching California, rather than being relieved of their fears they remained woefully ignorant of the true character of the Native American civilizations whose lands they had so recently traversed. This misapprehension born of prejudice and the prescriptive literature emigrants relied upon would allow the intensity of hatred and intolerance for Indians to persist unabated upon reaching California and ready to do its bloody work.

A second fundamental element to understanding Euro-American behavior toward Native Americans is emigrants' motives and attitudes as they set out for California. By looking at the newspaper articles, trail diaries, letters, and memoirs associated with westward expansion in this era, one can see that Euro-Americans imagined California before ever seeing it. And finding it unequal to what imagination had made it, they worked to remake California into their vision once they arrived. Whether one considers the individual musings of a Euro-American emigrant as he passed over the trail and considered the country around him—his country of birth, though he had never been there before—or the ubiquitous newspaper articles rooting for the settlement of western lands and the mining of rich gold deposits in California, the spirit of Manifest Destiny ties them all together, as if one mind had conceived almost all of them: the Euro-American mind.

Once emigrants arrived in California, convinced that their vigilance and strength of arms had brought them safely across, they found a place much different from what they had read about in the papers or heard as rumors. It was a foreign place. Indeed in 1846 it was a foreign country. But the foreign place and its peoples did not deter them. In part 2, "Perpetrating Genocide," I explore how Euro-Americans set about making their dreams a reality by rapidly remaking the legal and governmental systems to replicate structures they had known in the East and Midwest. Paramount to understanding how this process evolved is understanding how Euro-Americans engaged democracy to order their new lives in California. The opening rounds of the genocide were democratically organized by settlers and miners. While California had a state militia, it was the legally organized, heavily armed local volunteer units that committed most of the murders needed to speed up the dispossession and destruction of California's Native peoples. These men, often elevated to the status of local heroes, served as the most violently effective tool of a democracy aroused against Native Americans: citizen-soldiers engaged in acts of self-interest disguised as self-preservation.

Though it may seem counterintuitive to conceive of democracy as organized for murderous purposes, it was clearly the system employed by the many roving death squads known as volunteer companies in nineteenth-century California. Each company was raised by petitioning the governor through the collection of signatures of local male voters; often these petitions were covered by letters of support from locally elected officials, such as sheriffs and mayors. Local residents signed these petitions and letters claiming the need to protect themselves and their property and asking for the legal consent of the government to "chastise" fearsome Indians threatening them. They also reminded their democratically elected representatives that their duty and loyalty lay with those who elected them. Of course Native Americans had no voice, no vote, no representatives engaged on their behalf beyond the nearly powerless federal agents assigned to handle "Indian affairs" in California. Members of volunteer companies, even those not authorized by the state, voted to elect company officers and, as described by newspapers, exemplified the best aspects of patriotism and the pioneer tradition of the United States of America. Volunteer companies set out on hundreds of such "expeditions" against what they claimed were murderous, marauding Indians. Volunteers murdered thousands of Native people, including men, women, and children. Volunteers then often enslaved or removed those who survived but did not escape. After suitable "chastisement"—a euphemism of Euro-Americans that could refer to anything from outright murder to burning villages and driving the inhabitants into homeless exile to capture and imprisonment on crude reservations—or the legal expiration of their charters, companies disbanded and pressed claims for pay and other remuneration due them by state law. Similarly men suffering losses due to Native American raids on their property submitted claims for reimbursement by the state. The state paid these claims, and then pressed its own claim to the federal government to reimburse it for these Indian-related expenses.

The federal government paid the state of California millions of dollars in the 1850s alone in settlement of such claims. Such was the system engaged by everyday white settlers serving in volunteer companies and the state militia to bring about genocide, secure lands wrested from Native peoples, and obtain more land by their absence or demise.

In part 3, "Supporting Genocide," I consider the way the organs of government and the popular press responded to the wishes of white Americans. The process of statehood and the way Euro-Americans in California imagined the role of Indians show how settlers' motives were woven into the fabric of the political and social structures of the state. Euro-Americans created the state in such a way as to make being a Native American in California basically illegal. By using the democratic process and republican government to create a self-interested legal system that favored whites, Euro-Americans imposed laws that created injustice for unrepresented Native peoples. Perhaps believing that injustice could not be conceived by the democratic will of the majority, supposing that law always be equated with justice, Euro-Americans created a veneer of respectability in their own minds, ignoring the perspectives and interests of others. Even when they enacted laws that ostensibly afforded some protection to Native Americans, the state government, courts, and white citizenry ignored their own laws whenever and wherever these laws conflicted with their self-interests. Still worse was how elected officers of the state catered to the demands of their electorate in launching offensive operations against Native peoples, while ignoring the interests of Native Americans. Native peoples were forced to represent themselves in ways that Euro-Americans conceived to be illegal, dangerous, and uncivilized. Violent resistance by Native peoples was typically condemned by Euro-Americans as Indian savagery, never admitting their own complicity in bringing Native peoples to violent agency in order to resist genocide.

The process of the legal dehumanization of California's Indigenous peoples through the actions of the three branches of the state government of California, and to a lesser degree of local and county government structures, was also an element of genocide. In particular legis-

lative acts instituted a system of Indian slavery. Even in cases where
Native peoples escaped enslavement, laws regulating everything from
fishing to labor to landholding made it difficult to make a living or even
live in California. Legislators passed laws to please their constituents,
often violating the Treaty of Guadalupe-Hidalgo and usually ignoring
the primacy of the federal government in regulating Indian affairs in
order to deliver Native American lands and resources into the hands
of covetous settlers.[47] The governors of California signed these bills
into law, called for the funding of volunteer campaigns to devastate
Native groups, and used their influence as commander in chief of the
state militia to make sure weapons and ammunition flowed to the sites
of conflict. The judiciary, far from exercising judicial review to correct
inconsistencies of state laws or conflicts with federal law or the U.S.
Constitution, supported actions against Native Americans by ignoring
the predicament they faced under an assault that if taking place between a white and white one would otherwise call criminal. Moreover
even though it was technically illegal to kill Native Americans unless in
self-defense, California law did not allow nonwhite testimony against
whites, typically allowing injustice to reign in cases where whites were
brought to trial for crimes against Native people.[48] Perhaps worst of
all, local governments acted as something akin to governing boards of
avaricious homeowners associations in response to their constituencies'
demands, as local leaders and authorities petitioned the state for arms
and money to kill Indians, set scalp and head bounties, and looked
the other way as their citizens kidnapped, raped, and murdered local
Native people. Taken together the acts of local, regional, and state
governments in California show them to be complicit in the genocide
of Native American peoples.

    The federal government in California also demonstrated complicity
in genocide. The inaction and neglect of federal officials in California,
especially of Indian agents and superintendents, helped contribute to
the abuse and murder of Native peoples. Scholars have noted the lack
of federal involvement in California when compared with other regions
of the United States, but the U.S. government did act to fuel economic

development of the new state and to make minimal expenditures on Indian welfare. The Civil War lessened federal attention to California's Native population even further. By examining sources such as reservation reports, eyewitness testimonies, and the deceptions associated with the treaty negotiations of the early 1850s, one can observe the clear preferences given to the state and its Euro-American settlers, preferences that would both embolden local whites to commit consequence-free atrocities and open public land to white settlement at the expense of Native Americans. Reports were forwarded to Washington that presaged the extermination of Native peoples, warning that such was inevitable should policies not be changed. The response from Washington was typically to send in additional observers or agents to investigate, repeating this cycle periodically without making substantive changes to abate the disaster.

Like the state, county, and local governments, the federal government scrambled to meet the demands of voters in California. Historically the federal government had primacy in ordering relations between its citizens and Indigenous populations, but especially when one considers the physical difficulty in coming to or communicating with the state prior to 1869, the state of California exerted a great deal of autonomous control over Indian affairs. Indian agents and army officers were the most immediate representatives of the federal government, and as such were direct recipients of the demands of state officials, militia and volunteer officers, and citizens to chastise or remove bloodthirsty Indians. It fell upon these individuals to make decisions in the field, typically with little guidance or funding from Washington to support their resolutions. Federal officials in California, cut off from timely aid until the appearance of the transcontinental telegraph in the early 1860s and the transcontinental railroad in 1869, were often forced to lean toward the desires of the state rather than the national interest. In a situation complicated by the fraudulent and self-interested behavior of some of these federal agents on the scene and the neglect by officials back in Washington, Native peoples could claim almost no protection under the laws of the United States in any practical or reliable sense.

Nor could Native peoples expect much assistance or sympathy in the popular press. Rather the press fueled, reinforced, and countenanced genocide. The popular press, often called the "watchdog of democracy," acted as a cheerleader for Native American genocide, as publishers demanded that local, state, and federal governments work to dispossess, displace, and destroy dangerous Indians. Newspaper editors and publishers did what Serranus Hastings did in his letter, publicly reminding their representatives of the protections due them as taxpayers and citizens. While some far from the scene of Indian-white conflict from time to time called for reform or moderation, much of the popular press was suborned, as the state and national governments were, to the will of white settlers in California. Indeed it was far more typical for newspapers to repeat the calls of their customers for the abuse, neglect, and destruction of Native peoples. Even calls for restraint are telling in terms of timing: such calls for mercy came after all the Native people in the paper's vicinity had been exterminated, removed, or so devastated as not to pose a threat any longer. Newspapers published in the heart of areas where Native populations were at odds with white settlers acted in the opposite way, being the loudest proponents of murder and publishing editorials calling upon whites to "exterminate them."[49]

Magazine and newspaper publishers and editors, poets, artists, and authors, through the printed word and image, helped reinforce the popular perception of Indians as a savage people worthy of disdain, violent treatment, and ultimately murder. However, these perceptions were not their creations alone, but were also clear reflections of the people that consumed these publications. Beginning with the Gold Rush, California abounded with newspapers, and in view of the commercial nature of the press industry, newspaper publishers and editors of the era aimed to please their customers. Stories of Indian atrocities and depredations were reported frequently—daily in some papers—and usually without any attention to the truth or consideration of the Native American perspective.[50] The voice of Native people was absent in the press; indeed I never found any attempt in any paper to interview or otherwise publish the views of Native Americans in the period under study. As was the case in terms of democratic representation, being part of a nonwhite minority meant exclusion from the printed voice the press could offer. Yet these papers contain truths all the same, and by sifting through hearsay-generated stories and comparing them with eyewitness accounts, one can find kernels of truth and learn something of the reality of Native American life in California. One can also detect the similarity of attitudes toward Native Americans expressed in the press, from south to north and east to west in California: Indians were dangerous animals, and if they could not be moved, they must be killed.

When one considers the actions of the press, state and federal governments, and the citizenry as a whole, the result was the creation of an inescapable system of democratically imposed genocide that legalized and naturalized such atrocities as acceptable, commonplace occurrences, devised to fulfill the demands of the newly minted citizenry of California, only recently come from the United States. Native peoples in California became the object of the most destructive forces that a democratic system could contrive, and only barely survived through tough, extended resistance. The combination of limited appeasement, relocation, intertribal alliances and unions, and violent resistance during the period 1846–73 allowed Native Americans to occupy a shaky foothold that slipped to an alarming nadir by 1900, yet one that proved strong enough to recover its vitality in the ensuing twentieth century.

PART I

Imagining Genocide

Introduction

The most general condition for guilt-free massacre is the denial of humanity to the victim. You call the victims names like gooks, dinks, niggers, pinkos, and japs. The more you can get high officials in government to use these names and others like yellow dwarfs with daggers and rotten apples, the more your success. . . . If contact is allowed, or it cannot be prevented, you indicate the contact is not between equals; you talk about the disadvantaged, the deprived.

Troy Duster, "Conditions for Guilt-Free Massacre" (1971)

The people of the United States were not empty vessels to be filled with fear and hatred of Indians encountered as they headed west in the middle of the nineteenth century on the overland trails or after reaching California. These emigrants already brimmed over with terror and hatred of Indians, a hatred born of their culture. Before Euro-American emigrants went west to California to settle, mine, or otherwise make their fortunes, they had clear notions of what Indians were and what should be done with them. Ingrained thinking about Native Americans brought by emigrants to California arguably proved to be more significant than anything the emigrants learned on the roads west or from experience in their new home. This was significant to the pattern of Indian-white relations in California because Euro-Americans' view of Native Americans as inhuman animals helped to minimize any vacillation over whether or not to exterminate them. To borrow the words of Troy Duster, the "conditions for guilt-free massacre" of Native Americans had long been established in the social and cultural structures of American citizens.

White Americans' belief that Native peoples were less than human was a product of several centuries of racist sentiment codified and deployed in popular culture, education, and the press. This belief was part of the psychological foundations underpinning genocide. For settlers and would-be miners heading for California, the cultural demonization of Native Americans, deployed through education, books, and articles in newspapers, was a powerful influence on the way Indians were imagined in the collective Euro-American psyche. This cultural education was predisposed to teach the hatred or suspicion of barbarous Indians. This indoctrination, beginning in childhood, produced a powerful sense of righteousness in Euro-Americans when it came to the destruction of Indians, the boogeyman figure of North America until the late nineteenth century. Such thinking has historically played an important role in other genocides.[1] Even on westward trails the education of Euro-Americans about savage Indians continued. Trail narratives and guides were used as tools to make the journey from the East to the West safely. Native Americans of course were a key concern for potential emigrants and, perhaps because of this, for writers of emigrant guidebooks. Despite significant contemporary evidence that disease and starvation would be the great challenges of the trail, the attitudes and actions of emigrants suggested that they believed Native Americans posed the greatest threat. Strangely and sadly the typical emigrant experience of months of peace with Native people while heading west in the 1840s and 1850s did little to change emigrants' minds, deeply programmed as they were.

Euro-Americans' strongly negative predispositions were created by generations of negative interactions with Native American peoples. Whether one believed that Native Americans represented man after the Fall or some lower step in the hierarchy of race being constructed in the late eighteenth and early nineteenth centuries, Native peoples represented an obstacle to the growth and health of Western civilization. According to Irving Horowitz, genocide has often been exercised as part of nation building.[2] While Horowitz was referencing instances of genocide directed by a central authority, it seems apparent that the case in California shows genocide capable of being directed peripherally through the operations of democratic, republican forms, in pursuit of the formation and unification of a new portion of the United States. Many Euro-Americans believed that these savage obstacles could be overcome only by their destruction. The belief that a group was a "hindrance" to the progress or prosperity of another group has been a common element in other cases of genocide.[3] Settlers from the United States needed only to examine the national history forged by their ancestors for confirmation of Indian savagery. A knowledge of "Indian wars" in the eastern half of North America, fought to seize the birthright of all Americans—arable land—from undeserving savage hands, was likely known to every settler. Indians were obstacles in the past, and remained so in the present of the nineteenth century.

These commonly held ideas about Indian inferiority may explain most of the problems between whites and Native Americans. One can find examples where openly committed genocide was perceived by the perpetrating society not as a crime but as attendant to the march of progress and civilization, rightfully attained.[4] By the advent of the conquest of California the historical memory of the United States was already replete with uncritical interpretations of the past, as historians focused their efforts on celebrating the pioneer past and its connections with their present. Not simply an imaginative exercise, historians' efforts were also important in the present-day justifications of the work of expansion being carried on in the nineteenth century, and perhaps into the present. According to the anthropologist John H. Bodley, "Until recently, scholars in academic disciplines such as anthropology and history observed the destruction of indigenous peoples and sometimes contributed to it with their theories of evolutionary progress."[5] Of course in the case of historians such as George Bancroft that ideology of linked progress, advancement of civilization, and obedience to God's will was encompassed by the tenets of Manifest Destiny.

Manifest Destiny was not an idea conceived in 1845 by Stephen L. O'Sullivan; rather O'Sullivan gave the name to an ideology operating in North America since Europeans had first arrived. From the earliest days of British colonial settlement along the Atlantic coast of North America, settlers felt justified culturally, religiously, and legally in inevitably moving ever westward. Part and parcel of this trend was thinking about the character of Indians as inferior, impermanent populations. Manifest Destiny, as an organizing principle and ideology, provided a context in which genocide could take place. The notion of a divinely ordained progress of Euro-American settlers westward provided an essential relief to any moral qualms about Indian genocide. As Ervin Staub remarked, "Historical examples show that ideologies, including religious ones, powerfully affect human conduct.... Unfortunately, followers of ideologies often identify some people as a hindrance ... and commit horrifying acts against these people in the name of creating the better world, of fulfilling the higher ideal the ideology offers."[6] In this case the fulfillment of Manifest Destiny and its connections with Christianity meant a North American continent home to all the best elements of liberty and democracy. Fundamentally the westward push of Manifest Destiny against Indigenous populations was part of the "us and them" dichotomy a nascent Euro-American culture in North America had created between white, Christian "Americans" and so-called heathen, red "Indians."

In a disturbing way Native Americans were essential for the success of efforts to deliver the United States into its Manifest Destiny. Native people formed the foil for Euro-American efforts and were a key concern that helped unify them, albeit in genocidal ways. The people of the United States, as they still do today, disagreed on a host of issues. But few in the middle of the nineteenth century appeared to disagree on Indian affairs, at least in places where whites and Native Americans still lived near one another. "Real or imaginary threats" can help members of a group join together, as the threats "create antagonism toward an 'enemy.'"[7] Because of the perceived dangers of Indians, Euro-Americans were able to join together in pragmatic common cause, especially as they crossed the Plains and Rocky Mountains together. Trail guides and narratives served as printed reinforcement of the need for Euro-American unity in the face of a supposedly homogeneous, savage Indian race.

Hundreds of thousands of Euro-Americans headed west in the 1840s and 1850s with recent examples to guide them. Many emigrants used printed trail guides, government reports, travel narratives in books and newspapers, or what they learned by word of mouth to help them prepare for and then cross the territorial expanse between the eastern portion of the United States and California. These sources served twin purposes that many believed crucial for the survival of emigrants on the road westward: they educated about the trail and about the nature of Native Americans living along the way. The experiences of emigrants transmitted orally and in practical literatures offered suggestions for dealing with both challenges. Guides included two notions that were commonplace in travel instructions and advice: the use of democratic forms to effectively organize the company, and the warning that all should fear and guard against the hostile Indians they were certain to meet. One need not read the actual narrative or guide, though. This type of advice was often disseminated by word of mouth based on rumors and what other Euro-Americans had gleaned from government reports, trail guides, and travel narratives. In these ways emigrants found directions, warnings, and suggestions for a successful trip.

But the way that most of the hundreds of thousands of emigrants experienced the overland trail was much different from what they might have expected based on the stories circulated back in the United States, especially in newspapers, travel narratives, government reports, and emigrant guides. The trail was not the place of constant Indian danger and depredation created in the minds of many Euro-Americans. Despite the lack of trouble along the trail, emigrants' fear and hatred of Native peoples were so strong that their typically neutral or positive experiences with them along the trail were wasted. Despite the lack of evidence of emigrant-Indian hostilities, sensationalized accounts of violence and savagery, obtained by rumor and superficial conclusions in trail narratives and guides, were vivid in the minds of many emigrants. Given this pervasive foundation, emigrants were convinced that it was their vigilance and strength of arms that kept Indians at bay on the trail, and not the will of Indigenous people to trade peaceably or allow emigrants to pass unharmed. Upon reaching California, rather than being disabused of their ideas about Native Americans, they remained ignorant and fearful of uncivilized Indians and their bad intentions. Thus Native Americans in California, with no history of conflict with Euro-Americans, became inheritors of centuries of conflict, as emigrants seem to have used the prejudices of race and lurid stories, not experience, to prejudge California's Indigenous peoples. This willful misperception contributed to the intensity of the hatred for Native Americans rampant among Euro-Americans in California, contributing fundamentally to genocide in California.[8]

Genocide as a process, then, began not in California, but in the Midwest and East. Euro-American culture shaped the views and opinions of white citizens about Native Americans as savage animals. The core belief created within many Euro-Americans that this was the essential nature of Indians was the foundational step to genocide in California. The surety of the savagery of Indians was the nucleus for the "guilt-free massacre." According to Troy Duster, "The most general condition for guilt-free massacre is the denial of humanity to the victim." By dehumanizing target groups through marginalizing them in society, by applying negative appellations, and by racial essentialism, governments or strong majority groups can create the necessary conditions to embark on a campaign of genocide supported by a sense of righteousness and morality.[9] In numbers that quickly swelled to overwhelming majorities in 1849, Euro-Americans began a campaign of genocide against the Indigenous population in an atmosphere of hate they had imported into California. Nothing about California's Native people could or would have done much to abate this; these attitudes were brought across time and space to be applied to Native Americans in California, rather than being formed in reference to them after Euro-American arrival.

This is not to say that the attitudes of Euro-Americans toward Native Americans and other nonwhite groups were held in stasis in California, once transplanted. In nineteenth-century California, Euro-Americans continued to find, identify, and codify as inferior the nonwhite population as part of the process of claiming all of California for themselves. "Kanakas," "Greasers," "Niggers," "Celestials," and "Diggers" were shunted aside through the use of democratic processes, republican institutions, and laws acceptable to the white majority. The "Digger," the pejorative name Euro-Americans gave to California's Native American population, was the most ubiquitous hindrance of all, for he possessed most of the land in California. The Euro-American past shaped the future that settlers envisioned for the Native population. Settlers went to work at dispossession through genocide with the benefit of a long cultural education about the threat of Indians and how to deal with them. After having braved the terrors of the overland trail, convinced that the people of the United States were destined by God to own California, and given all Euro-Americans believed they knew about monstrous Indians, the guilt-free massacres began with a clear national conscience. The process of arriving at this moment was effortless: Euro-American culture had insidiously permeated citizens with potentially genocidal ideas for centuries. Euro-American thinking about Indianness combined with ideas about the virtues flowing from the spread of democracy to form the foundation of genocide.

1

The Core Values of Genocide

> California to us is no further now, than Arkansas or Louisiana was
> to our fathers, and if they possessed the nerve and spirit of enterprise
> sufficient, then, to settle where nothing civilized dwelt, surrounded
> by savages, more numerous and warlike by far, than the California
> Indians, why should we falter? ... The Pilgrim Fathers when they first
> landed on Plymouth Rock, had not a more laudable object in view
> when they left the mother country, with the ostensible purpose of
> worshipping God under their own vine and fig tree, and letting others
> do likewise.
>
> **D. G. W. Leavitt**, chairman of Committee of Arrangements, quoted
> in *Arkansas Gazette* (1845)

D. G. W. Leavitt's comments were part of a published notice in the
Arkansas Gazette, one of the numerous newspapers carrying similar
calls for the formation of westward-bound emigrant companies in the
nineteenth century. In this particular case the destination proposed for
the company was California. This notice, like many others prior to the
discovery of gold in California, followed a familiar pattern of language
and ideas that most would-be white settlers of the mid-nineteenth
century would have recognized.[1] Historians and journalists in particular used evocative language that connected with a series of Euro-
American core values and ideals: the pioneer spirit, Christian religious
teachings, national destiny, and the portrayal of Indians as an inferior,
dying race. All of these were commonplace themes when addressing
the prospect of moving westward.[2] Potential emigrants confronted

with these familiar themes were subtly asked: *Are you an American or not? Are you your father's son? Do you have what it takes to fulfill your American destiny? Will you let savages stand in the way?* It is the realm of ideas and questions such as these that one must investigate before embarking on a study of how emigrants from the United States could enter California and so swiftly embark on a peripherally organized campaign of genocide. And as one makes such explorations, it becomes clear that such preconceptions of identity help explain rationalizations associated with genocide.[3]

It would be a mistake to imagine that all nineteenth-century Euro-American emigrants, by culture and temperament, were people with hearts like stone, born killers who settled all of their disputes with blood. Much evidence exists to the contrary. Yet when it came to fearsome, savage Indians, they seemed capable of many terrible exceptions. Euro-American settlers, soldiers, and miners were able to kill infants, slaughter defenseless women and children in their homes, rape women and young girls, starve entire villages into death and disease, execute prisoners without trial, and murder dozens of people at a time to avenge the loss of a single cow or horse. Like many people in history who have committed monstrous deeds, Euro-Americans in California did not see themselves as monsters but rather as righteous, religious, pragmatic people. But how and why Euro-Americans, individually and in groups and communities all over the state, popularly—either by direct action or as bystanders—came to the collective decision to exterminate the perceived threat posed by Native American peoples using the organs of democracy and republican government cannot be explained by starting with their arrival in California and working forward to the atrocities. First, one must identify how the atrocity of genocide became naturalized as something other than a horror. As one investigates, even the gold fever of the early days of U.S. rule over California cannot explain the ability of Euro-Americans to indiscriminately murder entire communities of Native people, especially given that settlers and miners handled other nonwhite competitors for gold and land in nongenocidal ways. Rather than simple greed or experiences after departing the East, it seems more likely that Euro-Americans brought with them the ideological and systematic seeds of genocide.

After an investigation of the cultural and historical precepts of the white men and women who crossed the Plains or took ship for California in the foundational years of the state, one can argue that it was a set of ideas brought by emigrants, not something learned along the way or realized once in California, that served as the bedrock for a peripherally organized campaign of genocide. These thoughts included a national history that glorified pioneers and their destruction of savages, certainty of racial superiority over loathsome Indians, the basic beliefs of Christianity, and Western legal concepts of property ownership, all of which were used to declare null and void Native Americans' rights to land and life. Euro-Americans, faced with cultures and ownership practices that differed completely from their own, openly and pragmatically decided upon the extermination—either in body or mind—of Native Americans to clear the way for the full exploitation of the land and resources of California.

Nineteenth-century Euro-Americans viewed themselves and their connections with the past in very specific ways when it came to the concept of their place in human history. These views go far in explaining how they could eventually conceive of genocide as a convenient solution to problems associated with Indigenous populations. How Euro-Americans perceived themselves and Native Americans, as well as their shared pasts, informed their dealings with Native people on the trail and in California.[4] Many Euro-Americans had never met, let alone seen, a Native American before heading to the West; this was particularly true of the tens of thousands who sailed from the East rather than make the trek overland. The point of reference for many Euro-Americans regarding Indians was likely a secondary one. The nation's history was suffused with pioneer myth and absorbed in schools through the lessons of an often idealized "American history," and also through popular culture appearing in the biased and often inaccurate stories in the popular press. Both of these sources helped establish a seemingly clear, extremely negative vision of racially inferior Indians on the frontier before emigrants ever set foot westward.[5] By studying the popular narrative of American history created by scholars, politicians, and the press in the nineteenth century, one unearths ideas about race, religion, legality, and the pioneer past permeating the American psyche. These beliefs colored the perception of both self and Indian as Euro-Americans headed for California, and helped make genocide possible.

Euro-Americans cherished a national history founded upon a pioneer tradition that recalled a heroic past. As emigrants headed west they saw themselves as extensions of earlier generations as much as people undertaking a hard journey in the present. Prior to the Mexican-American War one can discern the repetitions of the move-settle-move pattern of pioneers and settlers that pushed Indigenous populations, willing or no, relentlessly west in the face of the popularly fueled expansion of the United States. Helping Euro-Americans to understand this process and its relationship to the present were historians, politicians, and journalists. Triumphal histories of the national past written by professional historians informed citizens of how the present connected with the past in meaningful ways. Much of what these scholars had to say about the past reflected the times in which they lived, and the popular press found easy connections with the current interests of their readers. Publishers and historians found that their fellow citizens, so focused on westward expansion in the 1840s and 1850s, were ripe to establish present-day links with the glorious past.

Historians of the 1840s and 1850s reflected the popular mood of the nation and U.S. citizens' demand for westward expansion. As they crafted a popular narrative shot through with Euro-American notions of race and religion historians were thinking about the inevitability of westward expansion, the pioneer past, and the threat posed to white civilization by uncivilized Indians. These ideas about the past, race, and religion led many to believe that by right of conquest and discovery Euro-Americans had legal title to all lands they settled or made claim to on paper. Indeed the commonly held belief of many Europeans and Euro-Americans was that non-Christian nonwhites did not count as legal occupants, and so the Americas lay there for the taking. Euro-American traditions celebrating great explorers and pioneers were operating in a related way. Euro-Americans knew that Native Americans occupied the West, but they also knew that their own progenitors had not let this stand in their way; these pioneers of the past opened lands closed by Native peoples. Euro-Americans of the nineteenth century wanted to show that they were cut from the same cloth. An analysis of historians such as William Henry Bartlett and George Bancroft reveals a strong continuity between seventeenth- and eighteenth-century Euro-Americans' view of the world and the worldview of nineteenth-century Euro-Americans.[6]

The most prominent American historian of the nineteenth century, George Bancroft, sought to explain to his countrymen the connectedness of their experience with past generations. Typical of how he conceived of his scholarly mission is this passage from the introduction to his seminal work, *History of the United States of America* (1854): "It is the object of the present work to explain how the change in the condition of our land has been accomplished; and, as the fortunes of a nation are not under a blind destiny, to follow the steps by which Providence, calling our institutions into being, has conducted the country to its present happiness and glory."[7] Herein lay one of the key Western tropes of the day: that it was not "blind destiny" but divinely directed fate that guided Christians in the conquest of the New World that "Providence" had ordained. Such ideas had abounded in Western civilization for centuries, and Bancroft, like the men of the Crusades and the Reconquista, invoked the dominion of Christians over an imperfect state of nature to justify their actions. Given this it is not surprising that an undercurrent of Christian religious teachings pervaded many of the ideas Bancroft and others expressed in their works. Prominent among those implied connections was the similarity between the pioneer setting out West to righteously exploit the land and the pious aims of the Pilgrims who went west across the Atlantic for much the same reason.

In this Bancroft was much like Leavitt and his notice in the *Arkansas Gazette*. By linking the proposed journey at hand, Leavitt, like Bancroft, recalled the reader to the responsibility placed upon him by

God in the beginning of the world and codified in the Bible, to exploit an imperfect state of nature and perfect it by their labor: "And God blessed them, and God said unto them, Be fruitful, and multiply, and replenish the earth, and subdue it: and have dominion over the fish of the sea, and over the fowl of the air, and over every living thing that moveth upon the earth."[8]

Similarly a simpatico between Bancroft and Leavitt exists in their direct connection between tilling the soil and the free practice of religion, which cleverly reminded the reader to recall how the religious foundations of dominion over the Earth given to Christians might be righteously spread.[9] Bancroft in particular mixed John Locke's labor theory of value with these self-righteous ideas to create a heady brew for his readers.[10] His writings proposed to teach how and why Americans had come this far, inspiring current and future generations to keep up the noble, prudential good work. Bancroft wrote that before Euro-Americans had begun to develop the continent "the whole territory was unproductive waste. Throughout its wide extent the arts had not erected a monument. Its only inhabitants were a few scattered tribes of feeble barbarians, destitute of commerce and of political connection."[11] Certainly Genesis and Locke were both apparent to him as he wrote about the national past. These beliefs born of religion underpinned legal definitions as well.

Euro-American concepts of law and property rights were founded on English common law, which took, as Locke did, a page from the Bible in its definitions of land ownership. Moreover these property rights were tied into legal systems that criminalized offenses against property, often with severe consequences. At the same time, and despite rhetoric laced with reference to equality and justice, Euro-American legal systems did not recognize all persons equally.[12] In fact, in the case of Native Americans it often treated them in an extralegal manner. According to Michael Stohl, one of the key factors that one must overcome in transitioning from being a bystander to genocide to a preventer of it is to overcome the "ostrich problem." Because individuals believe they have "the right to be an ostrich," one must criminalize such behavior or be faced with the ability of individuals to legally ignore genocide.[13] As our jurisprudence relies upon precedent and legislation to enact laws, Native Americans, like many other ethnic groups in the United States, went largely unprotected by law until well into the twentieth century. Without legislation or precedent preventing the "ostrich problem" in the nineteenth century, Native Americans could be starved or murdered, removed or outright kidnapped, with many white witnesses claiming that such was none of their business and feeling perfectly justified in ignoring what would be heinous felonies if perpetrated on a fellow white citizen. In other words, one could legally be an accessory to murder or other capital crimes if the victims were Native Americans. One must conclude that many thousands of whites witnessed such evils in the nineteenth century, yet the Bancroftian and later narratives recalled them as something much more palatable than accessories to murder.

Bancroft identified the success of the nation in overcoming such wastelands and savages with the heroic labor of the pioneer farmer. Where the "axe and ploughshare were unknown" before, and the land wasted all of its God-given fertility by producing "magnificent but useless vegetation," came the settler to farm the land into useful fruit-fulness.[14] Bancroft and his contemporaries believed that average white hands worked the lands of North America and delivered them into a divinely commanded state of perfection. As history became increasingly professionalized in the twentieth century, many historians began to separate the myths and legends from the truth. Out of the popular rhetoric created by nineteenth-century historians, newspapers, and popular culture a very different interpretation of history emerged in the hands of twentieth-century scholars. Today one can look back at the national past and discern the very obvious ways previous generations fostered the destruction of Indigenous populations as those celebrated pioneer farmers set their sights on conquering North America, almost from the moment they set foot upon its shores.

As early as colonial times Euro-Americans coveted and counted on western expansion as both a right and a duty. One of the earliest cases can be found in the colonial charter of Virginia, where the framers listed the western boundary of the colony as the Pacific Ocean, at a time when none knew who or what might lie in between. Moreover it could not have escaped the men of Virginia that much of this territory was already possessed by the empires of France and Spain. No matter. A strong sense of entitlement already permeated these early settlers of English colonies, an entitlement not even agents of the Crown could abridge.

In 1676 Bacon's Rebellion was fomented in part because of the refusal of Anglo-American colonists to honor reserves of land guaranteed to Native peoples by treaty. The force of righteous indignation demonstrated by the actions of settlers is another relevant case in point. The waste of land incumbent in leaving territory in uncivilized Indian hands was a major part of what informed the revolutionary ethic of the Virginia planters and settlers agitated by the terms of the treaty concluded between Virginia and the Powhatan Confederation.[15] The treaty, which reserved lands for settlers and Native people in order to keep them apart, seemed like a good idea to Virginians in the 1740s: the Powhatans were extremely powerful and threatened the colonists' existence. However, as the historian Gary Nash points out, by the 1760s the deal had soured for many Americans: the number of colonists had multiplied many times and the number of Native Americans had dwindled. The settler of the 1760s was no longer in need of protection from Native Americans, who had suffered at the hands of whites and the diseases they brought with them and now found themselves in a position of inferiority twenty years later. This was so much so that Bacon's Rebellion was begun on the pretence of Indian atrocities and sought, as its main goal, to take possession of Native lands. The white-on-white portion of the conflict (both sides were killing Native Americans) that ensued was a result of Nathaniel Bacon's and his followers' willful disregard for the promises of the colonial government to Native people of peace and friendship.[16] However, at the core of these men's thinking about the land reserved for the Indigenous population was the wastefulness of it all. The inability of savage Indian peoples to develop the land to its full potential called for a change in ownership; clearly Bacon and others believed that God meant for men to deliver the imperfect land into a perfected state by exploiting it, particularly through agriculture, and by Christianizing it through their presence. The colonists believed that the Crown's actions to protect Native American rights to the land were a violation of the social contract between the government and the governed. Such appears to be the same view Euro-Americans held in the nineteenth century. Bancroft reflects this in his coverage of Bacon's Rebellion, as he almost wholly disregards the standing treaties involved, and instead presents the self-serving interpretation of events that many of those rebelling held: that issues of representation and class were at the heart of their desire to rebel, not the greed for lands reserved to Native peoples.[17]

A similar example of how history became mythologized by Euro-Americans comes to us in the following century at the termination of the Seven Years' War, in 1763. Following the Treaty of Paris the English attempted a unified Indian policy in the form of the Proclamation Line of 1763. In establishing the Line the English recognized the problems and instability created by illegal settlement on Native American lands. The Proclamation forbade settlement west of the Appalachian Mountains and was designed to both reward the Native American allies of the Crown in the war and appease the considerable number who had sided with the French. Here again the colonists ran roughshod over the agreement and acted in total disregard of the promises the Crown attempted to make to Native peoples. Despite the clear fact that colonists had helped precipitate the French and Indian War by their illegal incursions west, and even when this long, bloody war was finally ended, colonists continued to illegally move westward in spite of the Line.[18] Here too Euro-Americans of the nineteenth century continued to maintain a biased interpretation of events in the historical narrative, focusing on the acts passed by the English Parliament as evidence of disloyalty to its own people, and which gave preference to savages and flew in the face of the destiny of the Anglo-Saxon race. In fact one might have thought Bancroft was channeling the ideas surrounding

Manifest Destiny in the 1840s and 1850s when he wrote about the postwar world of 1763 living in the hearts and minds of Americans, who by virtue of victory had become the master race of North America:

> Go forth, then, language of Milton and Hampden, language of my country, take possession of the North American continent! Gladden the waste places with every tone that has been rightly struck on the English lyre, with every English word that has been spoken well for liberty and for man! Give an echo to the now silent and solitary mountains; gush out with the fountains, that as yet sing their anthems all day long without response; fill the valleys with the voices of love in its purity, the pledges of friendship in its faithfulness; and as the morning sun drinks the dewdrops from the flowers all the way from the dreary Atlantic to the Peaceful Ocean, meet him with the joyous hum of the early industry of freemen! Utter boldly and spread widely through the world the thoughts of the coming apostles of the people's liberty; till the sound that cheers the desert shall thrill through the heart of humanity, and the lips of the messenger of the people's power, as he stands in beauty upon the mountains, shall proclaim the renovating tidings of equal freedom for the race![19]

With such an attitude, triumphantly echoed above by Bancroft, it should be no surprise that white populations moving west held little or no regard for Native American rights to land. Largely based on the belief that Native Americans had a natural inability to properly exploit land and resources, English colonists looked to wrest land from what they perceived as incapable, undeserving hands. Settlers crossing treaty lines looked to their government to support their interests and protect their persons. When the government objected to the continued westward movement of colonists and imposed taxes to pay the costs of keeping the peace and maintaining a standing army in the face of these treaty violations, it appeared to colonists that their government was supporting the savage interests of Indians. Parliament, many believed, was levying taxation without benefit of representation. It was this state of affairs, real and imagined, that led many English colonists to consider rebellion against the home country.

Such situations did not fade in the wake of the Revolution. Following nationhood for the United States, politicos typically embraced expansionism, at least in public. Echoing the demands of their constituents, politicians wrote public policy that built a continental empire in the United States. The nation turned westward in the late eighteenth century and the nineteenth, becoming an empire by gobbling up the lands of France and Spain, the unstable republic of Mexico, and numerous Native American nations in North America, all the while claiming not to be tyrannical or imperialistic. Euphemisms and platitudes were offered in the spirit of what the historian Walter Nugent has called the "democratic imperialist urge" of Euro-Americans who believed they were exceptional, blessed by Providence, and possessed of unique opportunities and resources not to be squandered.[20] As unpalatable as European empires seemed to the people of the United States, a North American "empire of liberty" was an altogether different matter.

The architect of this "empire of liberty" was President Thomas Jefferson, who justified the expansion of the United States as bringing prosperity and independence to the territory purchased from France. But following the Louisiana Purchase in 1803, Jefferson acted much the same as earlier Euro-Americans had acted when he ordered Meriwether Lewis and William Clark to survey not to the westward limit of the Purchase, but all the way to the Pacific Ocean. Jefferson knew his countrymen, and his agents helped map their future. His ideas about extending America across the continent and the acquisitive behavior of Euro-American settlers both preceding and following Jefferson demonstrate that desire for land overrode all other concerns for citizen and chief executive alike. That relationship, to borrow a phrase and argument from Frederick Merk's *Manifest Destiny and Mission*, reflected the "popular will" of Euro-Americans, ensuring that politicians would either respond to their demands as an electorate or be replaced by men who would.[21] Colonists had exercised such popular will through rebellion after the government displeased them by setting limits on westward movement in 1676 and 1763.

When the U.S. government seemed to be similarly inclined in the 1840s, Euro-Americans who protested such limits were only continuing a long tradition. This produced notable, political responses, including presidential platforms founded on policies of expansionism, such as the successful presidential campaign of James K. Polk in 1844 and in his subsequent administration.

The activities of western expansion exploded in the 1830s and 1840s. Euro-American settlers in Texas wrested the territory from Mexico in 1836, creating an independent republic. Polk ran on a platform of territorial expansionism in 1844 and won. In 1845 he began to make good on his promises. The United States annexed Texas, even as Euro-American settlers in Mexican-held Alta California were hoping to bring about a similar turn of events in the near future.[22] In 1846, nominally in response to a dispute over the U.S.-Mexican border, Polk sent troops to the area, helping to provoke a war that yielded up approximately 50 percent of Mexican national territory, adding a massive amount of land to the United States. With these acquisitions the fate of many tens of thousands of Native Americans, at least in part, passed into the hands of the U.S. government and its citizenry. Far from inclusion in its prosperity or independence, the continuance of the "empire of liberty" would mean death or relocation and forced dependence for the Indigenous people of the Far West. Indeed usually only white pioneer farmers benefited from Jefferson's vision or Polk's aggressive expansionism.

Such was only right according to many of the proponents of expansionism, including many holding political office. Politicians of the mid-nineteenth century saw the acquisitions of massive swaths of territory in 1803, 1845, and 1848 as proof positive of national exceptionalism, white racial superiority, and what became known as Manifest Destiny. Despite some protest against the cost to Indigenous populations and others, white Americans typically approved.[23] A prominent case in point is that of Caleb Cushing, an influential politician and ardent supporter of expansion and racist Manifest Destiny. Speaking to the Massachusetts State Legislature in 1859, Cushing described the limits imposed by race on his vision of equality:

> We belong to that excellent white race, the consummate imper-sonation of intellect in man, and of loveliness in woman, whose power and privilege it is, wherever they may go, and wherever they may be, to Christianize and to civilize, to command to be obeyed, to conquer and to reign. I admit to an equality with me, sir, the white man, my blood and race, whether he be the Saxon of England or the Celt of Ireland. But I do not admit as my equals the red men of America, the yellow men of Asia, or the black men of Africa.[24]

According to the historian John Belohlavek, Cushing's remarks gar-nered massive approval from the assembled body, arguably evidence of the similarity of views on race held by white men in Massachusetts and beyond. Cushing perhaps was also emblematic of what many po-liticos of the era of expansion believed of Native Americans: despite some objection to specific inhumane acts against them during national expansion, he believed destruction was the unavoidable destiny of back-ward Indians in the face of the inevitable progress of white, Christian civilization.[25] As the nation expanded to include more territory, the national narratives being assembled celebrated the best elements of expansion, leaving much else silent. In particular the story of those people who were acquired with the territory remained largely untold, and when they did appear, especially in the case of Native Americans, they were cast as would-be foils to whites, challenging God's will for the prosperity and progress of the people of the United States, among whom they were not numbered in the counts of Euro-Americans.

As William Henry Bartlett, a prominent colleague of Bancroft, once remarked, American pioneers by their "skill and power were gradu-ally changing the wilderness into a garden and literally making the desert 'rejoice and blossom as the rose.'"[26] Certainly Bancroft's self-congratulatory message, that free individuals had created the greatest nation on Earth, was familiar to Bartlett. Of course one was forced to consume this confection with solemn foreknowledge that there was more work on the western horizon, and some obstacles stood on the national pathway to completing the perfection of the continent. Decades later, when Bancroft released his final revision of his six-volume history in 1882, he left unchanged his introductory statement, confident that it captured the essence of America: "The intervening years have justified their expression of confidence in the progress of our republic."[27] By then events had made him sure that the obstacle posed by Native Americans was surmountable, something that he and other writers of the mid-nineteenth century had not always been so confident about.

Bancroft was also a purveyor of popular conceptions of Native Americans as a race, conceptions that Euro-Americans had held for over two centuries. In addition to static ideas about the glorious role of the pioneer in history and the justifications for taking land based upon religion and Indian inability to exploit it, ideas about race remained basically constant. Despite years of interactions among the different racial categories Euro-Americans had created—either by imaginative exercise or flawed inductive reasoning—ideas about the basic superiority of the Anglo-Saxon race remained unchanged in Bancroft's lifetime.[28] That is not to say that how these certitudes of racial superiority were arrived at had not changed. While many people subscribed to popularly held racist ideologies of Indians as animals rather than people, Bancroft was given to expressing his racial thinking in a newly developed "scientific" view of race emerging in the mid-1800s.[29] Describing the absence of law and order among Indians, claiming that what systems they did have were governed by whim or opinion, Bancroft believed that such processes for Indians "grew out of instinct."[30] He was pursuing a different course in describing the so-called savages of North America by employing ideas associated with Social Darwinism. Rather than positioning Indians as animals and not part of the human race, Bancroft judged that humanity was composed of gradations of superior and inferior races. He argued that Indians possessed the "general characteristics of humanity" and were certainly members of the human race, but of a lower order.[31] The lower the man, the closer to animal, but the Indian was not an animal. Bancroft shared his thinking in the early volumes of his history: "The red man has aptitude at imitation rather than invention . . . [and] he is deficient in the power of imagination and abstraction . . . [and] inferior in reason and ethics. Nor was this inferiority attached to the individual: it was connected with organization, and was the characteristic of the race."[32] Such inferior peoples were incapable of bringing the continent to its full potential. An enterprise of this nature would take a superior race of people.

Historians such as Bancroft and Bartlett and politicians such as Caleb Cushing knew what this would mean for Native Americans. Bartlett described their bleak future with a pragmatic fatalism: "It has always been found, by the authorities in the frontier settlements, extremely difficult, if not absolutely impossible, to impress upon the minds of white settlers the belief, that Indians might *not* be shot down with impunity; and that *their* lives were quite as sacred as their own."[33] Even as Bartlett seemed to depart from the mainstream apathy extant in the United States when it came to the killing of Indigenous peoples, he still lamented the situation as might a frustrated parent who gives in to naughty children, as if saying, "Boys will be boys. Let them play." But moments of clarity such as these did not prevent Bartlett from reinforcing those scenarios about Indian-white relations he seemed to have condemned at times; indeed like Bancroft, he disseminated ideas about race, religion, and the national past that would inform the opinions of many Euro-Americans, predisposing them to fear and mistrust of hostile Indians.

For instance, in the same volume in which Bartlett admitted the source of trouble between Native Americans and Euro-Americans as stemming from white settlers, he also reprinted a classic example of the epitome of the great pioneer. He retold the story of a Virginian named Dale, who became embroiled in a campaign sometime around 1812 against the Creek living along the Alabama River:

Some years before, he [Dale] was attacked by two warriors, who shouted their war-whoop as he was kneeling down to drink, and rushed upon him with their tomahawks. He knifed them both, and though bleeding from five wounds, he retraced their trail nine miles, crept stealthily to their camp, brained three sleeping warriors, and cut the thongs of a female captive who lay by their side. Whilst in this act, however, a fourth sprang upon him from behind a log. Taken at such disadvantage, and exhausted by the loss of blood, he sank under the serpent grasp of the savage, and a few moments would have closed the contest. At that instant, however, the woman drove a tomahawk deep into the head of the Indian, and thus preserved the life of her deliverer.[34]

This type of anecdote—one cannot know whether it is apocryphal in whole or in part—showed readers what the best man out on the frontier might do when faced with savages. It demonstrated as well what any good woman might do in defense of her man, particularly as he had saved her from the sexual threat all Indians were known to pose to white women.[35] This story, like so many others that speak of Indian savagery, included the subtle racist and religious connections to the oldest Western stereotypes of Indians as devils or demons. Here the Creek might be the literal "serpent" in the garden Euro-Americans are trying to turn into the Eden that God has willed. While some thinkers had tried to portray Native Americans as men "after the Fall," cast from Eden, a multitude of Adams and Eves looking for direction and a helping hand toward civilization, the idea of the "noble savage" typically appealed only to those whites not living near or among Indians.[36] Perhaps convenience, often one of the main motives for genocide, demanded the representation of devilishness be propagated in communities living cheek by jowl with Native populations, and the depiction of nobility discarded.[37] Historians were helping to do both.

Stories like Dale's were more appropriate for a people attempting to destroy Indians; indeed ennobling the people you were wiping out would work at cross purposes. Contained in scholarly works, fantastic narratives of pioneers like Dale became one more type of legitimizing notion that Indians were bloodthirsty savages to be feared, to be killed as they lay asleep, even, before they might wake and do murder. Given these perceptions of Indians, not eliminating such a threat would have dire consequences. "Fear that the failure to enforce vengeance," such as Dale exacted, could "ultimately allow the enemy to regain strength and inflict further punishments."[38] A people or a society, dreading its own extermination, can embark upon genocide fearing that similar destruction awaits them if they do not act.[39] Moreover attitudes revealed in tales such as these echo the "problem of identification." If one is unable to identify with the victims of genocide, particularly because of some concept of their inhumanity or utter otherness, there is little chance that one will become anything other than a bystander to genocide, unless one becomes a perpetrator.[40] In Euro-American culture the pioneer of the colonial era was a familiar, kindred spirit possessed of qualities many emigrants would seek to emulate in the nineteenth century; so too were the Indians of both eras portrayed as culturally alien and savage, always other.

The pioneer of every generation was an honorable, heroic, and necessary figure for the advance of Euro-American civilization. Even in the late 1870s historians not only continued to perpetuate the glory of the work of the pioneer, but redoubled their efforts to celebrate pioneers in their interpretation of the American past. For example, William Cullen Bryant and Sydney Howard Gay's *Popular History of the United States* (1879) described pioneers as men whose "names were known and dreaded by the Indian tribes, as they penetrated through all this unbroken wilderness,—men who have left behind them memories of mighty hunters and of mighty fighters, whose lives were filled with romantic adventure, with deeds of daring and endurance, which have no parallel in the history of the settlement of any other part of the continent."[41] But perhaps the finest distillation of Euro-Americans' perception of their past at the close of the nineteenth century was provided by Frederick Jackson Turner.

Turner, now long discredited by historians as regards the validity of his frontier thesis, should not be laid entirely to rest.[42] Turner should live and breathe again as a primary source on the attitudes of Euro-Americans at the turn of the twentieth century. Keeping in mind that Turner was educated in the Bancroftian narrative, one can discern the many ways his ideas attempt to perpetuate the vision of Bancroft for a new, industrial age that America was entering with some uncertainty. When Frederick Jackson Turner argued that "the existence of an area of free land, its continuous recession, and the advance of American settlement, explain American development," he was attempting to explain both the exceptionalism that many felt characterized the history of the United States and also why the West, not the East, was the source of national identity and values.[43] Turner was convinced, as were many others, that the United States was different from Europe and the rest of the world: more free, more individualistic, more just, more democratic. These and other traits were not simply reflections of institutions in the United States; they were also reflections of its people and their values. In particular Turner believed that the process of moving westward had shaped and redefined popular conceptions and systems of democracy in the nation, and lived, at least in the short term, as values rooted within the population of the current and previous generations.[44] "If, indeed, we ourselves were not pioneers," he wrote, "our fathers were, and the inherited ways of looking at things, the fundamental assumptions of the American people, have all been shaped by this experience of democracy on its westward march."[45] For Turner, as for Bancroft and Bartlett, the pioneer was the ultimate icon of patriotism. But as the twentieth century dawned Turner was searching for new pioneers to conquer new frontiers.

Turner was keen to make his point in 1903 and willing to ignore much of the contrary evidence that later historians would use to sandbag his thesis.[46] The frontier was closed by virtue of having been explored and occupied, according to the superintendent of the census in 1890, and so Turner was anxious to answer the question of what would happen to the country in the absence of a place that civilization, civilizer, and wilderness could keep this positive, democratizing process going. How would the nation "conserve democratic institutions and ideals" when the frontier was no longer there to preserve these values by its interactions with the borderlands of civilization?[47] Turner concluded that industrial capitalism and its great captains were the new pioneers blazing a broader trail for other Americans to follow. And that education, political systems developed in the frontier era, and the spirit and ardor of competition would preserve and protect the ideals born of the frontier and advanced by the pioneer.[48] Turner's reassurances that Americans of every generation might still be pioneers, that the glories of the past would live on, that democracy was preserved in a new competitive frontier, were powerful ideas, especially for historians. As the historian Patricia Limerick remarked, "To many American historians, the Turner thesis *was* Western history."[49] Indeed Turner and his ideas would shape the national historical consciousness for decades. But despite such prominence, Turner fell prey to historians of later generations, particularly in the 1960s and 1970s.[50]

Turner's whitewashed, masculine, and agrarian vision of the West—which was barely west of Appalachia and not really the West at all in terms of geography—was torn apart as ethnocentric and overly nationalistic. The fall of the thesis on these grounds should be no surprise: Turner and many other Euro-Americans in the late nineteenth century were ethnocentric and nationalistic, and his historical thinking reflected this. While he may not have been right about the role of the frontier in shaping the national character or the development of democracy, he did provide a window on how Euro-Americans perceived their history and national character. Turner's thesis was grounded in a skewed reality he and his countrymen had created for themselves, not in some imaginative exercise altogether his own. Given their inability to move beyond uncritical interpretations of history, race, and culture, Turner, Bancroft, and other historians cast Native peoples as villains rather than presenting the complex history of Indian-white relations and admitting that at its foundation, it is a relationship of invaded to invader.

Yet Turner was unlike Bancroft and historians of the previous generation in at least one very important respect. Where Bancroft had featured Indians as part of the process of civilizing the continent, Turner, reflecting his times, scoured them from his narrative. Once eliminated in body, Native populations began to be eliminated in popular histories, serving the narrative as little more than speed bumps in the Euro-American race westward.[51] He presented Indians as part of the landscape that needed to be overcome in the development of the continent, like a dangerous river to be forded or thick brush to be relentlessly cut back—natural obstacles, not human ones. Indians were receivers of action, never agents themselves. Turner's ideas reflected his and others' perceptions in the last decade of the 1800s. In his nearly bloodless and Indianless interpretation of the conquest of the frontier seemed to exist the fruition of the vision of William Henry Bartlett. Bartlett had observed in 1856 that "Indian affairs have gradually dwindled in importance as our history has proceeded" and were soon likely to diminish altogether.[52] If Bartlett had written "populations" rather than "affairs," his statement would have been truer with every passing day. Turner, who came to prominence when Native American populations were at their nadir, reflected as much in his work.

The rhetoric of politicians and the arguments of historians were not the only sources shaping the fears and attitudes of Euro-Americans. The popular press, by virtue of its role as educator, entertainer, and communications nexus, served a critical role influencing American perceptions. As institutions empowered by democratic ideals, newspapers and magazines were by their very nature supposed to be disseminating truth, serving as watchdogs against tyranny. As commercial enterprises, the press was also engaged in selling newspapers. In the case of Native Americans, both aspects—protecting the nation and turning a profit—worked together seamlessly as legitimizing forces spreading popular myths and stereotypes of savage Indians. A factor that gave the press much of its power to legitimize whatever it printed, fact or fiction, was the newspaper exchange system. It was commonplace, free, and legal for newspapers to reprint each other's stories. Filling an issue with stories was thus economical and easy.[53] The drawback of this practice was that all manner of unchecked news was given the air of legitimacy by its appearance in print.[54] Native Americans in particular would suffer from the press and its practices.

Like historians, the press used connections with the past. By connecting the past with current events, it attained a type of legitimacy in support of its rhetoric in the present. As Bancroft had done, D. G. W. Leavitt's published notice in the *Arkansas Gazette* associated the long jump through the unsettled Trans-Mississippi West to reach California with the decision of the "Pilgrim Fathers" who had braved the Atlantic to leap from England to Plymouth Rock. Leavitt implied that those not up to such an ordeal were not equal to their heritage and less than American. He built upon the historical connections to the pioneers of legend that historians like Bancroft and Bartlett were promoting, doing so as he described the "laudable object" of the Pilgrims' journey as going to a land where one was free to farm and practice religion and with a mind to let others do likewise in the nineteenth century.[55] These new Pilgrims too would "go out as peaceful citizens—we have no ambition, and have no sinister purpose to subserve.—We will 'in our right hand carry gentle peace to silence envious tongues,' and if we fall, 'in great attempts 'tis glorious e'en to fall.'" Of course over their left shoulder would be slung a rifle.[56] The end result of the connections between present and past in the news media, according to the scholar Richard Slotkin, was that the "raw material of history was immediately processed, conflated with ideology and legendry, and transformed into myth."[57]

Professional journalists and publishers such as John L. O'Sullivan echoed these histories and connected them in very practical, usable ways where westward expansion was concerned. Ideology and political trends that expressed popular sentiment about westward expansion were familiar to many Euro-Americans. So too were the stories of the national narrative disseminated in newspapers. Of greatest importance when it comes to the context in which emigrants saw themselves was the celebration of the steadfast, heroic pioneers of the Early Republic, in particular their righteous battles with hostile Indians as part of their mission to subdue the wilderness and deliver it into the hands of later generations to develop and fully civilize. As the Mexican-American War and the massive territorial conquests it achieved were concluded, Euro-American emigrants were ready to add their names and histories to the nation's triumphal historical canon. They would become proof positive that the threads of the national past and Manifest Destiny were bound up and operating inseparably in the present.[58]

But one should not make the mistake of believing that O'Sullivan created the idea he called Manifest Destiny by dint of imagination, or that Americans of the time would view the evidence the way one would today. O'Sullivan created the term based on the spirit of the age he lived in and in reference to the long-standing traditions and myths of the national past, which were also familiar to his countrymen. The cases discussed earlier in this work—Bacon's Rebellion, the Proclamation Line, and the journey of the Corps of Discovery—demonstrated the historical frame of reference available to many Euro-Americans, although as I have argued, critical analysis of the way many perceived U.S. history and tradition in the nineteenth century reveals much self-aggrandizement and self-delusion at work. Still, within O'Sullivan's famous phrase, "manifest destiny," lay deeply held Euro-American ideas about themselves, their past, and their future as engaged in a divinely ordained, divinely inspired, multigenerational mission to head west by strength of faith, force of arms and ethos, and through the breaking down of all man-made and natural barriers, until the United States lay exposed in its totality, "sea to shining sea."[59]

Manifest Destiny was an amalgamation of ideas that had been prevalent well before the 1840s.[60] These ideas were simply subsumed under the rubric of Manifest Destiny. Virginians in their colonial charter claimed all the lands west of their northern and southern boundaries to the Pacific Ocean, long before the Louisiana Purchase or the Treaty of Guadalupe Hidalgo. In other words, Anglo-Americans were determined in their righteousness and wanted to head west from the colonial outset. And as they spread, generations of Euro-Americans typically demanded lands from Indigenous populations, whose perceived inability to properly exploit the bounty of the lands they occupied was due to their racial or religious deficiencies. Such was the case long before O'Sullivan voiced ideas about the inevitable, divinely ordained creation of civilization out of unimproved, savage lands. That Euro-Americans were following in the footsteps of previous generations was not a foreign idea, but rather at the heart of national identity.

Not only did the press join historians in reconstituting history in palatable forms for its citizens, but the press also disseminated ideas connecting race with national destiny and religion. In determining how genocide came to pass in such a publicly acceptable way, one of the most important trends of the nineteenth century to understand concerns the commonly held Euro-American belief that the demise of the Indian race was inevitable.[61] This conviction permeated the national consciousness and informed perpetrator and bystander alike during the subsequent genocide of Native Americans in California and in other parts of North America.

Many Euro-Americans believed the Indian was a dying race, an idea around for centuries by the time of the U.S. conquest of California. Ironically Indians had been dying almost since Europeans had landed, and despite their continued presence in North America, little doubt remained that the outcome so long presaged remained the same. According to the historian Brian Dippie, this was because Euro-Americans believed the Indian was the "representative of a condition"; as savagery died, its carrier would die too.[62] According to the racial and cultural ideas of the nineteenth century, even change or adaptation were no escape. Based on the thinking of the day, for Indians, unlike whites, to change, adapt, or accommodate new elements of other cultures into their own was to become non-Indian.[63] The Indian as other than savage was an image impossible for Euro-Americans to accept because, as Dippie pointed out, savagery and Indianness were concomitant identities. Given that Indians needed civilizing to survive, yet were incapable of being civilized, they were inevitably doomed.[64] Emigrants to California, like other Euro-Americans, likely believed in this idea wholeheartedly. As the *Northern Journal* of Yreka, California, pointed out in 1860, "[The] red men of California are fast passing away."

The article, however, could not omit Euro-American complicity in the passing: "If left to roam at will around and in the settlements, a few more years will suffice to exterminate the race. . . . Dishonest by nature, they cannot resist a disposition to pilfer, and when caught in the act, and many times on a mere suspicion, a revolver or rifle ball closes the scene."[65] Killing people doomed to a slow death might easily be viewed as humane, pragmatic, and justifiable.

Not only were Native Americans assigned a dwindling life expectancy as a people, but they were also racially stereotyped in ways conducive to genocide. Native peoples all over North America were being grouped together in racially essentialized categories created through generalization, assumptions of inferiority, and the type of inductive reasoning required to prove their savagery. This essentializing was also a key in their genocide, helping to define the group to be exterminated; many Native people killed in the genocide taking place in California and elsewhere were killed simply for membership in the group called Indians "rather than . . . [for] individual guilt or crime."[66] The stereotyping of California Indians is the most fruitful example of essentializing to focus upon.

Complicating the picture of American racial attitudes toward Indians were the regional gradations of incivility among various Native tribes.[67] California Indians suffered particularly from this habit of classification; thanks to visitors preceding the waves of settlement of the 1840s and 1850s, emigrants believed that the state's Native populations were known quantities. Often called "Digger Indians," they were ascribed the lowest position among Indians in North America and most deserving of Euro-American contempt; emigrants were cautioned *against* respecting them.[68] The *Arkansas Gazette* asked rhetorically why the pioneers of the day should shrink from the journey to California when their forefathers had defeated "savages, more numerous and warlike by far, than the California Indians."[69] Many publications circulated in the United States only served to reinforce popular misconceptions about California's Native peoples, providing background information that emigrants would absorb as the factual basis for treating Native

Americans along the way and once in California. For instance, *Parley's Magazine* of New York offered this sketch of the California's Native population: "Equally inanimate and filthy in habit, they do not possess the ingenuity and perseverance which their northern neighbors can boast; sullen and lazy, they only rouse when pressed by want."[70] In another New York publication a correspondent offered a firsthand opinion: "The Indians I have seen in California are the most miserable looking wretches I ever saw; the poorest clad, and worst featured of any of the human family under the sun. They are a poor, cowardly race of men, living upon roots, nuts, and acorns."[71] It is not surprising, then, that emigrants arriving in California accepted that such destitution was the natural condition of California's Indigenous people, despite the fact that to do so meant to ignore the reality that Spanish, Mexican, and early Euro-American damage had provided a cumulative assault on Native peoples and their livelihoods dating back to 1769.

Prevalent views that Indians were both inferior peoples and a doomed race seem to partly explain the apathy of many witnesses to atrocity. According to one East Coast newspaper, the fate of the California Indian was simply part of what Manifest Destiny reserved for the unworthy. Making a clear connection between race and fate not long after California statehood, the paper argued that the "degraded 'digger' of California, standing lowest in the scale of the aboriginal tribes of this continent," would "soon enough disappear, in the inevitable course of that destiny which has opened the long-hidden treasures of the Pacific coast to the energies of civilization."[72] Time and experience seemed to do little to change the opinions of Euro-Americans in California during the nineteenth century. Indeed one newspaper, the *Chico Weekly Courant*, summed up in 1865 how attitudes had only changed for the worse after two decades of Indian-white relations in California: "nothing but extermination" and "a general sacrifice of the whole race" would protect their livestock. "They are of no benefit to themselves or mankind. . . . If necessary let there be a crusade, and every man that can carry and shoot a gun turn out and hunt the red devils to their holes and there bury them, leaving not a root or branch of them remaining."[73] Given such hatred founded on ideas of white superiority in a racial taxonomy and the righteousness of a "crusade" that any good Christian might undertake against such "devils," it is perhaps no wonder that so many Euro-Americans could countenance, if not directly commit, genocide.

Euro-American movements westward, then, occurred within a cultural framework made up of ideas about race, religion, history, legalisms, and national destiny. Identifying these movements—to themselves, their countrymen, their government—as righteous, legal, inevitable, and ongoing extensions of the national past into the bright future were the press, politicians, and historians. This is no small thing. As the scholar Herbert Hirsch has pointed out, "Memories, and the myths and hatreds constructed around them, may be manipulated by individuals or groups in positions of leadership to motivate populations to commit genocide or other atrocities." These memories can serve as foundational justifications for genocide and be "passed from generation to generation via the process of socialization, and the cycle of violence may be perpetuated by this continuous reinforcement of the memories of the hatreds that have been passed to succeeding generations."[74] In other words, atrocity can be naturalized, made the status quo paradigm by repetitively engraving a negative, racist view of Native Americans on the national consciousness. In the years leading up to the conquest of California and the genocide to follow, disparate forms and sources of such socialization—from a nascent, self-serving national narrative to sensationalized anti-Indian stories in the press to the triumphal statements by the political apostles of national expansion, all in a largely white-supremacist society—worked to prepare the American psyche not for a brand-new campaign to destroy Indians as savages undeserving of life and property, but for the continuance of a genocidal effort already more than two centuries old.

But as we will see, another group of people and another ideology played an important role as well. The ideas and experiences of the first two decades of overland emigrants to California, in the form of published trail narratives, emigrant guides, and letters communicated in the press and in books, served for many as the most credible sources for information about California and its Indigenous population. Two keys among their instructions for other emigrants lay in the democratic systems that were to be used to maintain order and the proactive prescriptions they recommended for dealing with hostile Indians on the trails to California. Overland emigrants to California—many of them educated by trail guides or narratives—went west attempting to operate as American polities in miniature, practicing democracy in the ways they organized, legislated, dispensed justice, and protected themselves from the threat of Indian attacks, all the while identifying their movements with the movements of the great American pioneer farmers. Coming to California in the 1840s and 1850s, emigrants disconnected from their homes in the East were yet connected with their past, conditioned to expect Indian savagery and to deal with it. Indeed with Euro-Americans of the mid-nineteenth century inured to such visions of the national past and the legendary pioneer, and already acquainted secondhand with the savage Indian obstacles that stood before them and the acceptability of clearing them by violence, no doubt some of them felt a close tie of kinship to the earliest settlers of what had become the United States of America.

2

Emigrant Guides

And in fine, we are also led to contemplate the time, fast approaching, when the supreme darkness of ignorance, superstition, and despotism, which now, so entirely pervade many portions of those remote regions, will have fled forever, before the march of civilization, and the blazing light, of civil and religious liberty; when genuine *republicanism*, and unsophisticated *democracy*, shall be reared up, and tower aloft, even upon the now wild shores, of the great Pacific; where they shall forever stand forth, as enduring monuments, to the increasing wisdom of man, and the infinite kindness and protection, of an all-wise, and over-ruling *Providence*.

Lansford W. Hastings, *Emigrant's Guide to Oregon and California* (1845)

As thousands of emigrants headed west in the 1840s and 1850s, they did so with recent examples to guide them. Many emigrants used printed trail guides, government reports, travel narratives in books and newspapers, or what they learned by word of mouth to help them prepare for and then cross the territorial expanse between the United States and California. These sources served the twin purposes that many believed crucial for the survival of emigrants on the road west: they educated about the trail and the savage Indians that lived along the way and offered suggestions for dealing with both challenges. Lansford Hastings's influential trail guide, published in 1845, was just one of many printed examples; it was perhaps the most infamous of guides due to its inaccuracies. Hastings's guide included two elements that were commonplace in travel instructions and advice: the suggestion that emigrants use democratic forms to organize themselves and the warning that all should fear and guard against the hostile Indians emigrants were certain to meet. This type of advice was also often disseminated by word of mouth or in the printed form of government reports, trail guides, and travel narratives that emigrants carried west to California and Oregon. The recommendations within such resources typically provided directions, warnings, and suggestions for a successful trip. They also often contained suggestions for employing traditional Euro-American ideals in a practical manner.

The direct democracy emigrants employed as an organizing principle and as a way of legislating rules, conferring executive power, and adjudicating disputes among the company was an important tool that embodied the practical application of emigrant values. As the excerpt from Hastings's guide attests to, this notion of democracy was not only concerned with the journey at hand, but was also bound up with the goals of reconstituting the United States wherever emigrants might settle, satisfying an inevitable "march of civilization" coming to be known as Manifest Destiny. Besides using direct democracy as their organizing principle, emigrants used race, religion, history, and national destiny, discussed in the previous chapter, to explain the context of their journey and the character of the Indigenous peoples they met. When one looks back at these pieces of advice, especially when democracy figured prominently, a sense of irony seems inescapable. When one realizes that these Euro-Americans were on the path to committing genocide, convinced of their racial superiority and all the while proclaiming a love of individuality, freedom, and equality—which they saw, along with God, as their guiding light—the contradiction is clear.

For the past thirty years or more historians have had a clear picture of what life was like on the overland trails of the 1840s and 1850s.[1] Emigrants undertook long, difficult, and dangerous journeys, but only very rarely was the danger ever due to hostility from Native peoples.[2] Sifting through the tremendous amount of available evidence provided by myriad diaries, letters, memoirs, and published trail narratives, one sees that few emigrants were attacked, let alone killed, by Native

Americans.[3] The historian John Unruh Jr., a well-known overland trail scholar, has calculated that no more than 4 percent of emigrants who died on the overland trails died from attacks by Native Americans.[4] Scholars like Unruh and those who have built upon his work have calculated that up to 90 percent of the deaths on the trail were the result of disease.[5] But one would not have known this from the rumors, stories, and trail literature of the nineteenth century; one would have believed the source of the deaths along the trail had savage origins.

A common notion existed among Euro-Americans that Indians were bloodthirsty savages and the main source of death along the trails west. This idea played a determinative role in emigrant behavior on the westward trails, and later in California as Euro-Americans interacted with the Native peoples there. Based on the sparse evidence of violence by Native peoples against whites, one comes to the realization that the Euro-American conception of animal-like Indians was so negative and deeply ingrained in their national psyche that the reality of positive relations with Native Americans meant little to emigrants on the trail or completing their journey without incident. As we saw in the previous chapter, many Euro-Americans believed Indigenous populations were members of a single, dying race. Some considered them little more than obstacles to civilization and a threat to life and property, despite the fact that many emigrants to California had never seen a Native American before. Resources for making the trip overland strengthened these existing perceptions. Even after making contact with Native peoples living along the trail, the secondhand foundation of Indian hatred trumped experience gained firsthand: generations of Euro-Americans *knew* what Indians were—barely human, mostly animal—and a few months on the trail were not going to change centuries of reliable truth. The fearful, racist ideas many emigrants entertained about Native Americans when they departed the United States arrived intact in California. The ideological basis of these misconceptions had some assistance in making its way to California unscathed and unchanged.

Notions associated with the threat and savagery of Indians were reinforced by rumors encountered orally and in trail guides, government reports, and travel narratives. In particular, printed resources built on already strong cultural notions regarding savage Indians, increasing the sense of fear and distrust of Native Americans already extant in the national consciousness, the legitimizing effect of publication being more convincing than mere rumor.

The prescriptive literatures of westward expansion often contained highly inaccurate directions and suggestions for making the journey. Hastings's, for instance, was one of the more popular guides, but also inaccurate in many ways, as the fate of the Donner Party proved by its disastrous example. Hastings's suggested shortcut through the Salt Desert proved longer, more difficult, and tragic for the emigrants of the Donner Party. In his and others' guides, insufficient directions on how to organize, camp, maintain sanitary conditions, and travel in an efficient manner all had negative effects physically and psychologically during the course of a journey to California—a journey that typically took four months but in worst-case scenarios could last over a year.[6] Hardship, hunger, and disease were typical challenges for many. But it was fear of the rare result, death, that captured the attention of most.[7] And among the ways to die, even though it was in reality one of the least likely ways, emigrants feared death by murderous Indians above all.

Given this, it is not surprising these works prescribed strategies for dealing with Native Americans that presupposed a hostile relationship between emigrants and the Indigenous populations they met. These practical manuals assumed an attitude not unlike other literature of the time that dealt with Native peoples: the uncritical and unexamined view that Indians were all the same, without variation and of a single savage category, and therefore worthy of suspicion. Given these assumptions, emigrants were typically advised to arm themselves when meeting with Native Americans. Such advice probably got more people into trouble than out.

Many examples of the prescriptive literatures of westward expansion survive. Although it is impossible to recover the word-of-mouth advice emigrants heard directly, one can glimpse its pervasiveness by reading memoirs, diaries, and newspaper reports, in many of which the authors refer to their source as rumors communicated to them before leaving home or while on the trail. Moreover, as many guides were written by persons not having made the journey themselves, a significant aspect of these works can be said to flow out of hearsay or perhaps even imagination. A study of some of the well-known works circulating during the foundational period of Euro-American emigration to California reveals much about the potential influences on emigrants. These works and their adherents help one understand the divergence of ideology and experience suffered by emigrants coming to California, as they attempted to maintain trail democracies in the supposed presence of savagery. In whole or in part, works such as Richard Henry Dana's travel narrative *Two Years before the Mast*, John Bidwell's memoirs, John C. Frémont's published government report on the two westward expeditions he participated in, and Hastings's *Emigrant's Guide to Oregon and California* reveal attitudes and opinions about race, national destiny, democracy, and the future of Indian-white relations. When one examines these narratives of travel to California and compares them with the practices of emigrants following in their footsteps, one can see that many Euro-Americans in the mid-nineteenth century shared a similar mind-set with these authors.

The autobiographical account of a sea voyage to California written by Richard Henry Dana helped inform Euro-Americans of what dangers lay in store for those taking the ocean route.[8] Dana's narrative rendered Mexican California from a Euro-American perspective, offering a particularly jaundiced account of the Mexican population and government, yet enthusiasm about what opportunities lay in wait for those emigrants prepared to seize them. However, Dana cautioned that no mere trickle of emigrants would deliver the fruits of Mexican California. He implicitly called upon the spirit of what was later termed Manifest Destiny to deliver California into its fullest potential, and perspicaciously predicted a flood of settlement from the United States, although his reason was based on abject racism rather than the actual draw, greed for gold.

Highly biased, racially denigrating prose characterized Dana's account, as he referenced a land like Eden filled with the unwashed, undeserving, and culturally backward Indians and Mexicans he believed occupied California in the middle of the 1830s. Calling the Indigenous people he met speakers of "complete *slabber*" that "cannot have been the language of Montezuma," he launched some of the first Euro-American print attacks against dirty, naked Indian peoples in California, who he argued were little more than a slave race for the Mexicans. At the same time he criticized the poor attempts at justice and democracy of the Mexican government, and the people as foolish, uneducated, immoral, and lascivious.[9]

Indeed Dana's Eden was filled with undeserving and civilizationally impotent peoples who could never exploit the land properly. This was the Anglo-American concept of landownership in its simplest, Lockean terms: to own property one had to exploit it; failing to do so, one was subject to its loss. A flood of Euro-Americans would be needed to bring true democracy, as anything less in numbers, Dana claimed, would fall victim to the "California fever" brought there by the Spanish, the "laziness" that would soon affect them by prolonged contact with Mexican California.[10] If California was to beat the disease, the civilization of the United States would need to be transplanted. As the historian James Rawls has argued, this vision of California and its people made a lasting impression. Many Americans looked upon their early dealings with California's Native population as a liberating, civilizing exercise to save victimized Indians from depraved papists and backward Hispanic culture.[11]

On top of the negative portrayals he included, Dana also provided a rosy picture of what California was like in spite of its current occupants. Painting California as a fertile, disease-free, monoclimatic, lush paradise, he shaped the American vision of California as an Eden, while ignoring the fact that he had seen only its coastal strip and knew neither its diverse interior population and geography, nor the ravages of smallpox and other diseases that decimated Native populations.[12] Dana's book, published originally in Boston in 1840, came out just before the initial ripples of emigrants tentatively began to flow in the direction of California. With Massachusetts contributing early emigrants to California and Boston being one of the main jumping-off points for "Forty-Niners" taking the ocean route to California, the story told by Dana was well placed to influence Americans.[13] Ultimately his message made sense for both generations of emigrants: "In the hands of an enterprising people, what a country this might be, we are ready to say."[14]

Settlers heading west to California, such as the Bartleson-Bidwell Party of 1840–41, demonstrated the spirit of Manifest Destiny contained in Dana's narrative. These settlers also exhibited many of Dana's prejudices, but also some ideas wholly unrelated to him, especially owing to their journey by land rather than by sea. In fact as one reads through the accounts of members of the group, one is struck by what was missing rather than what was included. Key among these absent ideas is national identity. The group was traveling to a foreign country, about to become, for all intents and purposes, expatriates of the United States. The land they hoped to settle would come either from a grant of the Mexican government or a lease or sale by an individual holding a Mexican land grant. While Mexico welcomed many emigrants from around the world under its Colonization Act of 1824, which was designed to help populate Mexican territories with naturalized citizens drawn from other nations, the members of this party seem to have had other plans in mind.[15]

With some exceptions, those who emigrated prior to the Mexican-American War came with the intention of settling large tracts of land and making California a place such as they had left behind. These early emigrants from the United States often arrived without papers or proper permission from Mexican authorities, and so were initially what one might call undocumented aliens living in California. Perhaps the best example was John Bidwell, one of the prominent men of the Bartleson-Bidwell Party.[16] In his published and unpublished memoirs one can glimpse how rumor and gossip spread from a few people to thousands, eventually gaining credibility by being incorporated into newspaper reports. Representing the first group of overland settlers from the United States to go west over the Sierra Nevada, they relied heavily on unconfirmed reports and anecdotes of California.[17] Their motives and trail experiences were emblematic of those of Euro-Americans passing the same way in the next two decades.

In 1840 no trail guide existed for the journey west to California. However, accounts obtained by word of mouth, reprinted in newspapers, and published in books such as Dana's did exist, and according to Bidwell were a key ingredient in the decision-making process of potential emigrants. Bidwell provided both positive and negative examples of how secondary accounts influenced interested parties. He consulted Joseph Rubidoux, a Frenchman engaged in trade with Indian peoples in the Southwest, who painted a lush portrait of California for Bidwell, calling it "a land of perennial spring," populated by hospitable Spaniards and friendly Indians, much like Dana's description of California as an Eden. According to Rubidoux, foreigners were welcome, land was abundant, and the government accommodating. The land was key, having been Bidwell's main motive for moving west once before. Rubidoux's reputation and glowing accounts of the land were enough to convince Bidwell to make the trip: "His description of the country made it seem like a paradise."[18] Bidwell did not realize it, nor would he likely credit it, but he was about to become a serpent in this Eden of the West.

Bidwell made common cause with hundreds of other Euro-Americans over the next few weeks. He spread the story told by Rubidoux, and in just a few weeks five hundred people had expressed interest in going to California. A committee was elected democratically to plan the journey; they created an organizational plan and a pledge that acted as a constitution. They called their westward-bound community the Western Emigration Society.[19] To increase interest, the group published calls for membership in regional newspapers, incorporating what they had learned from Rubidoux, which drew widespread interest. At the same time, another positive account of California began to circulate, this time in the form of a letter written by Dr. John Marsh, a well-known settler who had traveled by sea in the previous decade.

Although the people of the East did not know it, Marsh was some-thing of a con man. Like the more famous John Sutter, also a fraud of sorts, Marsh hoped to get Americans to come to California in order to profit by his position in the Central Valley, where he had large landholdings and practiced medicine as the only "trained" doctor in California, though he had no medical degree.[20] The Society published Marsh's letter in regional newspapers as well.[21] The tales of one French trader and one false doctor were now reaching thousands of would-be settlers and convincing hundreds to take an active interest in California.

Like the democratically organized Western Emigration Society, most companies of emigrants elected a man to command their group based on his merits, making him their "captain," often after some elec-toral campaigning by interested individuals. In the case of the Bartle-son-Bidwell Party, John Bartleson was elected by vote in 1840 to lead them westward. The male members of the party then elected officers for the expedition to support the captain. In the course of the journey, these representatives were not typically allowed to make momentous decisions, which the company as a whole voted on. When the group split unexpectedly, with Bartleson taking the swifter portion of the group ahead, Bidwell was elected the new captain for the remaining emigrants.[22] At the time, John Bidwell lacked much in the way of life or frontier experience, being just into his twenties. But he had the motivation shared by many Euro-Americans: a desire for land and a keen sense of entitlement to it.

Bidwell and his fellows played a part in achieving Manifest Des-tiny through the acquisition of land in the West. Before leaving for California in 1840, Bidwell had emigrated from Ohio, on foot, to the Kansas Territory. Working as a schoolteacher, he had originally planned to settle not far from the Missouri River in Platte County. This was real frontier country; settlers were living in close proximity to Native Americans in the region, protected by nearby Fort Leavenworth. Re-flecting the views consistent among those living in such circumstances, Bidwell wrote of the "intense longing on the part of the people of Mis-souri to have the Indians removed and a corresponding desire, as soon as the purchase was consummated, to get possession of the beautiful land." His motive for getting land of his own was a common one, although his view of how land might be got from Native Americans was relatively benign compared to the methods employed by other settlers and their representatives. Ironically, early on in his life, other settlers, rather than hostile Indians, stood in the way of Bidwell's dream. While visiting St. Louis for supplies, a man jumped Bidwell's land claim of 160 acres back in Platte County. Hoping for the law to settle the matter in his favor, Bidwell was disappointed to find that the law supported the squatter, who had built a home on the land while Bidwell was gone, something Bidwell had not done for lack of funds. Permanent residency in a house on the land was the key to legal ownership, and by the letter of the law Bidwell lost both the land and all he had invested into improving the acreage. Turned off of "his" land, Bidwell dared do nothing extralegal against the usurper, who was known to be a killer. Instead he resolved to head to California, where in unacknowledged hypocrisy he would, along with other Euro-Americans, turn Native Americans and Mexicans off their lands in similar fashion.[23] As W. W. Robinson wryly remarked, "Every American is a squatter at heart."[24]

The Bartleson-Bidwell Party experienced no loss of life due to Native Americans on the journey and, indeed, had several positive encounters with various Indigenous peoples, but arriving safe in California they remained as fearful of hostile Indians as they were when they set out, six months and several encounters earlier. Many emigrants shared such an experience: neutral or positive contacts with Native populations were the rule, rather than the exception. Yet the accounts communicated by emigrants and explorers from the United States seldom failed to put the paucity of trouble down to anything other than good luck or the product of the conspicuous armed might of vigilant emigrant parties. How could emigrants ignore reality?

Once on the trail, Bidwell noticed a curious thing about his fellow travelers bound for California: "If there is anything bad in a man's character, he will show it then. They used to say even a preacher could not cross the plains without swearing." One key element of the Euro-American character may have been fear of Indian savagery. Bidwell noted that most of the men in the company were quite courageous, but once they had gone far out into "Indian country," things began to look different to even the bravest. The terror of the unknown seemed to hydrate and reconstitute all of the many stories of terror and fear present in the Euro-American consciousness, planted there by educa-tion, newspapers, national myths, and popular culture. Mortal terror of Indians went West with the settlers. In one representative example, Bidwell recalled the terror experienced by a man sent out to round up the oxen the group had allowed to roam free and graze. Being encamped in an area skirted by rock outcroppings, the man, through tricks of light and distance, became utterly convinced and completely terrified that fearsome Indians had surrounded them. Rushing back to the camp, he raised the alarm. He even claimed the oxen were being herded off by the Indian raiders. When the men went out to investigate, they found his fears unfounded: no footprints anywhere, all the oxen present, and the terrifying shapes resolved into rocks, not Indians.[25] Emigrants on the trail often assumed that persons or animals that had gone missing had fallen prey to thieving Indians. Once, when Bidwell and others became separated from the body of the company, it was assumed they had been killed by marauding Indians. When the two groups reunited, it was not with silent apologies to the Native Americans they had wronged, but with overflowing joy that some-how Bidwell's lost party had cheated death and come together again. Not long after this incident, some oxen strayed from the party, and Bidwell and the infamously unreliable Cheyenne Dawson volunteered to recover them. Fearing attack all the while, the two men searched in vain for the lost stock. Dawson, true to his nature, abandoned the task as a bad job, leaving Bidwell on his own. As Bidwell stumbled upon the tracks of the oxen, he also noted the tracks of Indians. Discarding what he had learned by grim experience on the trail, that one should never carry loaded weapons, he carried his rifle and pistols loaded and primed. Better to shoot yourself than be shot by an Indian, apparently.

Finding the oxen unharmed, Bidwell journeyed all night to rejoin his party. But the next day it seemed that his nighttime bid to escape Indians had failed. In the light and heat of the next day, confused by a "mirage," Bidwell worked frantically to ready himself as two mounted Indians fast approached him. Panicking in the face of his approaching doom, he dumped his gun into a quagmire, putting it out of action by submersion in mud and water. He resolved to die shooting, though: "I was able to move and get behind the oxen. My gun was in no condition to shoot. However, putting dry powder in the pan I determined to do my best in case the supposed Indians came up; but lo! they were two of our party, coming to meet me, bringing water and provisions." Would he have shot the rescuers at long range if he had an operable weapon? One can never know for certain. Weeks later this experience seemed to have made little impression on him. Seeing a company of riders slowly approach, Bidwell and his company assumed hostile Indians were coming after them. It turned out to be the party led by Bartleson, who had split from Bidwell's portion of the company. Not only were they not a threat, but they were carrying supplies given them by Native Americans when they ended up near starvation in the Carson Lake area.[26] Still one could not be too careful around Indians, and no matter how many pieces of evidence were uncovered, the emigrants seemed to have little faith in their own experiences. For his part, Bidwell put his trust in only one thing: a good rifle.[27] And when the party did meet Native Americans, Bidwell implied, his fellows shared a similar faith.

Whenever the party of emigrants met Native people, Bidwell admitted that had they "not had an old mountaineer with [them], the result would have been certainly disastrous." This was the case because the party "was so easily excited" by the presence of Native Americans, even when the peaceful intent of the Native people was obvious. A Shoshone man, traveling near Bidwell's company, noticed that one of the emigrants had dropped a pouch of tobacco. Coming to the emigrant's camp, the Shoshone returned the pouch to the emigrant, who had already realized it was missing as his cravings took hold of him. Rather than thank the friendly man, the emigrant became angry and accused

the Shoshone of stealing the tobacco from him. "We had seen no Indians or signs of Indians for some days," recalled Bidwell; thus it could
not have been a case of theft.[28] The cooler heads of the party prevailed,
and the Shoshone departed, perhaps now wondering why he had gone
to the trouble to help. Luckily men like the old pioneer knew that Native Americans were not the bloodthirsty savages they were purported
to be, and counseled calm. Unfortunately for one of the emigrants in
the party, the old mountaineer could not be everywhere at once.

One day a member of the group was out hunting alone. The group
was passing through territory belonging to the Cheyennes, and the
hunter encountered a large party. The first indication of trouble was
the sight of the man running for all he was worth, only partly dressed
and without his mule, pistol, or rifle. Reaching his fellows, he shouted
a warning that he had been encircled by thousands of Indians, who
were even now pouring toward them following his escape. The captain
of the party tried without effect to calm everyone down, then put their
energies into forming a defensive perimeter with their wagons as a
barricade. Not long after they completed their defenses, the Cheyennes appeared. Forty of them, total. To the further amazement of
the group, the Cheyennes set up camp just a few hundred feet away.
This seemed incongruous with the story told by the fleeing man, who
claimed he had been robbed of his mule and weapons and only saved
himself by his flight. The captain and the mountaineer went out to
talk to the Indians, and after a time learned the truth of the matter:
when the party of forty Cheyennes had ridden up and surprised the
man, he had panicked. The Cheyennes had indeed taken his rifle: "He
was so excited when he saw them that they had to disarm him to keep
him from shooting them." The truth of this, already suggested by the
difference between forty and "thousands," was evident when the Cheyennes returned the man's rifle and mule to the two representatives of
the emigrant party. The pistol and some of his clothes, they said, lay
somewhere out on the plain, as the man had cast them off as he ran.
The episode was capped by the nickname given to the half-dressed,
humiliated man by his fellow travelers: "Cheyenne" Dawson.[29]

One might be tempted to laugh at Dawson, as certainly the emi-grants and perhaps the Cheyennes did, and catalogue this as a humor-ous anecdote, but one should do otherwise. Dawson escaped with his life, as did his countrymen, but how narrowly? What if he had pulled the trigger? His fellows would have told a different tale, if they lived to tell one at all. Dawson might have been killed by "bloodthirsty sav-ages" without provocation and stripped of his weapons. The rest of the party might have heard his unseen shot, fired in self-defense, not panic. In the real story, the Native people had the time and the opportunity to change the outcome of the encounter for the better. But one is left wondering, how many times did the Euro-American emigrant, seeing the Indians of nightmare, have enough nerve to shoot? How many killings or so-called massacres began as a fearful, unmanned emigrant discharging his weapon? One can never know for certain, but many emigrants attributed the success of their trip to a strong, well-armed company. In a related example, Pierson Barton Reading, writing to his brother in 1844, expressed with certainty how he and his fellow emigrants had come safely across the Plains: "Rifle by my side, ready at any moment to be called in defense of my life, from attack by the many treacherous and bloodthirsty savages we passed. Vigilance was our watchword and to it we are indebted for our safety."[30] Reading and his company, like Bidwell's group, went west with no losses at-tributed to Indians, yet convinced they would have been dead but for their arms and vigilance against the savages. As Unruh has made plain, such convictions were misplaced.[31] Yet Euro-Americans had faith that they *knew* Indians.

Certainly Bidwell and most of his company disliked and distrusted Indians, despite their positive experiences with several different tribal groups. Indeed at the heart of the group's split before reaching Califor-nia was how encounters with Native Americans would be dealt with. An unmendable rift developed between Bartleson and Bidwell follow-ing an encounter with a group of mounted warriors. One morning a "war party" of some ninety Native American men of an unidentified nation appeared. Many of the emigrants wanted to take up arms and stand out from the group to keep them at bay. Hearing this, Bartleson refused. He argued that presenting a hostile demeanor risked making a bad impression on the war party, saying, "Boys, you must not show any sign of hostility. If you go out there with guns the Indians will think us hostile, and may get mad and hurt us." Bidwell and four or five others ignored his orders and went out with loaded guns and stopped the riders from approaching. It turned out that the group was looking to trade. Despite this, Bidwell was convinced that had they not gone out to fight, there would have been a fight: "They might, and probably would, have killed us."[32] Again, Bidwell, like many of his countrymen, *knew* Indians.

The end of Bidwell's journey at Dr. John Marsh's rancho in 1841 was not the end for his overland memories and experiences. In addition to the letters he would send to family and friends from 1841 to 1900, he also wrote an extensive memoir of his trip to California and his life afterward. First published locally by the *Chico Advertiser* in the 1880s and later in New York in 1890 by *Century Magazine*, Bidwell's experiences influenced Euro-Americans in the short and long term.[33] He was known as one of the Founding Fathers of California, a general of the California militia, a state senator, and a prominent businessman, and his recollections in published and unpublished form were interesting and credible to most. Unfortunately his conviction that weapons had delivered them, not Indian diplomacy and forbearance, may have convinced later emigrants. But this should not be surprising, given that perhaps the most popular and widely circulated account of life on the overland trail reported a similar lack of Indian trouble, and for the same reason of armed vigilance.

Like Dana's book and the communiqués of emigrants in California in letters and rumors sent back east, the government report of John C. Frémont's exploring expeditions to California shaped the Euro-American perception of California and its peoples.[34] But because of the official nature of the mission, its exploration of the interior, and its scientific method of collecting data, the widely known and circulated copies of Frémont's report would become the blueprint for almost all trail guides published in the next twenty years. Indeed many guides were produced by men who had never been to California and had simply plagiarized Frémont's report to produce salable books.[35]

Frémont's report was filled with prescriptive advice for travelers west in the form of a narrative of his expeditions' experiences and findings. The expeditions, one to the Rockies in 1842 and another to California and Oregon in 1843–44, differed from those journeys undertaken by the emigrant companies that set out before him. Unlike the accounts sent east by early emigrant trains such as the Bartleson-Bidwell Party, traveling by the northern route, and the Workman-Rowland Party, which took the southern route not long afterward, Frémont's expeditions were focused on the future of American settlement west of the Rocky Mountains, not its present state; indeed in the case of his first and later a second visit, just before the advent of the Mexican-American War, Frémont and his companions were trespassers on Mexican territory. Interspersed among scientific data, tables of distances, map coordinates, and observations of the flora and fauna of California and the West were stories of dangerous Indians and methods of dealing with them. Because Frémont's report was the most influential trail narrative published, many emigrants would be exposed to it and the myriad guides that shamelessly borrowed from it.[36] Frémont's stories of fearsome Indians and his prescriptive solutions were critical contributions to the negative relationships between emigrants and Native Americans along the trails westward.

Describing his first expedition to the Rocky Mountains, Frémont revealed the anxiety plaguing the company of explorers, an unease that thousands of Euro-Americans would share in the coming decades. Despite the fact that they were well armed and organized and guided by the legendary Kit Carson, the men were in a constant state of fear from the Indian threat.[37] Frémont noted that "stories of desperate and bloody Indian fights were rife in camp," and as such false alarms of Indian attack abounded, especially at night. In one vivid example, when a camp guard shouted that more than twenty hostile savages were approaching, the men took up their arms and made ready. Carson, scouting the enemy position, soon returned to report that the twenty-seven Indians were actually elk.[38] But sometimes Native Americans were encountered, and Frémont's behavior is telling in itself and as a preview of the way later emigrants would think and react.

On one occasion, Frémont and another man were caught out in the open, not by twenty-seven Indians, but by more than two hundred mounted Arapahos. Frémont was carrying a rifle, a double-barreled shotgun, and at least two pistols. In the heat of the moment, facing the two hundred riders, the heavily armed Frémont drew his pistols and was getting ready to fire. Apparently, despite the impossible odds, he turned to his gun instead of his intellect; violence, not negotiation, was at the forefront of his mind. As he was about to fire, he heard his companion speaking to the Arapahos in their language. The man was a former trader who had met Arapaho people before. After a brief talk, the Arapahos decided to welcome the group to their village. They fed and supplied Frémont's men, and then allowed them to continue on their way. Yet Frémont, tellingly, implied that their survival was because of the trader, not the forbearance of the Arapahos at finding them crossing their lands; in fact the expedition ascertained that had they been Pawnees, the Arapahos would have attacked.[39] Clearly the Arapahos understood that their ways were not the ways of these strangers and allowed them to pass not only unmolested, but with gifts. At the same time, one can only speculate as to what this example reveals about those unsolved mysteries of emigrants killed by Native Americans on the overland trail. How many of them shot first, without considering inaction or talking to the Native people? One can never know for certain, but this and similar examples suggest that the preconceived negative mind-set of Euro-Americans may have been deterministic in such killings or disappearances.

Frémont was not the only man in the expedition to be convinced that conflict with Indians was unavoidable. His famous guide, Kit Carson, claimed that the group "could not escape without some sharp encounters with Indians" and set about writing his will in front of the other men. According to Frémont, this was "most unfortunate" as it increased the level of "alarm" among the men and resulted in the request of several members of the group for discharges.[40] The men were about to enter the territories of Indigenous peoples embroiled in war, and exacerbated by the fatalism of Carson, many were frightened.

However, this war was not between whites and Native Americans, but between different Native nations. Frémont's group was about to negotiate hundreds of miles of territory and resources contested by different Indigenous groups. Frémont adopted a strategy that might have proved beneficial had more Euro-Americans emulated it later. As Frémont and the expedition went west, they conferred with Native leaders, used guides from these groups to help obtain safe passage, and gave presents to pay their passage across the lands of various tribal groups.[41] In the many guidebooks based on Frémont's report, none that this historian viewed ever counseled the use of gifts to obtain safe passage; neither did they suggest bringing goods meant specifically to compensate Native peoples for passage over their lands or the use of their resources. This is perhaps not surprising, given that many Euro-Americans believed they owned all of these lands by virtue of the right of discovery and treaties with and purchases from Spain, Britain, and France. What emigrant guide authors might have learned from Frémont, to seek out Indigenous people and make agreements and compensations that recognized the power of Indian peoples on their own ground, instead seemingly failed to make any impression on them.

In this failure, readers of Frémont's report and later imitators of it ignored the successes of the strategy. Yet they can perhaps be forgiven, because often Frémont or his men seemed to forget these successes too. In one case, the expedition only narrowly avoided a conflict with a large, well-armed Sioux war party. Scouts of the expedition had spotted a group of Sioux, and after they raced back to the camp and raised the alarm, the company seemed willing to forget what they had learned from Frémont's nearly fatal mistake with the Arapahos. The men discharged a volley from their guns, reloaded, and set up a barricade with their wagons. But moments later their Indian guide and the former Indian trader went out for a parley. They quickly returned with two Sioux warriors, who confirmed that the group was looking for Crow people. In the course of conversations, Frémont's party also learned that these warriors had been part of a fight with emigrants the previous week. Although the men of the expedition did not know the particulars, "several of the men suggested shooting them [the Sioux envoys to the parley] on the spot." Frémont "promptly discountenanced any such proceeding." Not unlike Frémont in the heat of his moment of visceral fear, these men wanted to kill Native Americans brought in for a legitimate parley under truce, which would have certainly led to a fight with the balance of the Sioux waiting nearby. These Sioux were from just one of several powerful war parties ranging in the area. In this case, it was Frémont's cooler head that prevailed. He then made a gift of some tobacco to them, but he noted that this did not assuage their "bad humor" at seeing the hasty fortifications thrown up by the expedition and at being ringed by riflemen as they talked.[42]

The report also contained many less tense exchanges between the expedition and Native populations. On numerous occasions, the men of the exploring expedition sought out Native people to trade for provisions and ascertain local conditions, the best routes to take west, and where water and game could be found.[43] Using exchanges, negotiation, and diplomacy, Frémont and his men successfully completed their first expedition to the Rocky Mountains. But in spite of these many positive interactions and the satisfactory results they produced—no battles were fought and no men were wounded or died as a result of conflict with Indian peoples—Frémont's outfitting of his second expedition was telling in its composition. For his second expedition—this one exploring as far as the Pacific Coast—Frémont decided to bring along a brass howitzer manned by a crew of three. As anyone who has read trail narratives and diaries extensively will attest, one of the most oft-repeated complaints of emigrants was the trouble of transporting just about anything, no matter how dear. Given the lack of even light combat on the first trip, a brass cannon that discharged twelve-pound shells seems to fall into the realm of the altogether unnecessary. One can only assume that fear of hostile Indians continued to play a central role, despite the reenlistment of several veterans of the first expedition, including Frémont and Carson, who knew the reality of successful, peaceful relations with Native peoples.

In the second expedition, again the group relied on interaction with Native people and access to their resources. On this second expedition, in particular, the company attempted to eat anything other than the supplies they had brought with them, reserving these for periods when fish and game were unavailable along the way.[44] When it came to feeding livestock, once their initial small supplies of fodder ran out they relied exclusively on the grass and vegetation native to the regions they traveled in to provide all of the food for their horses and mules. The report also contained cautions about the care of horses and stock. Frémont warned readers that horses brought from the United States, having been fed on grain and hay since birth, did poorly on the Plains grass and that, even when tethered or hobbled for the night, animals worked themselves loose, which cost time to recover them, if the men even had the time to search for them. This observation was a critical one; a man could not count on his animal in the same way he did back in the United States, and even vigilance was no guarantee that an animal would cooperate. Threats such as the presence of buffalo and wolves also affected the ability of the group to retain its animals. Domesticated animals sensing the buffalo would run rather than encounter one, unless kept under strict control. "Animals are often lost in this way," and once away, "are rarely retaken." Sometimes, even when precautions were taken, animals escaped despite efforts to the contrary.[45]

One night a pack of wolves chasing a buffalo calf came near their camp. The pack, twenty or thirty in number, eventually caught and devoured the buffalo calf. As the men looked on from a distance, Frémont noted that had they had horses ready, they would have fought off the wolves and saved the little calf. This observation epitomizes the paradoxical Euro-American character of the day; according to the report, Frémont and his fellows had been killing buffalo all day long, just days before! In yet another example of contradiction, when the expedition ran across a red ox that had gotten loose from an emigrant train, the group claimed it as "a prize." As we will see later, Native people along the trail or in California found with a domesticated animal lost by emigrants ran the risk of being put immediately to death for doing what Frémont's expedition did without a second thought. When the ox escaped them as well, Frémont ordered that he not be recaptured; though the ox would have helped them survive lean times, he felt the animal deserved better after having escaped "so far among the Indians." Strangely, not long after, the expedition recovered a cow and calf that had strayed and decided to keep and consume these later, apparently without a second thought about their earlier actions.[46]

Euro-Americans' behavior was also often paradoxical when it came to Native Americans, as Frémont's report demonstrated. Many times Frémont disparaged the form and character of Indians, despite the massive amount of evidence available that he relied on many different Native American groups to survive his expeditions. Indeed at times he embraced them for their aid, and yet often displayed contempt for them. Without the help of Native Americans, their material aid, information, and tolerant forbearance of provocative actions, Frémont and his men might have perished on many different occasions. Yet Frémont would hardly credit this, despite the clear evidence he left behind in support of just such a conclusion. Much of this disconnection can be explained by his view of Indians as animals; one could rely on horse, mule, or oxen and yet have no real affection for them either. In one pregnant example of racism Frémont described their horses' skittishness around Indians as similar to their behavior around "any other wild animal." One tense meeting began with an Arapaho and Cheyenne war party boldly riding up, mistaking Frémont's encampment for a group of Shoshones attempting to escape. Once they had seen their error, the war party offered their explanation for the mistake and exchanged tokens of friendship before departing. But Frémont was not disabused of preconceived notions of Indian character, concluding rather that they had been lucky to avoid the "innate thirst for . . . blood" possessed by Indians.[47] Like many nineteenth-century Euro-Americans, Frémont possessed strong notions about race and racial hierarchies.

Frémont was one of the first to publish information about "Digger Indians." Rather than identifying them as Shoshones or Paiutes, Frémont instead displayed the essentialism that many Euro-Americans used to boil down what they perceived Indians were. Initially calling them the "tribe of *Root Diggers*," he went on to place these peoples within a racial hierarchy of Indians based on levels of animality: "Roots, seeds, and grass, every vegetable that affords any nourishment, and every living animal, thing, insect, or worm, they eat. Nearly approaching to the lower animal creation, their sole employment is to obtain food; and they are constantly engaged in a struggle to support existence." Given this description, one might believe that these people were cultureless subhumans grazing like cattle, leading a sleep-and-eat existence. According to Frémont, by observing them on the roads west, one learned all one needed to know of them. Despite the lowness of these "almost entirely naked . . . miserable" people, Frémont deigned to trade for some food from these Indians, who beyond their "lives spent in the rushes . . . seemed to have very little knowledge of anything." Even given this attitude, Frémont was at least willing to trade for the food. In one story related to Frémont by the famous hunter Joseph Redford Walker, Walker and his men surprised a Native American village somewhere in the Sierra Nevada, causing all the people to flee in fear. Entering the homes of the villagers, which they said were "abandoned," they ate their fill of the stores and took more for their breakfast the next day. In another example of Frémont's categorization of Indians as savage animals, he explained that hungry "Snake" or Shoshone people "eat every insect and every creeping thing, however loathsome and repulsive; snails, lizards, ants, all are devoured with the readiness and greediness of mere animals."[48] The irony, which was likely lost on a nineteenth-century audience, was that Frémont and his men in similar desperate straits ate the same food, sometimes eating dogs, ants, frogs, snakes, and skunks, among other unusual fare, deriving no shame from it, even as they ascribed an animal nature to Native Americans for doing likewise. The lowest, most inhuman peoples, Frémont argued, were the Indigenous people of the Southwest that he passed through to return home along the route south of the Rockies, where "savages hardly above the condition of mere wild animals" lived.[49]

Not only did Frémont comment on the inhumanity of Indians, but he also noted moments of sheer surprise at their undeniable humanity. While camped with a group of Shoshones, he observed laughter and merrymaking among the members of the village. This struck him as deeply nonsavage and "entirely different from the Indians [he] had been accustomed to see." Perhaps if he would have reflected more deeply, he had the answer before him. The Shoshones were no different from other Native peoples in their ability to laugh, cry, and carry on; their difference was that they did not live near whites, had little experience with them, and so still had much to laugh about. These "talkative" people made quite an impression on Frémont but did little to temper his prejudices. Most of what he chose to relate contributed in a negative way to the observations he included in the report. Their openness, intelligence, and laughter were un-Indian to him, and so exceptions to his rule of what Indians were like. This conflicted with the typical Euro-American view of what Indians were: a people who "prowled about like wild animals."[50]

This view of Indians seemed to be foremost in Frémont's mind when a member of his expedition, Mr. Preuss, became separated from the group while attempting to find another man lost bringing along some exhausted stock. Preuss volunteered to find the man and bring him back. The party decided to press on without seeing either of them, thinking that the two men would catch up. When the man originally lost with the stock turned up without Preuss, and Preuss did not come in later, the party realized they had abandoned their companion in a hostile country. Knowing that Indians were in the area, and that Preuss was unarmed, they "began to think his chance doubtful." The results of the ensuing search provided a stark contrast to what the Frémont expedition assumed had become of Preuss. After searching for days, the men found him. He had been saved by Native Americans. Stumbling upon a little village, near starvation and exhausted, Preuss accepted their hospitality and traded a pocket knife in return. Still Frémont could not help but comment that Preuss was alive because, encountering "only one man, they [the Indians] did not run off."[51] Frémont failed to realize that one unarmed white man could stumble into the midst of a village and have no need to fear. Instead he thought only of reasons why Native peoples might be afraid. Perhaps fear was prominent as a motivation in Frémont's mind because the men on the expedition were operating in a state of constant fear themselves.

Frémont often used aggressive tactics to discourage Native people from attacking, sometimes before even meeting them. Instead of firing a warning volley, as the party had done in the encounter with the Sioux, he decided on one occasion to load and fire the howitzer as they entered a valley full of Indian camps, cook fires, and activity. As these Indians were known as particularly courageous and hostile people, Frémont determined to take this added "precaution." After the roar of the gun and the explosion of the shell, Frémont reported that all the fires were quickly extinguished. What he was hoping for, though, was not deterrence, but capitulation. When the inhabitants did not come in to talk, he "determined to pay them a visit." His reaction to the local tribe's representatives spoke volumes about what he thought of Native Americans: "We were surprised, on riding up, to find one of them a woman, having never before known a squaw to take any part in the business of war. They were the village chief and his wife, who, in excitement and alarm, had come out to meet their fate together. The chief was a very prepossessing Indian, with very handsome features, and a singularly soft and agreeable voice, so remarkable as to attract general notice."[52]

Clearly Frémont contextualizes his dealings with Native peoples as part of a larger, ongoing war between Native Americans and Euro-Americans, rather than diplomacy being conducted by the representatives of sovereign nations. Similarly he assumed that these Native leaders knew they were doomed from the roar of the gun, rather than people who had come out to investigate the business of intruders. Frémont soon discovered that these were Klamath people. As he had done before, he inferred an inhuman otherness about them, saying they were "almost like plants" because of their adaptation of the soil and its resources. The Klamaths, apparently with no outward signs of fear, invited Frémont and his men into their village and discussed local intelligence and the lay of the land in a crude system of gestures the two sides adopted to bridge the language gap. Frémont demanded the assistance of guides, but the chief refused him, much to Frémont's annoyance. However, the day after his departure, the Klamath chief changed his mind, coming in person with a couple other men to help the party through the snows that blanketed the region. Frémont thought that the chief may have concluded that his decision not to provide a guide the day before had been rude, and so come to make amends.[53] One can never know, but it may be that the Klamaths wanted these men out of their country quickly or without receiving the help of local enemies who might benefit from the exchange. In any case, this act represented one more occasion among many where Native people provided assistance, despite the hostility exhibited by Euro-Americans at contact.

Not all the contacts the expedition had with Native peoples ended with such positive results. In one episode reported by Frémont, the group spotted some nearby fires and discovered a village. The expedition galloped straight into the heart of the village, terrorizing its inhabitants and causing them to scatter. Carson and another man tried to ride down some of the men, but the Native people living there could "run like deer" and so escaped using their "animal-like" powers of evasion. Returning to the group, Carson came across a woman attempting to hide her two young children in a bush: "She immediately began screaming in the extremity of fear, and shut her eyes fast, to avoid seeing him." They took her captive and brought her and the children back to the huts of the village. They learned that she was a Shoshone, but no matter how hard they tried, learning anything further was impossible given her terror. And although the explorers waited, the men who had run away would not return to the village while they were there. The fear of these people was frustrating, even though Frémont and his men had experienced several instances when they were surprised and made fearful by Native groups approaching their camp. Had Native

Americans attacked their camp, the men on the expedition and many other Euro-Americans would have condemned the act as terrorism and countenanced a violent, even deadly response. Frémont's company gave the frightened woman some presents and left, but Frémont remarked that what he had seen of them caused him to believe that these people lived by "instinct alone" and were "among human beings, the nearest approach to the mere animal creation." The party made the same racist judgment soon after, when, while traveling in the foothills of the Sierra Nevada, they stumbled across a lone Native woman. This time the woman was so afraid that she screamed incessantly until they determined simply to leave her alone. The group went away frustrated that they "could do nothing with her" she was so terrified.[54] The difference between the fear of the Euro-Americans and the fear of the Native Americans, in Frémont's mind, was likely that he believed the Native Americans' fears were completely unfounded and instinctual, whereas Euro-American fears were totally justified given the canon of knowledge they possessed on the subject of Indian savagery, depravity, and racial inferiority.

Frémont made numerous racist conclusions about Native Americans during his explorations. In one telling example, he showed his inability to recognize how his own actions might be perceived by Native people, indeed how his actions may well have suggested white savagery. Frémont was so desperate to retain a guide on one occasion that he kidnapped a Native man in order to secure his services. After a confused set of negotiations, during which the man seemed to accede to their demands for a guide, the expedition kept him under an armed guard that night, showing him loaded weapons so that he got the message about what would happen if he tried to escape. They gave him gifts for his services, but the gifts were clothes necessary for the inclement weather and rough terrain he would soon face. After four days on the trip, the man escaped, much to Frémont's disgust. While this man traveled with the party, the group had made additional attempts to bribe him to keep him compliant, but apparently he valued his freedom more highly. Frémont put it down, not to the forced manner of the man's inclusion in the party, but to his Indianness. "His bad faith and treachery," Frémont wrote, "were in perfect keeping with the estimate of Indian character, which a long intercourse with this people had gradually forced upon my mind."[55] Neither the dozens of positive contacts nor the lack of any armed combat with Indigenous people in over two years of traveling was enough to dissuade Frémont of his preconceptions of Native Americans.

Whether the result of a contact was positive or negative, Frémont's overall message to readers of his report was clear: the only way to deal with unfailingly savage, hostile Indians was with loaded firearms in hand. In a couple of lines describing a successful night of camping among Native Americans, Frémont explained how his party had come through Indian country safely: "Strict vigilance was maintained among the people. . . . There is no reason to doubt that these dispositions, uniformly preserved, conducted our party securely through Indians famed for treachery." For Frémont, as for later travelers to California, all of the moments of trade, cooperation, willing assistance, and friendship between Euro-Americans and Indigenous populations were ultimately meaningless. While there were reasons for "doubt that these dispositions" had preserved them, many chose to believe that armed might and distrust had been the key to survival. It was respect "inspired by . . . arms," above all else, that Frémont believed got them through alive. He made such assertions despite the fact that they had met Native groups several times that were better armed and outnumbered them by the hundreds. His evidence of success was the loss of only one animal to Indians on the trip to California; they lost thirty-two more of their original sixty-seven to straying, hunger, and exhaustion.[56] The same rate of success would not be had on the return home.

Although they had lost no men going to California, two men were killed on the way back. One died by his own hand, and the other was killed in a fight with Native people, but Frémont, like emigrants to come, would blame even the former case on savage Indians. While traveling home, the group met Mohaves near the Colorado River. The expedition exchanged gifts and information. The Mohaves warned the group of some Paiutes of the basin and range country who raided horses and controlled much of the territory the expedition was about to travel through. Not long after the warning, Frémont's party had a conflict with the Paiutes. They met a Mexican man and a boy out in the desert, leading a small herd of horses. The two were members of a Mexican party heading to California with horses and wagons, possibly from Sonora or New Mexico. The Mexicans had camped at a well-known water source and were surprised by a large force of, presumably, Paiutes, who swept up on the party. Instead of negotiating a deal with the Indians, the horses for their lives, the captain of the company yelled at the man and the boy to lead the horses to safety while the remaining two men protected two women and tried to fight about one hundred Indians. Frémont ascertained that the Mexican men left behind had been killed and the women and remaining horses taken captive. Coming to the site of the battle between the Mexicans and the Paiutes, Kit Carson and another man, Godey, volunteered to accompany the Mexican man to try to recover the horses that had been too far out of reach to save.[57]

The next day the three men returned with the horses and two scalps Carson had taken. Carson related that the Mexican's horse had given out, but Carson and Godey proceeded. The two men rushed a small Paiute camp where the stolen horses were picketed. The Paiutes resisted, but Carson and Godey shot several of them, killing two. "The scalps of the fallen were instantly stripped off; but in the process, one of them . . . sprung to his feet, the blood streaming from his skinned head, and uttering a hideous howl. . . . The frightful spectacle appalled the stout hearts of our men; but *they did what humanity required*, and quickly terminated the agonies of the gory savage." Carson, Godey, and the Mexican returned with fifteen horses. But in the mind of Frémont, they returned with much more than the stolen animals. He was fairly gushing about what Carson and Godey had done, believing it was the epitome of the pioneer spirit and moral righteousness. These men had not gone for horses merely, but to "punish the robbers of the desert, and to avenge the wrongs of Mexicans whom they did not know."

Frémont even connected the deed with his concept of racial hierarchy, writing, "We rejoiced that Carson and Godey had been able to give so useful a lesson to these American Arabs, who lie in wait to murder and plunder the innocent traveler."[58] It was soon after that Baptiste Tabeau was killed, the only man to lose his life in a fight with Native Americans on either expedition.

Tabeau had gone off by himself without permission to recover a stray mule and did not return. Frémont's men tracked him and found his dead body, naked and stripped of all possessions by the "Arabs of the New World." The men of the expedition, sure about who had done this, wanted revenge, but Frémont forbade it, and the party pressed eastward, homeward, now forced into constant vigilance by the inhumanity of Indians that "infested" their camps, "dogged" their heels, and "swarmed" around them.[59] It was within this haze of fear that the second man, François Badeau, died. The men, fearful of further reprisals, were traveling with loaded and primed rifles, pistols, and carbines. Badeau, retrieving a loaded gun muzzle-first, snagged the hammer on something as he pulled it toward himself. As the snag freed from the hammer, the hammer fell back and fired the weapon, shooting Badeau through the head and killing him. Although Frémont did not expand on the incident, it is logical to assume that the men were defying all the rules of safe weapons handling out of the necessity born of fear of Indian attack, hoping to be ready at a second's notice to fight. This was an often repeated scenario among Euro-American emigrants.[60] Even in the case of the very first set of emigrants traveling overland to California, the Bartleson-Bidwell Party, a man had killed himself accidentally by mishandling a loaded and primed gun.[61] Badeau was just one of the earliest in a long line of people along the trails of the West to be killed or maimed accidentally by a gun being kept loaded at all times to deal with the constant fear of Indian attacks.[62]

By the time the second expedition ended, Frémont and his men had traveled more than 3,500 miles in a little over a year's time. As in the first expedition, they had relied on the forbearance of Indigenous peoples and a strategy of negotiation, cooperation, and gift-making with Native nations as they crossed to California. They crossed sovereign territory, camped among tribes or at village sites not in use, and extracted the animal, water, and plant resources found along their path, both with and without compensation. They ate frogs, horses, snakes, ants, skunks, mules, and dogs—an unfamiliar menu for people not on the trail to California—and seemed to suffer no diminution of self. In short, they did many things that Native persons might do only at the expense of scorn or death at the hands of whites. Despite the clarity of the report, and all of these practices, strategies, and anecdotes that seemed to suggest hope for accommodation and cooperation with Native peoples, what many took away from Frémont's report was something altogether different from what one might suspect, as is demonstrated in the content of trail guides.

The most important of the three types of prescriptive literature was the trail guide. Trail guides were purchased by emigrants to be used as handbooks to get them safely across the mountains, deserts, and plains that lay between them and California. By examining emigrant guide content, one can glimpse both the lessons learned and not learned from the report of Frémont's experience—the guide that never referred to his report was a rarity—and how Euro-American presumptions about Native Americans continued to determine their hostile relationships. One of the most important guides in terms of use and negative results was Lansford Hastings's *Emigrant's Guide to Oregon and California*. Hastings's guide was unlike Frémont's report in two very important ways. First, Hastings's book was written with the goal of providing a set of instructions to bring emigrants west. Hastings himself made the trip in a wagon train of emigrants bound for Oregon, and later California. Second, Hastings's guide incorporates ideas about democracy as an organizing principle to help emigrants get to California, something that Frémont, as part of a militarily organized hierarchy, did not cover. Overall the guide, published in 1845, on the eve of the conquest of California by the United States in 1846, would help numerous emigrants before and after the discovery of gold to come to California.

For Hastings, democracy as an organizing principle must have seemed the natural choice in the increasingly democratized United States of the 1830s and 1840s. On his joining a company of westward-bound emigrants in 1842, no debate was convened about how the group would organize and conduct itself. Hastings recalled that he and his fellow travelers were "united in interest" in their quest for the "*El Dorado* of the West," and this was seemingly enough to make a start.[63] They did, however, take their first momentous step in formal democracy, electing a captain and officers from among their number before heading west. However, other steps toward "maintain[ing] order and a semblance of middle-class Protestant morality" as they "formed companies with constitutions and laws to replicate family and social institutions left behind" were soon required.[64]

The emigrants of Hastings's company were soon stymied by their lack of organization. With the "order and security" of civilization behind them, the "'American character' was fully exhibited" after just a few days. This character, which Hastings described as "all . . . determined to govern, but not to be governed," was at the heart of the problem. Even though they had elected their captain, individuals contested his decisions because, according to Hastings, they lacked the other elements of civilized government. A legal code was needed, which included some system of dispensing justice and enacting new rules fairly and for mutual benefit. Without such a system, men would be back in a "state of nature." The captain, the man in whom they had reposed executive power, proposed a halt and the creation of a system to organize the company and capable meting out justice. Fatefully a case presented itself, which according to Hastings was motivation enough for the emigrants to vote in favor of the halt and the new system.[65]

A man in the company had apparently voiced his intent to steal a horse belonging to a Native American. Some number of the party was transported by rage at the intended crime, which Hastings put down to an overzealous concern for "Indian rights." Given the arguments that followed, though, this must have been a small number, as most indicated that stealing from a Native person was "no crime at all." Hastings, a lawyer by training, recounted in some detail the trial convened in the presence of the company, whose members determined the outcome of by vote.[66] Although many, including Hastings, saw the outcry against stealing the horse as a misguided concern for "Indian rights," they may have been missing the point of those angry with the proposed crime. To steal the horse was perhaps to invite trouble in the same way Euro-Americans would view the theft of one of their animals by Native Americans. Yet in the heat of argument, Hastings and others seemed to see this as nonsensical, as might other Euro-Americans who may have viewed the West as theirs for the taking. But the matter was decided not on this point, but on an even more basic principle. The argument that clinched a unanimous vote of not guilty was this: because no law against stealing horses belonging to Native Americans existed among them, and the man had in any case not gone through with the theft, he could not be convicted of a crime.[67]

The decision was the second momentous democratic act for the group: "Thus terminated the first jury trial, in our little community, whose government was extremely simple, yet purely democratic." And so it was, for the time. The will of the majority, expressed directly by vote, was the law. The majority, of course, was a select one. No women voted or served on juries. The solution to preventing future problems of this nature, as well as other problems seen and unforeseen, was another matter. Another vote led to election of a judicial committee to draft a set of laws. After some deliberations, however, the members of the committee returned the opinion that the only law needed was already stored "in the breast of every man." This code, given to man by God, was enacted at Creation, and should, they concluded, serve them well as an arbiter of justice. The company voted and overwhelmingly agreed with this conclusion. This is not to say that no laws were enacted, just no "human laws." The company did indeed create a law that day: they ordered the extermination of all the dogs in the company. Not surprisingly, the law was born out of the fear of Native Americans. Many of the group believed that barking dogs would indicate the company's position to hostile Indians and so needed to be silenced, permanently. But when members attempted to carry out the law, a significant resistance developed that required yet another vote. This time the law rescinded.[68]

Referendums on laws were not the only democratic corrections the group made. Not long into the journey, the emigrants became dissatisfied with the leaders they had selected and elected a new captain and officers. This recall election divided the company, literally. Unwilling to emulate the Founders' concept of a loyal opposition, a significant minority, including those voted out of office, determined to go their own way west. Meanwhile Hastings found himself captain of their "infant *republic*" on the prairie. By the time the groups reunited at Fort Laramie, the secessionists had reconsidered their action and, after some hesitation, were allowed to rejoin the party. Apparently the two sides reconnected in fundamental ways, as future elections of officers, which seem to have been held regularly on the road without some divisive issue being necessary to produce a recall election, produced the reelection of Hastings and other veteran officers by democratic vote.[69]

The final momentous democratic step that Hastings and his fellow emigrants took came in the form of their behavior once in California. Making common cause with many of the earlier emigrants from the United States, Euro-American settlers hoped to make California part of their mother country. Hastings's closing remarks presaged this transfer:

And in fine, we are also led to contemplate the time, as fast approaching, when the supreme darkness of ignorance, superstition, and despotism, which now, so entirely pervade many portions of those remote regions, will have fled forever, before the march of civilization, and the blazing light, of civil and religious liberty; when genuine *republicanism*, and unsophisticated *democracy*, shall be reared up, and tower aloft, even upon the now wild shores, of the great Pacific; where they shall forever stand forth, as enduring monuments, to the increasing wisdom of *man*, and the infinite kindness and protection, of an all-wise, and over-ruling *Providence*.

As Dana had done years before, Hastings called for the transfer of California into, to borrow Dana's earlier words, the "hands of an enterprising people." This represented more than just a potential transfer of property and an end to corrupt government, though. It also envisioned the disappearance of Catholicism, which many in the United States in the 1840s were vehemently prejudiced against. In the true spirit of Manifest Destiny, democracy would sweep away backward Catholic, Mexican, Native American, and Spanish cultural forms in the righteous "march of civilization, and the blazing light, of civil and religious liberty." The source of the blistering radiance of civilization would be twofold. First, "genuine *republicanism*, and unsophisticated *democracy*," like the prairie democracy Hastings had partaken of, would bring justice and egalitarianism to California. Second, "an all-wise, and over-ruling *Providence*" bound up with national destiny would be sure to bless California, as it had blessed the United States thus far.[70]

The example Hastings presented in his guide was reflective of the way many emigrants organized.[71] The final words of Joseph Ware's popular *Emigrant's Guide to California*, which borrowed heavily from Hastings's guide and Frémont's report, were, like Hastings's, a meditation on the spread of democracy and American values to the West:

A word before we part, you are now in a country different from that which you left. Recollect that you are a component part of the country. Take no steps that will not reflect honor, not only upon yourself but your country. Oppose all violations of order, and just law. Unite with the well disposed to sustain the rights of individuals whenever encroached upon. Introduce at the earliest practical moment, those institutions which have conspired to raise our beloved country to the highest elevations of Nations: Let schools, churches, beneficial societies, courts, &c., be established forthwith. Make provisions for the forthcoming millions that shortly shall people your ample valleys, and golden hills—and above all recollect that *righteousness exalteth a nation*.[72]

These words reflected the high-minded thinking of other Euro-Americans in California, who in 1846 launched the Bear Flag Revolt against Mexican authorities, unaware that their countrymen were already at war with Mexico—some with a similar, albeit grander goal in mind. In an unsurprising twist of fate, John C. Frémont was on hand to help the Bear Flag rebels, and soon after, U.S. forces arrived to conquer and occupy California.

Unlike Frémont's, Hastings's purpose was to guide other emigrants like himself. He declared, "This I do in order to put future emigrants upon their guard, and thereby, to enable them, to avoid innumerable dangers and difficulties, which we encountered, and of which we were wholly unadvised."[73] Though Hastings and his fellows had difficulties that Frémont did not encounter, none of his group was killed by Native Americans. However, they did come into open battle with Native peoples on several occasions, resulting in the wounding of some of the emigrants and the deaths of many Native Americans. But this was perhaps to be expected, given the fact that they did not practice a strategy of accommodation and gifting. In spite of this, many similarities between the two men exist. Chief among these were racist ideas about Native Americans.[74] Like many of his countrymen, Hastings was the product of a culture popularly habituated to Indian hating. In his observations to future emigrants, he helped reinforce these racially essentialized views of Native peoples. As Frémont had done before him, Hastings interpreted almost everything about Indigenous peoples and their cultures as the result of their being the lowest form of humanity. He described a set of racial characteristics common to all Indians: they were naturally thieves; they were by nature cowards; they lived in "degraded solitude," in the rudest form of domiciles, which were constructed "in the most . . . artless manner imaginable."[75] And Indians in California in particular were "barbarous" peoples that lacked "all moral principle" and exhibited a "perfect destitution of intelligence," and as such, some of them had been "domesticated" by some of the missions to work as beasts.[76] One had to be particularly careful because they were not just animal-like in their racial character, but they also disguised themselves as animals to hunt and raid stock. Hastings claimed they wore elk hides and antlers and crawled "upon all fours . . . apparently feeding" as they went, fooling the guards into thinking an elk is among the horses; the thief in disguise could then cut the horses loose and chase them away with the "most hideous whoops and yells."[77] While some Native peoples in California hunted game in this manner, no indication that they attempted to infiltrate an emigrant camp in this manner has been found, including in Hastings's actual experience.[78] The likelihood of fooling anyone seems remote. Yet these were the devious savages that Hastings claimed Euro-Americans would find in California, standing in their way as they had stood in Hastings's way.

Simple tactics existed to keep oneself safe from such creatures. According to Hastings, firing a volley when Native Americans came too close was a prudent strategy, even when the Native people in question were otherwise deemed to be friendly. "Upon discharging a gun, they would, invariably, fall back, and flee in every direction, with the greatest confusion," was one such example for the purpose of maintaining a distance from *friendly* Indians who approached too close. Perhaps John Bidwell would have approved. Firearms were also useful in helping recover the stock of unknown emigrants. Seeing two Native men chasing a stray cow one day, Hastings decided to shoot them with a shotgun. After possibly wounding one or both of them, Hastings and his fellows recovered the cow. They did so not to return it to the rightful owner: they promptly ate the beast. What had been a crime for a Native American one moment was only what was right and proper when a Euro-American did the same. Still the use of firearms did come with attendant dangers. As had happened in Bidwell's and Frémont's parties, a man in Hastings's group lost his life from an accidental gunshot; the bullet passed up into the man's body through his groin, resulting in a slow and painful death. Unlike Frémont and Bidwell, Hastings explicitly linked the event to Indians. "While we were silently and solemnly moving on," he wrote, "under arms, 'to the place of the dead' [the grave they had dug], the sentinels were to be seen, standing at their designated posts, alternately meditating upon the solemnity of the passing scene, and casting their eyes watchfully aroused as if to descry the numerous and hostile foe, with whom we were everywhere surrounded, and thus, to avert the accumulating danger!"[79] Perhaps most telling of Hastings's thoughts as he "dreaded a fearful future" full of murderous Indians would be to note that at this point in the journey, the emigrants had not encountered any trouble with Native Americans and, indeed, seem to have met none thus far.[80] What was more likely causing this dread was their deep-seated fear before they ever set out on the road, fear accumulated from popular culture, education, and the racial essentialism of the nineteenth century.

Other tactics proposed by Hastings were costly in terms of time and the mental health of emigrants. He advised emigrants to stop well before dark and to make all fires for cooking early enough so that they might be extinguished by dark. This practice was not unheard of, and perhaps Hastings had learned the strategy by word of mouth.[81] He also advised that all animals be put out to graze before dark and then brought into a huge corral created by circling the wagons of the party. This formation would guarantee that strays would be rare and that raiders would have to work to get at the stock. The camp was to be ringed by sentinels, who were replaced every two hours. The manpower necessary would not be a problem if emigrants traveled in the numbers Hastings suggested, which should be large but not to exceed five hundred.[82] Of course, these precautions guaranteed cold nights, disturbed by cattle and stock moving and making noise all night. Yet the strategy would appeal to emigrants who were full of tales of marauding Indian thieves, stealing cattle and horses.[83] Native Americans did steal cattle and horses, but by most accounts other causes of lost stock far outweighed theft. Ironically, the strategy designed to keep thieves away from stock also made it necessary for Native Americans who wanted livestock to get past the emigrants, creating an opportunity for violence. Perhaps most important in the long run, Hastings's strategy packed emigrants together in slow-moving columns, and his recommendation to stop early each day added weeks to a journey.

But in spite of his advice and cautionary tales, Hastings could not help but admit that to his knowledge very few emigrants were killed by Indians. In fact he warned that emigrants were much more likely to die by each other's hands or by "accidental discharge," as had been the case in his company. Weapons, he cautioned, should be carried loaded but unprimed or uncapped to avoid their firing. But guns should be carried. According to him, a good rifle and two pistols were ideal, especially if one brought plenty of ammunition. One should be armed against the threat of Indian attack and also the threat of buffalo stampede, and to hunt buffalo for food.[84]

Implicit in Frémont's account, but nearly absent from Bidwell's and Hastings's narratives, was an understanding of the reciprocity that many Native American cultures demanded of relations between people. Many times Frémont and his party made gifts and trades with Indigenous people. This was customary and polite, especially given that he and his men were crossing lands controlled by these groups and often consuming their resources as they did so. In contrast, Bidwell's and Hastings's recommendation was to keep Native Americans away, almost at any cost. But Hastings was not completely blind to the uses of trade, advising the emigrant to "provide himself with some such goods, as are adapted to the Indian trade." However, he made no suggestions for how these items might be used on the journey. His party used exchange with Indigenous people to satisfy their own needs, not to show respect or offer compensation to Native Americans. He was clear that money was of little use because the "barbarous Indians . . . know nothing of money or its value."[85] Still, Hastings's vague advice concerning exchange with Native peoples on the trail was much more than most guides offered.

To my knowledge, no trail guides written for emigrants have been found that suggested packing trade goods specifically to be used as negotiating tools to secure safe passage or hire Indian guides or guards to take them along the trail in safety. Though this was obviously the strategy of Frémont's group, accounts of emigrants suggest that they felt no need to emulate his example on this point. Trade goods seem instead to be used in the way recommended by the example of Hastings: to get food from local Native populations. That is not to say that such exchanges did not occur, but they certainly seem to have occurred in the context of an inconvenience to emigrants; this would be particularly true of those emigrants reaching the end of their supply of staples, such as flour, sugar, and corn meal. In accounts of those instances when Native Americans were approaching with potentially hostile intent—most often with the taking of horses in mind—there is little evidence to suggest that negotiation occurred to emigrants. Despite the many examples available from sources like Frémont, where Native people and travelers met on uncertain terms, negotiated, and ended up sharing and trading together peacefully, most emigrants seem to have been convinced that the worst stories of inhuman Indian savagery were the only ones worth remembering in a crisis. As one examines the overland trail experiences of westward settlers, the strategy of force akin to that employed by Bidwell and Hastings seems the model many emigrants adopted.

3

The Overland Trail Experience

Digger.... I first heard the name from specimens of an abandoned class of the mountaineer type of white men. Some of these were indeed as degraded as it is possible to imagine. They seemed to think no more of killing an Indian than shooting a coyote. One of these men whom I saw boasted of the number of Indians he had killed, keeping the account by notches which he cut on his tomahawk handle that counted nearly a hundred. This was the sort of man that brought the name Digger from the Rocky Mountains to California.

John Bidwell to Miss Miller, December 28, 1894

The way that most of the tens of thousands of emigrants experienced the overland trail to California in the 1840s and 1850s was much different than what they might have expected based on the stories circulated back in the United States, especially in newspapers, travel narratives, government reports, and emigrant guides. The course advised by men like Hastings, when put into practice, often produced situations with much different outcomes. Moreover a variety of scenarios not anticipated in the trail guides occurred, offering myriad examples of Euro-American ideas of race, religion, national destiny, and democracy operating on the overland trails in an atmosphere of abject fear of Indian attack.

Ezra M. Hamilton's experience provides an important window on the way that anxiety and fear blended to create ridiculous scenarios that sadly helped to strengthen Euro-American hatred and disregard for Native peoples. Hamilton headed west in 1853 to prospect for gold. He traveled over the California-Oregon Trail with a company of emigrants, who, like himself, were concerned about Indian attack. The company followed the advice recommended in almost every trail guide: to go heavily armed and to keep a watch at night. Hamilton was armed with knife, rifle, and Colt revolver, plus plenty of ammunition. To defend against attack, each night the group mounted a two-man guard. One night, while on guard duty and finding his fellow guard sleeping, Hamilton determined to pay him out for his disregard of duty. He sharpened a stick of green willow wood about three feet in length. Creeping up to the sleeping man, he stabbed the shaft into his leg and retreated into the darkness to watch the outcome of what he considered a joke to pay the man for his laziness. But something much more than he intended followed. The man awoke, screaming and in pain, seeing the "arrow" sticking out of him. Already roused by his scream, the rest of the company rushed to him, and the man proceeded to report an Indian attack. The men of the company were incensed and immediately took up their arms and stood prepared to fight. So bloody-minded was the group that Hamilton dared not reveal his prank, knowing, he said, that he might be hanged on the spot.[1]

Native Americans were punished for Hamilton's joke gone awry. From that night on, the company proceeded with the full and true knowledge that savage Indians had attacked them. They redoubled their defensive efforts and stood ready to kill any Native Americans that might come too close. Luckily none crossed paths with the company, with the possible exception of Hamilton, but members of the group would contribute to the myth of Indian savagery and hostility, as they would tell others along the trail and once in California of the attack their group had suffered. They arrived in California with both fear and an unsatisfied desire for revenge for the false attack and all the days and nights of trepidation that followed. As one pair of scholars has pointed out, in the mind-set underpinning genocides, "vengeance is psychologically satisfying."[2] And as these travelers never exacted any vengeance on the trail, they likely sought it elsewhere.

Emigrants traveled west in a state of high anxiety and fear of attack by Indigenous populations, despite the reality that few emigrants encountered such. Rumor and disquiet, not reality, ruled the American perception of the Native peoples of the Trans-Mississippi and Far West.[3] This anxious state profoundly affected both how emigrants dealt with the Native Americans they came across on the trail and how they treated the Native population of California at journey's end. It also affected the minds of the emigrants in strange ways. Again, Ezra Hamilton provides an example of the ways rumor and myth operated along the trail. Hamilton describes one night on guard when he became convinced over the course of his watch that Indians had crept up on the camp, only to find that it was a tree stump shaped in his anxious mind like into the form of a prowling Indian. On another occasion, the same scenario played out, this time with sage brush rather than a tree stump.[4] Despite the fact that his fantastic fears were revealed as unfounded, Hamilton persisted in his belief that marauding savages were a constant threat along the trail. This can be explained in part by the argument that human beings have a "tendency to remember episodes of threat and fear more strongly than longer periods of calm and peaceful relations with other groups."[5] In other words, as emigrants headed to California, despite all of their neutral and positive contacts with Native Americans, one negative episode—perhaps even one perceived rather than experienced, as in the case of Hamilton's group—was enough to heighten the existing fear and hatred of Native Americans. Such fears could travel eastward as well.

John Unruh Jr., one of the most prominent historians of the overland trail, made a study of the effects of eastward migration on the trails normally taking emigrants west. As emigrants passed in both directions, information was exchanged. In particular, frontier outposts such as Fort Laramie served as a nexus for information exchange. According to one estimate, during the height of the 1850 rush to California, Fort Laramie handled hundreds of people and wagons in a single day. The information exchanged at these vital stopover and news-gathering points was particularly susceptible to the exaggerations and tall tales of eastward returnees. Two important trends in their stories have surfaced: first, they "were notorious rumor spreaders" and "tended to exaggerate the incidence of cholera, the insufficiency of grass, or the Indian threat"; second, they often contrived excuses for their own failure on the trail west, especially to cover up for disasters born of their incompetence. One telling example of the latter included men who had lost their stock through carelessness and ineptitude, yet blamed their losses on Native American thievery. The prevalence of the exaggerated horror stories told by those heading east was so great that newspapers sometimes cautioned westward emigrants not to take the tales at face value. One can safely assume that before the exaggeration became common knowledge, significant numbers of westbound immigrants were led to believe that marauding Indians were attacking or stealing from companies when no such action had occurred. This would have only reinforced already tainted perceptions of Native Americans. Even when emigrants had been forewarned, it was difficult for the bad information to be discarded because the true accounts carried by the eastbound were extremely important. Accurate directions and honest accounts of illness and Indian thefts and attacks did circulate without exaggeration, and what one was to believe or not believe was likely a tough decision. For many, the best and most reliable source of information about what lay ahead on the trail west came from the communications of the eastbound.[6]

Ezra Hamilton was the likely recipient not only of eastbound intelligence at some point along the trail, but also news exchanged when his company was reconstituted for another leg of the journey west. Traveling with a different company, he remained afraid and cautious, despite having had no trouble with Native peoples thus far. His fear of Native Americans this time almost led to the death of the man he worked for, a man traveling with his wife and children and employing him as a hired hand. Noticing that a horse was coming untethered one night, Hamilton's employer went to retie the animal. In a nighttime moment reminiscent of Bidwell's confusion at a daytime mirage, Hamilton, on guard and seeing a shadowy figure approaching the horse, believed it was a thieving Indian loosing the bonds of the animal, took aim, and was about to shoot when enough light was shed on the figure to reveal his employer.[7]

While no Native people that Hamilton need have feared presented themselves on the journey, one should note that by his own account he had done many things that would have provoked the violence of Native Americans along the way had they known of his actions and intentions. This was the case because, from a Native perspective, Hamilton had committed several misdeeds against groups along the way.[8] In one incident, he and his first company encountered raised platforms and trees containing funerary arrangements of deceased Native Americans. Rather than pass on, Hamilton ascended into the trees and disturbed the site to satisfy his own curiosity.[9] Had they found him at it, the Native Americans likely would have intervened violently. In any case the disturbance might have incited retribution or heightened defensiveness in the region later on, thus contributing further to the tensions between emigrants and Native Americans. Few Euro-Americans would have tolerated finding Native Americans engaged in similar disturbances of their own burial sites.

In two other cases that illustrate the variety of trail experiences, Hamilton sought to satisfy his own disturbed sense of humor. Apparently not dissuaded by the alarming results of his earlier "Indian arrow" prank, he decided to play some tricks on Indians. He conceived one such joke outside of Fort Laramie. Noticing how much the smell of bacon attracted Native people camped nearby to the company and the fort, he decided to get these curious individuals up close to his fire and pan of bacon. When he was sure they were close enough, and sure that they were focused on the pan of sizzling bacon, he purposely lifted a piece high over the pan and then pretended to accidentally drop it. Hamilton was pleased with the result: spattered and yelling from a spray of hot bacon fat, the Indians scattered. In another example of his twisted humor, and in a similar case of curious Native visitors, Hamilton described a joke he played in 1854 on an unsuspecting Native woman and her companions: "One day as I was handling quicksilver there come along about a dozen Indians and squaws. They saw the quicksilver [and] they wanted [it]. . . . I gave an old squaw a spoonful of it [to swallow]. She clapped her hand on her stomach and looked around. The quicksilver had went through her [and it now] lay on the sand [beneath her]."[10] Here again Native peoples might have acted otherwise had they known Hamilton or his motives better. Had they known the true properties of quicksilver, also called liquid mercury, they may have responded with violence. Although in the nineteenth century quicksilver was used in gold mining and even as a treatment in Western medicine, mercury is poisonous, and with enough exposure is lethal. Hamilton's joke not only demonstrated the disregard for Native people apparent in his other actions, but it also demonstrated the limits of Euro-American science and medicine. Confident of their knowledge, Western medical practitioners condoned the use of this toxic substance, and led Hamilton to poison an old woman, thinking it yet another harmless joke. As with his other moments of humor, this too had potentially far-reaching consequences, this time for a woman whose health he damaged in ignorance by serving her a half-pound dose of mercury. That Hamilton and others did not know that it was poison is of little value in their defense: Euro-Americans adopted a posture of superiority in culture and knowledge where Native Americans were concerned.

Such jokes were not reserved for Hamilton. In a third anecdote associated with playing malicious tricks on Indians, this one from shortly after his arrival in California, Hamilton related the case of a joke conceived by another Euro-American, with Hamilton playing the role of accomplice: "We had some sport while building this mill. When the blacksmith set up his forge and commenced to work the Indians collected to the number of about fifty or sixty to see him work. He had a large bar of iron to a white heat and laid it on the anvil [with the tongs] and winked to me. I hit it a furious blow with the sledge [hammer]. The sparks flew in every direction. In less time than it takes to write it there was not an Indian to be seen." Hamilton was sure that the Indians believed their pain came not from the discharge of white-hot fragments onto exposed flesh, but from "the devil or some other evil spirit" attacking them.[11] The humorous "sport" of burning unsuspecting Native people bears some resemblance to Hamilton's earlier bacon fat trick, revealing again the savage pleasures of Euro-Americans rather than Native Americans.[12]

In another instance, Isaac Gibson and his brother, traveling west to California in a group of emigrants, thought to trick a party of Sioux into trading a horse for their disobedient mule. The Sioux asked after the mule's behavior and Gibson lied to them, saying the animal was easy to handle and calm. What the Gibson brothers and their companions may not have known or considered was that they were endangering the lives of the Sioux by making this trade. Other emigrants, seeing Native Americans mounted on mules, shod horses, or in possession of domesticated livestock, sometimes assumed that these animals were stolen. As one emigrant put it, "Saw a party of Indians. They were a dirty miserable set and had a lot of horses, no doubt stolen, as they were shod."[13] Gibson tried to assure the Sioux by mounting the mule, but the mule immediately threw him.[14] Gibson's brother, J. Watt Gibson, wrote of the event, "I never saw anything give as much delight as this gave the Indians. . . . We joined the Indians and laughed as they; everybody enjoyed it but brother Isaac."[15] Though all but Isaac laughed, one can still detect the contempt emigrants had for Indigenous peoples. What if the mule, made skittish by a large group of strange horses and men, had not thrown Gibson? Likely only the whites would have laughed as they proceeded down the trail with a good horse, chuckling about the ignorant savages that had traded for the wild-tempered mule. The Sioux would have learned an important lesson about trusting whites coming through their country, a lesson that by its repetition might turn to something grimmer than laughter at a dishonest white man trying to swindle them in the future.

These tricks and demented jokes suggest a telling psychological aspect to what Hamilton and others were doing. In these moments, instead of mocking their own unfounded fears after meeting peaceful and curious peoples not bent on killing them, they chose instead to mock, maim, and cheat people who now seemed unworthy of being feared.

Perhaps they needed to release the tensions created by fear. Having been afraid for so long, and having had no opportunity to destroy the source of dread—that is, to kill—Hamilton and others perhaps looked for an alternative form of release.[16] Other groups released their pent-up fears in different but equally disturbing ways.

In the diary he kept during his 1862 crossing to California, George Harter described his discovery along the trail of a Native American funerary site. As the company passed the corpse, suspended on a platform by poles and wrapped in skins, one emigrant began to mutilate the dead body by using it for target practice. Harter, thinking the circumstances amusing, observed, "The boys were carrying their guns to shoot Indians and one of them tried his hand on this one, but I did not think it hurt him."[17] Harter is certainly mistaken; the defilement of the body and sacred site did hurt. Native peoples passing that way afterward would find the desecration and have one more reason to distrust and dislike whites. If Native people had opened the graves of Euro-Americans, it seems safe to assume that rage and outcry would have resulted. But such actions were no crime at all in the minds of Euro-Americans when committed against Native Americans. These unexamined releases to innermost fears are a clue to the way many emigrants must have felt having crossed the Plains with little or no trouble from Native peoples or as they poured into the Sierra Nevada foothills in 1849 looking for gold, only to find Native people peacefully living and panning for gold along the many watercourses that flowed down from the mountains.

When these emigrant trains reached their destinations safely and without bloodshed at savage hands, many may have been convinced that it was their proactive hostile stance that delivered them from the clutches of bloodthirsty savages. Such certainty, repeated in emigrant guide and trail narratives that sought to bring Euro-Americans safely to California, became self-evident truth for emigrants to California who suffered no troubles with Native peoples—statistically the majority of emigrants. As Frémont concluded in *Report of the Exploring Expedition to the Rocky Mountains*, "Strict vigilance was maintained among the people, and one-third were kept on guard during the night. There is no reason to doubt these dispositions, uniformly preserved, conducted our party securely through Indians famed for treachery."[18] Such certainty often flew in the face of experiences that suggested otherwise, as Native peoples in the 1840s and 1850s typically engaged in primarily friendly relations with emigrants. When considered together, these two related aspects of the Euro-American view of Indigenous populations helps explain how emigrants could travel thousands of miles without meeting any hostility from Native Americans, and yet remain fearful and aggressive toward them in California.

But despite the early years of emigration and its numerous peaceful encounters with Indigenous populations, as the United States took control of California, such evidence was not enough to disabuse successive waves of Euro-Americans of the erroneous stereotypes of Native Americans that had been constructed since the colonial era. Even with the safety in numbers granted by the massive relocation of whites to California during the overland sprint for gold starting in 1848, Euro-Americans continued to fear the Indian above all other obstacles on the trail. Even heavily armed companies of men lived in fear of Indian attack. A vivid example comes from Addison Pratt, who traveled as part of a Mormon company in 1848 from San Francisco to Salt Lake City. The company, which set out from Sutter's Fort in the second week of June 1848, was substantial: seventeen wagons, forty men, one woman, two hundred horses and mules, and 250 head of working stock and cattle. Perhaps most interesting of all the items they took east were two brass cannon they had purchased from John Sutter.[19]

Clearly the group anticipated trouble. The men divided into four ten-man companies and proceeded in military order for the journey. Much like Frémont's group, this was essentially a military company, not a democracy. They sent scouts out ahead and were particularly careful about reconnaissance because they had determined to break a new trail where they believed no white men had yet gone, but also believing hostile Indians were sure to be there and this might mean trouble. In this they were correct, because trouble did come.

Three of their scouts went missing and could not be located. After some progress eastward, a lone Native person was spotted. He was believed to be wearing a garment belonging to one of the men. Soon afterward they discovered an unmarked, unadorned fresh grave, which they assumed had been made by the murderous Indians to bury one of the missing men.[20] Pratt admitted that when the men had first gone missing, the group assumed that Indians had murdered them. The group camped at the grave site, making a thorough search of the area. They found bloody as well as unused arrows. They discovered an Indian burial mound, and after breaking it open, found *all three* of their missing friends. The men had been killed and stripped of their clothing and then buried in a mound "after the order of Indian burials." Who was buried in the first grave, then? What is interesting about the account, though Pratt did not find it so, is that the original grave was likely an Indian grave, as they were the only white men in the valley and their three friends now lay before them in the second grave. How had this person come to be killed? Based on Pratt's evidence, the whites believed their friends had been cut down while fleeing Indians in the dark. Perhaps one of the three killed an Indian, whom the three whites had buried before they were killed and buried together. However, it was and is impossible to know the order of events that produced the Euro-Americans' deaths. Pratt and the group, however, believed they had the measure of things as they reburied their companions in a grave they were careful to augment with stones and an inscription. Indians had wantonly murdered their companions.

After the investigation and the reinterment of the bodies, Pratt took a moment to reflect on the event, writing, "I have often read of such occurrences, but to be a participator in such a mournful discovery can not be easily obliterated."[21] This makes some sense of how stories circulated and reinforced earlier tales. For Pratt, the three had died in a way familiar to him, rather than in an event shrouded in mystery, as one with some perspective might admit. Of course, such deliberations on uncertainty were not part of Pratt's reflections. Based on the diary and on his later trip back into California, undoubtedly he communicated the story with a great deal of certainty to others, despite the lack of evidence his own account admits. One should not be surprised by this, because as Pratt explained, they knew what happened before it happened, and events were interpreted in this light. Other emigrants, with some luck, were able to be more circumspect, as was evidenced by the discovery made by the company with whom Jane Gould was traveling.

As Gould's company headed west in 1862, they heard rumors that a man had been killed by hostile Indians. The man had been buried in a shallow grave, on top of which were exhibited bloody arrows. As many wagons passed over the site, they unearthed the grave, and the truth. Puckered on the dead man's temple was a bullet hole.[22] It seems likely that the man had died by white hands rather than Native American. Fear of Indians was employed as a cloak to cover the crime. George Harter and his emigrant company actually encountered white men engaged in murder and a plot to blame Native Americans. After "his own company murdered him for his money" they told Harter's nearby party that Indians had shot him. Harter's group discovered otherwise as the night progressed, learning that white men, not Native Americans, had killed the man.[23] In the case of Pratt's company, though, the group's suspicions remained fixed on Indians as the culprits, and their assumptions did not end there.

The night they reburied the three men, the group was more fearful than ever. Pratt recalled that the company was in tight formation, with all the animals brought into in an improvised corral. The level of excitement was so high that Pratt and his fellows believed that the Indians "were on the alert for us," despite the fact that they had not seen any Indian since the day before the bodies were found.[24] Men not posted on guard decided to sleep on top of loaded guns. They also loaded the brass cannons with powder and shot. The trouble that ensued that night was perhaps much more typical of the trail experience of many Euro-Americans.

Several hours short of midnight, on a moonless night, the cattle in the corral suddenly shifted from one side of the enclosure to the other. This move was enough for the company to raise the alarm. As with the bodies, they knew the story before it was written. The men assembled quickly, brought the cannon around in a likely direction, and set fire to the touchhole. The six-pound gun not only produced a flash, a cacophonous boom, and a billow of smoke, but it also frightened all 450 animals out of the corral and into the night. As the smoke cleared and the echoes receded, no sign of Indians was to be found, though. When morning came, again with no evidence of Indians, the men began trying to recover their stock. During the next two days they found 449 of the beasts. The one that was not recovered, an ox, happened to belong to Pratt. And despite all evidence that no Indians had been at their camp that night, Pratt wrote in his diary that he and the others were sure Indians had stolen and eaten his ox. Yet when the ox was brought to him by the next group coming up the trail to Salt Lake, he simply recorded this and did not reflect on his and his fellows' error.[25]

Pratt returned to California in 1849, this time with an emigrant company organized in the Utah Territory. Comprising hundreds of men, women, and children, a thousand head of stock, and hundreds of wagons, the train was mammoth compared to his earlier, eastbound group. Leaving Salt Lake City on the first day of October 1849, the train took a southwesterly route down through what today is Utah and southern Nevada into southern California, their ultimate goal being the Rancho del Chino. Just nine days out, the train met Indigenous people of an unidentified group. Despite the party's campsite being located on one of the few water sources in the arid region, the Native men had come to trade fresh horses for rifles rather than defend the precious, scarce resource. According to Pratt, some members of the company obliged them with a trade. By October 21 the party had come over the Cajon Pass and was safely at Rancho del Chino, without loss of life or hostility from the Native populations of the Great Basin or the mountains.[26]

It is abundantly clear that Euro-Americans flooding into California in these first few years of the Gold Rush era came with an existing fear and hatred of Indians even though violence was actually quite rare between Americans and Indians on the overland trail during the

1840s and 1850s.[27] In the over two dozen trail narratives and diaries I examined, Indian difficulties are much feared and discussed, but never encountered. This fear was not dissipated by empirical proof of its falsity on the trails westward, and was still palpable once in California. Arguably it was this fear that was the source of Euro-American aggression and violence against Native Americans in California, or at least apathy about such violence. Despite the lack of evidence of Native American hostilities, sensationalized accounts of Indian violence and savagery, obtained by rumor and superficial conclusions in trail narratives and guides, remained vivid in the minds of many emigrants. Given this pervasive foundation, many emigrants convinced themselves that it was their vigilance and strength of arms that kept Indians at bay on the trail, and not the will of Native people to trade or allow emigrants to pass unmolested. As such, upon reaching California, rather than being disabused of their ignorance of Indigenous peoples on the journey across the continent, they remained ignorant of Native American civilizations and intentions, still eager to punish the "red devils" who were constantly lurking and ready to pounce. It appears, at least outwardly, that Euro-Americans remained convinced that they *knew* Indians and how to keep themselves and their property safe, despite the estimate that of the 90,000 Americans moving to California during the 1840s, only 115 died in conflicts with Native Americans. Ignoring the fact "that, in retrospect, they had felt more threatened by careless gunplay in their own companies than by hostile natives," emigrants celebrated their crossing as a triumph of arms over murderous Indians who had undoubtedly hoped to kill them.[28] This contributed to the intensity of hatred for Indians rampant among Euro-Americans in California. The violence it bred brought genocide to California's Native populations.

A second fundamental element to understanding Euro-American genocide of Indigenous peoples in California is an examination of motives and attitudes of emigrants as they moved to California. By looking at newspaper articles, trail diaries, letters, and memoirs associated with westward expansion in this era, one can see that Euro-Americans imagined California before ever seeing it and worked to remake California into their dream once they arrived. Whether one considers the musings of Dana on a relatively brief, geographically limited visit to California, or the reflections of an emigrant as he passed over the trail and considered the country around him (his country, though he had never been there before), or newspaper articles rooting for the settlement of western lands and the mining of rich gold deposits in California, the spirit of Manifest Destiny ties them together as if one mind had conceived them: the Euro-American mind. The Gold Rush in particular reshaped the course of the history of the United States. The discovery of gold in 1848 reached the United States in much the same way that news about California had reached earlier emigrants: through a government report, broadcast subsequently in the form of an address to Congress by President James K. Polk, followed by heavy coverage in the press. The Gold Rush emigrant was born. Hoping for a quick and easy trip to California, emigrants snapped up emigrant guides, listened to rumors, read travel accounts, and then went west, most intending to return rich, but few ever doing so.[29] They headed west to a place and people they already knew through education, national experience, and rumor. Some believed that the only thing that stood in the way of their getting the gold was Indians, described by *Harper's Weekly* as "hopelessly lazy and dirty, great thieves and liars, and treacherous and inhuman to the last degree."[30] In other words, the same Indians that many Euro-Americans believed they had always known. Euro-Americans numbering in the hundreds of thousands in the late 1840s and throughout the 1850s did not hesitate to go for California's gold, and no Indian would be allowed to stand in their way or in the path of the nation's Manifest Destiny.

The United States jump-started a new phase of Manifest Destiny, as thousands and then hundreds of thousands of Euro-Americans flooded California in its first decade as part of the United States. Most craved land or what the land offered in the form of gold. But, famously, most Euro-Americans did not strike it rich in California and were unable or unwilling to return to the East as failures. Whether continuing as frustrated miners panning for their dreams or as settlers trying to build a life in a new state from the bottom up, Euro-Americans found California's Indigenous population standing in their way. Approximately 150,000 Native Americans inhabited California in 1848. By 1900 their population was approximately 15,000, a shocking decline. What had happened? In the main, Euro-American hatred of Indians had mixed with the spirit of Manifest Destiny in California and created the perfect catalyst for genocide. Genocide became both an outlet for the pent-up terror of life among supposed savages and the mechanism necessary to deliver Native land into Euro-American hands, bringing national destiny in California to its horrifying fruition. Indeed one of the most murderous forces on Earth during the nineteenth century had come to California: the citizen-settlers of the United States of America. Looking back, California appears to have been the Murder State rather than the Golden State.

PART 2

Perpetrating Genocide

Introduction

The American as conqueror is unwilling to appear in public as pure
aggressor. . . . The American wants to persuade not only the world, but
himself, that he is doing God service in a peaceable spirit, even when
he violently takes what he has determined to get. His conscience is
sensitive, and hostile aggression, practiced against any but Indians,
shocks this conscience, unused as it is to such scenes.

Josiah Royce, *California: A Study of American Character* (1886)

Euro-American emigrants arrived in California by the thousands each
year during the second half of the nineteenth century. Those with the
means could take an ocean voyage, avoiding the perceived peril of Indians but facing instead a dangerous passage that could take five months
or more to complete or end in death by disease or shipwreck. Those
with less money traveled overland, often in terror of savage Indians
during a journey that could take three months or more. While most
arrived safely and experienced more danger from disease or starvation
than from Native Americans, few seemed disabused of the notion
that Indians had posed the greatest threat of all. Like Frémont and
Hastings before them, many believed armed vigilance had brought
them through alive. Flooding into the foothills of the Sierra Nevada
and congregating along the watercourses that flowed down from the
melting snows, thousands sought their fortunes by panning, rocking,
or hydraulic mining for gold. In 1848 there were perhaps only six thousand miners working claims, many of them Mexicans and Pacific Rim
peoples from Hawaii and China, plus an indeterminate number of

Table 1. Population Estimates for California, 1848–1910

Year	California Native Population	U.S. Native Population	California Non-Native Population
1848	150,000	n.d.	15,000
1850	n.d.	400,764	165,000
1860	35,000	339,421	379,994
1870	30,000	313,712	560,247
1880	20,500	306,543	864,694
1890	16,624	248,253	1,213,398
1900	15,377	237,196	1,485,053
1910	16,371	265,683	2,377,549

Sources: Stuart, *Nations within a Nation*, 52, 54, 57; Hyslop and Miller, *California*, 10; Hurtado, *Indian Survival on the California Frontier*, 194; Thornton, *American Indian Holocaust and Survival*, 109; Rawls, *Indians of California*, 171, 214. Data exclude Native peoples of Alaska and Hawaii.

Indigenous people. But after news hit the United States of the discovery of massive quantities of gold, more than two hundred thousand Americans poured into California in the next four years, bringing with them negative attitudes about Native Americans reinforced by deeply biased conceptions of race, religion, and national destiny, overwhelming nonwhites and driving many of them from the gold fields with a combination of violence, murder, and legal maneuvering.[1]

The Indigenous population of California, estimated at 150,000 in 1848, would suffer mightily at the hands of the gold seekers from the United States. As the Euro-American population increased dramatically each year, the population of Native Americans fell at an equally sharp rate. By 1900 the California Indian population was only 10 percent of what it had been in 1848 (table 1).[2] What had happened to cause such a demographic collapse?

Euro-Americans and democratically driven genocide had happened. Euro-American settlers, miners, and ranchers used the systems of democracy that they had employed in the East and on the trail to re-move the obstacles that Native Americans posed to their acquisition of land for farming, mining, or grazing. And whether one wanted mineral wealth, grazing pastures, or land to farm, Native peoples were ubiquitous in California at the outbreak of the Gold Rush. The Euro-American desire to remove or exterminate Native Americans from prime farming and grazing lands increased with each passing year, as Euro-Americans realized that the gold fields of California were not as advertised in the East. For example, in 1848 the six thousand non-Native miners in California extracted about $10 million in gold, or just under $1,700 per person on average. By 1852, the height of the Gold Rush in terms of the aggregate value of gold taken in a year, there were around one hundred thousand miners producing $80 mil-lion in gold, or $800 per person.[3] This average rate continued to fall for the rest of the 1850s. Because it could cost more than $800 to go to California, especially if traveling by sea, the Gold Rush proved to be a losing proposition for most. This aspect of the Gold Rush helps to explain the dramatic shift in what Euro-Americans did once in California. As more and more men realized that no easy money lay in the river or in the ground, many turned to pursuits that could make money more easily; often this meant charging new waves of miners outrageous prices for goods and services. Professions such as farming, ranching, and logging offered a cheap, easy, and profitable alternative to wading in cold, sometimes waist-deep water all day, panning for gold, or breaking one's back digging.

All one needed to get started was a little bit of capital, or an ax, or some cattle brought overland or bought from a *Californio ranchero*. The rest was there to be exploited from the natural landscape, at little or no cost. The U.S. government offered public lands for the meager sum of $1.25 per acre through a variety of programs, including the School Land Warrant system. In this system, the federal government gifted the state of California five hundred thousand acres that it had gained title to in the Treaty of Guadalupe Hidalgo with Mexico. The state was thus able to finance the creation of a public school system from the proceeds of the land sales. Given the massive inflation of prices and wages in California, and the decision of the federal government not to match the rise in inflation with a raise in the prices of land beyond $1.25, many Euro-Americans in California could afford to purchase large tracts of land.[4] Much of the five hundred thousand acres was land occupied for millennia by Native American people, who were now to be shorn of it via remote, uninformed decisions made in faraway Washington DC.

Soldiers from the recent Mexican-American War too had legal rights that they could exercise to obtain land, to the detriment of Native people. In 1847 the U.S. War Department issued a decree that public lands could be had as a bounty for participation in the war, depending only on an honorable discharge to claim it. While land was opened all over the West by the treaty with Mexico, California was undoubtedly the most desirable place to claim land. The generous bounty allowed one to claim up to 160 acres and also permitted claimants to transfer these claims to their next of kin in the event of their death. Even a man serving less than twelve months in the war was allowed a bounty of forty acres.[5] One could choose to take a cash payment rather than land, but the actual value of the land, even at $1.25 an acre, was typically worth much more than the cash offering. When one considered the potential money to be made by exploiting or even just turning around and selling the land in question, it must have seemed foolish not to accept the land bounty.

Given these options, much of the prime timber, mineral, and grazing public lands in California were, for all intents and purposes, available for the taking by emigrants and military veterans. Whether one was making a claim on land to farm, graze, or log, or surreptitiously using land with no legal claim at all for these same purposes, Native Americans entered into the picture in unavoidable ways. California, a state comprising approximately 100 million acres, had been only sparsely populated by non-Native peoples under Spanish and then Mexican control. When Mexico achieved independence, perhaps only three thousand non-Natives lived in California. By the 1846 outbreak of the Mexican-American War that culminated in the Mexico's loss of

California to the United States, fewer than ten thousand non-Natives lived there. Despite the fact that as many as eight hundred land grants had been made in California prior to the end of Mexican rule, perhaps only 20 percent of the available land was occupied by non-Natives. And given that the Mexicans typically let many Native people live within their grants, to say that they had complete control of even these lands would be an exaggeration.[6] For settlers from the United States, this would not do.

Euro-Americans came in massive waves by two main routes overland. The northern route, the Oregon-California Trail, was the main artery. The southern route, which included the Old Spanish Trail, the Santa Fe Trail, and the Gila River Trail, was of secondary importance. But though the southern trails constituted a secondary route for Euro-Americans bound for the Gold Rush, the route was an important main line for Mexican miners and traders coming up from Sonora, Mexico. As a result, from the beginning of the Gold Rush forward, Native Americans in northern and southern California had the experience of thousands of non-Natives crossing over their ancestral lands to reach the gold fields of the foothills of the Sierra Nevada and elsewhere. Worse still, as gold became difficult to find, Euro-Americans began searching the hills and mountains of California for new sources of wealth. As these dreams of quick riches faded, Euro-Americans began an assault on Indigenous populations in order to wrest the land itself from their control. Land and its productive capacity would be California's new gold—indeed, in the long term, its real gold.

Convenience and practical necessity, as in many other cases of genocide, drove genocide in California.[7] By launching a campaign of genocide, Euro-Americans were able to transfer control of land and resources from Native people to themselves. As they had believed before coming to California, Euro-Americans continued to envision Indians as wild animals; this also encouraged genocide as a pragmatic salve to their fears, allowing whites to justify extermination as necessary to avoid their own deaths at savage hands.[8] The key concern was how to effectively and cheaply bring about the demise of tens of thousands of

Native Americans in a relatively short span of time. Euro-Americans looked to their ancestors for answers to this quandary.

In both northern and southern California, the most effective way to accomplish this land theft by genocide was by utilizing democratic and republican institutions. By employing traditional practices and institutions, such as community cooperation, democratic decision making, and republican representation, small communities of Euro-Americans learned that they could effectively exterminate Native Americans legally, efficiently, and profitably. Without Indigenous populations to dispute or disrupt claims to lands and resources, Euro-Americans would be positioned to transform California into what many hoped would be the most free, most individualistic and entrepreneurial state in the Union. Many Euro-Americans seemed to think that only the murder of thousands of worthless Indians in the northern and southern halves of the state stood in their way. All they needed to do was get organized and proceed. Yet Native American communities resisted such efforts, sometimes with violence, which in many ways only intensified the genocidal efforts of Euro-Americans. The cycles of revenge that grew from acts of violence instigated mainly by whites, allowed Euro-Americans to soothe their consciences in yet another way.[9] As Indian people retaliated in kind against settlers, miners, and ranchers, Euro-Americans would add revenge to their existing justifications for genocide.

As Daniel Chirot and Clark McCauley have pointed out, there is a way to get "ordinary people to become butchers." The key, they argue, is to create distance between perpetrator and victim through dehumanization, ritual, and legalization. By disassociating themselves from the victims, the perpetrators are able to carry out horrendous acts with a minimum of self-loathing; without such strategies of disassociation, their actions would create feelings of revulsion out of the recognized sameness of victim and executioner. Using alcohol, military-style organization, and game hunting as practice for human hunting; taking trophies; making it lawful to kill certain groups; killing at a distance rather than in close contact—measures such as these were and are psychological rationalizations that allow human beings to brutally and repeatedly murder, and at the same time maintain a sense of their own humanity.[10] Many Euro-American settlers, miners, and ranchers in California employed many of these elements found in instances of genocide throughout history and around the world. Already predisposed to hate, fear, and distrust savage Indians, they found Native peoples in possession of the land and resources that could salvage their broken California dreams. As aggressive Euro-American pressures forced Native American defensive responses, the optimum conditions for genocide in California were achieved.

4

The Economics of Genocide
in Southern California

Cannot some plan be devised to remove them [Indians] from our
midst? Could they not be removed to a plantation in the vicinity of
our city, and put under the control of an overseer, and not be permitted
to enter the city, except by special permit of the Superintendent?
Our citizens who are in want of their labor could apply direct to the
Superintendent for such help as they might want, and when their work
was finished, permit them to return to their home.

Los Angeles Star (1856)

Despite their location away from the main gold fields of the Sierra
Nevada and its foothills, Native peoples in southern California faced
challenges to their very existence.[1] While Indigenous populations in
the northern half of the state experienced a massive influx of Euro-
Americans into areas previously unoccupied by Spanish and Mexican
settlement, in southern California Euro-Americans entered the "cow
counties" and grafted themselves onto existing systems of ranching and
farming. White Americans in the 1850s relied on Native Americans to
work large tracts of land in exchange for little or no hard currency. As
the Gold Rush boomed in the north, many rancho owners benefited
mightily, as they herded their animals into the Central Valley and
Sierra foothills to reap massive profits during the relatively flush years
of gold mining. Despite the relative lack of precious metals in southern
California, existence was no less perilous for Native Americans. They

faced genocide as Euro-Americans attempted to carve out fortunes that depended not on gold but on land. Destroying Native lifeways, economies, and people, Euro-Americans created an economy based on stolen land worked by what was, in many of its essentials, slave labor. Euro-Americans in southern California used multiple aspects of their traditional democratic forms to accomplish these goals.

Initially the Euro-Americans of Los Angeles County found a use for Native labor in an economy starved for laborers by the migration of people to the gold fields. Even in the middle of the 1850s, with gold fever near its cure, Euro-Americans still sought Native Americans as laborers, although typically only if they could be controlled effectively. The *Los Angeles Star* echoed the sentiments of its readers when it asked, "Cannot some plan be devised to remove them [Indians] from our midst? Could they not be removed to a plantation in the vicinity of our city, and put under the control of an overseer?" In such an atmosphere, Indigenous people who could not be removed to reservations or failed to remain in remote desert areas risked death. Euro-Americans had little use for Indians not harnessed to their interests. Only strong Native leadership, cooperation, and cultural resiliency prevented Euro-American success at obliterating Native peoples in southern California.

The example of the Quechan people living at the Yuma Crossing near the present-day confluence of California, Arizona, and Mexico shows the genesis of the genocidal intent of Euro-Americans and how democracy was harnessed against Native peoples in the southern portion of the state. As the Quechans, historically a powerful Native people living along the lower Colorado River, attempted to engage in commercial enterprise in competition with a gang of white outlaws, they found that Euro-Americans neither suffered rivals to their enterprises nor allowed nonwhites to exact justice on white men, even when they were murderous, rapacious, and evil.[2]

A group of Quechans living near the Colorado River in southeastern California in 1850 attempted to maintain a ferry business, running people, wagons, and stock over the river.[3] Since the colonial era, some Euro-Americans had argued that Indians' emulation of white labor and culture was key to their becoming civilized. The Quechans, however, were about to learn that such arguments were a pretense only. As had happened in the East, most famously to the Cherokees, Euro-Americans, except for missionaries, were usually not interested in living with and working near Native Americans or in allowing them to hold on to valuable resources. The Quechans were among the earliest victims of Euro-American hypocrisy in southern California.

Dr. Abel Lincoln was perhaps like many Euro-Americans of the Gold Rush era: he found mining hard work, competitive, and not the easy fortune advertised in the East. Lincoln decided to join a growing minority in and around California, the people "mining the miners" as they rushed to California or operated their claims once arrived. High prices, often paid in gold, could be got for almost anything in demand. Following the departure of a group of federal government surveyors who had established a ferry crossing of the Colorado River as part of their work in the area, Lincoln determined that this could be a profitable venture.[4] Without meeting or discussing his aims with local Native peoples, and indeed without having any title to the land from any government, he established the only ferry crossing of the Colorado River's meeting with the Gila Trail, the southern trail to California favored by thousands of gold seekers.[5] Despite Lincoln's decision not to enter into any negotiations with them, peace existed between him and the Quechans.[6] In just three months time, from December 1849 to February 1850, he brought in $60,000 from ferry traffic.[7] But beginning in the second week of February 1850, the ferry also brought in trouble.

A Euro-American named John Glanton came to the ferry with a party of men. Glanton was a former Texas Ranger and Mexican-American War veteran known for his brutality. By the time he met Lincoln, he was also a wanted man in Mexico, carrying an $8,000 price on his head for murdering and scalping Mexican citizens. Glanton had been engaged in a lucrative trade with the Mexican government, who paid bounties for the scalps of Apache men, women, and children. Likely finding the Apaches elusive and dangerous targets, he began murdering and scalping Mexicans and non-Apache Native peoples instead and passing the scalps off as belonging to Apaches. Discovered by authorities, Glanton and his men escaped from Mexico back into the United States.[8] At a loose end, he happened to hear about Lincoln's ferry.

Glanton forced Lincoln into a partnership with him and his men, then led the operation in new directions, embarking on a campaign of "robbery, extortion, and murder" that targeted gold seekers heading in both directions. Lincoln, faced with the choice of losing his cash cow or profiting by the Glanton gang's crimes, chose the latter. According to one account, kidnapping and rape were soon added to the gang's growing list of depredations. The group kidnapped Mexican women coming over the river, forcing them to remain in the gang's camp until the men were done with them. The gang also doubled Lincoln's already high rates.[9] As these crimes were committed mainly against Mexicans, Euro-Americans took little interest in bringing Glanton to justice. But justice came to Glanton, perhaps in a manner he least expected.

A Quechan ferry located downstream became a source of competition with the ferry run by Glanton and Lincoln. In fact the ferry operated by the Quechans had been constructed by a group of emigrants unwilling to be bilked by the high prices at Lincoln's ferry. Following their completion and use of the ferry, the emigrants turned it over to the Quechans, asking that they maintain fair rates for all. This the Quechans did, much to the outrage of Glanton.[10] The Quechans hired an Irishman, identified only as Callaghan in the historical record, to operate the business; this took business from Glanton's operation. Charging as little as a quarter of what Glanton and Lincoln charged, the Quechans transported many people, especially Mexicans up from Sonora, over the river in the first few weeks of April 1850.

Meanwhile, in Los Angeles, unrelated events were filling white imaginations with a terror of Indian attack. In a letter to the governor of California in 1850, Benjamin Hayes, the county attorney, requested executive authorization for a volunteer company in the absence of an official state militia, though he may have known that such a law was making its way toward passage in the legislature. Nearby Santa Barbara was experiencing trouble with Native American raiders, as was the eastern portion of Los Angeles County. As federal forces were unable to station troops in Los Angeles because of the cost and the need to send them where there was already conflict with Native peoples, Hayes argued that "a military company of citizens would answer every purpose of public utility."[11] Ironically, the brutal actions of John Glanton and his men not only failed to show Angelinos that their own countrymen were more of a threat than Indians, but also inflamed citizens against the Quechans.

Unwilling to compete with the Quechans, Glanton and his men destroyed the Quechan ferry after it had been operating for only a few weeks. They killed the Irish ferryman, Callaghan, and pitched his body into the river.[12] They also threatened to kill the Quechans, who responded not with violence but with negotiation. Quechan leaders suggested a compromise: Glanton's operation could ferry emigrants and cargo, and the Quechans would handle the animals. Glanton's answer was to beat a Quechan leader with a club.[13] Not long after the episode, the Quechans responded in an altogether different manner.

Led by Caballo en Pello, a respected leader who may have been the man beaten by Glanton, the Quechans attacked and killed Glanton, Lincoln, and nine others.[14] Three of the gang managed to escape.[15] Despite the fact that many people knew of Glanton and his character and the highway robbery of his ferry operation, they reacted swiftly and violently against the Quechans.

The way Euro-Americans perceived the event had much to do with the false, self-serving stories circulated by the three surviving gang members; how these tall tales meshed with existing prejudices against Indians was a mixture that could lead to genocide. In a letter to Abel Lincoln's family on May 10, 1850, the three surviving gang members described the event as undisguised Indian treachery and savagery, failing to mention the character of the men Lincoln had involved himself with, their murderous business dealings, and their offenses against Mexican and Quechan peoples in the region. They told much the same tale of white innocence and unprovoked attack to the people they interacted with in San Diego and Los Angeles. In a deposition taken in Los Angeles on May 9, one of them denied the rumors circulating about Glanton and the ferry, as well as the gang's destruction of the Quechan ferry.[16] In further depositions and accounts of emigrants and a scouting party to the area, it became clear back in Los Angeles that the Quechans had declared war on Euro-Americans. It was easy, perhaps too easy, for Euro-Americans to come to such a conclusion. As Lt. William Tecumseh Sherman, serving in California in the late 1840s, observed, "The Californians are very fearful of the Indians and are too apt to attribute to them seditious acts for which it would be unjust to punish them." The solution proposed by the United States prior to California statehood was to leave all civil affairs in the hands of the local *alcaldes*. The military would stay out of local affairs, even if it involved Native Americans.[17] Even after California created a constitution and applied for statehood, though, the state often handled Indian affairs itself. This did not bode well for California's Indigenous population.

In San Diego on May 1, 1850, following the departure of the three survivors and the rumors they had spread, a citizen committee was formed to contemplate action against the Quechan threat. As thousands of Euro-Americans would do in the coming three decades, the citizens of San Diego petitioned the governor of California, Peter H. Burnett, and the ranking army officers in California, Gen. Bennett Riley and Gen. Persifor Smith, for an immediate military response against the Quechans in the form of a permanent fort at the crossing. Meanwhile, in Los Angeles, authorities sent the depositions taken from the three gang members up to the governor. Apparently accepting the survivors' story at face value, the cover letter to the depositions called for the immediate dispatch of forces to the area to prevent further "bestiality [by] . . . these Indians." Soon the depositions, the calls for troops, and the conclusions drawn based on the gang members' account had taken on an unshakable air of credibility, as newspapers in Sacramento and as far away as Missouri picked up the story.[18] Glanton and his associates had taken on the character of martyrs rather than brutal criminals who had got what they deserved in a manner they well understood. Apparently only the outcome of what Glanton had wrought was of importance to many Euro-Americans, and Native peoples took the blame for protecting their lives and property. Ironically the actions of the Quechans probably saved the lives of many Mexicans and Euro-Americans, as Glanton would have continued to rob, rape, and murder when opportunity presented. Given the way that the story spread and the manner in which citizens quickly harnessed democracy and their representatives to take action, Euro-Americans presumably never learned of this irony. Instead, once again, Euro-Americans were learning a lesson about Indian savagery, a lesson that they likely found all too familiar, even though it was far from reality.

In June Governor Burnett succumbed to calls to authorize action. Even though forces of the U.S. Army were headed for the Colorado River to deal with the perceived threat, Burnett authorized the raising of volunteers in San Diego and Los Angeles. The volunteer force, to be composed of sixty men, was to rendezvous with Gen. Joshua H. Bean, commander of the California State Militia's 4th Division, who would lead the volunteers in a campaign in the Colorado River region. No representative of the state or national government visited the Quechans to hear their side of the story or to learn more fully of the situation outside of the depositions of the three outlaws who had survived the Quechans' retaliatory strike. Burnett ordered Bean to "proceed promptly to the ferry upon the Colorado, and pursue such energetic measures as may be necessary to punish the Indians, bring them to terms, and protect the emigrants on their way to California."[19] Such language serves as evidence that the outlaws' story had been wholly accepted and indicates what California's Indian policy would be for the next thirty years.

Based on Burnett's letter to Bean, it would seem that Burnett not only accepted the outlaws' story, but that all the depredations of the Glanton gang against emigrants on the southern trail into California had been shifted onto the Quechans. That the state of California needed to protect emigrants was apparent, and would become more apparent in the coming years, especially in the north, as companies of militia and volunteers operated *outside* of the state to secure westward trails.[20] The state of California often dealt with Native peoples on its own and without direction from or consultation with the federal government, who by law had charge of Indian affairs in the United States. Now Burnett ignored law altogether in his executive order to "punish" the Indians of the region, which volunteer companies interpreted as orders to kill. Burnett was not oblivious to this likelihood, as he cautioned Bean to restrain the men, using "prudence and as much humanity as may be consistent with the legitimate ends and object of the war."[21] Even so, the statement left a great deal unsaid and much to the discretion of the officers and men in the field.

Indeed the order to "pursue such energetic measures as may be necessary to punish the Indians" and achieve the "legitimate ends and object of the war" was tantamount to admitting that the ends would justify the means. Perhaps Burnett's greater concern at the time was money. Signs of this motive appeared here and in later instances. One order he was unequivocal about was that as soon as the ends had been achieved, the volunteers must be disbanded. Killing Native Americans was an expensive proposition, because volunteers were not strictly volunteers, but received wages for their service and sometimes reimbursement for other expenses. In June 1850 the potential costs increased. Burnett sent word to Bean that he had heard the situation was graver than first realized. The governor authorized the muster of forty more men, bringing the total to one hundred volunteers.[22] California would pay—and then be reimbursed by the federal government—millions of dollars to kill Native Americans in the 1850s alone.[23]

By July volunteers were in the field and incurring those expenses Burnett worried about. Bean had ordered the state militia's Brig. Gen. J. C. Morehead into the field, directing him to purchase rations, supplies, arms, ammunition, and animals to outfit "as many troops as [he could] muster" for an expedition to the Gila and Colorado Rivers. Bean also ordered Morehead to make a treaty with the Quechans, which might seem a humane measure, except that such a treaty would be illegal under U.S. law and therefore a hollow gesture. Finally, Bean confirmed the potentially genocidal message contained in Burnett's orders: "Make a treaty with the hostile Indians there—or if such is impossible you will there take the orders of his Excellency the Governor and Commander in Chief for your guide and act upon them as near as it is possible so to do."[24] If unable to sway the Quechans with the pen, Morehead was to put them to the sword, but with restraint. As Burnett had left Bean free to interpret much about his orders, so had Bean done with Morehead.

By September Burnett realized that his orders had not been explicit enough. Morehead had done little more than anger the Quechans in the weeks he had been on his mission. Following the Quechans' refusal to give up hostages drawn from their own people to secure peace and turn over any money taken from the Glanton gang, the Quechans and the volunteers set to fighting.[25] After a narrow escape from destruction, Morehead's volunteer forces remained in the field, impotent in the face of superior Quechan forces and with costs mounting. Burnett had heard nothing from Bean about the progress of efforts to bring the Quechans to justice. He had heard from other sources, however, and dashed off a letter to Bean requiring an explanation of what had transpired over the summer in the Colorado River region. Burnett told Bean that he had learned that U.S. forces were in the region, that the Indigenous people of the area were deemed not particularly hostile, and that Morehead had never mustered much of an effective force for service in the desert campaign. Most important, Burnett was convinced that men were still on the payroll and that his order to disband the company as soon as practicable had not been followed.[26] Morehead and his men were recalled. In all, the fruitless expedition had cost California $120,000 and yielded only further problems between Euro-Americans and the as yet unrestrained Quechans.[27]

The historian Joel Hyer argues that this episode taught an important lesson to Native peoples: "armed resistance to Americans as a viable alternative."[28] For better or worse, the Quechans realized that Euro-Americans understood violence and its application. The lesson of the incident and its outcome was not lost on the U.S. Army either. In 1851 the army built Fort Yuma in order to establish control over the Colorado River crossings connecting California to the rest of the Southwest.

The offensive actions of Glanton and the defensive response of the Quechans, followed by the actions of Morehead's volunteers and the creation of Fort Yuma by the federal government, precipitated what came to be known collectively as the Quechan War.[29]

Numerous Euro-Americans approved of the sequence of events as it supported the popular will. But the popular will was not static, even in the case of the conflict in the region around the Colorado River. This was confirmed early in 1851, when members of the California Assembly and Senate from southern California wrote to John Bigler, the newly elected governor of California. The representatives argued that the Quechan situation had cooled since the army had arrived, and that the rampant fears of an all-out war between whites and Native Americans were now calmed. Now their main concern was money, taxpayers' money. The men called on Bigler to "discharge at the earliest day possible to save further unnecessary expense to the State" those volunteers in the field not actively engaged against the threat posed by Native Americans.[30] The state could leave matters to the federal forces and turn to more pressing matters. The popular will had necessitated that the governor yield authorization of the volunteers, however unnecessary, to alleviate the people's fears. Now fiscal responsibility, which the people also demanded, necessitated new measures. The government's interests were its people's interests, not the reverse. The response to the popular will was devastating to the Quechans of the Colorado River region, as it was to other Native peoples.

The desires of Euro-American citizens were exercised frequently and with disastrous effects for Native peoples. While engagement of the democratic process and republican government were used to avenge Glanton and his men, in most cases such measures were employed by citizens living in small communities to protect or obtain property and remove troublesome Native peoples in the area or exterminate them if that proved ineffective. Such was the case of J. J. Warner, a businessman and state senator who harnessed elements of the democratic system to secure property owned by Native peoples. Warner too would precipitate a war between Euro-Americans and Native peoples.

According to one outraged letter sent to the *Daily Alta California* from Los Angeles in the first week of December 1851, Warner had caused trouble with local Native Americans, and they had in turn run him off his lands. This was not the first time he had to flee because of his behavior. But through protestations to the state, local authorities, the papers, and his neighbors, Warner had stirred up southern California near to the point of panic. Undoubtedly his position as a state senator afforded him inordinate influence as an individual living in the San Diego area. Nonetheless Los Angeles and San Diego were expecting an attack any moment and were operating as if they were under siege. Troops of the state militia had been called up for a campaign against the Indigenous people living on and around the Warner rancho. Even the leader of the powerful Cahuilla, Juan Antonio, had responded to the fears of the Euro-American population, offering them the services of the Cahuilla men he led. The correspondent to the *Daily Alta California* believed the results of Warner's cries for help, cloaked in the specter of general Indian hostility to civilization, were exaggerated and, above all, self-serving.[31]

No matter how self-serving Warner's claims were, though, many of his countrymen in southern California supported them. Warner was elected a state senator in 1851 and held considerable influence in the region. He was an important rancho owner in San Diego, one of those who had emigrated to California long before the Gold Rush. His presence and success in the senate were immensely important to southern California. Outnumbered in population by northern California at the time, the people of southern California fought to make sure their voices were heard in the state legislature. They faced a three-to-one population deficit, and the deficit in senate and assembly districts to go with it. As the population of northern California grew exponentially in the early 1850s as a result of the Gold Rush, representation soared while the south remained relatively static.[32] Pleasing Warner, then, may have been both an effort to maintain his good graces out of self-interest and an effort to attract a fair share of state spending to Los Angeles and San Diego Counties. Southern California's ranching economy relied on obtaining Native American land and labor to keep it vital and healthy. Cheap Native labor made maintenance of huge tracts of land not only affordable, but profitable. Disturbances of this land and labor supply, even minor ones, threatened the interests of many southern Californians. California in the early 1850s was a labor-starved state; Euro-American emigrants were looking for gold, not wage labor. Perhaps only fourteen thousand non-Natives lived in California at the outbreak of the Gold Rush, many of them also heading for the Sierra foothills. Indigenous populations, already important to the ranching economy, became even more crucial as they helped meet the gold seekers' demands for food, shelter, and stores.[33] In southern California, fortunes depended not on gold, but on sending herds of cattle north to the slaughter. Miners had to eat, and southern California was well placed to provide. Native American *vaqueros* and laborers were crucial to raising, protecting, and herding the animals.[34] Warner represented the men of the Californio rancho era, Mexican and Euro-American alike, whose stranglehold over land in the south was slowly being loosened by squatters, land commission decisions, and the imposition of Euro-American financial systems. He had settled there before the United States seized California in 1846. He represented both Euro-Americans who had accepted Mexican citizenship and place in the Californio elite before conquest, and also a new Euro-American California elite from southern California as an officeholder in the state senate in 1851.[35]

For former Mexican Californios, now U.S. citizens under the Treaty of Guadalupe Hidalgo, Warner offered perhaps the best chance for their voices and interests to be heard and old systems of labor relations preserved in the new state. Euro-American politics contrasted sharply with the systems in place in Mexican California. In the Mexican era, localized control by a system of *alcaldes* ran California. The Euro-American system of democratically elected representatives, multiple layers of government, and a tripartite system of distinct branches were new innovations in California.[36] Many Californios, though, were more concerned with the economic aspects of the transition. In Warner they likely saw a man with similar economic interests and with access to and an understanding of political circles in an increasingly Euro-American-dominated government.[37] Like other rancho owners, Warner believed that keeping Native populations suppressed and subservient was important to the economic and political stability of the entire region, and he supported those interests with his votes and proposals in the state senate.[38] The ability of southern California to maintain its traditional ranching economy depended heavily on pacifying and controlling Native Americans. Warner himself depended upon the Cupeño people to work his rancho at Agua Caliente. In a report prepared for his colleagues, he suggested that a proposed removal of Native Americans to some far-off location was not a logical measure for a labor-hungry California. Instead Warner sought to focus attention on the necessity of Native American labor in a counterproposal pushing for local reservations: "Here philanthropy and charity, hand in hand, might find a field in which to labor. From them, the farmer, the grazier, and owners of vineyards, might derive their accustomed and needed labors."[39] Creating local reservations to make Indian labor accessible, but otherwise removing Indians from contact with whites, was to Warner the best course. As several reservations were created by executive order in the 1850s and 1860s, Warner and his supporters got their wish in this respect. As California transitioned into a representative democracy, other laws made or supported by men like Warner would also play a crucial role in guaranteeing control of Native American liberty and labor.

Elam Brown was another representative of the new order working in the state government to preserve the old order of labor in the transition from Mexican territory to thirty-first state in the Union. Brown authored a bill that codified the desires of many of the members of the old regime, while at the same time appealing to the sensibilities of incoming Euro-American emigrants. Like Warner, Brown had emigrated to California prior to the Gold Rush and had established a rancho using Native labor to operate it. "An Act for the Government and Protection of Indians," principally authored by Brown while serv-

ing in the Assembly in 1850, codified an attempt to transplant the labor
relations of the old era to the new. In this effort, Brown and his supporters succeeded, at least in the short term. With the support of other
important rancho owners like Mariano Vallejo and John Bidwell, the
act became law.[40] It made California's Indigenous population practically
legal nonentities and the objects of legalized kidnapping, enslavement,
and murder, ensuring that access to Native labor would not only continue but would increase.[41] Efforts by Warner, Brown, and others to
suppress, dispossess, and marginalize Native peoples eventually resulted
in the Garra Revolt, the most significant pan-Indian alliance and revolt in southern California during the 1850s. The revolt would test the
resolve of Native peoples and Euro-Americans alike.

The troubled relations between Native Americans and Euro-Americans had roots deeper than the actions of Warner and other lawmakers,
of course, and the legal and illegal actions of many Euro-American
communities also played a significant role in the background to the
Garra Revolt. Euro-Americans attempting to occupy lands owned and
occupied by Native peoples encountered stiff resistance; many of these
Euro-American interlopers used republican and democratic forms and
legal niceties to steal Indigenous peoples' lands and resources. They
squatted on Native lands, used the legal system to gain title, and then
arranged for the white community to help them expel or kill Native
inhabitants unwilling to work on "their" lands. In this way some of the
best lands owned by Native peoples in southern California fell into the
hands of non-Natives.[42] Petitions by individuals and communities to
democratically elected representatives were common steps employed
when Native populations resisted these incursions. In February 1851
Euro-Americans in Los Angeles petitioned the governor of California,
John McDougal, for protection against Native Americans threatening
their lives and property. Their petition was forwarded by the commander of the state militia in the region, Gen. J. H. Bean.[43] As no
standing unit of the state militia was in the area, Bean recommended
in a cover letter to the petition that the governor authorize a volunteer
company of citizens to deal with the problem. One of the key rights

afforded to citizens, the right to bear arms and to constitute a militia for the mutual protection, was at the heart of this suggestion. The volunteer company, composed of citizen-soldiers who elected their captain and lieutenants, was the epitome of democracy in martial form. Bean himself had been elected to his command by the men of the California Assembly and Senate in joint session.

As the petitioners themselves did, Bean stressed the need for quick and decisive action without any reference to the Native American perspective of the situation: "My own impression is that a company of volunteer rangers of not less than fifty men should be immediately raised for the protection of the lives and property of the people of this section." While their representatives considered the issue, the petitioners decided to take matters into their own hands. As communities all over California would often do in this era of genocide, Angelinos took up a subscription to pay for volunteer armed forces to fight uncooperative Indians. These subscriptions would "defray the expense" until the state could step in to help.[44] In other words, the fifty-man company that Bean recommended the governor to approve was already taking shape in Los Angeles, illegally. However, one can safely assume that none of the participants believed he was doing anything illegal in forming this vigilante company early; participants included some of the most important city and county officials, conducted their meetings inside a courthouse, and voted democratically on their actions. The circumstances that prompted these measures were, however, not quite as clear as they had been made out to the governor.

The people of Los Angeles County, particularly Euro-Americans, had been engaged in depredations against the Indigenous peoples of the region for several years by the time the petition was drafted. Indeed in a separate petition sent to General Bean, the citizenry consciously ignored much of what had gone on previously, writing, "Without dwelling upon the details, we can say with truth that scarcely on the weakest frontier of the Union, or in the worst seasons of Indian hostility, had as much property been taken by the savages, as has been from this single county during this past year." The petitioners claimed the source of these troubles lay not in their actions, but in "want of proper military protection" in the face of the animal-like Indians in search of their "prey." The "details" they omitted, however, were suggestive of their real intentions toward Native peoples in and around Los Angeles County. Although they called on the governor and Bean to protect "lives and property," it was really the latter that was primarily threatened. The petitioners could not help but admit that only one man had been killed, and he in the process of chasing Native people defending themselves. The petitioners also succinctly described the fear inherent among those stealing Native American land and resources in southern California: "There is a deep-seated conviction in the community, that the lives of the inhabitants sparsely scattered over this extensive territory are exposed to savage vengeance."[45] They demanded that the government step in and save them from their own overreaching. The petitioners seem to have a sense of entitlement to such protection, and in this case Governor John McDougal agreed that it was the state's role to accede to the demands of his constituents.

McDougal responded in a manner that previewed the actions of the governors of California for the next decade or more. Even as the citizens of Los Angeles County were writing their second petition to implore Bean for aid, a letter from Governor McDougal reached Bean. McDougal wrote:

It having been represented to me that hostile tribes of Indians are committing aggressions upon our citizens inhabiting the Southern portion of the State, and the authorities having been invoked to aid in repelling these aggressions—You are hereby ordered to call out for this purpose fifty able bodied militia of the County of Los Angeles, who will be mustered into service at the earliest day practicable, under officers of their own selection, and proceed at once under your general command to punish and repel the aggressing Indians. . . . I presume the number of men ordered out will prove sufficient, and it is to be hoped no necessity will arise for an additional force. . . . Observe the most rigid economy in conducting the matters under your charge—incur no expenses which are not absolutely necessary, and require your disbursing officer to keep an accurate account of all disbursements made; and all expenses incurred and report to me.[46]

Several days later McDougal took the additional step to respond directly to his petitioners in Los Angeles, assuring them that he understood how the democratic system worked in the interests of its citizenry. To a brief letter acknowledging that he had directed Bean to form a volunteer company, the governor added, "You will be pleased to say to the people inhabiting the disturbed portions of our State that all and every means within the power of the Executive will be extended to their protection and interest."[47] In recognizing the interests of his constituency, McDougal related how those interests might be turned to genocide. If the electorate demanded action, action would be taken. McDougal's letter to Bean also contained a key contributing factor to genocide, one oft repeated by his successors to the governorship.

As McDougal's letter to Bean clearly demonstrates, he wanted the volunteer company to remain in the field for as short a time as possible, in the fewest numbers possible, and incurring the least expense possible. Implicitly almost everything about these instructions for proper economy suggested genocide as the logical way to fulfill McDougal's requirements. Expeditions that took prisoners, or were careful to kill only guilty parties or even just adult male combatants, took a long time and risked letting their targets escape. Moreover prisoners cost money to feed and house, especially if they were confined for long periods of time or transported to semipermanent reservations, which also cost money to maintain. Guards would be necessary to keep these prisoners contained in corrals, jails, or reservations, which also cost money. The cheapest, most expedient method to deal with recalcitrant Indians was to kill them all. In fact it is perhaps telling that McDougal did not set the limit on the volunteer company as short of the destruction of the marauders, but rather as a three-month tour of duty. Evidence from throughout the state suggested that volunteers took this as a time to bring about the maximum death and destruction possible while under the cover of the law. However, as was also the case all over the state, Euro-Americans engaged many more subtle measures to exterminate or control Indian populations than the overt force of volunteer companies.

According to the *San Diego Herald*, Native people simply walking on the streets of San Diego risked their lives. Shooting Native Americans for sport was common enough in San Diego that the *Herald* suggested one might think men were taking target practice for duels.[48] Three years later, little had changed in San Diego. In 1856 a group of men turned on a Native American man in the street and stoned him to death, apparently without direct provocation and for sport. The *Herald* noted that similar atrocities would likely "be repeated." This was undoubtedly because it was "considered fine sport" to kill Indians and that "magistrates don't trouble themselves about such matters."[49] Even the involvement of law enforcement provided no safety to Indian people, even when locked up awaiting trial. Native Americans arrested and placed in jail had an apparent proclivity for being found hanged in their cells, especially when jail attendants had stepped out briefly. This summary execution of untried Native American prisoners was practiced in southern California as late as 1880.[50] Not all crimes against Indians were so overtly brutal. Practices that deprived Indians of liberty and life occurred quietly and legally every day all over southern California.

White citizens used the legal system to their advantage. Horace Bell, a member of the Los Angeles Rangers volunteer company, described the "slave mart" centered in the city of Los Angeles in the 1850s. Bell noted that the labor provided by Indigenous people in the Los Angeles area was essential to Euro-American farming and ranching operations, as it had been for Mexican *rancheros* before them.[51] However, Euro-Americans introduced new complexities to the labor system through "An Act for the Government and Protection of Indians." The act replaced the informal, quasi-feudal relationship between Indigenous populations and Mexicans, in which Mexican *rancheros* had at least some measure of responsibility to their workers residing on their land grants. Euro-Americans harnessed laws contained in the act against Indian vagrancy and drunkenness to obtain a form of short-term slave labor from Native Americans. In fact the system depended upon neglect of Native American communities to ensure its successful operation. Keeping Indigenous people desperate and willing to work for next to nothing was key to the effectiveness and profitability of the system. Keeping Native workers healthy and alive was of no importance; many Euro-Americans already believed the "only good Indian was a dead Indian," and with thousands of potential replacement workers scattered all over southern California, illness and death were of little consequence.

At no time was this clearer than when it came to compensating Native American workers. Native workers would often be paid for their work with alcohol, which was illegal.[52] Employers used liquor as a low-cost means of maintaining access to cheap Native American labor by connecting the labor and justice systems. Indians found drunk or vagrant were arrested on Sunday, imprisoned overnight in a corral, and convicted on Monday. Because few could afford to pay the fine, the jail was kept stocked full of potential laborers. The *Los Angeles Star* reported on one darkly comic instance when the marshal had stuffed the jail so full of Native Americans that the jail door fell down and all the "Indians scattered in every direction."[53] Nonetheless jails full of Native Americans were what local employers wanted. Unable to pay the fines for their convictions, the prisoners were auctioned off in the "slave market." Usually they worked from Monday until Saturday after being bought for between one and three dollars by local employers, especially vineyard or rancho owners. Horace Bell believed Native Americans did most of the work in and around Los Angeles. Meanwhile the law required that one-third of the value of their labor be remitted to them at the end of the week. But the practice of illegally paying with spirits would be employed again, and the cycle begun again. Bell recalled, "Los Angeles had its slave mart, as well as New Orleans and Constantinople—only the slave at Los Angeles was sold fifty-two times a year as long as he lived." Bell believed that these repetitions were so damaging to Native health and welfare that one might expect to live no more than three years in such an environment.[54] At the same time, Indigenous people wanting to avoid arrest were forced to compete "fiercely for a limited number of steady jobs as house servants at wages reportedly from fifty cents to one dollar per day."[55] The repressive system wore down and killed Native Americans as employers provided only enough sustenance to keep them working during the week, and that only to the worker and not to his or her family. In off seasons and slow periods, Native Americans were left to fend for themselves without access to the fruits of their labor and often without access to their ancestral lands, which had been seized. In agriculture, the off season coincided with winter, when traditional food sources were typically scarce or even unavailable. Normally Indigenous populations would have been gathering food throughout the year to create stores for lean times, but the new labor regime did not allow this. Starvation was an omnipresent possibility for California's Native population. While this economy of slow starvation was not as direct as shooting Native people, it was just as deadly, if not more so in its long-term effects. According to Bell, by the time the vineyards had faded in Los Angeles, most of the Native American laborers had faded too.[56]

Harsh punishments meted out by employers were the norm for Native American workers. Native people found guilty of crimes were subjected to different punishments than whites. Four Native men convicted of stealing alcohol and a piece of clothing each received twenty-five lashes from a whip and an order to pay court costs, which likely landed them in the labor auction.[57] While touring southern California, Lt. William Emory found evidence that whipping was a common punishment for Native American laborers who displeased their masters.[58] J. J. Warner believed in using the whip to control his Native American workers. Many Native people chose to exercise patience in response to the actions of men like Warner; others did not.

Native Americans were not only laboring as slaves; the legal system placed Native workers in homes all over southern California through apprenticeship laws, also contained in "An Act for the Government and Protection of Indians." When bound to whites in this manner, Indians—especially children—received only room and board as their compensation. The spirit of the law indicated that apprentices were recipients of the most valuable compensation of all: exposure to Euro-American values and civilizing influences. Those apprenticed were unlikely to starve, but their work benefited non-Natives, not Native American communities. The style of labor imposed on Native peoples was corrosive to traditional patterns of work and social networks. Even worse, as males left villages to find work, communities were left undefended and subject to raids by outsiders.[59] But those employed outside the relative safety of Indigenous communities risked attack as well.

The case of one Kumeyaay or Digueño girl, dubbed "Emma" by the Chase family, who indentured her as a domestic servant in 1862, shows that female children and teenagers faced sexual abuse in the homes they were brought into.[60] When Andrew Chase originally considered bringing an Indian girl into his home in the San Diego area in 1857, his wife refused after learning from other women that their husbands had sexual relations with apprenticed Native American girls. The impetus for the intercourse, however, was blamed on the young girls, not the white males molesting and raping them. Andrew Chase confessed the temptation of an alluring young Indian girl might be too much for him, writing, "I should like an Indian Girl and had about concluded to send for one, but Mrs. C found by inquiry of ladies who had experience in this kind of *property*, that they [Indian girls] weren't to be trusted, especially if their masters are fond of *vanity*. Wife thinks *we* had better not run the risk, and I think if anything should *turn up* it would be awful."[61] The Chases waited five years before bringing Emma into their home; Chase's wife believed that because he was forty-five, there was no risk of his engaging in sexual activity with their servant girl. We don't know if Chase refrained from violating her or not, but at forty-five, he was likely still capable of what his wife had feared years earlier.

To make matters worse for Emma and other Native children, apprenticeship laws were repealed in 1863, but the practice of enslaving children continued through the legal system and informal networks

and agreements among Euro-Americans, including those laws governing wards and orphans in the state. Indeed Euro-Americans continued
to have Indian children in their homes well into the 1880s.[62] Scholars
have estimated that white Americans enslaved as many as twenty thousand Native Americans in California.[63] This slave system, disguised as
an apprenticeship in advanced civilization for inferior peoples, contributed to the genocide of Native peoples tremendously. By separating
families, depriving children of Native linguistic and cultural education, and inflicting mental and physical hardships, Euro-Americans
destroyed Native families, lowered birthrates, and committed physical,
cultural, and economic genocide.[64]

As conflicts between Euro-Americans and Indigenous populations
escalated throughout 1851, Juan Antonio's Cahuillas continued to support Euro-American interests in order to maintain their lands and
culture intact. A leader of nearby Cupeño people was not so willing.
Antonio Garra invited Cahuilla, Kumeyaay, Luiseño, Quechan, and
other local Native peoples to join him in an all-out war to expel Euro-
Americans from southern California in order to achieve freedom for
all Native peoples. Like Juan Antonio, Garra had at one time been
willing to negotiate with Euro-Americans, but his patience had come
to an end. Juan Antonio refused to support Garra, electing to continue
to accommodate Euro-Americans.[65] But this pan-Indian alliance appealed to many Native people who had experienced the depredations
of Euro-Americans. The man most responsible for the misery of the
Cupeños, J. J. Warner, would be one of the first people visited by the
forces organized by Garra.

Following the decision of San Diego County to forcibly levy taxes
on the Cupeños, Garra and a group of Indigenous peoples determined
to launch a war to expel Euro-Americans from southern California.
After inviting Hispanic Californians and area Native nations, including
the Cahuillas, to participate, Garra's forces attacked, some attacking the
Warner Springs rancho of J. J. Warner. Warner barely escaped with his
life, as his home was burned and possessions taken. Known for his brutality toward Native people, he was the prime target in the region. But

Warner was not the only target. The rebels launched attacks on live-stock herders and other emigrants too. Native American food sources were being destroyed by ranchers allowing their livestock to roam over crops and hunting into scarcity the local game Indians depended on for food. The rebels killed several Euro-Americans and captured several thousand sheep. Following these actions, attacks made in the Colorado River region by Quechan forces increased the scale of the rebellion.[66]

The Garra Revolt drove southern California into a panic. General Bean wrote urgently to Governor McDougal, "Aggressing Indians are devastating the whole country in the section of the State. I have according to your orders endeavored to show the people of the South that they would not be left defenseless—but that Your Excellency has a care for all portions of the State."[67] Both Bean and McDougal were aware of the justifiable paranoia of southern Californians regarding the imbalance of funding and representation between north and south. In the coming months, the fears of the public continued to escalate. As when Glanton had been killed, the public held citizens' meetings in San Diego and Los Angeles to form volunteer companies for "protection" against marauding Indians. In November 1851 a key meeting was held at the San Diego courthouse. The center of attention was Senator Warner, who told the assembled citizens of his narrow escape and the destruction of his home and property. The sheriff of San Diego informed his countrymen that Maj. Samuel Heintzelman offered the people of San Diego fifty muskets for use in suppressing the forces under Garra. Maj. E. H. Fitzgerald provided eighty more weapons, procured by the mayor of San Diego. But more than guns were volunteered by the collected citizenry. Cave Johnson Couts, federal Indian agent for the area, said "that he was confident that the persons needed no impetus of the Law, but would volunteer to serve in whatever capacity they could be useful." The sheriff promised to serve in a volunteer unit, even as a private. Fitzgerald volunteered too, as did many others. W. C. Farrell offered $100 toward the company's expenses, being unable to serve. The most important steps taken, however, were the citizen's democratic efforts to legalize their plans to attack the Native American rebels.

They drafted an extraordinary notice to the governor, stating, "For the mutual protection against the depredations committed by the Indians, an enrollment list, shall be opened for volunteers to place themselves under such officer as the company may nominate, and be subject to his orders, as long as the commanding officer may deem fit." This was voted on and unanimously approved by the assembled citizens, despite the reality that only the governor could authorize the formation of a volunteer company. With Couts's and Warner's blessings, and given the spirit of democracy that had been employed to constitute the meeting and carry out the business at hand, in a courthouse no less, the citizenry may have considered themselves the highest power in the state in their hour of need. The message to the governor concluded, "We the undersigned hereby subscribe ourselves voluntarily to do military duty, on behalf of the State of California against hostile Indians in any capacity that may be pointed out by our commanding officer, and for such a period as he may deem expedient to meet the exigencies of the case, said commanding officer to be elected by us."[68] The focus of past governors on expediency was certainly present in the hearts and minds of the assembled citizens of San Diego. The group elected Maj. E. H. Fitzgerald commander of the volunteer company, which became known as Fitzgerald's Volunteers.[69]

At about the same time, citizens in Los Angeles were also panicking and coming together to share their fears and make demands on the government for aid. On November 30, 1851, General Bean wrote Governor McDougal of the uproar created by Garra in Los Angeles. After giving McDougal a brief résumé of the events leading up to the present state of affairs, Bean argued that there was no doubt that the Indigenous population of the region had made common cause against the whites and were out for blood. Bean did not specify which Indigenous people or elaborate on their motivations beyond the fact that San Diego had been taxing them heavily. He described their attacks as "wanton butchery" and "aggressive war," not rebellion, defense, or active resistance to white depredations. He wrote, "All these things demonstrate the fact that an Indian war is upon us. The citizens sensible of this fact are taking the most energetic steps to meet the crisis." "Energetic steps" included democratic and republican measures. Citizens met and elected representatives to deal with the crisis. Bean and several others had been voted by the citizenry to act in their favor and to stop the "hostile tribes of savages that are devastating our country." This was an extreme exaggeration, as none of the combat had taken place in Los Angeles or the surrounding valleys. The action was mainly in the Agua Caliente region, in San Diego County, and east in the Colorado River region. Despite this, the democratic meetings conferred by vote "full and extraordinary power to guard the public welfare."[70] Again, the will of the people, especially when represented by a vote and recorded on paper, was law.

Bean was impressed by the will of the people represented in their response to his need for supplies in the face of the impending invasion, writing to Governor McDougal, "I am therefore thrown for resources entirely upon the patriotism of the citizens, and cannot but bear cheerful testimony to the prompt manner in which they are responding to the Emergency owing to their voluntary and praiseworthy generosity, there is no lack of means to get supplies." Of course, the citizens expected to be paid for everything they contributed. Certainly Bean was aware of this. He echoed Burnett's admonition of the previous year to be frugal as he requested arms and ammunition from McDougal: "If they are sent immediately it may save the State hundreds of thousands as by enabling us to strike a quick and effective blow the war may be suppressed, before it has broken out far and wide." Without alacrity, Bean warned, more rebels would flock to Garra's forces. Given the perceived necessity of the situation, Bean, like the people of San Diego, had overstepped the letter of the law. He acknowledged as much to McDougal, stating, "In this alarming state of affairs, wherein delay and indecision would be pregnant with the gravest and most pernicious results, I have upon the call of the citizens organized a company in San Diego, which marched on Tuesday or Wednesday last, I have before spoken of my arrangements here. I have had an eye to the impoverished state of the Treasury, and am using the strictest economy, I believe in acting as I have, I have only anticipated the orders of your Excellency, and confidently look for your approval."[71]

Bean concluded his letter to McDougal by imploring him to send men and equipment for the defense of southern California. McDougal received the messages of the people of San Diego and Los Angeles and sprang into action. He began by approving the extralegal measures taken in Los Angeles and San Diego, thus making the actions of the community and the men in the companies legal.[72] This post facto approval was a precedent he and other governors would repeatedly set, ensuring that when other crises arose later, the citizenry and their elected leaders would rarely hesitate to act first and ask permission second. Next McDougal used his influence as governor to call upon federal troops in the Bay Area to aid the people of San Diego. He asked the commander of federal forces in California to ship two hundred men to San Diego for immediate action.[73] Perhaps most incredible of all, he called for volunteer companies to form in San Francisco. The men would be shipped south to help prevent what McDougal clearly believed was impending disaster, convinced as he was by the petitions of "nearly all the State, county, and city officers of San Diego, together with names of nearly all the residents of the county . . . [and] the apprehension they experienced for the safety of their lives and property, concurred in by the Public Presses."[74] But news from Bean quickly reached him that changed his mind, causing him to disband the volunteers in the Bay Area just as they were about to board ships south. Despite not serving, the Bay Area volunteers demanded compensation.

By New Year's Day 1852 the rebellion was all but over. In December Bean had taken Antonio Garra into custody at San Gorgonio. But Bean had not apprehended them himself; the Cahuilla leader Juan Antonio had. Bean acted quickly to ensure that Garra and five other men captured would not cause further difficulties. He held a court-martial in Chino to try the five men captured with Garra, including Garra's son. Garra's son and two others were found guilty of murder by an impromptu military court. Two were immediately put to death by militiamen; the third received fifty lashes because he was a youth.

The punishment was hardly more than what Warner might have doled out to one of his workers for indolence or insolence. The remaining two men were found not guilty. Bean decided not to try the elder Garra in Chino, and instead transported him for military trial in San Diego, where he was convicted and executed by firing squad several weeks later. Bean also transmitted news that Major Heintzelman and his regular army forces had destroyed elements of the rebels. They too executed prisoners following summary courts-martial. In spite of the defeat of rebel forces, Bean was not convinced the trouble was over: "Notwithstanding what has been done, I do not consider that the difficulties are yet at an end. . . . I intend to move my command to the Colorado as soon as possible, to punish the Indians in that quarter." To accomplish this, he needed more arms and ammunition. He concluded his letter to the governor with a renewed promise that when matters showed that volunteers were no longer necessary, he would disband the companies immediately.[75]

To deal with the tensions in the region, a new Indian commissioner was appointed in 1852, Benjamin "Benito" Wilson. The reaction of the *Los Angeles Star* to the appointment showed the self-deceptive way many Euro-Americans viewed their role in relations with Native Americans. Praising Wilson for his knowledge of the "Indian character" and his constant energy to promote peace with them, the newspaper could not help but reveal its inability to acknowledge the role played by whites in causing trouble. The *Star* believed that peace would flow from Wilson's ability to deal with "all those tribes which have . . . been so troublesome to this county," rather than those Euro-Americans who had contributed or manufactured the trouble all on their own, such as Glanton, Warner, and others. The *Star* believed Wilson an ideal candidate because of his long experience with Native peoples in the area in and around Los Angeles. In fact the paper went so far as to conclude that the appointment alone was enough to secure a "permanent peace."[76] But what the paper failed to realize was that Wilson possessed ideas about Indian-white relations well out of touch with his fellows'.

In some ways, Wilson could not have been a worse man for the job. A longtime resident since the Mexican era, he was the product of a disappearing socioeconomic structure in California, a system that had valued Native American labor, even if it did not reward it fairly. Now the brutal Euro-American version of the system was becoming increasingly ambivalent toward their Native American labor source. In southern California, home of the so-called cow counties, Indigenous populations had long formed the majority of laborers on ranchos. As Euro-Americans entered and settled southern California, the reliance would slowly fade as settlers diversified the economy beyond ranching. Still, in the 1850s Native Americans in Los Angeles and San Diego Counties made up more than 50 percent of the manual labor force.[77] Wilson was one of about two dozen Euro-Americans who had settled in southern California in the Mexican period and collectively come to control approximately one-third of the land.[78] These emigrants and their landholding Californio elite neighbors relied on ranching for their prominent positions in society. As ranching declined and land holdings shrank in the 1850s, Native Americans were no longer needed by their old employers, and were distrusted and unwanted by many Euro-Americans who might otherwise have offered them new work.

The combination of a shrinking land base for Native peoples, a rapid increase in the Euro-American population, and deplorable labor relationships created difficult challenges for many Native Americans in southern California. Added to these difficulties was an imbalance of funds for the support of Native Americans in California, especially in the south; southern California Indian agents and subagents were typically ordered to spend nothing.[79] In 1852 the federal government allocated only $20,000 for the support of Indigenous populations in California, despite the fact that the state had the largest population of Indians of any state in the Union. Senator William Gwin, speaking before the U.S. Senate, summed up what Indian people faced in 1852: "We have taken their acorns, grasshoppers, fisheries, and hunting grounds from them. The ponds where the wild fowl assembled in winter, offering them for the time an abundant supply of food, is now the mining and agricultural region of our citizens. The Indian must perish from cold and hunger if this government does not interpose to save them. . . . If this is to be the policy of this Government towards this people, it will form a dark page in our history, if it does not bring the vengeance of heaven upon us as a nation."[80] Genocide by starvation would ensue.

The federal government, however, committed only $20,000 in 1852, just one-sixth of what the state spent to trying to kill the Quechans in 1850 to avenge the Glanton gang. Worse still, the federal government would spend millions of dollars in subsequent years reimbursing claims for campaigns against Native Americans all over the state. Exacerbating this was Wilson, early on, in his unpopular empathy for Native peoples. Over the course of the 1850s Euro-Americans in southern California would come to realize that Benjamin Wilson need not represent the only answer to all of their difficulties with Indigenous populations.

An unwillingness or inability to distinguish between groups during times of trouble devastated Native American communities unassociated with alleged crimes against whites. The Indigenous population living in the southernmost portion of the San Joaquin Valley and in and around the Tejon Pass, for instance, were often blamed for horse thieving, despite strong evidence that the raiders were actually Paiutes from the Owens Valley.[81] People living below the Cajon Pass were also blamed for the raids of Paiutes or Chemehuevis from the eastern side of the mountains.[82] The *Los Angeles Star* carried the story of these truths, but subsequent evidence suggested that it was either little believed or ignored as inconsequential. The only way the peoples of the southern San Joaquin Valley and Tejon could prove the truth of their statements was to deal with the thieves themselves.[83] Otherwise they would continue to be implicated. This was part of a larger problem for Native Americans all over California: any unexplained crime or murder was attributed to them.[84] Complicating matters was the fact that some Native people did indeed raid stock. While the Native population of Tejon was being accused of the thievery, Owens Valley Paiutes were engaged in these raids in order to survive in the face of increasing white settlement of their country. Euro-American mountain men and traders during the Mexican era had sent Native Americans into California to raid Mexican herds. In return for their services, these men traded goods to the raiders.[85] Paiute, Ute, and Shoshone peoples were often the raiders engaged in the trade of the stolen horses with Euro-Americans and others, waiting east of the Sierra Nevada or on the trail to Santa Fe. In the early 1850s only the targets had changed. Euro-Americans in the Owens Valley purchased the stolen horses that the Paiutes did not consume for food.[86] During the spring of 1853 the citizens of Los Angeles County finally recognized the clear evidence that the raiders from the east, not the Indian people of Tejon, were the source of stock losses, although they seemed not to have understood or cared that Euro-Americans were likely at the receiving end of the stolen property.

In April 1853 whites in Los Angeles proposed the use of volunteer companies to rid the county of the threat posed by the Paiute raiders from the east. To the editors of the *Los Angeles Star*, all other efforts had been fruitless. Soldiers had been stationed in the region, but they were unmounted infantrymen unable to pursue the mounted invaders. Treaties had been made, but they had no metal in them; they were, according to the *Star*, made of "straw" and useless.[87] Both measures had cost taxpayers money and only exacerbated the conflict. Euro-Americans were robbed of their property by Native Americans, and robbed through taxation supporting futile efforts by soldiers and Indian agents. Many Euro-Americans in the next two decades would come to the same conclusion as they contemplated Indian affairs in California. The solution to the problem came from an unlikely source.

Indian Commissioner Benjamin Wilson proposed the formation of a volunteer company to carry out an expedition against the Paiutes in order to deliver an object lesson to them on the inadvisability of stealing stock from Euro-Americans. Wilson, despite his professed empathy for Native peoples and initially temperate policies, was an experienced "Indian fighter," having fought against California Indians in the 1840s under Mexican auspices. The *Star* concurred with Wilson.[88] In the following months, the editors of the *Star* continued to express their support for the idea, calling on interested parties in the county to make common cause and root out the Paiutes.[89] Wilson, in charge of Indian affairs in several counties, made similar proposals elsewhere, including in El Dorado County, where he was elected to lead a volunteer company against outlaws while still serving as an Indian agent of the U.S. government.[90] This conflict of interest did not go altogether unnoticed.

More than any other California newspaper, the *Daily Alta California*, published in San Francisco, often took a sympathetic and humane tone when discussing relations with Native Americans. The paper's empathy for Native peoples may perhaps be explained by their relative absence in the area. As in the states of the Northeast, where Indian populations had largely been destroyed, San Franciscans could now afford to criticize depredations against Native populations, as they were no longer in the business themselves. The *Alta* observed that Wilson's plan of using volunteers posed a serious threat to Native Americans in southern California. Wilson, the *Alta* reminded readers, was a product of old California and inured to the violence employed by the Spanish and the Mexicans to control Indigenous populations. Perhaps worse still, Euro-American civilization in California seemed to be following in the bloody footsteps of Hispanic cultures. Euro-American volunteer companies, already operating throughout California, had a reputation for extreme violence. The *Alta* warned, "There is danger . . . that volunteer companies, not under sufficient restraint to check the propensity to profit by an advantage, may be guilty of indiscretions and excesses in the destruction of human life and appropriation of property among Indians, that will not be altogether creditable to the State, nor agreeable to the feelings of the Indian Agent [Wilson]."[91] In other words, volunteer companies were commonly known to steal, rape, kidnap, enslave, and murder Native Americans, and Wilson's suggestion implied that his goal lay along lines that could lead to the extermination of his charges. Wilson was as familiar as any Californian with Native Americans and volunteers, and likely knew full well what the outcome could be if a group of citizen-soldiers was put in the field. What he was suggesting was a path to genocide, although he seemed to favor cultural and economic genocide rather than physical annihilation. Where Indigenous populations were concerned, Wilson seemed to long for a return to the order of the old days of Mexican California, before the secularization of the missions. He believed that California's Native populations had been cast adrift by secularization and conquest by the United States, and that their progress toward civilization had been curtailed.[92] Unable to effect such a return, Wilson played an apathetic role at times, suggesting or doing nothing to interfere with Euro-American crimes against Native populations.

Contemporary with the Paiute raids in the area around Tejon was another incident of Euro-Americans creating serious difficulties with unoffending Indigenous populations. At San Gorgonio a man named D. G. Weaver had begun monopolizing water in the region, which was home to Juan Antonio and the Cahuillas. Weaver was also making land claims that interfered with standing agreements between Euro-Americans and the Cahuillas. To make matters worse, he was shooting Cahuilla stock that trespassed on what he claimed was his property.[93] The editors of the *Los Angeles Star*, among others, called on Weaver to release water to the Cahuillas. Juan Antonio was a powerful friend to the people of Los Angeles County, as he had shown during the Garra Revolt, and might prove to be an even more deadly enemy.

Weaver was well aware of these facts. In June 1851 representatives from Los Angeles and the San Bernardino area had met with the Cahuilla chief and secured a treaty, in which the authorities of Los Angeles County and local rancho owners promised the Cahuillas, "Since he [Juan Antonio] has always been considered in peace with all, and a friend to Order, he is hereby notified that he can return with his people to their homes, to live as before they left; and associate with his white neighbors; with a guarantee that no harm shall be done him, either by individuals or by the county authorities, because all consider him as a good friend, and will not consent to let him be injured, but will cooperate with force if necessary, to punish any person who may disturb the peace."[94] It was not surprising that they would describe Juan Antonio as a representative of "peace" and "order" as he and his men had only recently destroyed a band of outlaws, Euro-Americans among them, who had been terrorizing Natives and non-Natives alike throughout Los Angeles County.[95] The actions of the Cahuillas saved the lives and property of many people, including some of those who signed the treaty, such as Weaver. As Weaver was well aware, not only had the county made a treaty with the Cahuilla, but the state and federal governments had made treaties with the Cahuilla in 1851 and 1852 as well.

The logic employed by the *Star* in its plea to Weaver to relinquish the water was perhaps based on the faulty notion that all Euro-Americans intended to do justice in their dealings with Native peoples. The *Star* reminded Weaver of the treaty made by General Bean with the Cahuillas and the pledge that they would retain "uninterrupted possession" of their lands. Yet beneath these legitimate, legal reasons for Weaver to submit to the rule of law were serious flaws. Bean was a representative of the state of California, not the federal government. His treaty was not ratified by the U.S. Senate and was not legally binding, despite the belief by many Euro-Americans and Cahuillas that it was. In fact the federal government's treaty with the Cahuillas and other Indigenous peoples of the region, the Treaty of Temecula, was never ratified, though Native peoples were never told that no treaty existed with the United States. Put to the test in a federal court, the treaty made by Bean would not stand. Neither would the treaty made by the county, which if anything was less valid than the state treaty. The title to the land was not guaranteed either, then; it could be extinguished and passed on to any Euro-American manipulating the system. Finally, even if Euro-Americans believed the land was Cahuilla land, the water rights had not been specified in the agreements and thus were open to interpretation. The clear-cut case presented by the *Star* to Weaver was not as clear as the newspaper made it out to be. Weaver knew this and acted accordingly.

The Cahuillas did not respond with violence. Instead they sent a group of representatives to appeal to Indian Agent Wilson, who ignored the problem by redirecting responsibility. He told the Cahuillas that he could not help them because the issue was a state matter, not a federal one. Because he considered the issues to be about killing stock and stealing water, he believed he was speaking to a group of Native Americans attempting to charge a white man with a crime. Theft of water and the killing of stock were indeed crimes under state law, but they could never be successfully prosecuted in a state courtroom if only Native Americans stood as the accusers of a white man; state law prohibited Native American testimony against whites in state courts until 1872. Indians did have some legal recourse, however. By virtue of "An Act for the Government and Protection of Indians," Native Americans were able to press cases in a separate legal system through local justices of the peace. But before 1855 this process too had severe limits. The act specified, "In no case shall a white man be convicted on any offence upon the testimony of an Indian."[96] This meant that supporting evidence would have to come from non-Natives.

The treaty with the Cahuillas had also been made by the state, not the federal government. In a scenario that likely confused and certainly frustrated the Cahuillas, Wilson presented them with a hopeless case of legal injustice. Euro-Americans had made many promises, but when it came time to keep them, they used jurisdictional technicalities, legal injustice, and indifference to deflect blame, temporize, and avoid doing what was right. As a federal official, Wilson claimed, the best he could do was ask the local justice of the peace, the individual responsible for the justice system in Indian matters in California, to take a closer look at Weaver's actions.[97] The Cahuillas' request went unheeded, and Weaver continued to deprive them of land, stock, and water. The situation epitomized some of the root causes of genocide in southern California.

Bystanders play the most significant role in any genocide, but did so particularly in this case of democratic genocide. The authorities of Los Angeles County remained silent, even while the *Los Angeles Star* informed residents of the potential for renewed problems with Native people. By their inaction the county and its citizenry showed their true intent. To force Weaver to honor the agreements he and the county had made would have involved two key decisions by these bystanders: they would need to side with an Indian over a white man, which was an infrequent occurrence in California beyond the attention sometimes paid to the plight of Native peoples by Indian agents and Bay Area journalists, and they would have to risk being on the wrong side of their own laws, which clearly protected men like Weaver despite the obvious injustice of their actions. In the long run, even if whites had not wanted to be prosecuted for infringing on Weaver's personal and property rights, they could have used the democratic process to change the situation so that law might equal justice. Indeed they might have harnessed the very processes of democracy by means of the types of petitions they had sent to the governor, calling for the protection of Native American lives and property rights. One searching for this instance will not find it. Instead Euro-Americans in southern California engaged their right to emulate the ostrich, a behavior seen in other cases of genocide.[98]

The decision to remain bystanders to Weaver's actions flew in the face of what Juan Antonio and the Cahuillas had done for Euro-Americans in southern California during the previous two years. In particular Euro-Americans ignored Juan Antonio's decision to capture Antonio Garra and turn him over to General Bean, thus alleviating the worst panic over a possible Indian war ever experienced by Euro-Americans in southern California. Even as the Cahuillas negotiated, cooperated, and endured injustices, Euro-Americans ignored their willingness to participate in negotiation and exercise forbearance when wronged. Juan Antonio's later years epitomized what negotiation and accommodation wrought for many other Native communities. Over time Juan Antonio was no longer seen as an ally and protector of the people of Los Angeles and San Bernardino, but rather as conniving and self-interested, not to be trusted or admired. Most Euro-Americans shed no tears when he died of smallpox; indeed some Cahuilla people believe Euro-Americans purposely infected the powerful leader with the disease.[99] Other Native Americans in southern California, like Garra, became increasingly unwilling or unable to wait or negotiate with Euro-Americans. Ultimately the examples of Juan Antonio and Antonio Garra demonstrate that resistance and accommodation produced the same disastrous outcome: the impetus for genocide against Native Americans. Instances of armed resistance fueled Euro-American fears and desire for revenge and produced deadly armed responses. The worthless nature of treaty protections and the ineffectiveness of the justice system in redressing wrongs committed against Native Americans emboldened settlers to squat on Native lands and monopolize local resources. Both paths produced problems for Native Americans that threatened their existence at the most fundamental levels.

The Civil War years only intensified the neglect of the Indigenous peoples of southern California. The federal government reserved less and less money for Indian affairs, and consequently southern California even more so. Already the southern portion of the state, with its relative lack of bloodshed and nearly airtight system of Native American slave labor, commanded little of the funding allocated to the state for Indian affairs. Thomas J. Henley, the superintendent of Indian affairs for California from 1854 to 1860, had never even visited southern California. Angered at the deplorable conditions that their people were being subjected to, Native leaders complained to Indian agents. Native Americans were aware that the Indigenous populations in northern California, who fought frequently against the Euro-Americans and exacted heavy tolls on livestock, received much more in the way of funding for reservations.[100] The case must have seemed clear: those who fought were reviled but funded; those who negotiated were considered cowards and relegated to little or no funding.[101] The case of the Luiseño leader Francisco is illustrative of how the government dealt with such complaints. Following Francisco's attempts to get the United States to enforce Luiseño property rights, the federal Indian agent removed Francisco as chief and replaced him.[102]

Sometimes Native American attempts to achieve justice were greeted with bloodshed and ferocity. In 1861 American cattlemen began to scout the Owens Valley as a potential site for grazing, despite the presence of Paiute people in the valley and surrounding areas. A cabin soon joined the tule-and-willow houses of the Paiutes. In late 1861 Euro-Americans herded stock into the valley. By early 1862 Euro-

Americans made permanent settlements in the valley at Lone Pine and Bishop.[103] The construction of the cabin, the importation of cattle, and the establishment of a settlement at Lone Pine and Bishop were all accomplished without consultation or negotiation with the Paiutes. Trouble would soon flow from the Euro-American decision to ignore Indian property rights.

In many ways, Samuel Addison Bishop was typical of other settlers and ranchers in California in the 1850s and 1860s. He went west for gold, and after failing to make a huge fortune, he hit on cattle ranching as a way to make a living. Land and cattle were plentiful, and starting a business simply involved obtaining stock and finding a place unclaimed by Euro-Americans to graze them; Native American claims stood in the way of few. Bishop settled at the southern end of the Central Valley, in the Tehachapi foothills, and was the deed holder for the land where Fort Tejon was constructed. Evidence indicates that he made money on the lease of the land, as well as by supplying stores and raising stock for the U.S. Army. Like many Euro-American citizens, he joined a volunteer company and fought local Indigenous peoples for control of their land and resources. He fought in the Mariposa War and aided in the capture of Chief Yosemite. In 1861 he and his family decided to relocate to the Owens Valley to take advantage of the excellent water and grass.[104] As the cattle of men like Bishop began to spread throughout the valley, Native people, especially the Paiutes, began to resist the Euro-American presence in the valley.[105] Stock destroyed food sources and fouled the water supply. Native peoples responded by lighting cabin roofs on fire and raiding stock. Stock raiding became more important as the scarce resources of the area were consumed by thousands of domesticated animals. Many of the Euro-American settlers either failed to recognize what was going on or chose to ignore privation as a motivating factor for Native American action, interpreting the thefts instead as an expression of their nature and not a strategy for survival. This idea was so strong that Euro-Americans living in the area in the twentieth century continued to believe "temptation" and not starvation was the root cause of livestock raiding.[106]

Stock raiding quickly escalated into a mortal contest between Native Americans and settlers and ranchers. Seeing a Native American man leading away a cow, Al Thompson shot the man dead. Whether or not Thompson considered simply recapturing the cow and seeing the Native American off, one cannot know. Native people responded by killing a Euro-American almost in the same location in retaliation. Following these incidents, an opportunity for lasting peace presented itself in the form of a delegation of Native American leaders in the region. The two sides met and signed a treaty at St. Francis Ranch, each side promising not to interfere with the other. The treaty proved worthless, however, because a group of Native people living south of Mono Lake were not included.[107] When this group raided stock, the signatory Native groups were blamed and warfare broke out in the Owens Valley. The words of Henry Hanks, a miner in the region, summed up the sentiments of many valley residents as he appealed to his fellow white Americans and government representatives to secure their claims against the savage Indians of the Owens Valley:

I want you to use all your influence to have the reservation done away with, and to prevent a treaty until the Indians are punished severely. The citizens of this valley are exasperated to the extent that they will not respect any treaty until the Indians are completely conquered and punished. The Indians are a cruel, cowardly, treacherous race. The whites have treated them well, paid them faithfully for all services performed by them, and have used the reservation only after gaining the consent of Captain George, their chief. After living on the charity of the whites all winter, having gambled away their blankets and beads given them by the Government, they now, without giving us the slightest warning, pounce down like vultures, rob those who have treated them best, and murdered where they could without danger to themselves. They rush upon their prey like a pack of wolves, and not satisfied in filling the bodies of their victims with glass-pointed arrows, beat them into pumice with stones. Can we be expected to give such inhuman wretches a chance at us again? We call upon you, the people of California, State and Federal authorities, to have this reservation and this set of wild savages removed to some other point. This valley is the natural thoroughfare through the mountains, and destined by nature to be the seat of a large population.[108]

Apparently that population was not destined to be a Native American one. What had driven Hanks to call for the total destruction of Indian culture in the region? Hanks's cabin had been robbed while he was out prospecting. Even though the cabin was in an area described as a "natural thoroughfare" for all sorts of peoples, he did not doubt that thieving Indians were to blame. And given the problems between whites and Native Americans in the region, Hanks may have been correct. Genocide as punishment for theft was Hanks's typically Euro-American response, despite his admission that the government was giving blankets and beads to starving people. Certainly the blankets were useful, but the beads were an outdated Indian trade good that would purchase nothing. Blankets and beads were no defense against hunger. As the months passed in Owens Valley, and with the Native land base cut into by more and more ranchers and their animals, stock raiding increased as Native people in the region stole to survive.

During 1862–65 coordinated attacks against Native peoples by volunteer groups and the U.S. Army attempted to put an end to resistance. At the same time Indians from the west, at Tejon, and the north, at Mono Lake, aided the Owens Valley Paiutes in resisting the settlers and ranchers. According to one report sent to Governor Leland Stanford in July 1862, at least six different Native groups had joined the Paiutes to fight whites in the region. Stanford's representative, James Allen, believed that over one thousand warriors, some with firearms, were arrayed against the settlers and the army. Allen also reported, "The original aggressors . . . were the Whites, by recklessly herding their stock upon the cultivated and artificially irrigated grounds of the Indians." He explained to Stanford the problems of the treaty made at the St. Francis Ranch. But Allen, like the ranchers, believed that the Native American signatories of the treaty were accountable for the actions of all Native people. An Indian is an Indian. Allen told Stanford that the U.S. Army had created a post in the region, Fort Independence, and sent over two hundred cavalrymen into the area to put an end to the Native uprising. Allen believed that these men were "sufficient to keep the Indians in check and maintain peace." But were they enough to deal with all of the inhabitants of the valley and prevent future trouble? Allen certainly believed that Indians were only part of the problem: "The commanding officer, whoever he may be, should be particularly instructed to guard the rights of the Indians as rigidly as those of the Whites."[109]

Allen's words seemed to suggest that his countrymen were at fault, but that was not fully the case. He commented, "If the Indian Reservation System had been carried out, honestly and intelligently, the late difficulties would not have occurred, and the blood and treasure, expended in suppressing them, would have been saved."[110] Allen felt that the federal government, especially its Indian agents, was to blame as much as anyone. As did many people of the West in the nineteenth century, Euro-American populations in California relied on the federal government to address many of the problems they themselves created. This has been a lasting source of irony, given that Euro-Americans living in the West have traditionally claimed their independence from government is unrivaled in the United States.[111] With a large body of troops to aid them, the Euro-Americans of Owens Valley fought numerous actions against the allied peoples of the Owens and Mono region.

Actions could be bloody on both sides, but Paiute tactics focused on the destruction of property; the Euro-Americans focused on destruction of lives. In April 1863 sixty Indians raided a ranch and slaughtered cattle. Euro-American forces pursued them, killing fifty-nine in retaliation for the dead animals. Less than two years later, one of the most disturbing episodes in the history of the Owens Valley brought the war to a close. Following the murder of a white woman and child, apparently by Native American hands, settlers in the valley marched on a local village and killed one hundred men, women, and children in retaliation.[112] However, the actual culprits were more likely two Americans, named Newman and Flanigan. The two men had stopped in the home of the woman and her son, who ran a kind of rest stop in the valley. After the bodies were discovered, a party trailed the two men and caught up with them. Flanigan and Newman claimed that Indians had attacked the house while they were there, set it on fire, and then waited to kill the occupants. They said they implored the woman and boy to come with them, but they refused. The two men made their escape safely. After hearing the story, the party threatened Flanigan and Newman with death if they ever returned to the valley. Though some believed that Flanigan and Newman had killed the mother and son, set the fire, and blamed the Indians, it was not enough to stop retaliation against the Indians. Following the butchery at the village, additional evidence seemed to indicate that, at the least, the wrong Indians had been killed.[113] Still, Euro-Americans had achieved what they wanted: Native American resistance after that became sporadic, and eventually faded.

Euro-Americans in the Owens Valley, however, continued to stir up trouble between themselves and the Owens Valley Paiutes. In March 1866 a man named Spray committed one of the innumerable crimes against Indigenous peoples based on racist perceptions of the Indian character that were common supports to the genocide. Spray, while heading for his home in the Owens Valley, stopped to rest at a house in Adobe Meadows, just west of Mono Lake. He laid down his pistol on a table. The house containing children, their mother stored the weapon for safety. When it came time for Spray to depart, the weapon was missing. Suspicion immediately fell on a Native man employed by the household. Protesting his innocence and claiming that perhaps another man who had recently visited had taken it, the alleged thief volunteered to find the man and get the pistol back. As the man frantically tried to mount his horse, Spray concluded that he was guilty and likely attempting to flee. Spray, and perhaps some companions, shot the defenseless man three or four times, killing him. Shortly after the murder, the woman discovered the pistol, having looked for it in the wrong place earlier. There is no indication that Spray or his companions were ever charged, let alone convicted of any crime. Indeed the narrative suggests rather that except from Native Americans in the area, there was little outcry at the murder. Native people around Adobe Meadows were angry and demanded that Spray be brought to justice. Unlike many Euro-American settlers, the Native peoples of Adobe Meadows were willing to let the legal system in California operate rather than turn immediately to vigilante justice. Uproar among Euro-Americans followed, as the Native community decreed that they would kill ten whites in retaliation if something was not done to bring Spray to justice.[114] Ultimately the Native people determined to forgo vengeance, likely because they were unwilling to reignite the war only recently ended.

As would be repeated in northern California, Euro-Americans in southern California used land and resources in a manner that was unsustainable, permanently damaging to ecosystems, and detrimental to the Indigenous population. The historian Donald Worster has pointed out that this type of misuse was "explicitly democratic." The popular demand for government to support ranching and farming through irrigation was at the heart of this issue in southern California. Like those in many Western nations, Euro-Americans in the nineteenth century accepted that they had to tear down nature and reconstruct it to suit them. They believed that nature could be brought to perfection only by the intervention of men. In the case of diverting and exploiting water resources, democracy was the means and the end. Many Euro-Americans believed "a rearrangement of nature . . . would save the nation and the state for democracy" by "making possible small-scale autonomous communities, egalitarian harmony and justice." This was particularly true in southern California, where water was a scarce and valuable commodity. It was not necessarily hard for Euro-Americans to find, though. All they need do was locate the site of Native American villages or camps, as the Mexicans and Spanish had done before them. Then they could make claims under state and federal laws on Native lands containing valuable water resources, or claim lands nearby and then manipulate these same laws to redirect water to them and away from Native peoples. The democratic voice of the people in their demand for water to irrigate crops and satisfy the thirst of herd animals was the mechanism by which these laws and ordinances were created during the first four decades of California statehood. Because the water represented life and livelihood for settlers and ranchers, irrigation projects were much more than public works projects: "irrigation was a *cause*" that American settlers fought for.[115] Water was also vital for Native communities, but given that Native Americans could not bring suit against whites in state courts until 1872, little could be done legally.

Euro-Americans also continued to structure their laws so that their animals could roam freely over Native lands, consuming health- and life-sustaining plants and water. Complaints were not tolerated. And Euro-Americans and their representatives were even less tolerant of stock raiding, which incurred harsh punishment. In one terrible example, an Indian agent, Cave Couts, caught two Luiseño men raiding stock. Even though the men were stealing to feed their people, Couts whipped them so savagely that both men died. The stock raiding continued in the area, but now with increased hatred for Euro-Americans.[116] Couts, like other local, state, and federal officials, acted in reference to what Euro-Americans wanted, not what decency, justice, or even the law demanded.

In northern California many of the same challenges faced Native peoples. But because of the location of the Gold Rush, the inordinate number of Euro-Americans, and the collapse of many miners' dreams of quick riches, northern California's Native population faced a genocidal assault perhaps unrivaled in North America in terms of its ferocity, bloodiness, and loss of human life. As in southern California, northern California's impotent federal agents and apathetic bystanders looked on as many thousands of Native people died directly and indirectly at the hands of whites. While some sympathetic voices called for justice and restraint, they were often drowned out by the voices of the killers and their supporters. As the anthropologist Florence Shipek once remarked about a similar situation in southern California, the confusion stemmed from the fact that people who hated Indians often proposed the same solution as those who cared for them: to remove them for their own safety.[117] Removing Indigenous populations into camps where they could be used for labor or neglected until they died was often the way Euro-Americans in the mountainous regions north of Sacramento handled their Indian affairs.

5

Democratic Death Squads
of Northern California

The Indians have committed so many depredations in the North, of late, that the people are enraged against them, and are ready to knife them, shoot them, or inoculate them with smallpox—all of which have been done.

"Exciting News from Tehama," *Daily Alta California* (1853)

As Euro-Americans flooded into, and then out of, the gold fields of California in the 1850s, they harnessed democracy to achieve a new dream of wealth and security based on landownership. Using new state laws and their rights as citizens, they quickly and bloodily transitioned California's land base from one controlled mostly by Native peoples into one controlled almost completely by Euro-Americans. The development of the conflict over land was central to beginning the transfer. Euro-Americans placed themselves in close proximity to Native Americans, preventing them from gathering food, trading, and living in traditional ways. As conflicts evolved, Euro-Americans turned to traditional ways to take advantage of Indigenous populations. The process of doing so involved the clever manipulation of democracy and its various institutions: local and county governments, the press, and the state legislature, executive, and judiciary. Often failed miners and recent emigrants to California themselves, the men who worked in these institutions found it easy to identify with settlers and their interests. In most cases, governments were at least willing to turn their heads, if not send help, when Native populations were being exterminated. Yet above all else, settlers, ranchers, and miners, like their brethren in the southern portion of the state, used voluntary, democratic associations to greatest effect in bringing about the genocide of California's Indigenous people.

Judge Serranus C. Hastings provides an example of how one operated within democracy to acquire and exploit Native American lands. Hastings had obtained school land warrants to purchase all of the Eden Valley, though he seldom went there and never lived there.[1] Instead his purchase was the beginning of a stock-raising venture. Hastings sent hundreds of head of horses and cattle into the valley under the care of H. L. Hall, to whom Hastings and a partner promised one-third of the valley in exchange for his stewardship of the stock and the property. However, Hall would have no easy time getting his payment. The valley was home to several hundred Native people, the Yukis.

The Yukis inhabited the areas in and around Eden Valley, Round Valley, and Long Valley, cut by the diverging courses of the Eel River and its tributaries in what became Mendocino County in 1850. Like other Indigenous populations in California, they had their own distinct language, traditions, and subsistence practices. They were not one people politically, but rather several autonomous groups, sharing a language and culture but each community having its own leadership. Other Native peoples, such as the Wailakis and Wintus, lived nearby. The Yukis traded, intermarried, and sometimes fought with these groups and other Yuki communities. But each village was autonomous.[2]

Settlers and ranchers began to graze stock and settle in these valleys. From time to time emigrants would pass through on their way elsewhere, and miners would periodically inspect the rivers, foothills, and mountains of the region, hoping to find a new source of gold. These intruders put a strain on the Yukis, as such incursions did all over the state. As Euro-Americans pushed deeper into these valleys, they attempted to push Native peoples out. Settlers and ranchers exhibited the same combination of hate and fear possessed by many other Euro-Americans, despite recent emigrant experiences that seemed to suggest that the Indians of childhood nightmares were not the "devils" portrayed in trail guides, newspapers, history books, and rumors and tall tales. Nevertheless over time the strain on the Yukis and other Native Americans living in proximity to white settlers and ranchers reached a breaking point, forcing normally peaceful Indigenous groups into the necessity of taking livestock, or more rarely violent action, in order to survive. This would give Euro-Americans confirmation that the savage Indians of their childhood fears were the same as the Indians of their adult reality in California.

As would be repeated hundreds of times throughout California, the presence of settlers and ranchers and their domestic herds spelled disaster for local Indigenous populations. The oxen, horses, mules, cattle, sheep, pigs, and hogs brought by settlers and ranchers ruined the lands Native communities depended on for food, shelter, and fuel. Herds of domesticated stock drove off native species. Euro-American industry, especially logging, also took a toll. Sawdust discharged into rivers killed fish and deprived Native peoples of a traditional, reliable food source.[3] Mining waste did much the same thing. Other Euro-American activities created problems as well.

Euro-American hunters, both professional and recreational, reduced the game population in areas where Native people lived, removing an important source of protein and upsetting traditional roles played by Native men. Some of the earliest conflicts were between Euro-American and Native American hunters and trappers who met on Native lands. Knyphausen Geer recounted the story of the death in 1854 of Charles Hicks of Humboldt County. Hicks was hunting and became lost, so much so that he stumbled right into a Native village, uninvited. The Native men of the village, identified as Salt River Indians, attempted to disarm him. Whether it was to protect their people or to get possession of his valuable firearm or to kill him, one cannot know for certain what the villagers intended. In the struggle that ensued, the Native men took Hicks's rifle. Either in the struggle or as he ran, one of the Native men shot Hicks with his own weapon. Badly wounded, he was able to make his way from the village, apparently without pursuit.

It is unlikely that the villagers had initially meant to kill him, because they could have done so without taking the gun. In fact, if they could struggle for a time with him, and then take possession of the gun, and then shoot him, it would seem that they intended something else besides killing him. Similarly if their intent was robbery and murder they could have easily pursued Hicks, killed him, and despoiled him of his remaining possessions. Geer believed that the men probably just wanted the gun, not Hicks's life. Native people living along the Bear River later discovered the wounded Hicks and sought help on his behalf. He was brought back to a camp he shared with other hunters and trappers, where he died under a doctor's care.[4]

Despite Geer's relatively benign interpretation of events, the hunters in the camp were not so circumspect in their judgments. Hicks's partner, a man named Holly, was infuriated by Hicks's death. He immediately organized a party to seek revenge, saying, "Who'll go with me? I can't eat or sleep in peace till I kill a Goddamned Digger." Following Holly's call for vengeance, six men from the hunter's camp gathered local residents to aid them in avenging the death of Hicks. Geer was a rancher with 160 acres in Humboldt County and had a keen interest in preventing disturbances to his business, even if he suspected that Hicks had died unnecessarily. Geer became one of the five local settlers added to the group seeking revenge. The eleven white men proceeded to the Salt River camp of the Indians in question, finding between thirty and forty Indians there. According to Geer, some of the Native people were obviously visiting from the Eel River region, and not members of the offending group. The party of eleven men, after waiting overnight, attacked at first light and slaughtered the entire village. Geer recalled, "We fought and killed quite a lot." What made matters easier was that the villagers did not want to fight them, but attempted to hide and so were shot down without resistance.[5] The motive for the massacre, revenge for the death of Hicks, led eleven men to slaughter not just the man who killed Hicks, but also the other men, women, and children in the village. Such overreaches of vengeance often play a role in cases of genocide; in this case, the victims were considered so devoid of humanity that the men could kill those simply cowering, offering no resistance. Indeed what resistance could helpless women and children offer? According to the genocide scholar Bruce Wilshire, it is typical for "genociders [to] lump all of *them* together," making few distinctions among victims, seeing all as totally alien others.[6]

Recreational hunting also took a toll. In one example of thoughtless excess, three men hunting for recreation in Tehama County shot 148 quail between them.[7] To make matters worse, the sportsmen were hunting during the vital time of the year when Indigenous peoples were attempting to collect winter stores. Euro-Americans could not help but realize that their hunting threatened Native survival.

The activities of ranchers and their animals were particularly troublesome. Ranchers hunted the deer and elk that competed for forage with their cattle and horses, devastating wild herds. Domesticated animals ate the plants that Native people and indigenous animals depended on for survival, upsetting the ecological balance of entire regions. Only eventual damage to commercial agricultural resources created any noticeable impetus for changing the practice of allowing free range to herds of domesticated animals.[8] But many years would pass before Euro-Americans addressed the issue as it pertained to them.[9]

Many Native peoples were forced to find new means of subsistence. There is evidence that Euro-Americans were aware of this, especially in areas where Native labor could prove extremely valuable to settlers and ranchers.[10] Pierson B. Reading believed that the destitute state of the Native Americans living on land recently granted to him was a "very good advantage." He felt that they could be made to work like the "negroes in the South." And given that there were some three hundred men, women, and children on his land, he felt he could "convert them into useful subjects" and do quite well for himself on his forty-five-square-mile ranch.[11] Native Americans who attempted to get nourishment by eating the livestock that was destroying their lives died at the hands of white Americans who exacted payback for lost cows or horses by murdering human beings.[12]

This cycle of starvation of Native peoples, their stock theft for food, and the bloody, retaliatory vengeance by settlers and ranchers, exacted often with self-righteous fury, was the key sequence of events leading to the Euro-American claim that extermination of Indigenous populations was a practical necessity. And the cycle only worsened over time. As settlers and ranchers, many of whom were unharmed by the thefts, hunted down and killed Native Americans, many of whom were not associated with the thefts, the cycle changed. Native peoples living at higher elevations or areas hit with heavy winter snows needed to prepare for winter long before winter arrived. With emigrants filling the valleys and lowlands where game and edible plants flourished spring through fall, it was difficult enough to survive on a day-to-day basis, let alone prepare for winter. Soon Native Americans began to attack settlers and ranchers in addition to taking their stock. Various Native American groups in Tehama County, for instance, chased off white hunters up to the late 1850s, but by the early 1860s sometimes killed them.[13] The level of violence on the Euro-American side escalated in retaliation. In what may be an underestimation, the anthropologist Robert Heizer judged that "for every white man killed, a hundred Indians paid the penalty with their lives."[14] In the case of the valleys in and around Mendocino, Tehama, and adjacent counties, one can use the experience of the Native peoples and their Euro-American competitors for land and resources as a model that shows clearly the democratically driven genocidal events unfolding all over the state in the nineteenth century.

H. L. Hall was twenty-three when he took up stewardship of Eden Valley on behalf of Serranus C. Hastings and his partner, Thomas J. Henley, the superintendent of Indian affairs in California. In addition to his stock-raising duties, Hall began to farm on a portion of Eden Valley that Hastings promised him as compensation. When Hall moved into Eden Valley in August 1858, no other white settlers lived there; he claimed that no Native Americans lived there either.[15] In the heat of the summer perhaps no Indian peoples lived down in the valley, but instead resided along the banks of the river or in the coolness of the surrounding higher elevations. But Native people did live there.

In August and September Hall drove nearly four hundred horses into Eden Valley. The herd belonged to Hastings and Henley. In the next two months Hall discovered that an Indigenous population did live in the valley, later recalling that over one hundred people came down and camped near where he was living. He called them "my Indians" because they were on his land, and he believed them peaceful. His life remained undisturbed until December 1858, when something happened: "My Indians told me that one mare had been killed and before I went out after them they reported three or five [more] killed."[16] Hall reacted quickly and decisively to protect the horses, but he did not use the laws in place to punish horse thievery or summon an Indian agent or justice of the peace. He felt that Indians deserved an entirely different standard of justice when applying punishment for crimes. Like a fox killing chickens or a bear killing cattle, death was the solution for dealing with animal-like Indians. Indeed after reading the new state law regulating horse and cattle thievery, one Euro-American commented to a crowd, "If an Indian steals a horse, or a steer, he shall be whipped, with not less than 25, nor more than 39 lashes. And if a white man does the same, he shall be imprisoned for several months, and fined $1000. Now, gentlemen, what sort of law is that? A damned Digger to get off with 39 lashes . . . *that* law won't work! . . . Well, stranger, if I catch an Indian stealing from me, I'll shoot him, by God!"[17] Hall was of a like mind, and he knew of a local Native American village that seemed the likely culprit.

Seeking the help of three white men living in nearby Round Valley, Hall attacked the village without warning or investigation of their involvement in the theft. Even though the villagers ran as Hall and his fellows approached, he and his men still shot down and indiscriminately killed half of the twenty people living there. After the main episode of killing, the men entered the village to see if these were actually the responsible parties. They found another "buck" and executed him after setting fire to his hiding place, forcing him to come out and be shot to death instead of burned to death.[18] They found some horse meat and went away, apparently satisfied that killing ten Indians compensated them for the lives of four or six horses. This was not an isolated event. Euro-Americans often determined likely culprits without any sure knowledge of guilt or innocence.

As was the case on the overland trail, stock was typically unattended as it grazed in the valleys and foothills of California. Ranchers often had a difficult time locating stock, although they had little trouble placing blame for the losses. Animals missing for an extended period near Native population centers were typically believed stolen by them, despite the evidence that abounded in local papers of all the ways an animal might be lost or killed by forces other than Native Americans. Plant life that was unfamiliar to new emigrants and poisonous to cattle and horses grew in the valleys of central and northern California. One "noxious weed" killed two oxen in 1857 between Red Bluff and Fort Crook. Luckily their owner saw them consume this strange plant; otherwise they might have been considered killed by marauding Indians.[19] Even greater numbers of cattle were confirmed dead for similar reasons in Humboldt County, north of San Francisco on the Pacific Coast.[20] Emigrants to California were learning a similarly harsh lesson on the eastern borders of the state, as cattle consumed a plant that could kill them in only thirty minutes.[21] Outbreaks of disease also claimed the lives of horses and cattle.[22] In cases where owners observed the onset and terminal conclusion of the affliction, Native people were safe from retribution. But animals dying away from their owners' locations might easily have joined losses attributed to Indian thievery. Weather was also an important contributor to livestock mortality. Flooding, heavy snows, and other natural phenomena often claimed the lives of animals. In one case, four horses corralled during a summer storm were struck by lightning, killing them all.[23] If the horses had been loose, there would be little chance that their owner could know that lightning strikes, not Native people, were to blame. Winter storms also claimed the lives of animals, attended or not. Such was the case for Simon P. Storms, who lost five mules in icy weather that hit in November 1859 while he was running a pack train.[24] In the early 1860s a well-known sequence of devastating floods and then drought nearly destroyed the cattle industry in California, killing hundreds of thousands of animals in four years. In 1874, just south of the Oregon-California border, hundreds of animals perished from a series of frosts and floods.[25] But nature was not always the responsible party in herd losses.

What one might characterize as man-made disasters were even more prevalent in claiming the lives of cattle and horses and giving local settlers and ranchers the opportunity to place unqualified blame on Native Americans. Non-Native cattle rustlers and horse thieves abounded in California. Euro-American horse thieves were often mentioned in the newspapers when caught or spotted in the act, but when thefts went unwitnessed, newspapers did not conjecture that whites had committed such crimes.[26] Rather they typically attributed the crimes to Mexicans or Indians. Blaming Indians may have seemed the natural conclusion, given the common stereotype of Native Americans as thieves. The *Butte Democrat* reported on November 19, 1859, "Horse Thief Shot—We are informed that Mr. Owens, of Round Valley, a few nights ago shot at and wounded a Spaniard, who had been caught stealing horses. Mr. Owens first endeavored to arrest him, but owing to the darkness, could not, until he had brought him up with a bullet. Four animals that he had stolen were recovered. *His arrest has possibly saved some Indian's life.*" The "possibly" is interesting. Whether or not the *Democrat's* editor intended to suggest that other victims of thefts might ignore the fact that a non-Indian horse thief was among them, that some would not be convinced is obvious. Unconfirmed reports of herds of animals being run off by marauding Indians also circulated and informed the subsequent decisions of communities to rise up and seek retribution through murder. In very real ways, these assumptions and false reports of Native American guilt cost many lives. In two similar instances, citizens organized parties to retrieve cattle and kill thieving Indians after reports swept through communities in Yreka and Lassen, only to be called off after finding out that the animals had simply wandered a bit farther than expected and were recovered without loss.[27] What might have happened had those animals evaded recapture another day or two? Or had they been taken by other whites? Given the ubiquity of losses by means other than Native people, well-publicized means at that, one might assume that settlers and ranchers would have at least been more circumspect in their assignment of blame for stock losses.

A great number of unchecked stories and wild rumors of missing whites also led to hasty assignments of guilt to Indigenous populations. Numerous accounts of missing men filled the pages of newspapers, often accompanied by charges that savage Indians had kidnapped or killed them. The *Daily Alta California*, the leading newspaper in the state, reported the "probable murder" of three miners in the Shasta area and "feared that they had been murdered by the Indians."[28] The fact that the missing men were traveling in the rough terrain of the Cascades in the winter seemed to play no role in the thinking of the writer. In Yreka a volunteer company was formed to seek revenge in a similar case of missing men, even though no bodies had ever been recovered, the names of the persons and their numbers were unknown, and no physical evidence of murder existed. Given this, the party's mission was twofold: finding the bodies and "chastising the Indians."[29] The paper included no comment as to what would happen if they found those presumed guilty before finding the bodies. Examples abound of unexplained absences and unwitnessed murders explained as Indian devilry.[30]

In some cases, newspaper editors had to admit that they, like their countrymen, had been premature in their judgments of Native American atrocity. The *Red Bluff Beacon* cheerfully reported that a party led by Captain Weatherlow had *not* been massacred by Indians, as had been reported. Weatherlow and company had turned up in Shasta, untouched and apparently unbothered by Native Americans. Learning that the newspapers had been reporting their deaths, they wrote to assure the *Beacon* they yet lived.[31] Of course, these reassurances and the pseudo-retraction printed by the *Beacon* did not help any Native peoples in the region who ran afoul of vengeful Euro-Americans in between the time the false report was printed and the error corrected. This was not the *Beacon*'s first mistake. Only a year before it had reported the death of three Americans at the hands of the Klamaths.

Two weeks went by before the paper received word that the men were not killed, but had gotten lost and taken some additional time to reach their destination. Whether or not any Klamath people suffered for this error, one cannot know. The *Beacon* temporized about its error, reporting to readers that many miles away some other men had been killed, most likely by Indians.[32] Certainly men did disappear, and sometimes because they really were killed by a group of Native Americans, but in some cases whites were killed by other whites.

Seldom, though, was a newspaper able to identify which group of Native people had perpetrated the alleged murder or why they had killed their victims, instead using the word "Indians" to describe the culprit and attributing the motive to savagery. Perhaps the Euro-American mind, inured to this common representation of Indianness, readily accepted the explanation. This situation contributed to the random slaughter of Native Americans unassociated with a given crime. Euro-American criminals exacerbated this by disguising themselves as Native Americans as a way of displacing blame, undoubtedly with potentially fatal consequences for Native peoples wrongly blamed for white men's misdeeds.[33] Even the apprehension of white criminals posing as Native Americans failed to stem the hate and violence directed at California's Indigenous populations. As when animals went missing, the impulse among editors seemed to be always to blame supposedly savage Indians. Men who died without witnesses contributed to the fear and suspicion of Native Americans. Suicide by gunshot, by accident or on purpose, was common enough in the boom and bust times of the second half of the nineteenth century in California. Unless one was near to witness the act or accident, one might never know if a wound was self-inflicted or homicide. As was common on the overland trail, accidents frequently happened; one might as easily call a lone body with a bullet wound a mischance as a murder, perhaps depending on the proximity of an Indigenous population.[34] Who, for instance, could distinguish between men killed by Native Americans armed with firearms and those killed by the many highwaymen infesting California in the 1850s?[35] Despite the irrefutable fact that whites killed and stole from other whites, the propensity to place blame on any other people besides Native Americans seemed beyond the capability of many settlers, ranchers, and miners. In examining these moments where much doubt should have existed about the whereabouts of men or animals, instead one finds a high degree of certainty of what lay behind the losses: murderous, thieving Indians.

Hall and his employers continued to put pressure on the local Yuki people as winter deepened in the valley. Just days after his punitive expedition, Hastings sent up 230 head of cattle to add to the hundreds of horses.[36] Now well over six hundred animals alien to that part of California roamed the valley, unfenced and unwatched on a daily basis, while hundreds of the Yukis and indigenous animals in the depths of winter had to accept their presence, remove to another location, or find a way to coexist. Leaving animals unfenced and free to roam was commonplace in California at this time. To have fenced the land of such huge claims was impossible in this era before barbed wire. Ranchers believed that animals that could not be rounded up or otherwise found had fallen prey to Indians. As the *Lassen Sage Brush* phrased it a decade later, "The Indians, it would appear, are becoming emboldened by their successes for the few months past and are hanging around as though they had made the conquest of the country." Settlers and ranchers neither wanted Native Americans thinking that California was their country nor assuming that they were willing to share lands with them.

Within days of Hall's taking his latest delivery of stock, the major commanding the local detachment of federal troops paid him a visit. Major Johnson and his command remained in the valley for a week. Hall made no comment as to why the troops came to stay for such a time; it might have been a routine patrol or maybe to investigate Hall's massacre of the Yukis. The troops departed after a week, perhaps hearing that a white man named McDonald had been killed in Round Valley. With the departure of the troops and news of the death reaching Hall in quick succession, he grew afraid. McDonald, it seemed, had been killed by Native people in Round Valley.[37] Most likely they were the Yukis, the same people who lived in Eden Valley. Since Hall was no stranger to the region, he might have known that McDonald was guilty of at least one serious offense against the Yukis of Round Valley and suspected it was a revenge killing.

In 1855 McDonald had kidnapped Native Americans, a woman and two children, intending to sell them. Luckily for the trio, they managed to escape back to their people.[38] The practice of kidnapping Native women and children was common throughout California and normally practiced with much more success than McDonald's attempt. According to one account, the practice was widespread in the Round Valley region the same year as McDonald's failed attempt. According to the Indian agent Simon P. Storms, white settlers enslaved many Yuki women and children. Two Americans, the Asbill brothers, kidnapped Indian boys and girls; they forced the boys to hunt game as part of a hide-tanning business they had established, and they traded the girls for horses. The fate of these young girls seems disturbingly evident. In one transaction alone, the men traded thirty-five Yuki girls for 105 horses. The Asbills enslaved so many Yuki children that a Yuki chief visited the Indian agent at the reservation and lodged a complaint. Sadly, according to Redick McKee, the Yukis had been undergoing such raids stretching back to the Spanish colonial era. In the early 1850s McKee attempted to bring the Yukis to treaty talks with great difficulty as a result of their fears of Euro-American abduction. By the late 1850s matters were much worse, especially in areas that contained reservations. Euro-Americans used the reservation as markets to pick up Native women and children. These reservations included the Nome Cult Farm and Nome Lackee reservations, where many of the Yuki people had been taken against their will or convinced to relocate for protection from white settlers. The relocations only made it easier for whites to kidnap them, essentially concentrating the targets of the slavers in one convenient spot. Conditions were worse in mining areas, where Euro-Americans vastly outnumbered Native populations. Miners kidnapped Native women and drove away or killed Native men as they appropriated everything and everyone they desired by weight of numbers. What they did not take they burned to keep Indigenous populations from coming back.[39] This was the tradition that McDonald was carrying on when he attempted to kidnap the Yuki woman and children. Despite his failed attempt, he continued to live in the area and may have committed additional crimes against the Yukis. In 1859 the Yukis killed McDonald. It appears that an opportunity to avenge either McDonald's initial or later crimes had presented itself. However, local white citizens interpreted the Yukis' action as wanton savagery, not self-defense or revenge. Similar circumstances and reactions surrounded the first recorded deaths of whites at Yuki hands in Round Valley. William Mantle and John McDaniel, killed in 1857 and 1858, respectively, were both infamous for depredations committed against local Native peoples. McDaniel was noted for his recreational shooting of Indians, whom he endeavored to kill at ever-increasing distances as a challenge to himself.[40] Both men were described as keeping what whites called "pet Indians" in their homes. In fact McDaniel had reportedly been killed with his own gun by one of these "pets" he kept enslaved.[41] Local army officers reported the deaths of both men to their superiors as retribution for their crimes against Native people.[42] Even though Mantle and McDaniel were known as unsavory characters, their neighbors still avenged their deaths. After Mantle was killed, according to Isaac Shannon, whites went out and killed fourteen Yukis in retaliation.[43] Based on Hall's reaction to the story of McDonald's killing, and his likely knowledge of the cases of McDaniel and Mantle, he may have seen a similar demise in store for himself if he did not act quickly.

Not surprisingly, given his own transgressions against the Yukis, Hall immediately sent a letter to Hastings, asking for protection. Hastings responded with his own letters to the governor and the commander of the federal forces in California. The response of the federal government was slow in reaching Eden Valley. After two months of waiting, Maj. Edward Johnson and his troops returned to Eden Valley for a second visit, but finding no trouble brewing, they departed.[44]

As February 1859 was coming to a close, Hall found the remains of one of Hastings's stallions. He assumed that the animal had been killed by Indians. Shortly thereafter clearer evidence presented itself in the form of a cow wounded by an arrow. This was another moment that required Hall to take quick action. He rode to Round Valley to see the company commander of the federal forces stationed there, Lt. Edward Dillon. His request for the troops to deal with the Yukis of Eden Valley fell on unsympathetic ears. Dillon clearly believed that settlers and ranchers were the source of the trouble. Hall claimed that Dillon told him that for all he cared, the Indians could "kill all the stock in Eden and Round Valleys."[45] Dillon was well aware of the crimes being committed by white citizens against Native peoples all around him. He reported to his superiors in 1859 that he had received intelligence that during a two-week expedition by Hall and other citizens, some 240 Indians were killed.[46] Dillon later wrote in a letter dated 1861 that in just a few months of the new year, as many as fifty Native children had been kidnapped by whites and sold into slavery. Although he had no authority to make war or exact justice on whites, he did have the ability to avoid helping them in their depredations.[47] Hall, like other settlers in the region, would soon grow to hate Dillon, as he regularly refused to exterminate Native Americans, and indeed spent most of his time interfering with the settlers' attempts to kidnap or kill them.

Other than his private foray of the year before, Hall claimed he had not joined in any of the expeditions against Indigenous populations launched in the region. But based on the intelligence received by Lieutenant Dillon, this statement seems doubtful. The death of the horse and cow, coupled with Dillon's flat refusal to help him, changed Hall's mind about participating in a volunteer company. Instead of returning to Eden Valley, he visited local men and told them his story. The next day Hall and five men rode back into Eden Valley to hunt down and kill the Yukis who had killed the cow and, allegedly, the horse. Following a branching trail used by the Yukis, they discovered a Yuki village of some thirty people. The six white men attacked, managing to kill eight men. Following the slaughter, they found no trace of horse flesh and no sign that the Yuki villagers had killed any stock. Undeterred, and apparently unrepentant for killing innocent people, the men pressed on to find the real culprits. It appears that to Hall and his fellows, an Indian was an Indian. Finding another camp of Yukis some two miles up the trail, they entered the nearly deserted village to find no evidence of involvement and only "one sick buck" there to meet them. Still they managed to threaten the sick man before leaving, warning him that his people would be exterminated if they took stock from whites in the valley. Four miles farther on, the group found what they had been looking for, a village with fresh-killed cattle and horses. However, all of the men were away, and only women and children were present. Undeterred, Hall and the group took them all prisoner. Later, under questioning by a member of the California State Legislature, Hall was asked if any of the women or children were harmed. After attempting to evade the question, he at first admitted that he knew of one "squaw" who had been mysteriously shot during the encounter, but claimed that he had no idea who had done it or why, despite his presence at the village and his leadership of the party. But then his resolve to hide the truth gave out, and he told the committee what had happened on the road home: "I think all the squaws were killed because they refused to go further. We took one boy into the valley and the infants were put out of their misery and a girl 10 years of age was killed for stubbornness."[48] In other words, Hall and the men had killed defenseless women and children, including infants, because they were scared, crying, or hesitant to go to the homes of these men, where they might find rape, enslavement, or both as their fate. What these men failed to realize was that the "misery" of these Native peoples was misery created by them.

In all, Hall and his men killed as many as eight Yuki women and children on this one expedition, in addition to several men. Why Hall had even hesitated to admit this immediately is unclear, as the justice system in California rarely punished white men for crimes against Native people, with the exception of selling liquor to them. According to Lieutenant Dillon, many brutal crimes committed against Native peoples, no matter how gruesome, could not be prosecuted in the region. In one case a white man named Dodge chopped a Native man into bits with a hatchet for stealing a knife. In another, Dodge shot a

Native woman in the head for slaughtering a pig. And in another, a white man known as Texas publicly raped a Native woman. In each case witnesses were present, yet justice could not be done. Either the witnesses were Native Americans and unacceptable to the justice system, or they were whites. And whites, Dillon admitted, would "not testify against each other."[49] Meanwhile Hall and his group had in their possession another child, the only Indian boy seized in the raid. Bringing him back to Eden Valley, Hall planned on making him work. This, too, was perfectly legal under California law.[50] But after only a few weeks the Yukis "stole the boy" back.[51] Hall obviously considered the boy a piece of his property now. But this would become the least of Hall's troubles. According to a hired hand working for Hall, even as Hall, his men, and their single prisoner were returning home, the Yukis were driving off large herds of animals belonging to Hastings and Henley. Their strategy seemed to be that if no animals were left, the ranchers would have no reason to stay.

In March and April the Yukis escalated their attacks on the stock guarded by Hall. By mid-April they had killed twenty-five horses, and thirty cattle were killed or missing. More than just six white men would be needed to put an end to the problem this time. Hall went to meet Hastings directly. In the short term the Yuki strategy seemed to have won the battle at hand: Hastings and Hall removed the remaining stock from Eden Valley and brought them to pasture not far from the Eel River, where Hastings had recently brought nearly seven hundred more animals.[52] He had planned on putting them in Eden Valley, but the resistance of the Yukis was too strong to risk the herds.

After discussing the situation, Hastings and Hall agreed that the best course of action was to use their rights as citizens. They harnessed democracy by circulating a series of petitions in Round Valley and the surrounding area. After getting local men to sign the petition for a volunteer company, they sent the petition to the governor of California, asking permission to field the company for "protection" from the marauding Indians. If authorized, this would make nearly any act that the company committed legal, as the Militia Law of California allowed the governor to empower volunteers with the legal authority to defend the lives and property of citizens if the regular militia was unable to do so. They sent not one petition, but in excess of a dozen community petitions and citizen letters to the governor.[53] According to a later petition, these petitions were "unanimous" expressions of the will of the people.[54] A community representative, J. G. Doll, was elected and sent to Sacramento to press the citizens' case in person. Hastings also appealed to the governor on his own, using a terse letter to argue that he, not the Indians, was entitled to protection. In his letter to Governor John B. Weller, Hastings wrote, "Now sir I have purchased of the State of California Eden Valley with School Land Warrants. I have by the laws of this State the right of possession—I demand protection from the State. . . . I am attacked by Indians in front and the tax collector in the rear." Hastings demanded quick action, claiming that delay in preference for a response by the army would be disastrous.[55] For Hastings this was especially true. Not only was he partnered with Hall and Henley, but he was also partnered with other men in the area. In fact according to one account, almost every piece of stock in Round Valley and Eden Valley was owned in whole or in part by Judge Hastings.[56] While the citizens of Tehama County waited for the governor's reply, the situation escalated.

The Yukis continued to take animals belonging to Hall and from places ever nearer to his home in the valley. Hall turned to Lieutenant Dillon again, asking him to protect his home and property. This Dillon was willing to do, sending a squad of men to watch the house and surrounding area. The men eventually spent over a month watching the property. They were fairly effective in discouraging theft of stock until late May 1859, when, within sight of Hall's house, two horses were stolen. Hall demanded the soldiers accompany some local men and him to punish the Yukis. The soldiers refused; either Major Johnson or Lieutenant Dillon had forbidden the soldiers to do anything more than defend against attack.[57] To make matters worse, three more horses were taken in the night. Likely angry but certainly undeterred by the refusal, Hall and his neighbors set out on their own mission to retaliate.

While Hall and some men pursued the Yuki raiders, on May 27, 1859, the citizens of Tehama County held a meeting at the Masonic Hall in Red Bluff to draft new petitions. The citizens voted to elect a chairperson, secretary, and representative committee to articulate their grievances and draft a petition to the governor. After questioning a local army officer, Captain Flint, about his orders pertaining to suppressing Native populations, the citizens were left disappointed. Apparently Flint, like Dillon, was unable to simply arbitrarily exterminate the nuisance of local Native Americans. After a brief recess, the townspeople elected a new committee of three men to pursue their main desire: "to raise a company of volunteers in this county to commence in martial action against the Indians." The male citizens elected another committee of three to draft a petition to Governor Weller asking that he fulfill this wish for the people of Tehama. The committee produced the petition for review and signatures two days later, on May 29, 1859. In the petition, the people of Tehama County expressed their lack of faith in the U.S. Army and its troops stationed nearby, a company that had been sent by the federal government in response to a request by the governor after an earlier petition from the community. The committee argued that despite the local citizens "giving him [Captain Flint] what aid and advice [they] could, in obeying his instructions," the company was wholly ineffective. As the recent meeting had confirmed, the soldiers were either unwilling or unable to exterminate the local Indigenous population: "We consider the company of U.S. soldiers entirely insufficient to meet the demand and exigencies of the case." They argued that although there were likely only around two hundred Native people in the area, the soldiers were unsuited to the difficult task of moving over harsh terrain. And, more important, the troops were unaccustomed to dealing with Native Americans in an effective manner.[58] "Effective manner" likely referred to the citizens' desire for the pragmatic killing of the Indigenous population, a pragmatic outlook born of a desire for convenience seen in other cases of genocide.[59] In reality, this meant that Flint's orders forbade him from killing Native people in cold blood, which was exasperating for the citizens. A group of the local white citizenry, familiar with the region and experienced in dealing with uncivilized Indians in an effective manner, was the only alternative.

The committee explained to Governor Weller what this experience had already entailed. Although no white men had been recently killed, much stock had been taken and the people were seized with terror. The committee advised the governor of their recent acts of self-defense, carried out by men like Hall. The following account of an expedition by Tehama citizens, taken from their petition, seems to anticipate that news of their savagery might come to Governor Weller's attention, possibly by reports of Flint, Dillon, or some other army officer. Rather than deny it, they admitted their actions:

> A few weeks since, a party of whites, to recover some stock the Indians had driven off, pursued them into the mountains and surprised a rancheria [Native village] in which there were a few Bucks and a greater number of squaws and children, and I am pained to say that in the heat and excitement of the attack, exasperated with the recollection of the many injuries they had suffered from these Indians, cornered them and then a war of extermination, by shooting down the women and children. And it is since then these Indians have commenced the fearful work of burning houses.[60]

A "war of extermination" had been launched and the citizens of Tehama County were not afraid to admit it, even to the governor. In fact their petition was, in effect, asking for funding to continue the extermination.

Yet time was short. The committee could not avoid mentioning that the local Indians had responded in kind. Native Americans were setting fields on fire, and the representatives of Tehama admitted that if the grass had not been so green, the fires would have done great damage. The fires may actually have been unrelated to the conflict; California Indians traditionally burned grasslands in many parts of the state to keep brush low to prevent wildfires, to reduce screening for game animals, and to control or harvest insects, especially grasshoppers. Most important, the brush clearance provided nutrients to the soil and protected the acorn supply. According to one settler, William Bull Meek of Indian Valley, some white residents appreciated the practice for the benefits it offered.[61] In Tehama, clearly the settlers and ranchers did not, and clearly they contextualized the fires as retaliatory.

Though no lives had been lost, the committee told the governor that the people were full of fear and terrible anxiety because of the Indian threat. Such fears have been common among those committing genocide.[62] The governor had the ability to relieve these tensions by allowing a volunteer company and, more important, paying for it. "We have contributed of our money and time and lost some lives in protecting ourselves from this common foe," the Tehama petitioners wrote. They demanded action against the hostile Indians threatening their "peace and wellbeing." Weller needed to remember that a democratic election by his peers made him a tool of the people. He was sworn to protect his people, the white citizenry, not the savage, animal-like Indians: "You understand who these marauders are; where they live and how they live."[63] Weller would show that he understood his constituents and Indians alike.

While the petition was being drafted and then sent to Weller, Hall and four other men set out on the trail of the most recent raiders. Discovering a group of between twenty-five and thirty Yuki people butchering the meat they had taken off the stolen horses, Hall and his men attacked. As the Yukis fled, some loosed arrows at Hall's party, and others leaped into a nearby brook. None of the arrows found its mark. By the time the fight ended, Hall's party had managed to kill at least ten men and one woman. After searching the camp, they decided to leave the butchered meat, but only after lacing it with strychnine in hopes of killing the unsuspecting survivors.[64]

By the time Hall returned home, the governor had replied twice. First, responding on June 2, 1859, to the numerous petitions sent in May, the governor judged that federal forces in the area would be

more than enough to stabilize the situation in Tehama.[65] In Tehama
County, Native people continued to retaliate against the settlers and
ranchers, and the soldiers continued to remain unmoved by the situation created by the citizens. The *Red Bluff Beacon* called on the community to flood the governor with new waves of petitions for action.[66]
Weller's second message responded to the May 29 petition drafted by
the three-man committee. Apparently convinced by the citizens and
what they ascertained from Captain Flint, Weller assented to their
demands and gave his approval to form a company. But Hall and other
settlers seemed to operate well enough without the commission, and
with clear consciences. The main difference now would be money. The
state of California, by law, would be paying the men wages and supplying them with food, stores, and ammunition. These supplies would
come from local businesses and individuals, who would then submit
claims for reimbursement.[67] These bills, however, could be difficult to
collect and often also rested on additional petitions to the government
for settlement.[68] This difficulty in being reimbursed seemed to cause
more hesitation for some than the realities involved in the genocide,
namely the slaughter of innocent, defenseless people.

In June and July the company failed to take the field. Ironically
the problem was money. Dryden Lacock, the man elected to the cap-
taincy of the company by his peers, felt that the likelihood of receiving
compensation for his services was too chancy to risk signing on for
an extended tour of duty. A section of the Militia Law of California
governed the formation and operation of volunteer companies and
established rates of pay for officers and men. The finer points of the
law seemed to cause him to balk at the mission, for Lacock was no
stranger to killing Native Americans. Since 1856, he admitted, he and
others in the Round Valley region had been going on cooperative Indian hunts, much as Hall had been doing with his neighbors. Lacock
said, "The result was that we would kill, on an average, fifteen or twenty
Indians on a trip." He admitted that he and his fellows had done this
so often that he could not remember how many times; in some cases
they went out "two or three times a week" in Round Valley. In July

Hastings was no longer willing to wait for Eden Valley to be made safe for his cattle and horses. Using his considerable influence, he suggested that the community form a fresh company under a new leader, using the old permission issued by the governor. According to Lacock, Hastings offered to front the money to fund the company, which still did not convince Lacock to take the commission assigned to him by the governor.[69] Other men also distrusted Hastings's promise to pay, especially when he nominated a different captain and a new course of action in the wake of Lacock's refusal to lead the volunteer company.[70]

At Hastings's suggestion and with his approval, the community elected Walter Jarboe as their captain.[71] Though the governor had not commissioned Jarboe, Hastings suggested that the commission for Lacock might be used for Jarboe until official approval came from the governor. Unlike Lacock, Jarboe took quick action to form the company and put it in the field, despite the fact that he held no commission from the state. Under Jarboe, the company, sometimes called the Eel River Rangers, quickly won approval from the community. This was not surprising, as they were doing exactly what their fellow citizens wanted: killing Native Americans. Hall joined the group, which consisted of a standing company of about ten men. Hastings and Henley, the men with the most to gain by the company's success, initially outfitted the men and later made claims upon the state for reimbursement. The company carried a letter from Hastings, which promised those who supplied the company in the field would be reimbursed. When in need of food and unable to secure supplies from local settlers and ranchers, Jarboe and his men simply—and ironically—killed the cattle they found loose in the fields and hills they traveled in.[72] Hall claimed that Jarboe tracked who the cattle belonged to, presumably by their brands, and reported their consumption to the owners. The owners could then make a claim on the state for reimbursement. Well outfitted and provisioned the company set out to reimburse their benefactors in a different coin: they immediately went into Eden Valley and sought out the Yukis who had threatened the stock of Henley and Hastings. Their inaugural mission was typical of the results they would achieve.

On their first day out, the company pursued a group of unidentified Native people to the west of Eden Valley. The chase resulted in
one death. Hall recalled that they shot one "squaw" by accident as
they pursued the band, the rest apparently getting away.[73] By the time
the Eel River Rangers returned to Eden Valley, a new wave of stock
raiding had commenced, possibly in retaliation for the earlier attack
and killing of the woman. The raid's location also strongly suggested
that the woman and the people attacked were Yukis. After two days
of raids on horses and mules belonging to Hastings and Henley, the
Rangers went out again, this time following the trail left by the stolen
animals. Following a day in the field and a fruitless search in rough
foothill country, the volunteers returned without sighting any of the
stock or the thieves. The men did not stay idle long.

Following Hall's discovery of several cattle carcasses, Jarboe and the
company went in pursuit of the Yukis they believed committed the
theft. Coming upon a village of between twenty-five and thirty inhabitants, the volunteer company attacked without warning and without
ascertaining if these were the same people who had taken and butch-
ered the cattle. Only a third of the Yuki villagers managed to escape, as
the Eel River Rangers killed an estimated dozen men and took eight
more people prisoner, including women and children. The one adult
male was tried by court-martial, empowered, they felt, by virtue of the
governor's commission and the Militia Law. There was no evidence to
suggest that the man tried was represented or was allowed to defend
himself or that he even understood English. The man was found guilty
by the court-martial and put to death on the spot, in clear violation
of state law, which required that the man be brought before the local
justice of the peace. What is more, the penalty for stealing cattle and
horses was twenty-five lashes or a $200 fine under "An Act for the
Government and Protection of Indians," not death.[74] The remaining
four women and three children were taken to the nearby Nome Cult
Reservation.[75]

The company, even after destroying an entire community, continued
to patrol the area, now apparently looking for any Indian rather than

people guilty of the recent theft. A scouting patrol sent ahead by Jarboe met two Native men in the wilderness and killed them somewhere near the forks of the Eel River, their crime apparently crossing paths with the Rangers. The group then returned to the Eden Valley region, deciding to patrol the southeastern portion of the valley. Stumbling upon a group of Native people attempting to hide in the brush, Jarboe and his men attacked, killing another two or three people. Again, the crime seemed to be that they were Indians. When the Rangers got back to Round Valley, they found that the governor had officially approved Jarboe as captain and leader of the company and approved the company under Jarboe for the purposes of protecting the community.[76] The way the citizens chose to define protection as offensive rather than defensive was typical of many communities raising volunteer groups.

The group continued to operate against the Indigenous population in the region. According to Hall, between getting the official approval and November 1859, the Eel River Rangers killed approximately forty more men and took one hundred more prisoners. In November Hall got a man to take his place in the company, and he mustered out.[77] The company continued to operate.

Throughout his service with the Eel River Rangers, Jarboe sent the governor's office regular reports of his activities. Although the governor had approved a company for protective purposes, Jarboe's reports clearly indicated offensive operations in the region. He often failed to mention the full details of his activities and methods, however. According to accounts of members of the company and local settlers, the company was known to raid white-owned ranches looking to kill Native Americans held under guardianship or working as laborers. In several cases, the company did kill Native Americans who had been under the protection of local settlers and ranchers.[78] Based on a comparison of the accounts of various members of the company, the number of women and children reported killed, as well as the dispositions of prisoners, varied widely; some were unwilling to say that any had been killed, and others admitted that some had.[79] The company also operated in a state of drunkenness at times, reflecting the behavior of others engaged in genocides past and present.[80] By using intoxicants, men have historically overcome the restraints basic to human beings when it came time to slaughter other people. Over time, as one became habituated to killing, inebriation was no longer necessary to perform genocide.[81]

The Eel River Rangers' movements and statement of losses inflicted in their first month on duty provided the governor with a clear idea of the intensity of action in the Eden Valley and Round Valley region, if not precisely all of their methods. The numbers Jarboe reported to the governor, however, failed to capture the true damage done to Native peoples. While Jarboe and his men killed dozens of allegedly dangerous Indians and captured many more, the company, which at times had grown to twenty-one members, suffered none killed or captured and only two men wounded. Eventually the Eel River Rangers would claim hundreds of kills. The campaign, which took place during the fall months crucial to Indigenous populations in preparing for winter, left many Native groups without men to hunt and protect villages, women to gather and prepare food, and stores to survive the winter, which hits hard in the mountains of northern California. Governor John B. Weller, though reviewing some of the startling Native American casualty figures (sixty-two killed, fifty prisoners taken) provided by Jarboe for the first month of operations, was likely oblivious to such consequences.[82] However, Weller did realize defense was not what the Eel River Rangers were about.

Just days after Jarboe's first report to Weller, the governor sent him a brief letter reminding him and his men to attack only those certain to have stolen property. In one sense, Weller was calling for restraint. He implored Jarboe, "Human life must not be taken when it can possibly be avoided and the women and children under all circumstances must be spared."[83] To encourage restraint, Weller was careful to mention that he had alternate sources of information about the operations of the Eel River Rangers. This admonition hinted that Major Johnson and Lieutenant Dillon were in contact with the governor, as later correspondence proved to be true. But in another sense, the state was sanctioning death as the penalty for Native people who stole cattle and horses, which was clearly well beyond the limits of the penalties imposed under state law. Weller empowered Jarboe to act as judge, jury, and executioner. Jarboe's personal determination of innocence or guilt was to be the arbiter of the fates of Indian peoples in the region. This too was clearly well outside what would be acceptable among whites in California, or anywhere else in the United States, in terms of the normal system of justice. Jarboe's response could not have encouraged Weller.

In his second report, stating that he had reached full strength for his company, twenty men, Jarboe added, "If I had forty men in the field, I could in a very short time take every hostile Indian out of the mountains."[84] But Jarboe's second report did show some improvement, when compared with his first; in their second month of operations, the Eel River Rangers had killed only twenty-five "Bucks" and taken a hundred prisoners. On the volunteers' side, Jarboe lamented the loss of a "valuable dog." He also mentioned that the citizens of nearby Long Valley were petitioning him directly for help, rather than the government.[85] Jarboe was also sending reports to Judge Hastings, some of which have survived and found their way into archives. Just days after his second report to the governor, Jarboe revealed plans to go on the offensive against another Native community, this time five hundred Wailakis believed to have driven stock off of G. H. Woodman's ranch in Long Valley.[86] Apparently Jarboe had accepted the petition of the Long Valley citizens as binding upon him, and determined to go to their aid with or without Governor Weller's approval. On October 16 Jarboe reported to Weller on his expedition to relieve the people of Long Valley. Following an unsuccessful attempt to get Lieutenant Dillon and his men to help them, Jarboe's company launched an attack against the Yuki people; the Eel River Rangers killed eleven "bucks" and captured thirty-three others, although nineteen were able to escape on the way back to Round Valley. The Yukis, Jarboe believed, had also been responsible for the death of a local white man, John Bland, one of the few settlers certainly killed by Native peoples in the region in 1859.[87]

Governor Weller was not happy. In a terse reply to Jarboe's report, he reminded Jarboe of his previous cautionary note. He also voiced new concerns about Jarboe's decision to operate outside the limits of Round Valley and Eden Valley: "Your company was organized to protect the lives and property of the Citizens in certain localities and not to wage a war of extermination against the Indians."[88] Jarboe returned to the Round Valley area and continued his operations.

The prolific Jarboe reported to Weller on October 28 that he had resumed normal operations. In the two weeks since his previous report, the Eel River Rangers had killed nine and taken 120 prisoners. One of the prisoners, however, had apparently been raped by William Daley, a member of the Rangers. Jarboe euphemistically reported his discharge for "imprudent conduct with a squaw."[89] As the woman raped was a "squaw," no penalty other than dismissal was forthcoming.

As Native people prepared for the early winters that often hit the northern quarter of the state, Jarboe and the Eel River Rangers remained active. Given the impossibility of obtaining access to many traditional winter food sources, Native people of the region began to take livestock as a substitute; the alternative was death by starvation. Even in spring through fall, Native people on reservations were sometimes forced to steal stock, lest they risk, as Treasury Agent John Ross Browne phrased it, "absolute starvation." According to Browne, leaving the reservation to "procure subsistence . . . by the instinct of self-preservation, [they were] shot down on the most frivolous of pretexts."[90] This put Native people in the sights of volunteer companies, including the Eel River Rangers. Jarboe and the Rangers made sure that the choice to leave the reservation, to take livestock, meant death, as those who voted to empower them intended. And not just for the Indigenous populations of the Eden Valley and Round Valley. Against instructions, Jarboe and the Rangers returned again to answer the call for help from Long Valley residents. Over the course of November the Eel River Rangers killed thirty-six and took fifteen prisoners, again taking no losses themselves.[91] In November terrible winter storms hampered the volunteer company's efforts to kill Native people. Native Americans, meanwhile, caught and butchered livestock to survive, though some stock may have already been killed by the snow and freezing temperatures. One cannot help but notice that the livestock being protected was left to roam in this severe weather, but losses were still mainly attributed to Native Americans, not the weather. Despite Jarboe's willingness to please the communities that depended upon him, no matter the source of stock loss, it may have been a petition of his neighbors that deprived him of his company and led to its disbandment.

In an undated petition by nine Round Valley residents written sometime in December 1859, citizens asked Governor Weller to relieve Jarboe of his command. Most of the men were not ordinary residents of the valley, but employees of the local Indian reservation. Their complaint: the company cost too much money because of how Jarboe ran the group.[92] Undoubtedly this stemmed from the way the company financed its operations through promises of later compensation by the state. Jarboe and his men consumed local cattle for food—ironically the same as local Native peoples—and the owners worried that losses would not be recompensed by the state. This would go doubly for reservation employees, for Jarboe took not only government stock but their personal stock from the lands they owned around the reservation. Whether it was in response to this petition or to Jarboe's second visit out of bounds to Long Valley, Weller acted.

In a terse note to Jarboe on January 3, 1860, Governor Weller ordered the company disbanded. Giving no reason but thanking Jarboe and the men for their service, the governor stated that the company was no longer needed.[93] Public outcry was immediate. In one vivid example, a petition of eighty-two citizens of Mendocino County called upon Weller to reinstate Jarboe and the company less than two weeks after it had disbanded. Citing Indian depredations at a new level of intensity, the petitioners also asked that the company's size be doubled. What the petitioners failed to realize was that the depredations that the Rangers had "held in subjugation" during their service were actually retaliations against them for the Rangers' actions.[94] Meanwhile an unlikely source of resistance to the possible restoration of the Eel River Rangers under the command of Jarboe had developed: the men of the Eel River Rangers themselves.

In a petition to their fellow citizens of Mendocino County, and forwarded to the new governor, Milton Latham, the men of the Eel River Rangers expressed their desire to renew their service, but under a commander other than Jarboe. Several of Jarboe's actions had angered them. First, they were constantly hungry and forced to eat only "half rations" because Jarboe was always attempting to reduce costs—ironically, the very thing the petitioners from the Round Valley Reservation charged he was not doing effectively. Second, the men believed that Jarboe's concern for Native welfare put them at risk and that "he did not value their live[s] above that of a Digger." Third, he had discharged "good and true men against the Protestation of the company for no other reason or offense than that which he was himself guilty of and first set the example." In other words, Jarboe had been the first to rape a "squaw," though William Daley and others were discharged for doing so.[95] Fourth, they charged that he was defrauding the citizenry and the state, charging the people for full rations and supplies, but issuing much less and keeping the difference.[96]

Despite the serious and specific accusations, the Rangers recanted their charges ten days later in a second petition sent to the governor, explaining that they had written their petition in a "moment of Excitement" and included in it "misrepresentations" about Jarboe. They asked Latham to disregard their "errors committed in the heat of passion" and return Jarboe to the head of the company, claiming that they now better understood the exigencies of command that Jarboe faced and that, in hindsight, his actions were something altogether different than what they had originally thought.[97]

Nothing came of the request to reinstate Jarboe or the company. Governor Milton Latham surrendered the governorship to take a seat in the U.S. Senate made vacant by a death, and when John Downey succeeded to the governorship, he took no action to reinstate the men. The Eel River Rangers were through except for the money owed to the men and citizens. On February 18, 1860, Jarboe sent Governor John Downey the bill for the company, claiming that they fought twenty-three actions and killed 283 Indians in five months; the state owed

$11,743, of which $5,779 was payment due the men. Hastings reneged on his promise to guarantee payments, creating much animosity in the community.[98] His goals accomplished, Hastings apparently abandoned the pretense of concern for his neighbors. Many residents found it hard if not impossible to collect on the debts incurred by Jarboe under the cover of Hastings's promissory note, which he apparently denied existed.[99] The people of Round Valley would begin a new round of petitions, this time to successive governors and representatives trying to recover their losses to other whites.

Settlers and ranchers not only petitioned their representatives at the county, state, and federal levels for help against Native populations and for the remuneration of claims, but they also acted in concert at the local level, using democracy to fund Native American genocide directly. White citizens sometimes took up a subscription to fund campaigns against Native Americans when their requests were not fulfilled in what they judged to be a timely or effective manner, especially when federal officers refused point blank to exterminate local Native groups. Some U.S. Army officers, such as Lt. Edward Dillon, proved unwilling to resort to the quick and easy expedient of wiping out Native peoples wholesale. Dillon reported to Pacific Division headquarters in San Francisco that settlers, not Indigenous populations, caused the disturbances in Round Valley and Eden Valley. His reports also belied the wild claims of settlers that many whites had been killed. In fact in 1859 he reported that only one white man had died by Native American actions, and that was when he tried to abduct a Native woman.[100] This contradicted the vague claims of settlers and ranchers, whose petitions rarely identified by name people killed by murderous savages.

This may have caused governors of California to hesitate to give permission to their constituents to form volunteer companies, although they almost always submitted eventually. One way local settlers got around such inconveniences was to take up subscriptions, given voluntarily by local citizens, for the purpose of funding settler campaigns against the Native communities. Funding genocide had become democratic, a grassroots process. According to the *Marysville*

Weekly Express, the people of Red Bluff, which was the county seat of Tehama County, had "adopted . . . [a plan] to chastise the Indians for their many depredations during the past winter. Some men are hired to hunt them, who are recompensed by receiving so much for each scalp, or some other satisfactory evidence that they have been killed. The money has been made up by subscription."[101] In Humboldt County the people of Uniontown and Eureka voted for a tax to be levied on residents "to prosecute the Indian war to extermination."[102] Taxes and subscriptions such as these were inherently democratic, in the view of some Californians. They represented the recourse that any community might turn to in the absence of what they deemed effective government responses at higher levels. In Red Bluff, Tehama County, the citizens tied the collection of subscriptions to the failure of the state and federal governments to adequately represent the wishes of their citizenry by failing to exterminate the Indigenous population of the region.

For some, however, having to come up with additional monies to fund their own campaign of genocide smacked of taxation without representation. One man published his opinion in the official newspaper for the county: "Were we a band of outlaws who denied the authority of the courts, or an isolated community where tax-gatherers never come, we could submit to neglect like this without a murmur, but, situated as we are, contributing, as we do, more, perhaps . . . than any county in the State . . . we feel that we are entitled to have the protecting arm of the State thrown around us."[103] Thus citizens used subscriptions and special taxes as alternate means of obtaining representation. In the 1850s and 1860s this meant subscription and tax funds were being used to arm, outfit, and provision groups of men looking to root out Native Americans living nearby and then kill them.

Often the killings included Native American women, children, and elderly. Given that many Euro-Americans thought Indians were animals, it was easy to rationalize killing them as something more akin to killing a pesky animal near one's home or herd, rather than accepting it as murder of another human being. As the *Chico Weekly Courant* described it, "Nothing but extermination will keep them from committing their depredations. It is a false notion of humanity to save the lives of these red devils. There should be no prisoners taken, but a general sacrifice made of the whole race."The editors and publishers of the *Courant* certainly believed in genocide as the concept is understood today: killing by category. But the *Courant*, reflecting the philosophy behind the slaughter of predatory animals, did not stop there, claiming, "They are of no benefit to themselves or mankind, but like the rattle-snake live only to slay. Like the wild beast of prey they are necessarily exterminated by the march of civilization. The tribes of Indians upon this Coast can no more be civilized than the jaguar." But how was one to meet such a threat posed by wild animals? "If necessary let there be a crusade, and every man that can carry and shoot a gun turn out and hunt the red devils to their holes and there bury them, leaving not a root or branch of them remaining, then we shall record no more massacres."[104] In other words, let there be an outright elimination of all Native Americans.

Even more overtly economic incentives helped drive genocide in California. In Tehama County a company paid for by subscription was not raised for the duration of an emergency or to settle a specific conflict with Native Americans by arms, but for a two- to three-month tour of duty. In that span of time, they would operate "to clean out" any Native people they might come across.[105] Members of the company were cared for by the community during their tour, receiving supplies and medical care and compensation for their time from the subscription fund.[106] Because California law stipulated that reimbursement was due to citizens who supplied volunteer companies, it was potentially profitable and desirable for Euro-Americans to promote conflict with Indian people.[107] Subscriptions, then, were one way of funding such crusades over extended periods of time. Other ways of ridding an area of Indians existed, and settlers employed these as part of their geno-cidal campaigns as well. Scalp and head bounties were instituted in some towns and counties. In one example, a county paid 50 cents for every Indian scalp and $5 for every Indian head brought in. In Shasta City a local man attested to interest in claiming such rewards, as he noted that one man brought in as many as twelve Indian heads on one trip alone. In the community of Honey Lake, the life of an Indian was worth much less, as they paid only 25 cents for an Indian scalp. Besides heads and scalps, in some communities "some other satisfactory evidence" of the extermination of an Indian might do in place of a scalp.[108] Given that the average daily wage for a miner in California in the late 1850s was $3 per day, bounties could afford one a good living when unemployed or in a pinch for funds.[109] The funds to pay out the bounties were often collected by community subscriptions too, as in the case reported by the *Shasta Herald*: "A meeting of citizens was held a day or two before at Hazelrigg's store, and measures taken to raise a fund, to be disbursed in payment of Indian scalps, for which a bounty is offered."[110] To make matters worse, the *Sacramento Union* reprinted the story, informing an even wider audience that money was to be made directly by killing Indians to the north.[111] In other cases, private individuals put up the funds, as when John Bidwell reportedly placed a $500 bounty on the head of a Mill Creek Indian who was interfering with his business. Sadly and ironically, a Native American brought back the chief's scalp as proof of the kill.[112] Perhaps the most shocking bounty opportunity was one suggested by the editors of the *Lassen Sage Brush* in 1868, a $500 bounty for "every Indian killed." This would be such an incentive as to make killing Native Americans tantamount to California's new Gold Rush. Any Indian found not on a federal reservation would be worth $500 dead. This, they argued, would stop the "brutal savage."[113] And given the amount proposed, it likely would have produced the absolute destruction of California's Indigenous population, down to the last child. Rewards that necessitated the killing of Indian people, guilty or not, were obviously genocidal in their intent, as they encouraged wanton slaughter for profit rather than allowing for self-defense, as Euro-Americans often falsely claimed to be their real intent. Native Americans were killed because of who they were, rather than what they had done. Such killing by category epitomizes the core definition of genocide.

Murdering Indians was not only economically incentivized; there were also important social connotations to scalp and bounty taking that contributed to genocide. Many Euro-Americans considered their countrymen heroes when they returned home with scalps. This may explain, in part, why men were given to displaying scalps and other trophies. According to one account published in the *Sacramento Union* in 1852, based on a report of a raid against Native peoples in Yreka, men returning from the bloodbath proudly adorned their rifles with Native American scalps taken in the raid and displayed captured weaponry.[114] The anthropologist Robert Heizer discovered that the raid was more akin to a massacre than a retaliatory raid. According to Gen. Ethan Allen Hitchcock, a volunteer company led by Benjamin Wright, the same company mentioned in the *Sacramento Union* article, had invited a group of Indians to a peace conference and then murdered them. This foul act, commented Hitchcock, would undoubtedly produce an "inexhaustible desire for vengeance" in the local Native population.[115]

Wright sent an Indian woman out to a local group of Native Americans whom the volunteers had been attempting to catch without success. They convinced the woman and the Native people she met with that they intended to make peace with them. The woman was successful in bringing in forty-eight Native men of an unidentified group. Once they were in camp and surrounded, Wright opened the slaughter with pistol shots. The ambush produced shocking casualties: thirty killed and, curiously, none wounded. According to Hitchcock's report, the men scalped their victims, adorned themselves with these grisly trophies, and returned to Yreka. Once back in town, Wright "entered in triumph, his men bearing on their rifles the scalps of the Indians and . . . with a general welcome by the citizens of the town."[116] The taking of trophies, especially the mutilation attendant to beheadings and scalping, was elemental to the genocide of Native peoples. Reinforcing the savage, animal, and inhuman nature of their victims lay behind the collection of such trophies by the perpetrators.[117] Wright and his men were rewarded economically with bounties paid by the community and reimbursement and pay by the state, and socially with adulation from their local communities. In part, this helps to explain the rise of a category of men known as "Indian hunters," who came to prominence in northern California during the 1850s and 1860s.

Harmon "Hi" Good, Robert Anderson, Jackson Farley, John Ross, Sim and Jake Moak, and others worked as professional assassins on behalf of local communities and the state. The notion that these men were dedicated "Indian hunters" is misleading, though, because most of them were much like their neighbors who hired and helped them: they were settlers in the region. In fact Indian hunters were usually members of the citizenry that set out to exterminate local Native Americans at the head of a column of their neighbors. Jackson Farley headed a citizens' volunteer company based in Long Valley, where "about one hundred voters in the Valley and vicinity" had become tired of Indian depredations. Gathering together, not unlike the emigrant communities electing a captain and officers for their overland passage, citizens voted to elect volunteer company captains and officers to lead them against the Indians. Like the people of Eden Valley and Round Valley, Farley and his fellows used their power as white citizens to call upon the state and federal governments to defend their lives and property. Farley was a farmer and rancher in Long Valley. He had experienced three years of seasonal stock raids, all of them occurring in the two months immediately preceding winter. Though it might seem obvious today that Native people in the area were hungry, were regularly denied traditional food sources, and were attempting to get food to survive another winter, for Farley these were simply acts of wanton thievery by "wild" savages. In three years he lost a total of four horses and two cows, though one of the horses he only "believed" to be his own.[118] Like many farmers and ranchers of the era, his stock was roaming free, sometimes unattended for days or weeks. William Frazier admitted that he and his neighbors could not in fact say with certainty how many head of stock they lost for this very reason. Frazier had seen the remains of animals outside Native villages, but had been unable to verify how the animals had perished or if Indians were culpable; indeed verification was even more difficult given the fact that Native Americans could own cattle themselves and sometimes received stock as gifts from federal Indian agents. In some seasons "the grass was short" and animals had to stray up into the hills to graze. In fact when pressed by an investigative committee, Frazier had to admit he had no idea how many of his animals had been lost or to whom.[119] Despite all the many reasons a cow, horse, or mule might go missing, Farley, Frazier, and their neighbors were sure they knew who had taken their livestock.

The loss of six animals in three year's time was too much for Farley to take. He solicited his neighbors for help. They formed a small party and went out to "punish" the guilty. According to Frazier, they heard a report that a rancheria of Pomo people had some beef, and they attacked the camp without warning and without investigating the source of the meat, which might even have been a gift from the local Indian agent at the reservation attempting to induce the villagers to come onto the reservation. All but one of the Pomos escaped; one man was killed during the escape, when the white men "shot his head off."[120] The group continued to operate. After killing "three or four of them" as a punishment—they tried for more but they escaped—Farley and his party seemed satisfied that the lives of four Indians for six animals was enough for the time being.[121] However, a more formal organization was soon needed, and Farley was elected captain and Frazier lieutenant.[122] This became necessary because the Pomos they had "punished" changed the motivation behind their raids from subsistence to retaliation.[123]

Farley quickly lost eleven horses following the attack he and his neighbors made. His neighbors also began to suffer heavy losses. The stock this time was not being carried away and consumed; the Pomos simply killed the animals in retaliation. Local white citizens responded using democracy. The residents of Long Valley sent two petitions to the governor, demanding action and the approval to form a volunteer company to further "punish" the Pomo. Some individual settlers, such as G. H. Woodman, also sent personal petitions. Woodman argued that a company could perform the work of "guarding and protecting themselves against the incursions of Indians."[124] In December 1859, after gubernatorial approval, they formed their official company. Farley's company was very effective at killing Native Americans and emblematic of the way many companies operated by loosely interpreting what "guarding and protecting" meant. They established a patrol in the mountains between Long Valley and adjacent Round Valley. This decision was especially disastrous for Native people, because as men like Farley and Frazier pushed Native peoples out of these mountains toward Round Valley, companies of men such as the Eel River Rangers under Jarboe were pushing others out of Round Valley toward Long Valley. Native people such as the Yukis and Pomos were caught in a deadly trap, with bloody-minded volunteer companies applying a genocidal constriction. In fact all over California, Euro-Americans were mainly concerned with driving Native Americans from their midst, giving little thought to the fact that they were driving them into similar situations elsewhere. The way Frazier's company attacked was also typical. According to Frazier, a typical engagement took place at dawn and usually lasted only minutes, as in the company's first raid: "[At dawn] we attacked and killed 20 consisting of Bucks, Squaws and children and also took 2 squaws and one child prisoner. Those killed were all killed in about three minutes. . . . We found in this rancheria no sign of any depredation having been committed by these Indians." Then the company delivered their prisoners into the hands of local settlers, "who promised to take care of them," that is, make them legal slaves on their farms and ranches under apprenticeship statutes.[125]

Farley, Frazier, and company continued to raid villages. They indiscriminately killed Native men, women, and children. Calling the men "bucks" and the women "squaws" was habitual. Frazier in particular graphically described killing elderly women, children, and wounded men without any compunction.[126] In their first genocidal campaign, Farley and Frazier led forty-six citizens of Long Valley against the Indigenous people of the region in a bloody three-month campaign that led to the deaths of between 150 and 200 Yukis and Pomos. The company took only twenty-two prisoners, who were sent to the Indian reservation at Mendocino or to settlers, where more horrors awaited them under the jaundiced eye of federal Indian agents or under the bloody hands of some of the same men who had killed their families and friends. Following this initial genocidal campaign to "punish" Indians, the company remained in operation intermittently, waiting for Farley to call them into action whenever Indian peoples of the region threatened stock in Long Valley.[127] Ten years later their macabre success was obvious.

When the citizens of Long Valley elected Farley and Frazier to lead them, in excess of four hundred Pomos and an indeterminate number of Yukis lived in Long Valley. Within a decade not one Native American remained in Long Valley. The community was able to take a new step at this juncture: in 1868 the people of Long Valley decreed, "No Indian is now allowed under any pretext whatever to come in to the country."[128] It had literally become illegal to be a Native person in the valley. What perhaps made it all the better for non-Native residents of Long Valley was that not one member of the community had ever been killed—not in raids, not by unexplained murder, not in action as a member of Farley's company.[129] In fact no evidence exists of any Euro-American even being wounded.[130] Hundreds of Native people had died to make sure cattle, horses, and oxen could roam free.

Miners acted no better than settlers and ranchers when it came to the treatment of Native Americans. In fact the democratic institutions employed by mining camps in California and other parts of the West in the 1850s were the very definition of what Lansford Hastings had lauded as "unsophisticated democracy" come to fruition. In the words of one historian, "The mining district, within the governmental meaning of the term, might well have been hailed as a perfect, municipal democracy."[131] Certainly many miners must have thought so, because their future depended on the ability of these democratic associations to protect their rights, especially when it came to mining claims and property rights. The California Gold Rush took place, for the most part, on unsurveyed public lands—lands owned and occupied for millennia by Indigenous peoples but taken from them by virtue of the Treaty of Guadalupe Hidalgo. Located far from the population centers of Euro-American settlement, the camps organized, adjudicated, legislated, and executed their own systems of government. The ultimate goal, according to one set of mining district regulations, was to use democratic cooperation: "The isolated position we occupy, far from legal tribunals, and cut off from those fountains of justice which every American citizen should enjoy, renders it necessary that we organize in body politic for our mutual protection against the lawless, and for meting out justice between man and man; therefore, we, citizens . . . do hereby agree to adopt the following rules and laws for our government."[132] When it came to encounters with Indigenous populations, "those fountains of justice" would run with blood.

In 1848 and much of 1849 Native populations entered the gold fields of California easier than most. They lived there. In 1848 perhaps as many as half the miners looking for gold in California were Native Americans. Native people, especially the Maidus, Nissenans, and Miwoks who lived in and around the Mother Lode region, acted both as independent miners and miners for hire. As independents they traded the precious metal, for which they had no cultural use, for goods they did use. As hired miners they were either brought by their rancho-owning employers or hired out to work on behalf of an individual for as little as a dollar a day. In either case, many non-Natives looked to cheat them. However, the arrival of the massive waves of white miners from the United States in 1849 and throughout the early 1850s changed much. After just a few years of Euro-American invasion, an Indian openly prospecting for gold was almost unheard of in California.[133] The unwillingness of Euro-Americans to compete with other peoples, especially Native Americans, lay at the heart of the disappearance of many nonwhites from the gold fields.

Redick McKee, an Indian agent in California, described the genocidal actions of a group of miners in a report to Commissioner of Indian Affairs Luke Lea. McKee learned that as many as forty Native men, women, and children had been massacred at a camp on the Klamath River. Following the shooting of a Native man by a local white miner, the unidentified Native people in question went to the nearby mining camp and complained to the miners about the shooting, leaving peacefully after their protest. The miners felt certain that the Native group would soon turn violent. Holding a camp meeting, which was the way miners democratically regulated most everything in a mining camp, the men determined on a policy of preemptive extermination of the dangerous Indians, before the same was done to them.[134] They descended upon the Native village and exterminated the entire population. This was a reflection of how miners solved many of their problems democratically, among themselves or with others. When a crime was to be adjudicated or punished, the miners met and discussed matters. Decisions were made by the group, with "the whole power of the camp . . . ready to support such decisions."[135] James Mason Hutchings, an English immigrant to the United States and later the California gold fields, detested this system. At first, Hutchings recalled, the mines were disorganized and unsafe. But following the mass organization by Euro-Americans to implement law and order, enforced with the lash and hangman's noose, an even more "deplorable state of things" existed.[136] The miners, in their single-minded zeal, had taken the law into their own hands and created an orderly tyranny of the majority. As a foreigner, Hutchings was appalled, as the miners from the United States applied harsher standards and more brutal punishments to non-Americans. But Hutchings was lucky that at least he was white. The ability of nonwhites to compete with whites was severely limited by whites' propensity for violence in matters complicated by race. Such was certainly the case when it came to the competition and threat posed by Native peoples to Euro-American interests.

Euro-American miners also instigated trouble that devolved into genocide by attempting to kidnap and rape Native women. According to the captain of a volunteer company leading Native American prisoners through a mining district, miners descended upon the volunteers and took possession of all the "squaws" for their own uses—likely meaning they raped them or forced them into slavery in their camp.[137] Only trouble came of such acts, as Native men became enraged and took up arms to reclaim their wives, mothers, sisters, and daughters from the rapacious miners. According to Josiah Royce, the "American character" was to blame. Royce observed that some "Americans" were "cruelly bigoted men, who encouraged the ruffians of their own nation to ill-treatment of the wanderers of another, to the frequent destruction of peace and good order."[138] Nothing could have better described the actions of white men who would never countenance rape of white women. Native American standards of reciprocity led to a much different standard of behavior toward non-Natives.

According to an emigrant named Alexander Hamilton Willard, in California for the Gold Rush in 1850, Native Americans who were treated with respect were easy to get along with. Even when provoked they could still maintain control of their fury. On one occasion, a member of Willard's emigrant company raped the daughter of a local Native leader from an unidentified group. The chief visited the leader of Willard's company at their camp and offered a solution to make matters right between them: if the man who had violated his daughter would come forward, he would exact justice where justice was due. If not, he would slay all of the company. After a time, one of the young men came forward and confessed. After "the Indians tore out his heart," they let the rest go in peace.[139] Had the scenario taken place at a mining camp, the result would almost certainly have been different, as white miners concentrated in great numbers would have been unwilling even to let armed Native Americans into the camp, let alone treat with or execute one of them. But because the company of emigrants was small in number, a mutually satisfactory result was achieved. Since the retribution was carried out with full knowledge on both sides of what had transpired by testimony of the girl and the admission of guilt by the rapist, the parties settled the matter with a minimum loss of life and satisfaction that justice had been achieved on both sides. However, most cases of crime against Indigenous peoples and subsequent actions to achieve justice for the victims resulted in much more bloodshed, and mostly on the Native side. Sometimes, however, even when white miners outnumbered Native people, retribution was achieved despite the odds. In 1849 two parties camped on opposite sides of a river one day. On one bank, five white men set up a camp. On the opposite bank, three Native people, a woman and two men, did the same. The following day, the whites crossed the river and murdered the two men and took the woman to be a slave for them. Unknown to the murderers, the woman was either a medicine woman or the wife or child of a medicine person. Preparing dinner for the five, she laced their food with a soporific plant that caused them to fall into deep sleep. The woman summoned her people and they killed the murderers by burying them alive. Years later a descendant of the Indian woman's people decided to return the bones of the dead men to the authorities. He noted that for a time the bones accompanied the group to each new village and acted as a strong protection for the people.[140]

Despite such incidents, white miners massed in mining districts had less fear of Native Americans than isolated settlers or ranchers. And they had their democratic mechanisms to organize revenge when Indigenous populations had the temerity to challenge them. According to one miner, in their regular meetings miners settled all matters that might affect the community by group "resolutions that were adopted . . . [and] carried out, and no back talk." The backing of large communities of well-armed miners shielded individual miners from crimes even more horrendous than rape or murder of just a few people. In fact rape was just one of the despicable recreational activities some miners engaged in. Others included gambling, prostitution, drunkenness, and using Native Americans and their villages as target practice. At other times, rape was mixed with murder, arson, and thievery, leading to campaigns of extermination of entire communities.[141] But not all elements of the genocide of Native peoples were as visible as murder, arson, or even rape. As a result of malnutrition, rape, and forced cohabitation, disease was destroying the health and fertility of Indigenous peoples throughout California.

Since the Spanish brought venereal diseases to California as part of their Sacred Expedition in 1769, California Indians had struggled against unseen killers like syphilis and gonorrhea.[142] As with influenza, smallpox, and other communicable diseases, California's Indigenous population had no natural immunities or resistances to these diseases.[143] Soldiers, sailors, and settlers from Spain, Mexico, and the United States transmitted these diseases to Native populations. What might be a mild or even unnoticed case to whites, who had built up immunities or robust immune systems, were fatal to many Native Americans. In the case of venereal diseases, contracted through rape, prostitution, willing intercourse, or forced cohabitation with non-Natives, the ability of Native women to conceive or bring a healthy child to term was damaged. Euro-Americans in particular were responsible for spreading disease to much of the Native population of California simply by virtue of attempting to claim or inhabit what seemed to be every square mile. The spread of disease in conjunction with the genocidal campaigns, which led to death, malnutrition and starvation, and demographic collapse, helped transition California's land base out of Native American hands into that of a society promoting the spread and use of "unsophisticated" frontier democracy as its organizing principle and its mechanism for genocide.

Settlers, ranchers, and miners, however, did not rely solely on the "unsophisticated democracy" represented by local communities in their use of resolutions, petitions, mining camp districts, and volunteer companies to organize, fund, and execute genocide at the local level. White citizens in the nineteenth century also used their power over state and federal governments and the press. And government and the press responded to the will of the people, acting as sponsors, enablers, bystanders, and perpetrators of genocide in order to please those they served, the white citizenry of California.

PART 3

Supporting Genocide

Introduction

> The tyranny of the government is ordinarily *added* to the greed of the colonists. Though the Cherokees and the Creeks be settled on the soil that they inhabited before the arrival of the Europeans, although the Americans have often dealt with them as foreign nations, the states in whose midst they are have not wanted to recognize them as independent peoples, and they have undertaken to subject these men, scarcely come out of the forest, to their magistrates, their customs, and their laws.
>
> Alexis de Tocqueville, *Democracy in America* (1835)

Although Tocqueville was observing Indian affairs in the decade preceding the U.S. conquest of California, his observations held true for how the state of California would approach dealings with its Indigenous population. Native Americans were often seen as obstacles to be removed from the paths of Euro-Americans. As Tocqueville observed, the state was an *additional* factor in the assault on Native Americans, not the foundational one. He reserved that dubious honor for the settler. At least in this respect, Tocqueville understood democracy in the United States during the antebellum period very well, especially how citizens put their government to use, rather than the reverse. But unlike the world Tocqueville observed in the East in the 1830s, where the typical steady trickle of settlers was followed by often repetitive cycles of war, negotiation, and removals, in California the timetable for conflict, negotiation, and removal was contracted by the Gold Rush. It was as if one hundred thousand white Americans appeared out of nowhere in twelve months to inundate non-Native communities structured at the time to support less than 20 percent that number.

During California's first few years as part of the United States, the Euro-American population quickly exceeded that of Native Americans, especially as malnutrition, disease, and conflicts began to devastate Native peoples throughout the state. After ten years of American statehood, the Indian population had fallen by 80 percent, while the white population had increased at an even greater rate.[1] Much of the way Euro-Americans were able to destroy the vitality of Native communities was accomplished by land seizure, legalized murder and injustice, and the creation of reservations that in some cases resembled burial grounds for the walking dead. The state and federal governments, as executors of the popular will, played crucial roles in creating and legitimizing laws and institutions to bring these genocidal measures into being.

The state government played the most immediate and vital role in supporting genocide in California. Governors of California responded to popular calls to exterminate Native Americans by authorizing deployment of volunteer and militia companies. Governors also helped fund community efforts to destroy or remove Native populations by representing the will of the people to the legislature, as well as federal officials. Most important for the economy of the state, governors worked diligently to make sure the genocide was not paid for by the citizens of California, but by the federal government. This is not surprising given that most of the governors serving in the first two decades had never held any other office, were often failed gold miners, and were free to operate in an isolated state as yet unburdened by layers of bureaucracy and entrenched political groups.[2] Particularly in the 1850s, California governors were free to represent the people who had elected them: white male U.S. citizens.[3]

The legislature was similarly free to act in favor of the electorate. Members of the California Assembly and Senate were akin to those holding the governor's office in many ways. Most were newly arrived in the state, few had any political experience, and many had failed to strike it rich mining gold, though many had become prominent and successful by profiting on the following waves of miners panning away in rivers of fading dreams. As emigrants to California realized that riches in gold did not abound for long, if at all, especially in a corrosive economy of massive price inflation, they turned to land and other resources to make their fortunes. Kindred spirits to those who had elected them, legislators helped by passing laws supporting settlers and disenfranchising Native Americans.

The judiciary played a role typical to a legalistic society. Whatever they might judge to be right or wrong on a personal level, the law was the key to the work of the courts and the judicial process. Courts made their decisions based on the law, not what was right or moral between Native Americans and Euro-Americans, and certainly not what was right or wrong from a Native American cultural perspective. With a spate of anti-Indian legislation on the books in the first year of statehood alone, Native Americans' chance of receiving justice in the courtroom was hamstrung.[4] In fact Indian people were not allowed to access justice in the regularized court systems in California. Instead they had to rely on the justice of the peace in a given area in order to seek legal redress, and then with limitations.[5] California's new judges, though many had legal training or even some experience as a jurist, were nonetheless similar to their fellow emigrants. Perhaps none more so than Serranus Hastings, first chief justice of the California State Supreme Court and, later, attorney general of California. Men like Hastings, however, would have few chances to exercise their authority in cases involving Indians given the separate systems created by the state to deal with them.

Taken as a whole, the tripartite system of checks and balances designed to keep democracy from devolving into a tyranny of the majority failed in California. Rather than three branches of government balancing one another, California had three parts of a settler's government walking in lockstep with one another. More like a homeowners' association than a representative democracy, judges, lawmakers, and governors walked arm-in-arm, kicking Native Americans and other minority groups before them, on behalf of their constituencies. Even if so inclined, the federal government could do little to break apart state sponsorship of genocide.

In the antebellum United States, state power waxed in relation to central government. Even in the last third of the nineteenth century, after the federal government entered a period of ascendancy following the Civil War, it did little more than write the checks to pay for the costs of killing or removing California's Indigenous population. And when the United States dispatched Indian agents or professional soldiers into communities around California to help deal with Indian-white relations, the loyalties of federal officials were often oriented toward their own countrymen. This was particularly true of Indian agents, who in California were often members of the local community. Many of them owned or would come to own land around reservations established for the protection of Native peoples but instead turned to the exploitation of Indigenous lands and labor. This obvious conflict of interest would help make a mockery of the reservation system in California, as agents misappropriated land, funds, and labor for the benefit of themselves and local white settlers and ranchers.

Soldiers were no better placed to help. Though some men resisted the call of settlers to exterminate Indigenous populations, others did what their countrymen wanted. Federal military forces participated in the slaughter of thousands of Native people in hundreds of engagements.[6] Settlers treated those federal soldiers who resisted their will as pariahs, calling them traitors to their country for resisting the genocidal impulse that had captured so many in California. At best these officers could stem the tide of genocide for but a little while, and only when left free by orders to act on their own judgment. If ordered to kill Native Americans, even these officers did so.

Even what some of the Founders intended to be the watchdog of freedom and a check on the government, the free press exercising the right to free speech, operated very differently in California when it came to Indian affairs. As with any commercial enterprise, the press served a customer base in California, which included white settlers, miners, and ranchers, not Native Americans. The desire to please customers was reflected in the stories printed and reprinted in California's newspapers. Newspaper publishers, as settlers themselves, were doubly interested in making sure local whites triumphed over the challenges Indigenous populations represented. The sad result was that the popular press in California was a vociferous supporter of genocide. Some notable exceptions did exist, however, and spoke volumes about how the Euro-American mind operated.[7] Newspapers in areas shorn of their Native populations soon turned a critical eye on those vicinities where Indian-white conflict continued to rage. Apparently as soon as once-fearsome Indians were obliterated from view, Euro-Americans could step back and assume a more circumspect attitude about the genocide being perpetrated elsewhere.

With the branches of state government arrayed against them, the federal government engaged in a policy of neglect, and the press acting as a voluble cheerleader for genocide, Native peoples in California found that settlers had powerful, democratic institutions as allies supporting efforts to exterminate them. Had Tocqueville visited California in the 1850s, perhaps he would have still come to his earlier conclusion: "The tyranny of the government is ordinarily added to the greed of the colonists."[8] Perhaps no better example existed in the nineteenth-century United States than in California, where the government was truly peopled by the colonists.

6

The Murder State

That a war of extermination will continue to be waged between the two races until the Indian race becomes extinct, must be expected; while we cannot anticipate this result with but painful regret, the inevitable destiny of the race is beyond the power and wisdom of man to avert.

Peter H. Burnett, governor of California, "Address to the Legislature" (1852)

As these words by California's first U.S. governor demonstrate, California's Indigenous population was abandoned to the whims of white citizens by the state government from the beginning. Burnett's conviction that the "inevitable destiny" of Native Americans was extermination was commonplace among many Euro-Americans in California, as they were in the East. Like thousands of others who had come to California to strike it rich, Burnett believed that God had ordained the end of Native peoples as part of Manifest Destiny. He abandoned any thought of stemming the tide of such extermination because as part of God's master plan, genocide of the Indian "race [was] beyond the power and wisdom of man to avert."[1] Indeed in the minds of some nineteenth-century Euro-Americans, to turn away from genocide would be to contravene God's plan. More important, in Burnett's mind, to do other than let the extermination move forward would ignore his constituency's demands upon him as their top elected representative. In this Burnett was not alone. His successor, Governor John Bigler, wrote in 1852, "I deplore the unsettled question of affairs in the North [of the state]; but the settlement of new countries, and the progress of civilization have always been attended with perils. The career of civilization under the *auspices of the American people*, has heretofore been interrupted by no dangers, and daunted by no perils. Its progress has been an ovation—steady, august, and resistless."[2] Clearly Bigler contextualized his role in much the same way Burnett did, as an instrument of the people to be wielded in concert with, not contradiction of, the historic forces of Manifest Destiny and the popular will of the citizenry. Expressions of the popular will concerning Indians were most often seen in the form of citizens' petitions to the governor's office.

Every governor of California received petitions from local communities during the 1850s and 1860s asking that the state do something to curb the "Indian troubles" in their region. Some asked that the governor make an appeal to the federal government for troops, hoping that pressure from California's top official would convince the army to take stronger measures against pestiferous Native groups. Other petitioners asked that the state militia be called up, reminding the governor that he was empowered to do so as its elected commander in chief. But many groups of citizens asked rather that the governor empower them. Drawing up petitions at town hall and county meetings, citizens called attention to the threat posed to their lives and property by Native Americans in their vicinity. As the Special Joint Committee on the Mendocino War, convened in 1860, would find while interviewing many of these petitioners, it was really a threat to property rather than lives that drove men to petition the governor. Yet despite this realization, the majority of the Committee's members concurred with the settlers' motives. As most of the men in government in California in its first decade were, like the petitioners, failed gold seekers going in new directions, the petitions found a great deal of sympathy from them. In fact the Committee was convened not to investigate Native American genocide, but why the efforts to exterminate them had cost so much money to achieve.

Reporting to their colleagues in the California Senate and Assembly, members of the Committee sought to identify why hundreds of thousands of dollars had to be expended to solve the problems of

Native-white relations. The majority and minority reports that followed in the wake of their 1860 investigation, which took dozens of depositions from settlers and ranchers in the region, but none from Native Americans, painted a bleak picture of what life had become for Native peoples.[3] Most striking were the open admissions of complicity in genocide. Many admitted under oath to killing Native Americans, including men who were not part of authorized volunteer companies, who were simply killing in order to protect their self-interests.[4] Such admissions to killing noncombatants or killing while not under the authority of the government were admissible in court and could have been used to prosecute men. Many of the those killing Native peoples legally, under the protection of gubernatorial authorization to form volunteer companies, exhibited a callousness that might have given elected officials pause about allowing any further use of volunteer units. Clearly the reports demonstrated that volunteers had organized to answer theft of their livestock with the murder of entire communities. The majority report admitted that judging by the horrific results, "either [the] government, or [the] citizens, or both, are to blame." The report also admitted that white settlers had often initiated the hostility with Indigenous populations. Yet when it came time to affix blame, they ignored the immediate context and instead contextualized blame in the grand scheme of American history. "The same relations and condition of things [exist] between white settlers and Indians in Mendocino County," wrote the majority committee, "as has always been the case from the first settlement of our country to the present time, whether on the frontiers or in the more thickly settled districts, where the Indian has been permitted to inhabit the same country with the white settler." What might be done by the legislature to respond to this state of affairs? Help in the extermination: "History teaches us the inevitable destiny of the red man is total extermination or isolation."[5] Lawmakers such as these, and like Governor Burnett, saw the genocide of California's Indigenous population as an inevitable component of bringing about Manifest Destiny. In the view of the majority committee, the true problem was that although the present state of affairs was necessary, it was currently inefficient and unnecessarily cruel. They saw the killing of Native Americans perhaps as something akin to the humane euthanasia of a dying race, and relocations to areas so barren and remote as the only possible way to prolong the life remaining in the race. Extermination or relocation, in short, should proceed apace but be as painless as possible. Ultimately the outcome would still be the disappearance of Native Americans.

Addressing the problems of inefficiency, the Committee admitted that settlers had manufactured an unnecessary war in which "a slaughter of beings, who at least possess the human form," took place. The citizens had used the governor to authorize its conduct. The Committee did not fault the governor for his authorization, though, because he had only done what the petitioners wanted. The governor, like the legislature, was a tool of democracy wielded by a sovereign people. Instead state officials shifted much of the blame to the opportunities for trouble created by the federal government. Despite the fact that California's Indigenous population had no formal treaty protections under federal law in 1860, the Committee believed the federal government had been foolish to allow Native Americans to continue to occupy productive land. When settlers and ranchers were determined to move onto such attractive lands, who could stop them? Certainly, few obstacles would be erected by elected representatives at the state level, especially when the federal government was traditionally responsible for Indian affairs. When Native peoples objected and resisted, the state government could do little other than aid its constituency. The results of the aggressive dispossession of Indigenous populations by white settlers, according to the majority committee, had produced massive population decline among Native communities: "Within the last four months, more Indians have been killed by our people than during the century of Spanish and Mexican domination." One way to preserve the remaining Native population was to press the federal government to remove and concentrate them on land that no white settlers were likely to want. Because only about one-fourth of Indigenous peoples resided on reservations in 1860, the majority were scattered in and around white populations predisposed to dispossessing them, if not killing them. The majority committee charged the federal government with neglect of and apathy toward Native populations. Yes, the Committee admitted, settlers had taken land and killed Native peoples, but the federal government had put these settlers in this unavoidably tempting position by not getting all of the Indigenous peoples off of these attractive lands and out of white sight.[6]

Another solution was to let matters continue as they were: "The question resolves itself to this: Shall the Indians be exterminated, or shall they be protected."[7] The Committee thus left genocide on the table by not appending any unequivocal statement calling for the practice to be stopped; in a democracy, the will of the people expressed by their elected representatives might well continue the process of extermination. Perhaps this is not surprising given that they had noted in their report that Native Americans were possessed of "human form" but not humanity. To protect Native peoples the majority committee proposed the creation of larger reservations. However, their recommendation contradicted their own conclusions on the state of affairs, given the desire of Euro-American settlers for more and more of the best available lands. Describing Round Valley as beautiful and desirable, the majority committee suggested that it be fully reserved for Native peoples, as currently only 25 percent of the valley was reserved in the form of Nome Cult Farm.[8] Given that depositions taken in the formulation of the report indicated that white settlers were already squatting illegally on federal property in the valley, and others were leasing lands legally, the suggestion seems disingenuous. What miracle would protect an enlarged reservation in Round Valley from depredations by whites when they were already happening on a smaller reservation there, the Committee did not mention.

The minority report of the Joint Committee better represented the majority of Euro-Americans in California; it was a microcosm of the power wielded by individual white citizens in their war with Native Americans in California. The minority report was written by one man, J. B. Lamar, who also represented the single dissenting minority opinion of the committee. He attacked the majority report as a mis-apprehension of all the facts learned through citizens' testimony. He indignantly criticized the majority for calling the war in Mendocino unnecessary. In Lamar's view, nothing could be more necessary. He too pointed the finger of blame at the federal government; he described the federal troops stationed in the valley as the next thing to useless. Lamar referred to history as well, claiming that soldiers had a tradition of ineffectiveness in dealing with Native Americans.[9] He might have qualified his remark by adding that this ineffectiveness was usually in the face of white settlers being present in such instances and doing much to complicate or destroy the peace that soldiers arranged. Such was certainly the case in Round Valley at Nome Cult Farm.

Unlike the majority of the Committee, Lamar offered solutions representing the actual state of affairs in California. He believed the way to solve the problem of Native-white relations was with the adoption by the state of "a general system of peonage or apprenticeship, for the proper disposition and distribution of the Indians by families among responsible citizens. General laws should be passed regulating the relations between master and servant, and providing for punishment of any meddlesome interference on the part of third parties."[10] In short, Lamar proposed a system of slavery for all Indigenous peoples that gave masters nearly absolute authority over their slaves. Only the scale of the proposal was surprising, because the system of slavery mentioned had already been in existence since 1850, as "An Act for the Government and Protection of Indians."[11] In this manner, Lamar argued, all reservations would soon be emptied and the former inhabitants placed under the care of their individual masters. Such a measure would also relieve the state of any future financial burdens, as Native communities would be broken up, with individuals living in discrete family units, susceptible to the control of white male heads of household. Such a plan was never enacted on this scale, yet Lamar was openly proposing a campaign of cultural genocide, designed to destroy Native American groups by destroying them as cohesive civilizations.

As the various suggestions of the Committee were considered, money was always a key issue as California lawmakers considered what course of action to take regarding Indian affairs in the nineteenth century. As the legislature examined the Indian wars of the 1850s, this was particularly true. The state government had spent millions of dollars in the 1850s paying for the expenses and wages of volunteer companies and the state militia. By January 1, 1854, the state of California had already spent $924,259 on Native American genocide. Some of the money had been reimbursed by the federal government, but much remained unpaid. The state resorted to issuing war bonds to pay for the costs of campaigns against Native Americans. In a sense, this was democratic capitalism at its best and worst. Like the subscriptions taken up for scalp bounties or the funding of local volunteer companies, purchasers of Indian War Bonds funded the genocide of Native Americans. In addition to the blood on their hands, those investing between $100 and $1,000 collected interest at a rate of 7 percent; for wealthier investors, an issue of 12 percent bonds for $1,000 investments was offered.[12] By 1860, with bonds mature and many not yet paid, bondholders were clamoring for their representatives to make good on their investments. For many, far from the scene of the wars between whites and Native people, the massive transfer of land into Euro-American hands was not enough. Legislators, however, had little hope of recovering the state monies spent fighting and exterminating Native Americans in a timely fashion through federal reimbursement.[13] Inefficient and unreliable funding were the rule in state-federal financial relations in the early history of the state of California.

According to State Comptroller John Houston, in 1851 the federal government was not inclined to offer assistance to California because of the lack of revenue the state sent to fund the general government.[14] In 1860, despite the nearly $1 billion in gold extracted in the state since 1848, California contributed relatively little to federal coffers. As the California Gold Rush took place on unsurveyed public lands and in the absence of a federal income tax, the best the federal government could hope for was to make indirect revenue as commerce increased between California and the East or to make money on the sale of public lands once surveyed and offered for settlement. In addition to attempts to obtain money from the federal government, California legislators also looked for weapons from the federal government. In 1852, by joint resolution, California lawmakers petitioned their representatives in Washington for twenty thousand rifles and one thousand revolvers. The state legislators asked their senators and representatives to make it clear that "hordes of savages" threatened the citizenry of California.[15] The legislature then turned to the governor to oversee remuneration. In 1855 the California Senate and Assembly enacted legislation placing the responsibility of seeking compensation for Indian war expenses on the governor. By law the governor's office was to seek out the $924,259 the state felt the federal government owed California for operations against Native Americans prior to 1854.[16]

The state legislature also used the democratic process to call on federal agents to modify federal Indian policy in California. In a joint resolution in 1858, the state government called on the superintendent of Indian affairs for California to remove all Native Americans from any county where the board of supervisors of the county requested it.[17] The superintendent at the time, Thomas J. Henley, already found it impossible to keep Native Americans on what he claimed were underfunded reservations. Henley lacked the authority to comply even had he been so inclined. Besides, based on Native-white relations in California in 1858, one cannot imagine any county not making this request. In 1860 the legislature proposed something even more radical, and deadly. The California Assembly and Senate, again by joint resolution, called upon the federal government to relinquish control of all Indian affairs to the state after ceding to the state all reservation lands. Moreover because settlers were living on reservation lands in Round Valley, the resolution called upon the federal government to pay settlers for the land and improvements they had made. No mention was made of the fact that these settlers were illegally squatting on federal property.[18] The federal government did not acquiesce. In 1862 another joint resolution was transmitted to Congress by the state legislature. Now the California Senate and Assembly asked that all "undomesticated Indians" be removed from the presence of whites, so as to be "protected from molestation on the part of the whites." These relocations were to be permanent.[19] Again federal authorities refused. Judging by the language contained in the resolution, the legislature clearly believed that Native Americans not under white control as laborers would inevitably be molested. Native peoples were already being murdered, kidnapped, and dispossessed, even as these votes were taking place and the resulting resolutions delivered to Washington. Moreover the legislature had been funding the "molestation on the part of whites" for many years and knew very well the hypocrisy of their claims that removal would avert trouble between Native Americans and whites in the long term. The resolution also reveals that maintaining the supply of Native American labor to benefit white employers was still an important concern lawmakers maintained on behalf of their constituents.

The state was running into financial problems year after year. Because the Gold Rush took place mainly on federal lands, the state was unable to tax gold seekers for the profits taken out of the ground and rivers of California. As early as 1851 the state comptroller had spotted difficulties in securing enough revenue to run the state. The expenses for militia and volunteer companies were particularly high, and many men were unwilling to register for service or to pay a "commutation tax" to avoid having to serve. Likewise, local authorities seemed indisposed to collect the tax or to force men to register for the militia. Comptroller Houston encouraged the legislature to either mandate enforcement, reduce the tax to encourage its payment, or repeal the law.[20]

The original law governing the formation of militia companies anticipated the unwillingness or inability of federal forces to respond in the manner citizens desired, the financial impossibility of maintaining a standing state militia for extended periods, and the tradition of opposition by citizens to standing armies. A well-defined law served to codify how local communities could petition the state governor to legally and temporarily form volunteer companies to deal with emergencies requiring an armed response. The system was designed to avoid regular costs associated with maintaining permanent forces. Community meetings, petitions for forming a company, and the manner by which officers were to be elected, among other concerns, were covered.[21] As earlier chapters have shown, white citizens were well acquainted with the law and how to put it to effective use exterminating or driving off Indigenous peoples. Other laws protected the financial interests of individuals at the expense of the state. Laws stipulating rates of pay, reimbursement for expenses, and per diem were enacted. Even the rate at which the government would compensate volunteers for wear and tear on their horses was legally defined. A man serving as a private and supplying his own horse, for example, would make $5 per day in pay and $1 per day for the horse, plus his food, ammunition, and other equipment were either supplied to him or their cost reimbursed. Officers, quartermasters, and noncommissioned officers could make double or triple what a private made.[22] That is not to say that volunteers felt these wages were enough, even though many were also engaged in securing their own interests by eliminating or relocating Native Americans while serving in a volunteer company.

Many volunteers in the early 1850s demanded high wages to kill Native Americans. In 1850, for example, when the gold was still relatively plentiful in the Mother Lode region of the Sierra foothills, men demanded higher compensation because of the gold they expected to miss out on while campaigning against Native Americans. According to a report by the state militia's Brigadier General Winn to Governor Peter Burnett, men expected to be paid $8 per day for service as a private, and officers expected at least $16. This wage was in addition to the food that each man expected, which amounted to another $2 per man. Given this system, costs could mount fast. For instance, a body of 250 men mustered under Sheriff William Rodgers at Mariposa cost the state $24,500 per week to keep in the field, fighting Native Americans.[23] Money, probably more than inhumanity, may have caused Burnett to conclude, "We cannot anticipate this result with but painful regret, the inevitable destiny of the race is beyond the power and wisdom of man to avert."[24] Indeed the decisions to allow the democratically conceived death squads to operate were likely influenced in part by simple economic necessity for a cash-strapped state.

To keep costs down, militia and volunteer companies needed to kill with alacrity, and they were constantly reminded of this fact in veiled communications from the state to "punish" or "chastise" Native Americans and then disband as quickly as possible. In practice, identifying and capturing the real culprits in stock raiding would take time and patience, something not countenanced in the commissions issued to volunteer companies. It is likely, then, that some of the bloodiness of the campaigns was due to financial constraints of this type. A second cost-cutting measure adopted by the state was perhaps equally bad for Native people. The number of volunteers in a company, suggested General Winn, should be kept to the bare minimum. This may have contributed to the forces' use of ambushes and shoot-first policies rather than risk being overwhelmed by superior Native American numbers. Nonetheless Winn believed that until the federal government could supply sufficient forces to deal with Native Americans, the state should fund troops. These forces required "the strictest economy" in their operations and should be limited to one hundred men, "properly armed and supplied to do all that [was] necessary." The challenge of using only one hundred men instead of the 250 Rodgers mustered was not a problem for Winn, who reminded Burnett of "the character of [the] people in the immediate vicinity of the Indian difficulties": "And we know that one white man is equal to 10 Indians in combat."[25] Burnett approved the reductions suggested by Winn. Although some companies in excess of one hundred men were mustered by the state after 1850, these cases were relatively rare.[26] Burnett set a standard in terms of force size and the demand for alacrity in bringing a conclusion to "Indian difficulties" wherever they were encountered. His successors would emulate his precedent, especially in their demands for cheap and timely performance.

Governor John McDougal, Burnett's successor, inherited the difficulties at Mariposa. McDougal held true to Burnett's course. Following the receipt of numerous citizens' petitions demanding the state assist settlers in the San Joaquin Valley, McDougal ordered Sheriff James Burney to muster volunteers and head into the field. McDougal wrote:

The officer in command will then proceed to punish the Indians engaged in the disturbances which have occurred. One hundred men it is believed will prove sufficient for the emergency, but should such not be the case the commanding officer is directed to report to me without delay that such efficient steps may be taken as shall effectually and speedily quell the disturbances and afford protection to our citizens against the hostile tribes.

The call above ordered to be made must, under the circumstances, be for volunteers, whose compensation will have to depend upon the action of the State or General government, one or the other of which will, I make no doubt, provide for their pay. The Commanding officer will use all necessary caution and energy in conducting the expedition. He will not keep more men in command than may be indispensable to accomplish the object, and will disband the same at the earliest day when it may be done with safety.[27]

McDougal was unconcerned with how the men would "punish" the Native population, but he was obviously worried about how much money it would cost the state. In fact McDougal likely knew that the volunteers would simply kill many of the Native Americans they encountered. The governor's main concerns were rather "efficient steps" taken "speedily" and not by more troops than were "indispensable to accomplish the object."

McDougal stressed these financial necessities when he informed the legislature that he had authorized the formation of militia companies after receiving petitions from the citizenry of Mariposa County. He pointed out the responsibilities that the executive and legislative branches have to their constituents: their common duty was to do everything in their power to protect the lives and property of the citizenry. As the federal government was currently failing in this charge, McDougal believed it fell to the state to take up such protection in the interim. From McDougal's perspective, his executive powers had already dealt with the physical threat to the lives and property of the citizens in Mariposa County. What he looked to the legislature for was a solution to the financial threat posed by forming expeditions to violently subdue Native Americans. The governor argued, "Up to this time arms, ammunition, provisions and other munitions of war have been supplied by individuals," most of whom were miners. "The State," he claimed, "owes it to them to see, that they are compensated." McDougal recommended "that provision be made by law for the payment of whatever claims be justly due, for, and on account of services which have heretofore been rendered by its citizens in repelling Indian aggressions." He forwarded a similar message to U.S. Army headquarters, preparatory to the state's seeking repayment for what state officials believed to be a federal responsibility.[28] This course of events—citizens' petitions to the governor, legal authorization and payment of volunteer or militia companies, and communications of the governor to the legislature seeking financial redress for volunteers, first by the state and then by the federal government—became the standard procedure the state of California used to authorize and fund genocide. Laws, especially the Militia Law and its later amendments, made it easy for citizens to take the correct steps to legally allow them to commit genocide, and then be compensated for its perpetration.

Citizens were plainly aware of the law, and lawmakers and the governor could do little but require their constituents to adhere to the steps prescribed in law. Influential citizens such as Judge Serranus C. Hastings, angry at the loss of property to Native Americans, were well aware of their rights and how to engage the law to support their interests. Such men used petitions, letters, and their rights as citizens to spur the state government to action. In Hastings's petitions to the governor he lambasted the weak efforts of federal forces in the region and their failure to stop thieving Indians. Hastings was so agitated that he claimed the army was in league with the Indians, representing not the citizenry's interests but the welfare of Native Americans. Federal officers were traitors, he claimed. He paid his taxes to the state, and he wanted his due.[29] Hastings demanded that the system function as any citizen might expect from his elected leadership: representatives empowered by a democratic majority should represent that majority, not some inconsequential minority group, and certainly not a group of nonwhite noncitizens that had neither the vote nor many other legal rights in the state. Hastings and others demanded that the governor order the formation of volunteer companies to solve the problem of Indian affairs in the region—in other words, to take up the practical tool of Manifest Destiny, the rifle. As discussed in previous chapters, governors responded positively and repeatedly to their constituents' demands. However, another branch of the state government played an even greater role in fostering Native American genocide in California.

The state legislature, even more than the executive branch, created an environment that was not only conducive to genocide, but encouraged it. With the 1846 occupation of California by the United States, a rapid transition began that would subject Indigenous peoples to a multifaceted system of violence and murder. This descent into hardship, privation, and death was not begun by the armed forces of the United States, but by the Euro-American settlers already present in California and the addition of hundreds of thousands more that would follow in search of gold and land in subsequent decades. These miners, ranchers, and settlers quickly overlay their laws, institutions, and ideologies on California. While Euro-Americans had long dealt with Indigenous populations in the central and eastern portions of the United States, the way they treated California's Native peoples was in some ways unique. Native people in California became the object of the most destructive forces that a democratic system could contrive. Ironically Native peoples in California might have appeared the epitome of what one would hope for in a civilization. Most exhibited widespread representation within autonomous groups, a tradition of reciprocity underlying their justice system, and a lack of social classes that might create problems of self-interest.[30] In the nineteenth century, democracy in California represented white male citizens alone. This segment of the population, through its elected representatives, created a system of justice in California poised to destroy Native American communities, cultures, and economies. In other words, the legal system was foundational in the genocide to come.

The cornerstone of legal genocide in California was Chapter 133, or "An Act for the Government and Protection of Indians." Implemented in 1850, Chapter 133 legalized genocidal crimes such as the enslavement of Native peoples. The process of passing Chapter 133 began the prior year, 1849, when the California Constitution was ratified. It began a long tradition in California of marginalization, persecution, and prosecution of nonwhites by legal means. California's Indigenous population was only first in a long line of ethnic groups—including peoples of Hispanic, Asian, and African ancestry—to find whites in California willing to legally disenfranchise them or worse.[31] Building on the inequities codified in the constitution, the legislature erected additional walls against Native Americans and other peoples interfering with white domination of California. Using this constitutional foundation, lawmakers added numerous laws to exclude or control Native Americans.

Laws passed in the legislative session of 1850 also dealt with Native peoples prior to the passage of the omnibus Chapter 133. Perhaps most important among these was California's criminal code, which prevented Native peoples from serving as witnesses against whites, being judged incompetent on account of race: "No black or mulatto person, or Indian, shall be permitted to give evidence in favor of, or against, any white person."[32] Because of this law whites could kill with impunity as long as no white witnesses observed their actions. Not until 1872 could Native Americans offer testimony against whites in regular criminal or civil proceedings. Evidence, however, shows that even in cases where whites did witness criminal offenses against Native peoples, few ever came forward to serve as an acceptable witness on a Native person's behalf. In Santa Barbara, for instance, when a white man named Edward Simmons was found brutally murdered, authorities immediately arrested and charged a Native American man based on the "strong suspicion of his being the guilty party." If the role of victim and supposed perpetrator had been reversed, no white man would have been charged, let alone held for such a crime. The unidentified man was found guilty based on the "desperate character" of his Indian nature.[33] James Hilan, arrested for the murder of two Native

men by pistol-whipping them to death, was acquitted with the help
of a sheriff's deputy and on a legal technicality that would never have
allowed a Native person to go free. In this case, one of the arresting
deputies destroyed the physical evidence of Hilan's guilt by cleaning
and refurbishing the murder weapon prior to Hilan's trial, making it
inadmissible as evidence. Strong circumstantial evidence still existed
of Hilan's guilt, including the testimony of the local sheriff who had
seized the murder weapon. Despite this, the judge ordered Hilan to be
pronounced not guilty, but not due to evidentiary matters. The judge
ruled that because the names of the victims were not known, their
true identity remained in question, and a man could not be charged
or convicted of murder without the victim's identity being known.[34]
Ransom Paul, another white man, stabbed a Native woman to death
with a knife in public. Paul was arrested, indicted by a grand jury, and
subsequently acquitted of the murder charge by a local white jury, all
by due process of law.[35] In Santa Barbara a Native man was stabbed to
death in public by a white man. When several Native Americans who
had witnessed the killing took the murderer before a judge, the white
man was set free. With only Indian witnesses having come forward
there was no need to press on with a case.[36]

Sometimes the justice system obviated the need to investigate crimes
against Native Americans. In one case, a justice of the peace closed the
case on the killing of a Native man found murdered in a vineyard based
on the fact that the owners of the vineyard had heard nothing, and it
was supposed that other Native Americans had killed the young man.[37]
The supposition went unquestioned, as the justice of the peace was fully
responsible under Chapter 133 for adjudicating the matter. In another
instance, a coroner's inquest was all the investigation that followed the
brutal murder of two Native men before the case was closed.[38] A Native
man called Bacilio received similar treatment when a judge deemed
his "death from intoxication, or the visitation of God," and closed the
case without further investigation.[39] Many Native people never reached
a judge or justice of the peace before receiving what Euro-Americans
deemed justice for Indians.

Whites in California were well aware of the authority of the citizenry acting democratically and in large numbers. At no time was this truer than in the 1850s, when Californians famously created vigilance committees to expedite justice in central California, especially in San Francisco. These episodes of mob violence in the name of justice were an outgrowth of the popular belief that individual white citizens, acting in concert and achieving a majority, were empowered to act to preserve public order—even when elected officials, court officers, and law enforcement disagreed. The famous vigilance committees of San Francisco were not concerned with Native people, but numerous groups of vigilantes throughout California aped the actions of their more notable counterparts, as they treated Native Americans to a form of justice they called "Judge Lynch." In southern California two Native men taken by the citizens of San Gabriel were hanged after a summary decision by the gathered mob.[40] In Marysville, after a Native American leader objected to the recent murders of his people, a group of whites seized him and brought him as a captive back to a local ranch, where other citizens waited. No legal trial was held; the citizenry voted unanimously to hang the man, which they did.[41] Miners, located well away from the institutions of the California justice system, nonetheless used democracy to make their private justice system legitimate in their minds. In one instance, five Native American men were caught and held prisoner by miners for several days, after which time they were convicted on suspicion of committing "several depredations" and hanged.[42] Even custody or acquittal by lawful authorities was no guarantee that the justice system would operate, at least not in the face of a mob of citizens who knew how to carry out justice on savage Indians. In Susanville a mob of citizens relieved a local constable of a Native American prisoner accused of murder and hanged him from a tree.[43] In another case in Susanville, following the acquittal of three Native men on murder charges, a mob seized the three men anyway and hanged them.[44] In few ways can it be clearer that white citizens believed the majority, not laws or officials, made distinctions of right and wrong when it came to Native Americans.

Landowners too exercised illegal but often unchallenged authority over Native Americans working for them or allegedly committing crimes on their property. A Native man and woman caught gathering clover on a white man's property near Clear Lake were punished by having three ferocious dogs set upon them. The man survived the mauling, but the woman died from her wounds, which included having her breasts torn off by the dogs.[45] Landowners beat and whipped Native employees and interlopers for a variety of reasons. One Native man caught stealing a calf was "severely horsewhipped" by the ranch owner.[46] As previously discussed, the brutality of J. J. Warner against Cupeño people helped to precipitate a war. Many white citizens knew what their neighbors did to Native people, but most remained silent. One U.S. Army officer observed of Native peoples, "[They are] not blind to the feelings entertained towards them by the people who surround them. They know they will have no justice." According to the same observer, "No white man would be harmed for killing an Indian, and it would certainly be a force to bring such a case before any tribunal in this country, as I am afraid it would be equally so in any of the adjoining counties."[47] In other words, short of the U.S. Army invading these counties and imposing martial law, settlers would continue to kill Indigenous peoples without significant repercussions, except when Native people fought back in self-defense.

Legal punishment was also meted out in a different way for Native Americans. Native peoples sentenced for crimes were forced onto work gangs or auctioned off to pay fines, while non-Natives typically were not.[48] Whites were not whipped in public spectacles, as were Native Americans. In the case of two Native men charged and convicted of cattle theft, a justice of the peace ordered that each man receive twenty-five lashes at a public flogging. In the course of their examination by the justice, the men had revealed a Euro-American ringleader who had assigned them the task of stealing the animals.[49] But because the two men were Native Americans, the testimony against the white man was inadmissible under the penal code and Chapter 133.

With the authority and protection of Chapter 133 and other laws

that legally disadvantaged Native Americans, whites committed genocide of Native peoples. This can be seen in an examination of the legal
system, particularly in Los Angeles County. During the 1850s and 1860s
the local- and county-level legal system in Los Angeles participated
in creating and perpetuating a system of debt peonage that led to de
facto slavery for many Native Americans. By repeatedly convicting
Native Americans under vagrancy and drunkenness laws, magistrates
provided cheap Native labor for the benefit of the local economy. Such
was the case in 1855, when six Native men were convicted of assault
and sentenced to a fine of "$25 cash, to be cancelled by a requisition
to work for the public not exceeding six months."[50] The punishment
required some wages be paid beyond the settlement of the fine, but
these were well below those paid to whites, and often below levels paid
to Native Americans engaged in free labor associations with whites.
This situation was exacerbated and made cyclical by the use of alcohol
as payment in lieu of cash. Under Chapter 133, as well as other state
laws, it was illegal to sell or provide alcoholic beverages to Native
Americans. However, the practice was ubiquitous and largely went
unpunished. Part of the reason was that it was profitable. In the cases
tried in court against those trafficking liquor to Native Americans, the
fines levied upon conviction were almost always paid immediately, in
cash, by the defendant—the implication being that it was so profitable
that the statutory fines were no deterrence to the practice.[51] In one
notable departure from this state of affairs, a man named McDonald
was arrested and convicted of selling liquor to Native Americans and
was ordered to either pay a fine of $40 or serve ten days in jail. The
man happily accepted the jail term, arguing that he knew of no way
to "make four dollars per day easier." McDonald knew that he could
not be made to work off the fine, and instead "went to board at county
expense."[52] Perhaps in disgust, the judge released the man after he
served less than a week.[53]

  Those employing Native people, especially those bought at auction
for short-term labor in payment of criminal fines, used alcohol to
ensure a steady flow of labor. The example of Los Angeles demon-

strates well how the system worked. Selling liquor to Native Americans was illegal under Chapter 133 and under Los Angeles city law, yet a thriving and allegedly unstoppable trade existed. The *Los Angeles Star* lamented as much, saying, "It does not appear that the Liquor Ordinance has done much good. . . . Still the Indians get their liquor the same as ever."[54] The inattention to the laws on liquor sales stands in sharp contrast to the efforts to round up intoxicated Native Americans. Drunkenness was used to arrest and auction Native Americans or to collect fines when those in question could afford to pay. The *Los Angeles Star* noted with some suspicion, "The City Marshall and his assistants . . . spend the Sabbath in arresting and imprisoning Indians, supposed to be drunk, until Monday morning, when they are taken before the Mayor and discharged upon paying a bill of two dollars and a half each, one dollar of which is for the Marshall. . . . Now we have no heart to do the Marshall the slightest prejudice, but this leading off Indians and locking them up overnight for the purpose of taking away one of their paltry dollars, seems to us a questionable act."[55] For those unable to pay the fine, labor punishment was used to settle the debt. In fact this was the more common routine. Native Americans labored Monday through Saturday on farms and ranchos as hands or domestic servants. On Saturday evenings those whose terms were up were discharged with whatever payment was due them. Payment was seldom made in cash but more often in the form of food or spirits, despite the prohibition of providing liquor to Native Americans.[56] The following day was typified by a common occurrence the *Star* described: "Negro Alley is the principal resort of these Indians especially on the Sabbath, when the little money they have been able to get during the rest of the week, is spent for liquor."[57] They were then subsequently arrested, jailed, and auctioned on Monday to the highest bidder. Each week this cycle was repeated.[58] It is important to note that whites were never auctioned; those unable to pay a fine did jail time.[59]

Moreover the practice of paying wages in full or in part in alcohol prevented Native Americans from earning cash wages on a level capable of fully supporting themselves or their families, which led to a state of debt peonage. This was made manifest as Native peoples endeavored to find steady work and keep out of the hands of law enforcement officials looking to arrest them on vagrancy charges. Fierce competition for steady work drove wages down. Auctioned by the court in order to work off fines or hired for meager wages by employers, Native Americans in California were forced into labor relationships with non-Native peoples. This not only reduced the standard of living for Indigenous peoples, but it also eroded traditional subsistence practices. The end of this cycle came only when local need for Native American labor ended. The need for Native labor declined in part due to the lack of a reliable supply of Native American laborers, as populations were savaged by genocidal practices leading to demographic collapse.

Under California law Native American existence was closely regulated in order to both assuage white fears and harness Native labor in an otherwise labor-starved California.[60] In the early years of statehood, finding people willing to labor away from the gold fields was difficult and costly. Many workers demanded high wages to forgo the potential riches of the Gold Rush. Chapter 133 was key in feeding labor-hungry California with low-cost Indigenous laborers. It did so in part by codifying the relationship between labor and punishment.[61] Chapter 133 allowed for justices of the peace to decide all matters of law and justice pertaining to Native Americans, thus circumventing the legal systems in place for whites and other non-Natives. Locally appointed justices of the peace were responsible for maintaining the many remaining provisions of the act and communicating to local Native Americans their responsibilities under the law, particularly those sections dealing with labor.[62]

The most important and insidious provision of Chapter 133 for harnessing short-term labor was section 20, which allowed justices of the peace, mayors, and town recorders to render judgments in matters of alleged Native American vagrancy. Walter Jarboe, the infamous leader of the Eel River Rangers, was a justice of the peace, so it is not surprising that so many Native people encountered legal injustice.[63] Chapter 133, section 20, required that Native Americans maintain an "honest calling" or otherwise face criminal penalties. Of course an "honest calling" included only work in a manner and mode acceptable to whites. Being out on the street with no money in one's pockets was cause for arrest; those who could not pay the fines imposed were publicly auctioned off for a work term of up to four months. Longer terms could be imposed for crimes judged worse than vagrancy. The money received at auction, minus the fine and "expense for clothing for said Indian," was either added to a general-purpose Indian fund or paid to the family of the indentured Indian. Not only Los Angeles, but communities in the northern half of the state had similar auctions.[64]

Section 5 of Chapter 133 allowed citizens to avoid the need to attend an auction to obtain labor. Anyone wishing to "hire" a Native American simply went to the local justice of the peace for approval of a contract between a Native American and an employer. The only proviso was that the laborer was not already engaged by another employer. This contract was only "obligatory on the part of the Indian," so whites could make and break contracts with impunity. The rates and terms were decided between laborer and employer, yet what these typically were or whether they were clearly understood by those hired under them is unclear. Some certainly were aware of the paucity of wages for work in agriculture and construction, far below what whites might expect. Nonetheless, according to the historian William Bauer, Native people in Round Valley industriously blended old and new work habits to create a "multi-source economy" allowing for the subsistence and survival of their communities.[65] Despite such cases of successful adaptation, as discussed in chapter 4, these provisions were the foundation of economic genocide for California Indigenous people. Chapter 133 also provided support for their physical and cultural genocide.

The most sinister component of Chapter 133 in support of genocide was the indenture of Native children permitted under section 3 of the law:

Any person having or hereafter obtaining a minor Indian, male or female, from the parents or relations of such Indian minor, and wishing to keep it . . . shall go before a Justice of the Peace in his Township, with the parents or friends of the child, and if the Justice of the Peace becomes satisfied that no compulsory means have been used to obtain the child from its parents or friends, shall enter on record, in a book kept for that purpose, the sex and probable age of the child, and shall give to such person a certificate, authorizing him or her to have the care, custody, control and earnings of such minor, until he or she obtain the age of majority. Every male Indian shall be deemed to have attained his majority at eighteen, and the female at fifteen years.[66]

Because Native Americans were prohibited from testifying against whites in regularized courts under California law before 1872, there was no way to challenge the system outside of taking one's case to a justice of the peace. After 1855 Native testimony could be accepted in cases involving whites taken to justices of the peace, yet it was justices of the peace who would have granted the indenture in the first place. In the research for this study, no evidence was ever uncovered suggesting the reversal of an indenture. Though Chapter 133 had a section prohibiting the kidnapping or unlawful forced labor of Native people, two realities are clear. It would be extremely difficult for Native Americans to charge a white with kidnapping or any other crime against a Native person, even if they had white sponsors or witnesses to bring all of the charges on their behalf. No evidence of such assistance was uncovered in the preparation of this study. And even if a case were pressed successfully, the penalty under the law for kidnapping Native Americans was a fine of no less than $50.[67] Kidnapping Native Americans was not considered a heinous crime. The vague phrase "friends of the child" can lead one to deduce nefarious purposes of unscrupulous people using this legal leeway. Indeed a thriving trade developed between southern and northern California that supplied Native child laborers during the Gold Rush era. Whites in the north were anxious to harness Indigenous laborers under the guise of apprenticeship, and whites in the south were seemingly apathetic about the Native American children kidnapped and sent north to work. The combination of white indifference and legal ambiguity led to few instances of legal action against this slave trade.[68] The government and the public were well aware of the trade, as newspapers often published stories about the kidnapping of Native Americans. The *Humboldt Times* described the dilemma faced by Superintendent Thomas J. Henley. Charged with managing Indian affairs in California, Henley fought a losing battle against his neighbors in northern California. Kidnapped Native people were bringing "from $50 to $250 each" in the region, and Henley was at a loss to stop the practice.[69] What offended him, though, was not that Native Americans were being placed in white households all over California, but that men were profiting from it. Henley himself allowed the apprenticeship of Native people from his reservations. Indeed he had Native people working for him as a private individual, as did the white men he employed on the reservation. In the most telling example of how partial federal officials were to Chapter 133, the former Indian agent Vincent Geiger had eighty Native Americans legally apprenticed to him, whom he promptly took out of the state to Washoe in Nevada, possibly to engage in mining operations.[70]

Men engaged in the illicit trade of Native Americans circumvented Henley's and other federal, state, and local officials' authority and made future relations with Indigenous populations extremely difficult, because typically the apprentices were children whose parents had been killed or injured by the slave traffickers.[71] Similarly troubling, many volunteer companies openly reported to state and federal authorities that their Native prisoners were handed over to white citizens who wanted apprentices.[72] In fact some volunteer companies went out as much to capture Native people for apprenticeship as to seek revenge. Harmon "Hi" Good, a notorious "Indian fighter," led an unauthorized company of volunteers in northern California. In a letter to Governor Leland Stanford, Good wrote openly of the actions of his company, despite the fact that Stanford had not approved its formation. Good, however, seemed to believe that because the community sanctioned their mission, that was approval enough. Good reported on his activities, including daily entries such as the ones for August 2–3, 1862:

August 2nd intercepted an Indian on Antelope Creek East of Tuscon Springs (3 miles) laden with Beef [F]irst took his scalp and then his trail running South East

August 3rd at break of day surprised a camp of about one hundred large + small. Killed seventeen and wounded many more and captured Six children 3 Boys and three Girls ranging from one to 8 years old. We numbered eleven five men being in camp 12 miles distant We found but two guns one of which was stolen from Deer Creek when passing with the young Hickok, a prisoner We returned to camp same day packing the children on our backs.[73]

Obviously Good's description of scalping and aggressive surprise attacks on Native villages indicated a lack of fear of any repercussions. Indeed based on the remainder of Good's communications with Stanford, the man seemed to want the governor's congratulations and his official commission. Good also revealed that part of the mission of the company was to deliver Native prisoners into the homes of whites in the aftermath of massacres. The prisoners from the August 2 attack, for instance, were given up to two local families. "One Boy and one Girl," wrote Good, "were left in families who wish to adopt them. . . . I would also observe that applicants are numerous Who would take all I have or expect to bring in hereafter and raise them in their families if such a course should meet your approbation but none of the Boys should be left on this side of the River or where they ever could discover from whence they came."[74] Though Good feared no retribution from the state, he certainly feared Native American retribution. The ill will and desire to seek vengeance for their children created by men like Good led Native people to both resist violently and disbelieve any white man claiming to offer aid.

Because of the practices of kidnapping and enslavement, Henley found it difficult to convince Native peoples to come to reservations. Many Native American parents told Henley they thought the reservations were a "trick to deprive them of their children."[75] Behind the problem, at its very root, was that there was a market for these slaves. In 1861 the *Marysville Appeal* lamented the practices associated with enslaving Native Americans. Following the capture of several Euro-Americans engaged in killing Native people and enslaving their children for sale in and around Marysville, the *Appeal* published an article condemning the barbarity of the practice. Perhaps the editors failed to realize that some of their readers were purchasers of such slaves. The indignant *Appeal* wrote, "We have not the space at this time to comment upon the matter, but it is enough to chill the heart of man to know that these vile kidnappers in human flesh are making a regular business of killing the Indians in the mountains, or running them off, and kidnapping their children, packing them about the country, like so many sheep or swine to sell, at retail or wholesale."[76]

Though one might judge that the language of the *Appeal*'s correspondent was metaphorical in referring to them not as children or human beings being marketed as slaves, but as animals being sold, a follow-up article suggested otherwise. Calling the rescued children "young sprigs of heathendom," "brats," "poor little creatures," and "shrivelled-legged, pot-bellied and dirty," the correspondent constantly degraded the character of the children. Similarly the children, appearing in court as their kidnappers were arraigned, were described as awed by the practices of white men and their courts. Despite the evidence, the case was thrown out on a legal technicality that needed to be rectified before charges could be brought again.[77] The kidnappers were rearrested once the letter of the law had been obeyed and brought to a second arraignment. Each man promptly made bail, absconded, and was never tried for his crimes.[78] In an outcome typical of how the justice system treated Native peoples, the children, saved by authorities from being sold as slaves, were promptly apprenticed to local white families who wanted slaves.[79] The fact that the nine children recovered from the kidnappers so easily found homes in Marysville is telling. The reason why men like

Thomas J. Henley and other Indian agents found the problem of kidnapping and enslavement so prevalent was a function of demand. Local white settlers and ranchers wanted Native laborers to work in their homes and ranches and found a ready supply as slavers and volunteer companies brought kidnapped children into communities like Marysville. Such arrangements had long been available in California. One source claimed that California's system for rounding up Native American slaves had been in operation as early as 1850, comparing the state to the "far-famed slave-market at Washington." The anonymous author commented, "The process is, to raise a posse and drive in as many of the untamed natives as are requisite, and to compel them to assist in working the land. A pittance of food, boiled wheat or something of the kind is fed to them in troughs, and this is the only compensation which is allowed for their services. Their condition is worse than that of the Peons of the Yucatan, and other parts of Mexico, and yet there are no slaves in California."[80] By the 1860s in Marysville years of violent Indian-white relations had done little beyond resituating the supply of slaves to places farther afield. At one time situated among Indigenous communities, by 1861 Marysville's citizenry had killed or driven off local Native people. They were now well away from the shrinking Native population of the region, who sheltered in the local mountains for safety. Thus when slavers called, many buyers were to be found in Marysville and communities like it around California.

In 1860 an amendment to Chapter 133 was passed that not only expanded the scope of the apprenticeship laws but also demonstrated the state legislature's willingness to openly condone and perpetuate the slave system euphemistically called the apprenticeship system. Despite the common knowledge of the abuses and outrages linked with the system circulating in the press and in testimonies taken by the legislature itself, the legislature passed an amendment expanding the age limit of apprenticeship to include even adults. The lengths of indenture were also increased. Children apprenticed under fourteen could be held until twenty-five (for females twenty-one) and children over fourteen but under twenty could be held until thirty (for females twenty-five).

Adults—those over twenty—could be held for ten years from the date of apprenticeship.[81] The willingness of lawmakers to take such steps may be the result of what the historian Vanessa Gunther argues is a byproduct of the fact that "during most of the 1850s Pro-Southern democrats controlled the legislature in California. . . . By the outbreak of the [Civil War] almost 40% of California's inhabitants were from slave states."[82] Unlike eighteenth-century Anglo indenture laws that required money and/or clothing to be given to the freed servant at the end of his term, little beyond keeping the indentured person alive was required under the terms of indenture in California. And if one were found not properly feeding or clothing a Native person under apprenticeship, the penalty under the law was a $10 fine.[83] The anthropologist Robert Heizer estimated that in the thirteen years the apprenticeship section of Chapter 133 operated, at least ten thousand Native people were enslaved through sales, indentures, and apprenticeships.[84]

The willingness of Euro-Americans in California to engage in a form of slavery and slave trade stemmed in part from an extreme labor shortage in the 1840s and 1850s, as available labor from around the state became concentrated in the gold fields and their promise of instant wealth. However, fortunes could be made outside of the mines as well. Men with the ability to supply the needs of the miners and labor-strapped northern California could make fortunes without needing to pan or dig. Instead they harnessed labor in the southern portion of the state to feed demand in the north. As Superintendent Edward Beale mentioned in a report to Commissioner of Indian Affairs Luke Lea in Washington, "Los Angeles County is the cattle market for the state." Native Americans, Beale believed, "must be neglected" in order to better serve civilization.[85] With northern California relying heavily on Los Angeles County for beef, Beale highlighted the necessity for controlling southern Native American groups in order to maintain the steady and efficient supply of cattle northward.

The necessity for placid relations required either harnessing Indigenous labor or destroying those Native Americans who attempted to live outside of the parameters of their existence set by whites. In the case of the former, ranchos needed more Native American labor to support their ranching operations to capture the "tenfold increase in price" for cattle.[86] Ranchers also needed peaceful Native Americans who did not steal cattle or interfere with the cattle drives north. In the case of the latter, law enforcement, both public and private, became an important focus of everyday life—indeed the most important focus for local government, whose function in terms of public opinion was often limited to public safety and water and land title rights issuance. Vigilance committees were organized to augment law enforcement patrols. These groups were not confined to the Bay Area. Citizen militia groups, such as the Los Angeles Rangers and the Los Angeles City Guard, were formed to allay fears of potential Native American uprisings.[87] Los Angeles also passed a city ordinance that enumerated the many crimes for which Native Americans could be arrested and auctioned, including disturbing the peace and loitering. In practice, the historian Ronald Woolsey notes, "individuals could apprehend Indians or confiscate their belongings merely because they suspected them of unscrupulous activity."[88]

In addition to taking Native Americans into indentures and apprenticeships for the sake of harnessing labor, whites also hoped to change their behaviors through these laws. By repeatedly convicting Native people under vagrancy and drunkenness laws, magistrates sought to control their behaviors and benefit local whites and other non-Natives. The sentencing patterns in these cases show that Native Americans were punished by their assignment to labor for government or private individuals in order to work off their debt to society in ways acceptable to whites' views of proper avocations and a largely Protestant work ethic. As the *California Star* phrased it, "The vagrants should be schooled to labor."[89] Edward Beale counseled as much in a report to his superiors. Reminding them of the extensive work undertaken by the Spanish in building the missions of California, Beale noted that the benefits to the Native Americans were manifest in these works: "Every useful mechanic art, all necessary knowledge of agricultural pursuits, was here taught under a system of discipline at once mild, firm, and paternal.... It is this system modified and adapted to the present time, which I propose for your consideration ... which would preserve this unfortunate people from total extinction, and our government from everlasting disgrace."[90] One doubts that the source of the disgrace to the government was the extinction of the Native Americans; rather it seems that the shame would be in failing to use an available resource to the fullest benefit of the United States. Whichever might be the case, Beale's proposal to establish a mission-style system of labor and discipline never came to pass and was only weakly echoed in the reservations established in California—which were, in paternalistic terms, only shadows of the later reservation systems of the late nineteenth and early twentieth century. Beale might well have been mistaken as an employee of the state of California rather than the federal government. Following his dismissal as superintendent of Indian affairs for California in 1854, he became one of the largest landowners and employers of Native Americans in the state. Using the laws that had made his earlier work impossible, he thrived in his pursuit of his own self-interest.

Additionally, the practice of paying wages in whole or in part in alcohol prevented Native Americans from earning cash wages on a level capable of fully supporting themselves or their families, which led to a state of debt peonage that forced them to labor for local whites and non-Natives even when not forced to do so by a conviction under state or local law. In a system where Native Americans could ostensibly come and go as they pleased, state and local laws both eroded traditional means of survival and forced Native Americans to rely on whites more and more for subsistence. Special Agent John G. Ames undertook a tour in 1874 of villages occupied by Native Americans classified as former "Mission Indians." In his report to the commissioner of Indian affairs, he wrote, "The whites of that section of California [San Bernardino County] have been largely dependent upon these Indians in the care of their farms. . . . Many of the land-owners would have been subject to great inconvenience had not this Indian labor been available." However, Ames noted that such benefits were absent from the Native American experience of the relationship: "In the mean time the Indians have reaped no permanent advantage from their labors; they have only become demoralized by their contact with whites."[91] Whether Ames knew it or not, he confirmed Beale's perspicacious words of twenty years before, "They are fading away," in the same tone of impotent sympathy.

Ames's and Beale's reports provide interesting bookends to the most detrimental period for Native Americans in California's history. Beale entered California as the state government and the local communities it sought to govern, protect, and organize were just coming into being. Laws requiring Native Americans to labor and adopt white ways were described as benevolent paternalism gifted from prosperous Euro-Americans to the miserable and misguided savages. Yet even in this nascent stage, Beale sensed in California what had already been occurring in the East: continual displacement and destruction of Native Americans. The only hope for California's Native Americans seemed to be employment on a scale unheard of in the rest of the United States. By the time Ames wrote his report, the vague yet looming dread that permeated Beale's words was fully formed and realized. Ames noted the inefficacy of liquor laws and the total subordination of Native Americans to the whims and "lusts" of "corrupt white men."[92] One wonders whether Beale would have predicted that the genocide that took two centuries in the East would take only two decades in California.

That the limit of the Euro-American vision for Native Americans was to create laborers and not pseudo-whites of them became clear in the aftermath of significant shifts in California's economy in the 1870s. The end to this cycle came only as the result of an end to a local need for Native American labor. Only part of "An Act for the Government and Protection of Indians" and its 1860 amendment were repealed in 1863. Native American slavery continued. The historian James Rawls notes that Native Americans continued to be held as slaves at least until 1866.[93] The real end for Native American slavery in the Los Angeles area arrived with the influx of white and minority laborers riding the newly built railroads in southern California in the 1870s and 1880s, and with the decline and relocation of ranching and farming to California's Central Valley and to other western states. Whites now had other whites and a growing population of Asians and Latin Americans to labor for them. Native Americans were no longer a necessity, and so Beale's ironic lament came to full fruition: "Humanity must yield to necessity." This time the necessity was not that they work, but that they die quickly and quietly. Other state laws introduced conditions destined to speed genocide, even after Chapter 133 ceased to operate as the legal focal point of Native-white relations.

As Euro-Americans attempted to "school" Native peoples to labor, they also attacked traditional cultural practices that might obviate the need for Native Americans to accept the demeaning, unrewarding labor that whites offered them. Native American acorn gathering, seasonal hunting, and domestic mobility did not fit the Euro-American vision of permanent domestic arrangements funded by year-round farming or ranching. In one clear case of Euro-Americans harming themselves as well as Native Americans, laws throughout the state prevented them from setting large grass fires. Native peoples had been doing this for centuries as a way to protect acorn supplies, drive game, and reduce pestilence. Grasshoppers, once controlled by grass fires and an easy source of food for Native peoples, destroyed crops and caused havoc for white farmers throughout the nineteenth century, as they were no longer kept in check by Indigenous populations.[94] At the same time, whites took to destroying the trees that supplied Native Americans with acorns to build homes, mills, businesses, and flumes for mining. Damming or redirecting water courses destroyed traditional fishing grounds, and land claims encompassed and restricted traditional hunting grounds. Combined with a lack of state and federal concern for Native peoples displaced by Euro-American settlers, Native American people starved. Even the *Los Angeles Star* was outraged when Congress in 1852 decided to appropriate only "20,000 dollars" for the maintenance of California's Indigenous population when, after all, whites had "taken their acorns, grasshoppers, fisheries, and hunting grounds from them."[95] The readers of newspapers, white settlers chief among them, were not similarly inclined to outrage. No mass movements to ameliorate the conditions of Native American peoples were launched in California. White laws and practices were designed to force Native Americans into reliance on whites and their ways in order to survive, something that patently benefited whites living in California. The historian Douglas Monroy argues that laws aimed at Native Americans did nothing less than attempt to criminalize nonwhite labor systems.[96] The same held true for subsistence practices, as the state sponsored a legal system beholden to white interests and blind to those of Native people.

The presence of settlers and ranchers and their domesticated animal herds spelled disaster for local Native peoples in other ways. The livestock introduced by settlers and ranchers lay waste to lands Native populations depended on for shelter and subsistence. Herds of domesticated stock drove off native species. Whether whites realized this threatened Native American survival or not at first, it became clear over time and they could not help but realize the connection. These animals ate native plants that Native Americans and animals depended on for survival, upsetting the ecological balance of entire regions. The laws in California, though, protected the herds, not the Native Americans. Only eventual damage to agricultural resources owned by whites would create any impetus for changing the practice of allowing free range to herds of domesticated animals. Once farming became widespread in California, the problems suffered by Native peoples became the problems suffered by whites. Euro-American and Native American crops were attacked by domesticated animals allowed to roam free. Hogs became such a menace to whites' crops that laws were enacted to protect the white citizenry.[97] Other laws against allowing the free range of herd animals followed in short order.[98] Most of the laws coincided with the gradual transition of California from a mining and ranching economy in the 1850s to an agricultural economy beginning in the mid-1860s. These laws were too late in coming, though, for many Native Americans in California. Many Native peoples died as an indirect result of practices such as allowing cattle and other stock free range. As food supplies dwindled, and as settlers and ranchers defended their stock, some Native people succumbed to hunger and others to bullets as they tried to feed themselves and their families. Sometimes laws protecting the supply of fish and game were enacted yet did not necessarily benefit Native peoples.

Native American hunting and fishing, which allowed Native people to survive without having to resort to stock raiding, was curtailed by law. Beginning in 1852, California put game laws on the books that prevented anyone from taking fish and game out of season.[99] When Native people violated such laws, often unknowingly, the penalties were harsh. In the case of two young Native American boys fishing to augment the diets of their families, punishment came not from the law, but the citizenry. One white hired hand protected the property rights of his white employer by discharging both barrels of his shotgun into the boys. The older of the two boys caught both barrels full in the face, leaving him partially blind and in critical condition. A local doctor removed fifty-four pellets from the boy's face. Though the local newspaper was filled with outrage immediately following the heinous act, a search of subsequent issues reveals the likely case that the man was never punished. When punishment was meted out, courts continued to deal more harshly with Native defendants. One Native man, identified as the chief of local village, was caught fishing out of season and received ninety days in jail for his crime.

In 1854 the state enacted a law against selling firearms or ammunition to Native peoples. This interfered with their ability to hunt and to defend themselves against whites, this latter reason being the idea behind the law.[100] The law also ensured that Native Americans would have to engage in theft or illicit trade to obtain arms, causing additional trouble between Native Americans and whites. Some legislation was less direct. In 1852 an act designed to stop the use of fish dams or weirs to catch salmon also had consequences for Native Americans relying on salmon for food.[101] Laws such as these precluded Native peoples from engaging in traditional subsistence practices. As such laws had no power on federal public lands the laws were unable to attack the real source of danger to California's salmon population: mining and logging. Euro-American logging operations negligently dumped sawdust waste into rivers, wiping out fish populations. When miners could no longer find gold near the banks of watercourses, they redirected the path of entire rivers to expose the gold where deeper water flowed; this too killed fish and destroyed fish runs. Native people who depended on annual appearances of trout and salmon were forced to find subsistence elsewhere. Actions such as these by loggers and miners also made the water undrinkable by people and animals living below their operations, further damaging the local ecology.

Settlers, miners, and ranchers also directly and purposefully attacked the local ecology. Top predators in the food chain, such as bears, wolves, and mountain lions, and smaller predators, such as rattlesnakes, coyotes, and wildcats, posed a threat to the investments of settlers and ranchers, as these animals killed a variety of stock and sometimes threatened the men themselves. Efforts to eliminate them were highly successful, yet produced negative consequences, especially an explosion of the vermin population. According to California's first governor, Peter H. Burnett, "Before the country was inhabited by Americans, these pests were not very troublesome, because ... their excessive increase was prevented by coyotes and snakes, then very numerous." State and local bounties on animals, the commonplace killing of predatory or pestilential species on sight by settlers and ranchers, and parties that hunted as much for sport as for ridding the region of such pests decimated predator populations. The consequences for the environment were obvious as the population of predatory species declined. For example, while squirrels declined in agricultural lowlands and pasturelands inhabited by whites, their numbers skyrocketed in the foothills and mountains because many of the top predators and rattlesnakes had been killed. These squirrels, now unchecked by nature, went to work overproducing at the expense of the plant life of the region.[102] Among the hardest hit species were oak scrub and trees that produced acorns, the staple of the Native American diet in most of California.[103] Harvested in October and November each year, the acorn was a vital store for winter, especially among Native

Americans living in the foothills and mountains of the northern third of the state. Heavy snowfalls were, and are, common to this region. With whites infesting the lowlands and the valleys between the hills and mountains, Native people were forced to remain away from these intruders for survival, suffering colder temperatures and deeper snows as a result. Acorn and pine nut supplies began to fail. Many others died by disease or violence. Without the nutrients of their traditional diet to support their immune systems, even Native Americans obtaining alternate sources of food stood an increased chance of contracting an infectious disease. Others, as they attempted to get nourishment by eating the livestock that was destroying their lives, died at the hands of vengeful whites who exacted disproportionate payback for lost cows or horses by murdering human beings.

Laws were also purposely ignored by whites where they might benefit Native peoples. When the stock of settlers and ranchers repeatedly invaded the reservation at Nome Cult Farm—after the settlers had pulled down the reservation's fences—no charges were brought against them, despite a standing law designed to punish just such invasion of property by herd animals.[104] When the depredations of local whites had wrecked the ability of federal reservations to house and feed Native peoples, the California Senate and Assembly set about trying to close the reservations and make the land made available to Euro-Americans. Nome Lackee was the first to get such attention from the legislature. In 1864 the legislature sent a joint resolution to Congress asking that Nome Lackee be closed, reasoning, "The Indians who were on [Nome Lackee] . . . have mostly died, and the remainder have scattered through the country." They called for Nome Lackee to be "as speedily as possible thrown open to pre-emption" so that Euro-American settlers might finally put the land to good use.[105] Of course the resolution neglected to mention the white settlers already squatting at Nome Lackee illegally. In 1868, several years after Nome Lackee was closed and the desired preemptions begun, the state legislature sent another joint resolution to Congress, this time asking that Mendocino Reservation be closed to Indians and opened for white settlement.[106]

Table 2. Native Children Living in Non-Native Households

Year	Children under 5	Children under 17
1863	n.d.	4,522
1864	n.d.	5,987
1865	n.d.	5,920
1866	427	1,629
1867	578	1,809
1868	324	1,558
1869	295	1,558
1870	382	1,551
1871	254	1,561
1872	247	1,526
1873	322	1,392
1874	206	1,348
1875	262	1,376
1876	290	1,405
1877	241	1,291
1878	372	1,552
1879	379	1,463

Sources: Annual and biennial reports of the superintendent of public instruction of the State of California, *Journals of the Senate and Assembly of the State of California*, 1864–80. The flow of data from various school districts during this period was often incomplete or sporadic; figures should be considered conservative totals.

Laws not initially intended to deal with Native Americans sometimes became significant over time. Following the end to the legal practice of adopting Native American apprentices, whites kept their Native children as long as they liked under the auspices of the regular child guardianship laws of California. Though it was more difficult to obtain Native American children legally following the 1863 repeal of section 3 of Chapter 133, it was still possible. Native American children living in white households numbered in the hundreds well after the apprenticeship code was repealed. As table 2 reveals, even without an apprenticeship law in effect, hundreds of Native American children younger than five continued to be adopted by whites. Clearly families such as the Chases and their adoption of Emma were actively obtaining Native American children through other methods besides the provisions of Chapter 133.

The data in table 2 are from census records of school districts making plans to educate Native American children living with whites.[107] To attend school, Native children had to be under the guardianship of whites. However, the local school board had to vote to allow their entrance on a case-by-case basis, which the white guardians could appeal. This may explain the lack of evidence that Native children were educated alongside white children in the nineteenth century, even if their guardians were inclined to enroll them. The law did allow Native children from Native American households to attend Indian schools, which were authorized if ten or more families wanted to send their children to school and provided the local board of education approved their request.[108] Based on the records of the superintendent of public instruction for California in the nineteenth century, many Native American children lived in communities that met this requirement, yet few of the children received an education outside of Indian boarding schools or tutoring by private individuals and churches.

Few persons spoke up on behalf Indigenous peoples to their state representatives. One of the rare instances came in 1873, when Lydia B. Lascy wrote to Governor Newton Booth to recognize the state's responsibility for what was being done to Native peoples in California by her fellow citizens. The daughter of an Indian trader and a Quaker mother, Lascy had a great deal of sympathy for Native people in need. Her letter assumed many of the same things her genocidal countrymen assumed in their petitions to the governor. She too believed that Indians were a dying race, but she believed that whites were the disease killing them rather than some divinely ordained fate. She also believed in representative democracy. "In a certain sense," Lascy wrote, "you are placed in your position in order to look to the just rights of all in this State both great and small." Lascy's fellow Euro-Americans, however, asked that the governor remember only the interests of the "great." Lascy implored the governor to do something to ameliorate the condition of the Native Americans in California through labor and education. "But there is one way in which they can be helped," she wrote, "and it is *this* I demand for them at once and without delay."

A Bounty can be paid to them for all the Bear, Fox, and wild cat skins they bring in since there are so many vineyards in this neighborhood the Foxes have become so numerous that we all suffer by them, even coming and carrying off chickens before sun down. Three or four years ago the acorns were killed, as they are this year and the poor creatures died of starvation and exposure at a fearful rate. I kept one family alive for two months they came almost daily to my door for soup, beans and bread. I did not think it possible for two of them to recover health but when spring opened, they slowly gained strength, and overcame their dreadful coughs, at that time I sent some Fox skins to San Francisco for them and could get but twenty five cents a skin for them I paid them fifty cents a skin, for I wanted to encourage them to hunt them, this summer I have bought fifteen skins paying them fifty cents apiece for them and I could obtain but ten cents apiece for them, my means are very limited and I have a family of young children to raise and educate, I am willing to do all in my power toward any and all good but I certainly think that government owed the Indians something. It is probable that one hundred dollars a year would be enough to pay fifty cents apiece for every Fox skin they would bring in and this small amount would enable them to buy powder and lead and flour to replace the acorns destroyed by frost and so avert the suffering which surely lies before them if some small help does not reach them. You will see that there is no time for legislation upon this matter and indeed it is too small for that, still it is not too small to involve a deal of human woe.[109]

Lascy received no reply from Booth, and her plan was never put into effect. In reality, what she proposed would have likely only further eroded the ability of Native people to exist in their small enclaves around California, as the proposal would have certainly destroyed their already fragile ecosystems. Though Booth did not reply, Lascy was aware of what people thought of her idea. In fact she included in her letter the reactions of some people she had shared her idea with: "I spoke to two persons about this matter, one ridiculed me and told me I was foolish to trouble myself about such miserable wretches, the sooner they died the better, another simply remarked 'oh dear! I should think you would be afraid to touch their skins there might be small pox in them?'"[110] Many Californians scoffed at the idea of doing anything to save a doomed people. Oddly enough, while the state sponsored genocide by funding it, making it legal, and pressuring the federal government to assist them, an unlikely group of allies helped, however ineffectively, to stem the tide of genocide in California: select officers and men of the U.S. Army.

7

Federal Bystanders to and Agents of Genocide

We desire only a white population in California; even the Indians amongst us, as far as we have seen, are more of a nuisance than a benefit to the country; we would like to get rid of them.

Californian (1848)

California was seized by U.S. forces on July 7, 1846, as part of the conduct of the war with Mexico. Federal military governors went on to supervise the government of California until December 20, 1849, when the military governor surrendered power to an elected governor and California began life as an unadmitted state.[1] This transition began the genocide of California's Indigenous population in its most pervasive, physical form. As the editors of the *Californian* suggested, most Euro-Americans wanted Native Americans out of California, and the institution of a state government responsive to the wishes of white settlers, ranchers, and miners was a key first step. Admission to the Union followed on September 9, 1850. However, the federal government continued to play a vital role in California: the role of a bystander and enabler of genocide. With as many as 150,000 Native Americans living in the soon-to-be state, California had by far the largest Native American population in the Union. The federal government was the legal authority responsible for dealing with Native peoples, who were considered people of sovereign nations in terms of diplomacy and treaty making. In the course of the next two decades, though, the federal government would prove reluctant to contradict the will of the white citizens in California in their democratically driven campaign of physical extermination through violence, kidnapping, exposure, and compulsory starvation.

Until 1849 the War Department had responsibility for Indian affairs; that year, the duty was transferred to the Interior Department, and federal Indian agents replaced army officers as the primary managers of Indigenous people. These agents, often with little or no experience with Native Americans, remained connected with the War Department in a crucial way, though. Much of federal Indian policy relied on intimidation of Native peoples in the face of treaty violations, usually by citizens rather than Native populations. Treaties were the arbiter of affairs between the United States, represented by its agents and army officers, and Native peoples. Concluded on a nation-to-nation basis, treaties inherently recognized the limited sovereignty of Indigenous nations.[2] California was no different from the rest of the United States in its earliest days as a state. Federal treaty commissioners were chosen in 1850 by the U.S. government to negotiate treaties with Native populations. George Barbour, Redick McKee, and Oliver Wozencraft were selected. None of the three had any knowledge of the Native peoples of California; indeed they had little knowledge of the state itself. The task of the three commissioners, however ignorant of the Indigenous population, was to conclude treaties that would keep Native Americans and Euro-Americans apart, in hopes of avoiding in California the failures common to other treaties made by the United States with Native peoples.

The commissioners needed to make treaties with Native people that set aside federally protected reserves of land for their use. Native title to lands not reserved would be extinguished and the land made public.[3] The arrangement was as much for the protection of Euro-Americans as for Native Americans. Euro-Americans had a long history of violating the treaties their government made with Indigenous populations. When settlers came onto lands protected by treaties or abused, raped, or killed Native peoples, Native Americans often found themselves in nearly hopeless positions, as the U.S. government and its military forces were seldom willing to exact retribution of its citizens who violated the sovereignty of Native nations. Native Americans were forced to either accept these violations, renegotiate treaty terms for a further loss of territory, or fight the intruders themselves, which almost always produced an armed response by the United States to protect its citizens. It was this repetitive scenario that produced what Vine Deloria called the "trail of broken treaties."[4] Following illegal incursions and subsequent Native American armed responses or diplomatic overtures, new treaties were concluded, Native peoples relocated, and the cycle begun again. However, this was not the case in California because of the inability to move Native peoples any farther west.

Americans descended upon California from nearly every direction during the height of the Gold Rush and settled near Native peoples within the first decade of statehood. Native Americans living east of California had for centuries been pushed westward, but in California that option was unavailable, lest one push California's Indigenous population into the Pacific Ocean. It was not that this idea did not cross the Euro-American mind: one proposal sought to strand Native Americans on an island in the Pacific.[5] As the three commissioners entered California in late 1850 and began negotiations in early 1851, then, the situation was already critical given the proximity of the two populations. The failure of concluding successful treaties would be particularly disastrous given the lack of the traditional safety valve available to the populations east of the Sierra Nevada. Unfortunately the treaties were doomed to failure from the start of negotiations.

Complicated by the widespread belief of white citizens that all land in California already belonged to them by right of conquest, reinforced by the provisions of the Treaty of Guadalupe Hidalgo, several other factors prevented lasting peace through the treaty-making process, including communications and the acceptability of the final arrangements by all parties concerned.[6] The commissioners spoke no Native languages, so communication was usually indirect, typically translated one or more times during negotiations. Such translations were frequently imperfect for two reasons. First, it was not always possible to find an interpreter who spoke the language of the Native delegates at the conference. More often, a translator spoke Spanish to Native people who acted as intermediaries. Second, and more important, the concepts being discussed were completely alien to many of the Native attendees. Land cession, the primacy of U.S. sovereignty, and other stipulations contained in the treaties were concepts foreign to California's Native cultures. Indeed words to express such concepts did not always exist. And then there are the realities of the treaties as documents: most of the Native American signatories were illiterate and signed by making their mark (the legally acceptable "X"), and therefore could not have understood fully what it was they had agreed to.[7] Even if one were to assume that everything that transpired between the two sides was fully understood, one would be mistaken in believing that the treaties could be acceptable to both sides.

Euro-Americans, traditionally unwilling to understand Native American people, likely could not understand the role played by diversity within the Native American community in California, perhaps more than anywhere else in the United States. There were more than one hundred different Indigenous dialects, and the state's Native Americans generally eschewed large confederations in favor of local, village-level autonomy, so any attempt to deal with anything less than every group would automatically produce some degree of failure.[8] To have concluded publicly, as the commissioners did, that the eighteen treaties they negotiated between April 29, 1851, and August 22, 1852, fairly extinguished all title to unreserved lands was either patently ignorant or an outright falsehood. Evidence suggests the latter. Some Native Americans were forced to the negotiations at gunpoint; many others never attended, either out of fear or because they were not invited. In the case of the Wiyots of the Humboldt Bay region—future victims of the Indian Island Massacre in 1860—nobody could be found who could translate negotiations into Wiyot, so they were purposely bypassed.[9] Unsurprisingly, the land the Wiyots lived on was covered by one of the treaties anyway. The commissioners knew of these problems, but given the public pressure to conclude agreements and move forward with the transition to white land ownership already progressing unabated, they had little incentive to do otherwise. Indeed according to some scholars, the commissioners did well to conclude treaties that did offer some protections and incentives to Native Americans.[10]

The greatest problem with the treaties did not come from the Native Americans the agreements claimed to represent, but from the United States. The U.S. Senate, despite initially having requested that President Millard Fillmore appoint and dispatch the treaty commissioners, then rejected the concluded treaties outright. Senator John B. Weller, who later became governor of California, was one of the state's two U.S. senators when the treaties came up for ratification in July 1852. Even though California's representatives to the Senate two years before, William Gwin and John C. Frémont, called for the creation of treaties with Native American tribes, California's senators in the summer of 1852 were vehemently against ratification. The California Senate and Assembly met in committee, voted a resolution against ratification, and communicated the unacceptability of the treaties to Weller and Gwin.[11] Weller believed that his duty to the white citizenry of California precluded his ratifying the treaties, despite the good faith negotiations carried on by the United States and the sacrifices the Native leaders had been willing to make to secure a home for their people for generations to come. Weller believed that to proceed with ratification was foolish and shortsighted; white citizens would never abide by the treaties, especially as they already did not support them. Senator Weller was a tool manipulated by the citizenry, to be wielded to express their desires, not his own or the treaty commissioners'. Speaking to his colleagues, he argued against ratification, saying, "We who represent the State of California are compelled, from a sense of duty, to vote for the rejection of the treaties, because we know that it would be utterly impossible for the general government to retain these Indians in undisturbed possession of these reservations. They [the commissioners] knew that those reservations included mineral lands and that, just as soon as it became more profitable to dig upon the reservation than elsewhere, the American man would go there, and the whole army of the United States could not expel the intruders."[12]

Like many of his colleagues, Weller agreed with the white citizens of California that the treaties were too generous. They focused on securing territory and providing material, vocational, and financial assistance to Native Americans, and maintaining them would require millions of dollars.[13] The commissioners had foolishly or benevolently allowed approximately 7 percent of all the land in California to remain legally occupied by Native Americans. In the nineteenth century the federal government derived revenue from, among other things, land sales. Having no income tax, the only way the federal government received a taste of the California Gold Rush was through the sale of public lands bought with gold.[14] Millions of acres left in possession of Native Americans could not generate revenue. Gold, Weller noted, was potentially contained on these unsurveyed lands. As had happened to the Cherokees in Georgia, even when the law was on the side of Native Americans being overrun by gold seekers, enforcement was unlikely when Euro-American interests were set against Native welfare. Weller believed that the government ought not to put itself in conflict with the interests of those who had chosen them to represent their interests. Besides, few whites would lift a hand against another white to defend a Native American.

The ultimate arbiter of the fate of the eighteen treaties was divorced from consideration of California's Indigenous population. Instead the Senate focused on white public opinion, especially as it pertained to government expenditures. Cost concerns were magnified because California prices for food, labor, and other goods were many times higher than in the East, all due to the inflationary effects of the Gold Rush. The costs incurred in negotiating the eighteen treaties, when combined with the expenses of the three commissioners, approached $1 million.[15] And the future costs of meeting treaty terms promised to be many millions of dollars more. The massive overrun in expenses—the commissioners had been budgeted for only $50,000—convinced the Senate that the treaties were deeply flawed and worthy of rejection. California

Senator William Gwin joined Weller in condemnation of the treaties, calling for haste in rendering a decision because many of the Native Americans had already been moved onto reservations guaranteed by as yet unratified treaties and were now consuming government-supplied food and becoming accustomed to their new homes.[16]

In a vote held on July 8, 1852, the U.S. Senate unanimously rejected all eighteen treaties; Weller was absent. Following the vote, the Senate ordered an injunction of secrecy on the treaties, which were hidden from public view until 1905, when hearings on Native American land claims brought them out again. That was the day when the descendants of the treaties' signatories found out that the United States had failed to approve the treaties. When the Senate rejected the treaties, new negotiations did not transpire. Senator William King argued that new negotiations were not required because the old negotiations were not required either. The United States had already received title to all Native American lands by virtue of the Treaty of Guadalupe Hidalgo.[17] Native Americans acted in good faith, moving onto reserved lands or waiting to be moved when the time came, not knowing that the United States refused to accept any binding agreements.[18] Instead the U.S. government took weak steps toward cobbling together a makeshift strategy for administrating Indian affairs in California.

At the same time, implicit in the treaty negotiations was the belief that Native Americans were not citizens of the United States, despite some suggestion that in the Mexican cession, which included California, they were. According to the terms of the Treaty of Guadalupe Hidalgo, citizens of the Republic of Mexico were to be afforded U.S. citizenship unless they chose to retain Mexican citizenship. The United States and its representatives chose to ignore this portion of the treaty where Native Americans were concerned. In Mexico, Native Americans were citizens, at least by the letter of the law; in California, under Mexican rule, this had been the law but not typically the practice. Few Native Americans were afforded the rights and privileges of Mexican citizenship in California. In the transition to U.S. statehood, California state law excluded Native Americans from the benefits of citizenship based on the idea that they had not been citizens of Mexico. California practice rather than Mexican law was the foundation of the exclusion. Former Californios, accepting U.S. citizenship and serving in the constitutional convention and later as legislators, encouraged this willful ignorance. As large landowners dependent on Native peoples populating portions of their grants, there was great potential for land loss to Native Americans imbued with all the rights and protections of citizenship. California's Indigenous population, then, assumed the same status as Native Americans outside of California, who also were not usually considered U.S. citizens.[19]

The means the United States proposed for controlling Native Americans in the absence of treaties was executive action. The Interior Department appointed a superintendent for Indian affairs for California, who was tasked with residing in California and acting as the intermediary for Indian affairs in the state. The superintendent would help identify regional Indian agents and subagents who, with assistance from the U.S. Army, would oversee the management of reservations created by the federal government. Created by executive orders or acts of Congress, the reserves created over the next several decades were not to be the property of Native peoples protected under treaties, but rather federal property where Native Americans were housed.[20] These early reservations bore little resemblance to the reservations of the 1870s and later; they were designed to quickly create locations to remove Native populations, hoping to limit interaction with whites in order to protect the Native Americans. Little attention was paid to education, vocational training, Christianization, or any of the other assimilationist measures imposed at later reservations. Instead these reservations were places where Native Americans could be concentrated in great numbers so that they could be fed and watched over at minimal expense.[21]

The first superintendent, Edward F. Beale, was much like the earlier treaty commissioners: he had no experience with California's Native population and did not speak any of their languages. Beale had supported the treaties before they were rejected, believing them "proper and expedient."[22] Once in California, and operating without treaties,

Beale saw little hope for Native Americans. The Senate had not created a long-term plan to manage Indian affairs in California. Money
to pay the expense of regulating Indian affairs was represented by a
one-time appropriation of $100,000 to be used for the purchase of
blankets, clothes, and other material goods. The money was to placate
the Native Americans until other arrangements might be made.[23] They
were not envisioned as long-term commitments, perhaps in a nod to
the commonly held belief that Native Americans would soon be extinct.
According to Senator Weller, the money represented an attempt "to
soften the blow that strikes the Indians to the earth."[24] In other words,
Native American genocide was inevitable, but it would be better that
they go to their graves as quietly as possible. Because no funds were ear-
marked for food, and perhaps under the influence of the cold logic that
feeding them extended the period of obligation, it is possible the Senate
envisioned the demise of Native Americans through starvation. The new
superintendent, limited by funding and the apathy of lawmakers, would
find an even worse state of affairs following his arrival in California,
with settlers and miners engaged in open conflict with Native peoples
at Mariposa and other places in proximity to gold deposits.[25]

Beale arrived in California in September 1852. His first report to the
Office of Indian Affairs presaged the genocidal results of the planned
neglect adopted by Congress:

Driven from their fishing and hunting grounds, hunted themselves like wild beasts, lassoed, and torn from homes made miserable by want, and forced into slavery, the wretched remnant which
escapes starvation on the one hand, and the relentless Americans
on the other, only do so to rot and die of a loathsome disease, the
penalty of Indian association with frontier civilization. This is no
idle declamation—I have seen it; and I know that they parish by
the hundreds; I know that they are fading away with a startling
and shocking rapidity, but I cannot help them. Humanity must
yield to necessity. They are not dangerous; therefore they must
be neglected.[26]

Beale's words, emanating from the person responsible for Native American health, safety, and welfare in California, did not bode well for the Native people put in his care. Beale did not wholly abandon Native Americans in California, though.

Beale requested an appropriation of $500,000 to help finance reservations and provide military protection to Native people. The cornerstone of his plan was to make each reserve into a farm, where Native Americans would grow food, become self-sustaining, and require little in the way of federal appropriations. Congress countered with an appropriation of $250,000 to be spent on five reservations. Agreements were made between the U.S. government and California's Indigenous population, but were not formal treaties.[27] The first reservation, Sebastian Military Reserve, was established at Tejón at the pass in the Tehachapi of the same name.[28] Opened in 1853, the reservation was on land that was still part of disputed Mexican-era land grants. Years later John Grice, writing to Commissioner of Indian Affairs George Manypenny, described Beale's decision to site it there as a dubious one:

The location was made no doubt for the purpose of fleecing the government out of a large amount of money for the purchase of the title. By referring to a map of this place you will perceive that two thirds of the Reservation is surrounded by tall mountains, the base of which is about three miles distant and the summit about ten. The other third is an opening out to the Tulare Plains in which is located those large lakes, the first of which is about fifteen miles distant. You will perceive that the local attraction forbids its ever raining much on the Reservation at this remote distance from [the] coast, where the soil cannot absorb any moisture from the fogs of the ocean, it is not safe to rely on more than one crop in five. During last winter it frequently rained hard in the mountains and not any on this place. The brook that is supposed to water the Reservation, although large enough to run an overshot mill where it strikes the Reservation is afterwards taken up to a great extent by absorption and evaporation, so that it is not sufficient to irrigate a large crop. In as dry a year as this has been it is impossible to raise a crop by irrigation for there is not water. The soil is generally a poor red gravelly thirsty quality which requires a great deal of water to raise anything.[29]

The government had not only funded the purchase of nearly worthless land, but had located the reservation where there was little chance that the Native people held there would ever be self-sufficient.

Beale became embroiled in charges of fraud and mismanagement. Congress responded by cutting appropriations in half, reducing the approved number of reservations from five to three, and seeking, and getting, Beale's removal as superintendent.[30] As Congress had done in the case of the overruns of the three treaty commissioners, Beale's mistakes led to Native American degradation. Native Americans, not the officials in question, were punished because of the mismanagement. Beale's replacement, Thomas J. Henley, would lead the federal effort in Indian affairs to new lows, helping to enable genocide and limit other federal officers from serving as much more than bystanders to genocide.[31]

The case of Thomas J. Henley and the reservations of the Round Valley region demonstrates how federal apathy allowed citizens and officials of California to organize a genocidal campaign against Native Americans. At first Henley seemed to reverse much of the damage. He received an additional $150,000 appropriation and permission to operate five reservations, as had been originally authorized. He opened the system's second reservation at Nome Lackee, in Colusa County, and he appointed a subagent at Tejón and Nome Lackee charged with managing the Native peoples there and interfacing with federal troops stationed on or near the reservations.[32] Over the next two years Henley opened additional reservations at Mendocino and Klamath and received permission to open temporary reserves at Fresno, King's River, and Nome Cult. By 1858 seven reservations were operating. Henley reported them as smashing successes, and many area newspapers concurred. But the positive reports by Henley and the approval of the press did not sway federal investigators sent to the reserves to perform audits and investigate conflicting reports on conditions beginning in the mid-1850s.

In 1855 John Ross Browne, a U.S. Treasury agent empowered as a special investigator for the federal government, was sent to inspect Indian affairs and conditions on California's reservations.[33] After reviewing reports made by other investigators and conducting a series of investigations and interviews of his own, Browne excoriated Henley and other federal agents associated with Indian affairs in California. In a series of reports to the commissioner of Indian affairs in Washington DC, he described the corruption apparent on the reservations he visited and the utter waste of federal funds. In particular he noted the shady dealings of officials, including Henley. In one telling report, Browne said that private enterprises by the officials were sited on the reservations and seemed to make use of Native labor, federal funds, and land set aside for the care of Native peoples on the reservation.[34] Timber from federal land was being harvested without recompense, and the discharges of a sawmill were destroying the fisheries Native people depended on. Much of this, Browne charged, was for the profit of Henley and other whites living on the reservation.[35] Indeed his many reports charged that those empowered to carry out the operations were inept, ineffective, or downright corrupt.

These corruptions were not petty ones. Funds in the thousands of dollars meant for the subsistence and care of Native peoples were being expended on for-profit ventures of federal employees and whites settled on reservation lands. Some idea of the level of embezzlement Browne charged can be judged by the reservation roll Henley claimed at Mendocino. He listed the population of Native Americans being funded by the federal government as 3,450 in 1857, while Browne discovered in 1858 an actual population of about 250 in various stages of deprivation, ill health, and misery. The pecuniary losses paled in comparison to the human toll. According to Robert White, who witnessed the devastating consequences for Native people on the reservation, "Many of them actually died of starvation. . . . It made his heart bleed to hear them beg for food, without the power to relieve them. Had the force of able bodied men employed upon the mill, been detailed to [assist] the aged and decrepit in procuring food, the probability is they would have suffered less." Such starvation was not by accident at Mendocino in 1858. Browne reported that only Indians who could work in the reservation's legitimate or illegitimate enterprises received food. Families of workers, the aged, and the infirm had to fend for themselves. This and similar testimony was corroborated from multiple sources—some Euro-American, some Native American—by Browne.[36] He went so far as to tell Henley outright of his conclusions, giving him a written copy of the charges. Henley responded by circumventing Browne, sending evidence of his own directly to Washington to refute the claims.[37]

Browne also reported the attitudes of the local white settlers toward Native peoples, clearly describing the people of Humboldt County as having "repeatedly avowed their intention to exterminate them if ever they were let loose upon them again."[38] Never one to shy away from publicity, Browne also published many of his observations in public forums. In Washington officials likely were not surprised by such attitudes in the 1850s and 1860s, as some citizens petitioned the federal government directly, making plain such attitudes in letters and petitions. Even a citizen's petition otherwise quite sympathetic to the plight of Native peoples—the 140 signers were willing to admit there were some *good* Indians deserving protection—nonetheless readily admitted that "settlers have hunted the Indians and in most cases killed them indiscriminately when found."[39] A petition from citizens around Fresno and Tulare advised one Indian agent that they had undertaken Indian removal on their own authority. The petition demanded the removal of any remaining Indians and called on the agent to ensure that those already removed not return, or they would be "harshly dealt with" and "summarily treated."[40] To make matters worse, the Native people in question were forced onto the Fresno Indian Farm, where there was no food to feed them, nor indeed enough to feed the people already housed there.[41] Federal officials clearly knew of the dangers faced by Native populations from these official and unofficial sources, but beyond the creation of the reservations, Indian policy did not undergo any radical changes in the 1850s and 1860s.

Browne did not leave the intelligence he provided to the government solely in their hands. He publicized many of his negative opinions of Indian affairs in California and the West to an intrastate audience in Bay Area newspapers and nationally in *Harper's Monthly*. Reading one of Browne's diatribes against ineffectual Indian policy would leave few in doubt that problems of some type existed on the reservations at least. Browne also publicly objected to the neglect and violence directed against Native people, and risked public censure to state as much in newspapers and magazines.[42] He made clear to his readers that inhumanity characterized dealings with Native people, pointing out that reservations were often expending their foodstuffs feeding whites, not Native peoples, and that many on the reservation were being slowly starved to death or dying of disease brought on by malnutrition or their weakened state. According to the scholars Frank Chalk and Kurt Jonassohn, "genocide by starvation" was the most significant form of genocide directed at Native North Americans. Whether due to the often insufficient food supplies on a reservation, or the purposeful withholding of food from those who did not labor, or destruction of traditional food supplies off the reserves by settlers, ranchers, and hunters, the resultant starvation had a domino effect in California. As has been seen in other examples of Native American genocide in North America, disease proliferated in hunger-weakened populations, and birthrates dropped in the face of rising mortality. Though not quite the romanticized, tragic tale of the destruction of the buffalo and the genocidal results to the Indigenous population of the Great Plains, nonetheless the destruction of elk herds, rattlesnakes, rabbits, acorns, and other flora and fauna had no less devastating a consequence for California's Indigenous population.[43]

Those not perishing slowly by starvation or disease on reservations sometimes died by violence, including approximately 150 men, women, and children housed on the Nome Cult Indian Farm. Browne argued, "What neglect, starvation, and disease have not done, has been achieved by the co-operation of American settlers in the great work of extermination."[44] Browne understood that a combination of neglect and violence coordinated to bring about extermination of Native peoples was transpiring. It was this type of exposé that typified Browne's writing and made him unpopular with many. According to the scholar Peter Wild, Browne was notable as a writer who "irked both local westerners feasting at the public trough and logrolling politicians in Washington by producing reports that exposed the corruption riddling federal agencies."[45] Still Browne was not wholly the friend of Native people. He himself took two "Digger Indian" children from the Nome Lackee Reservation, naming them Friday and Sally, and later took a third child—an Apache girl, Lupe—from Arizona. All were made to work as servants for his family.[46] Nonetheless Browne and some federal officials like him clearly demonstrate that the federal government had employees that worked diligently to achieve some semblance of humane treatment for Native people, attempting to get them the funds set aside for their care and calling for reservation boundaries to be secured against white encroachment. Although Browne's calls were not heeded, his reports did attract some further investigations.

The government took Browne seriously enough to dispatch other investigators to confirm his observations. Godard Bailey visited the reserves in 1858 and found that Henley's reports were gross overstatements of the level of success. Bailey called the reservations failures, reporting that although Native Americans did indeed live there, they were few and living in squalor. At best the reserves were panaceas that provided no real relief and no hope for the future.[47] What Bailey found was a scenario that exemplified the challenge faced by California's Indigenous populations in all regions with reservations. The federal government had left Indian affairs in the hands of Henley and a few subagents, with little financial support, separated by several thousand miles from Washington. The result was that the state of California was able to exercise a great degree of control over Indian affairs, responding to the demands of its citizens by pressuring federal agents and army officers to side with the settlers and miners against the local Native peoples. As Bailey observed the reservations in 1858, what he may not have known was the complex interplay of soldiers, Indian agents, settlers, volunteer companies, and Native peoples that created much more misery than was caused by a simple dearth of reservation funding.

Henley and his subordinates were not the only federal officials embroiled in the conflict between white Americans and Native people in California. U.S. Army officers and enlisted men served continuously in California beginning with the 1846 occupation during the Mexican War. Army officers were the recipients of all sorts of requests in the first few decades of statehood, from the governor down to ordinary citizens, as whites attempted to harness the might of the U.S. Army to deal with Native Americans. The openness of the genocidal intent of white American citizens was obvious to senior army commanders early on in California.

Ethan Allen Hitchcock was an experienced army officer when he was posted to California in 1851 and given command of the Pacific Division. A West Point graduate, a veteran of campaigns against the Seminoles in Florida, and a former Indian agent, Hitchcock was a critic of U.S. expansionist policy in the Mexican War and an opponent of the way Native Americans were dealt with by settlers and governments. Although prevented from public criticism of the government by his officer's oath and the accepted limits placed on individual officers against criticizing their superiors, Hitchcock kept a diary of his dissatisfaction with the state of affairs in the West, particularly California. As such, he was a difficult officer to deal with for Indian agents and state officials. He was also a keen observer of the brutal and hostile attitude of white Californians toward Native Americans. Perhaps the most disturbing moment of General Hitchcock's tour in California came on July 31, 1852. While visiting a Methodist minister in San Francisco, Hitchcock met a man also calling at the minister's home. The unnamed man, who seemed outwardly respectable at first, turned out to suggest something that Hitchcock could scarcely believe would be uttered in the presence of the minister. The man told the minister and the general his suggestion for dealing with California's Indigenous population: "Providence designed the extermination of the Indians and . . . it would be a good thing to introduce the small-pox among them!" While Hitchcock noted that the minister and he certainly did not share such a sentiment, the general also grimly admitted that it was all too true that many Californians would agree with the man.[48] Perhaps unexpectedly army officers and their troops often played the role of protectors of Native Americans and deterred settlers, ranchers, and miners in their attempts to commit genocide against Native peoples. Hitchcock, being in command of the entire Pacific Division, was able to influence many of his subordinates to carefully consider actions against Native people, although the immense size of the command hampered this effort. Whether or not an officer was free to direct his energies in support of Native Americans depended largely on the orders he received from superior officers in charge of local commands.

Some soldiers found themselves entangled in a miasma of bureaucratic technicalities and legal niceties that made it nearly impossible to please settlers or care for Native people in their charge. As an example of the former, Capt. H. M. Judah, commanding officer of the Fort Jones Reserve, where he was also acting Indian agent, attempted to get Superintendent Henley to send food and supplies for Native people there—some 150 persons, mostly women and children, who were the survivors of massacres by whites in the area. They were near to starving and freezing to death as winter approached, but Judah's several attempts to get Henley to aid them were hampered by ill-organized lines of government communication. As Judah waited in frustration, only army rations and the generosity of some local white settlers fed and clothed the Native people. Ultimately his attempts failed because of the bureaucratic policies adopted by Henley, who refused to send the supplies, claiming that the Native population of Fort Jones was to be relocated to Nome Lackee, having ordered as much months prior. Their refusal to go to Nome Lackee essentially exonerated the government from any further liability. Henley concluded his letter to Judah, "I have no doubt of the mutinous character of those Indians, but I regard the policy of feeding those who refuse to go to the Reserves as injurious to the policy of colonization as contemplated by the system now in operation."[49] Unilaterally and against the advice of Captain Judah, Henley decided to let them starve rather than acquiesce.

In a case of legal niceties, soldiers who arrested a white rancher named Vanpelt for the murder of an unarmed Native man were forced to turn him loose, even though the man had admitted to the killing. He was freed on the technicality that it could not be proven that the Native man in question had a written pass to be in the area, despite the fact that such a pass had actually been issued by a reservation employee. Indeed a witness confirmed that the Native man carried not only a written pass, but also a white flag. S. G. Whipple, the Indian agent reporting the matter, called on Henley to press the federal government to create some means to affect the "punishment of outrages committed upon innocent Indians by evil disposed Whites" in federal courts.[50] No such system was forthcoming.

In the Round Valley region, Maj. Edward Johnson and his subordinates, Lt. William Carlin and Lt. Edward Dillon, attempted to relieve the suffering of Native peoples by interposing themselves between local settlers and threatened Native groups. These officers of the U.S. Sixth Infantry, assigned to operations based at Fort Bragg, were tasked with protecting Native Americans from Euro-Americans, and vice versa, in and around the reservations at Mendocino, Nome Cult, and Nome Lackee. In short order, the trio came to be despised by Superintendent Henley, reservation agents, and white citizens of the region. Johnson was a West Point graduate with twenty years of experience and several citations for bravery. He assigned Dillon to command the detachment stationed at the Nome Lackee Reserve. When Johnson and Dillon arrived in Round Valley to establish their post, ranchers had just massacred forty Native people in retaliation for stock stealing.[51] The pair quickly found out why the area was such a hotbed of Native American resistance by the local Yuki people.

Whites in Round Valley loathed Johnson and Dillon, who sided with Native Americans whenever local whites committed depredations or injustices against them. The two officers had no tolerance for vigilante justice. Dillon was especially unpopular. When the young lieutenant caught a white man clubbing a Native person on the reservation, he arrested the man and imprisoned him against the advice of the Indian agent at Nome Cult Farm. Soon a group of angry citizens entered the reservation and threatened to break the man out of the guardhouse if Dillon did not release him. Dillon invited them to try. The citizens armed themselves with both weapons and a petition calling for the release of the man. Dillon refused the petition. The tension was ended that night, when the man broke out of jail and left the reservation. Because Dillon had no power to arrest the man off federal property—another legal technicality that led to injustice for Native peoples—the matter was essentially at an end. Major Johnson believed that Dillon had done the right thing but cautioned him to leave future arrests to the reservation officials; the Interior Department's appointed agents had jurisdiction over Indian affairs, not the army.[52]

Superintendent of Indian Affairs Thomas J. Henley supported the settlers of Round Valley in this and other disputes. This was not surprising given that Henley's two sons were members of the angry mob of white settlers. Henley wrote a letter of complaint to the War Department about Dillon's arrest of the citizen, claiming that "only the escape of Dillon's prisoner had prevented a fight between soldiers and civilians." A rebuke directed at Major Johnson from the War Department followed. Johnson was to ensure that his command did not interfere with citizens off the reservation and to follow the directions of the Indian agents and superintendent while on the reservation. Dillon was empowered only to escort violators of reservation property off its grounds. He was specifically prohibited from arresting any of the citizenry. In other words, Johnson and Dillon could do little to stop settlers from harming Native peoples, save by physical interposition or bluff.[53]

Johnson wrote his own letters of complaint to his superiors. He believed it impossible to protect Native Americans from the settlers if the only way to do so was by physically being there to intercede. Johnson argued that the only way to stop stock raiding was to end famine among the Native population. He believed that getting all the Native Americans of the valley onto the reservation would solve the problem of starvation.[54] But few Native Americans showed interest in living at Nome Cult. The reservation was already familiar to some, and word had spread among local Native groups that food was scarce there, and disease common. White settlers often went to Nome Cult to catch and kill Native Americans for stock theft, whether or not they were guilty, and for other, darker purposes. In one particularly despicable case, a settler named Murphy went onto the reserve and raped a Yuki girl "12 or 14 years of age, perhaps younger." Native men attempted to stop the man, but he was armed; being housed on the Nome Cult Reservation, the Native American men were unarmed.[55] The soldiers were powerless to apprehend the man.[56]

Following an investigation by the federal government, including the report tendered by Bailey, Henley was sacked for mismanagement and accusations of fraud. The press carried Henley's side of the story. Among other counteraccusations, he accused Johnson of cowardice and slander. The only outcome that benefited Native Americans was that many soldiers and their officers became reticent about attacking or apprehending Native Americans accused of crimes by reservation personnel or white settlers. Senior army commanders soon became aware of the problems faced by their subordinates, and also began to decline to aggressively prosecute campaigns against Native Americans at the requests of settlers or their representatives in state government. In June 1859 Major Johnson reported that the citizens of Round Valley had been engaged in a bloody, self-serving private war against local Yukis. Johnson claimed that more than six hundred Yukis of all ages and both sexes had been killed since 1857 and argued, "The Indians and not the Americans require protection." He noted that because of the actions of Jarboe's volunteers, especially their destruction of villages, regular subsistence practices had ceased. Only stock theft kept Native Americans from starvation.[57] But to take stock meant a death sentence for Native people caught in the act or for those caught in the vicinity, guilty or no.

As fear grew among Native Americans, Johnson and Dillon convinced them to seek protection on the reservation. However, once there, these hundreds of refugees found little food and a prevalence of disease. From eight to ten Native Americans were dying per day from disease and malnutrition. Conditions such as these regularly drove Native people off reservations out of self-preservation.[58] According to the reports of John Ross Browne and others, it was sometimes the practice to allow Native peoples off the reservation to forage when, whether from mismanagement, corruption, or poor harvest, the government reservations could not feed those whom they had promised sustenance.[59] These foragers would then face extermination by local whites.

The practice of kidnapping women and children from the reservation also continued. Much of this problem can be attributed to Henley, who had been hiring out Native Americans as laborers or allowing them to be indentured.[60] Henley also led parties of reservation employees to forcibly bring in local Native Americans. In one instance, Henley either killed or had killed a lame Native man who "looked like a bad Indian."[61] Further undermining the attempt to make reservations a safe haven were volunteer companies, especially those seeking bounties. Johnson called Jarboe and his men "assassins," as they used area reservations as a site to collect and kill Native Americans.[62] Given the reports by Browne, Henley had reason to see such companies as a threat to his illicit businesses on the reservation, for which Native people served as the unpaid labor force. Many white residents of the region, though, believed their actions were justified, both morally and legally.

Charles H. Eberle, who had moved to Round Valley in 1857, believed his neighbors were righteous, upstanding people. Eberle participated in the petition process that demanded aid of the governor against the local Indigenous population. He was also a local magistrate, empowered as a justice of the peace for the area.[63] Under state law, he had the power to deal with Native Americans in the state, separate from the federal government or the state courts. When the state legislature dispatched an investigative committee to the region, Eberle was a key witness. In his deposition he staunchly defended the actions of his fellow citizens as righteous responses to thefts and murders. Eberle knew of only three deaths in the region, those of William Mantle, John McDaniel, and John Bland, and used the three as examples of how good men had been needlessly killed.[64] Mantle, whom Eberle described as a "quiet, peaceable man" was well known to him, and Eberle claimed that he "never knew him to molest Indians in any way." John Bland, the most recent man killed, was also described as a "quiet peaceable man."[65] Eberle's portrayal, though, contradicted what was widely known about the men, who were all known to have abused Native Americans in the area.[66] Eberle and other citizens believed Bland was killed by Yukis from Nome Cult Farm. When asked how he knew this, Eberle recalled that the last time Bland had been seen, he was in the company of a Native person from the reservation whom Bland had taken to be his guide on a hunt. Bland never returned, but a few weeks later Eberle spotted the Native American guide and captured him at gunpoint. The Native agreed to take Eberle to see two other Natives who knew of Bland's last whereabouts. Eberle went to the reservation, met with one of the men, and then arrested him. Eberle delivered the Native American man into the custody of George Rees, the reservation agent. While Eberle sought out an interpreter, Rees held the man in custody. By the time Eberle returned with an interpreter, though, the prisoner had escaped. Through their Native American interpreter, Eberle and Rees learned that a Native woman on the reservation knew where Bland's body could be found. Capt. Walter Jarboe and his Eel River Rangers were summoned to go out and recover Bland's remains.

As news of Bland's death spread, Eberle and local white citizens pieced together an account of the last days of Bland's life. Apparently Bland had gone on his hunt and returned successfully. According to people in Tehama, Bland made a visit some time after the hunt. While away, his locked cabin was broken into and burglarized. Bland found a couple of Yuki people from the reservation wearing some of his clothes. He did not report the incident to U.S. soldiers, the reservation agents, or the magistrate. Instead he captured the two men and whipped them.

The Native Americans, however, did follow the proper procedures: their leaders complained to Major Johnson. Johnson attempted to locate and arrest Bland, but Bland evaded capture. According to James Wilsey, a local stock raiser, Bland spotted Major Johnson's patrol, and he was forced to flee. The soldiers did find a "rather a good looking squaw" at his home, whom they took back to the reserve. Wilsey noted that he too sometimes had "squaws" at his home. Although soldiers had never tried to recover them, some of the reservation agents had. The woman liberated from Bland's home was put under guard at the army outpost on the reservation.[67] Major Johnson's attempts to arrest Bland angered the white citizenry, including Eberle. Despite several years of "constant depredations" by local Native Americans, including stock raiding, the soldiers refused to offer the level of protection demanded by the community.[68]

Wilsey's own words belied the certainty with which settlers and ranchers charged Native Americans with crimes:

This winter two years ago I lost I think between 25 and 50 head of cows steer and calves I know some of them were killed by Indians. I have seen some of the carcasses. I have been on expeditions against the Indians. I believe they were all killed by the Indians—I have lost stock off and on ever since. The last I lost I think was in January last. Last winter I lost about as many more. Since then I have lost a good many but I cannot say how many. Of my stock and those under my charge I brought 700 head into the valley.[69]

Like many of his fellow stock raisers, Wilsey let the animals roam free over the rugged terrain of the valley. Despite the many perils animals faced, from predators to floods to falls to non-Native thieves, all losses were put down to Indians. According to one reservation agent, whites were the greatest predators of all. George Rees claimed, "I know there are large bands of stock driven in to the mountains by American men which range from 7 to 10 miles from the Valley."[70] These white cattle rustlers, not Indians, preyed upon loose stock too. Despite public knowledge that white outlaws operated in the region, Bland's death was inexorably linked to Indian savagery, just as were stock losses.

Lieutenant Dillon captured one of the Native American men believed responsible for Bland's death. To the chagrin of Eberle and others, Dillon refused to issue summary justice, and instead had the Native man transported out of Round Valley to await further instructions. Dillon was likely aware of the justice the citizens had in mind. In the months previous to Bland's death, the Eel River Rangers had been operating in the region with a self-confidence born of public consent. Eberle described the volunteer company system as legal, efficient, and responsive to community needs. Following the petition process, Jarboe and his Eel River Rangers went into action. "When stock was stolen," Eberle said, "the owner informed Jarboe of the fact and he acted accordingly and went I presume according to his orders." Whatever Jarboe had been doing, Eberle claimed that it was working. "I have not heard of so many depredations in the last two months and I think the settlers have been benefited by the operation of this company. I think the most of the Indians have gone back towards Long Valley."[71] Though Eberle had never been a member of the Eel River Rangers, he assured the state that Jarboe acted properly in all respects, so far as he knew. In fact Eberle believed Jarboe and his company were sure to be needed in future. The Native people previously driven out were believed to be coming back from Long Valley, and the soldiers were useless. Dillon and his men protected Native Americans, not whites.

William Hildreath, a member of the Eel River Rangers, concurred with Eberle's assessment. Hildreath was part of the effort to punish the Yukis following the death of Bland. They killed eleven men and captured ninety-eight more men, women, and children in a series of raids. Hildreath claimed that they were "sure to always get the guilty Indians and not punish Innocent ones."[72] How Jarboe and the Rangers determined guilt or innocence, however, went unsaid. Certainly evidence existed that local whites, if not the Rangers themselves, deviated from any practice attempting to afford true determination of guilt or innocence. Just days after the discovery of Bland's remains, a Native boy went missing from Nome Cult. A few days later the dead boy was brought back by the local Native people. Rees recalled, "His throat had been cut and he had also been shot."[73] According to Hildreath, such treatment would have been impossible; Native Americans captured by the Rangers, he claimed, were well treated. But what represented good treatment for Native Americans in the mind of Hildreath was quite disturbing. Years later, in 1865, he murdered a Native American he claimed as his property. Finding his alleged servant engaged in work for another settler, Hildreath roped the Native man's hands together, tied the other end to his saddle, and spurred his horse. The horse, panicked by the screaming man, bolted out of control, throwing Hildreath and dragging the Native man away in terrible agony. Eventually the horse was caught, but not before the bound man "was terribly mangled, his arms being twisted off his shoulders."[74] Hildreath was later released without punishment. In his testimony to the state legislature, however, he was convinced of the generosity and justice the Rangers meted out: the wounded were treated and prisoners were taken. Prisoners were not sent to Nome Cult, however, but to the Mendocino Reservation.[75] The Ranger's apparent goal was not to contain Native Americans near their community, but to remove them altogether by death or deportation. To Native people, this represented much more than confinement on a reservation. Mendocino was not their home, and the relocation was rather a wholesale abduction of a Yuki community.

Removal to a reservation in California involved many hardships for Native peoples after their arrival as well. Hildreath, like many settlers and ranchers in Round Valley, had intimate knowledge of the reservation's operation. Hildreath had worked on the reservation for a short time. He admitted that conditions were not good at Nome Cult, but he claimed that Native Americans who performed the work they were directed to did well enough. For eight hours of work, Hildreath recalled, a worker received six ears of corn. Native Americans who did not, or presumably could not, work received nothing. Native Americans were not allowed to eat meat.[76] Such treatment made it hard to keep Native Americans content on the reservation or remain patient in the face of other difficulties, or resist the onslaught on their population by Euro-American diseases.

According to Lieutenant Dillon, settlers and ranchers used Nome Cult Farm's pastures to graze their own animals, obtained Native Americans for labor, and cut through the reservation when traveling to the valley beyond. When reservation agents put up fences to redirect whites around the reserve, the settlers and ranchers responded by pulling the fences down, though they accused Native Americans of doing so. Dillon investigated the matter, finding not only downed fences, but fresh wagon tracks leading through the openings. The Yukis did not use wagons, but local settlers did. The problem represented much more than simple trespassing. Dillon testified, "From observation and conversation with various parties I am firmly of the opinion that it is the object of certain parties to get rid of these Indians on the reservation for the purposes of possession themselves of the land occupied by the Government and to still further to extend the stock range."[77] George Rees, the overseer of Nome Cult Farm, described the resultant damage as loose stock owned by whites trampled or consumed crops. Two white squatters had even gone so far as to build homes on reservation property.[78]

White men looking for housekeepers and seamstresses found a way to get some Nevada women to leave Nome Cult, perhaps by offering better food or pay than what the reserve provided. Two Native American girls may have been abducted for these reasons. But they may have been taken for more disturbing reasons as well. Rees recalled, "One of them is about sixteen and the other twenty years of age. They are tolerably good looking. They appear to be contented on the Reserve." Rees and his men were forced to recover the two girls from the homes of local white men. Rees had to lock up the girls each night, to both punish them and keep them from being taken again. Despite a padlocked door, the girls went missing again, one of whom Rees later recovered at the home of James Wilsey. The problem of abduction was an old one. As early as 1855 Superintendent Thomas Henley was fighting against kidnappings of Native Americans from reservations. According to a newspaper account, Henley discovered a group of men who were abducting Native American children, selling them "from $50 to $250 each."[79] Ironically Henley's son later abducted Native Americans and refused to return them. In one memorable case, George Henley abducted perhaps the most valuable Native worker at Nome Cult and refused to give him up. Only with the help of Lieutenant Dillon and his men was the man recovered by force. Rees also objected to the behavior of other white men formerly associated with the reservation. Like George Henley, former reservation agents such as Simon Storms used reservation Native Americans to work their lands as unpaid labor, sending them back to the reservation for feeding or when not needed.[80] George Henley, Storms, and others, however, were not ashamed of their behavior and felt they had done nothing wrong. George Henley in fact complained to state officials that Rees had stolen his Native boy back from him.[81] Simon Storms admitted that he attempted to stop Nome Cult reservation agent Vincent Geiger and Lieutenant Dillon from placing Native Americans he wanted on the reservation.[82] Other men, so-called "squaw men," used Native women and girls for sexual purposes, with and without their consent.

"Squaw men" were a subset of white males throughout California. These were single men who kept Native American women or girls in their homes, and were believed to be engaged in either forced or consensual sexual relations with them. It is unlikely, though, that much concern existed among Euro-Americans for the Native women or girls. In one telling example, occurring in 1881, a local newspaper suggested that the way to avoid future problems was to keep Native men from getting drunk, in which state they had the bravery to avenge the rape of Native women and girls.[83] Many communities despised "squaw men" as a pollutant of Americanness and as a source of trouble with Native Americans, and the attention devoted to their elimination became an important element in Native American genocide.[84] Indian savagery, apparently, was contagious. Some communities went as far as to create laws against white men cohabitating with Native Americans.[85] Most communities were more informal, however. At the town of Antelope

Mill, it was discovered that "pale-faced digger" thieves were encouraging and allying with some Native Americans in the region to commit crimes.[86] In Butte County "squaw men" or those pretending to be them were committing crimes, hoping to shift blame onto Native Americans.[87] The strongest public warnings to "squaw men" appeared in newspapers, such as the notice published in the *Red Bluff Beacon* of May 26, 1858: "For those filthy and abandoned beasts in human shape, who have squaws, with whom they live in concubinage, we hereby give notice to every one of them, that they and their bitter-halves have to be parted asunder, or both must leave the country. This is the only warning we will give them, and they had better take it, for if they continue to keep their squaws about them, we shall view them as nothing better than Indians themselves, and act accordingly."

The *Chico Weekly Courant*, perhaps the most vehement champion of Native American genocide in its repeated calls for extermination, adopted a similar line for "squaw men": "Exterminate the [Indian] fiends, together with those who . . . live with their squaws."[88] While abject racism was certainly part of the hatred for "squaw men," fear of Native American retribution for the kidnapping of their women was an even more important issue in fostering cycles of violence between Natives and whites.

Over a year before Bland's death, George Lane of Cold Spring Valley had a Native woman and boy in his household. In April 1858 the woman and boy made their escape. Shortly thereafter Native American warriors raided Lane's home and the homes of some of his neighbors. The citizens in the area got up a volunteer company and killed fifteen Native people in retaliation, despite the fact that Lane had started the trouble.[89] The problems created by such men help explain the resentment directed at Euro-Americans by Native Americans all over the state. In the case of John Bland, who was charged with abducting a Native woman, federal authorities tempered the public outcry for revenge with knowledge of what Bland had done to the local Yukis.

In the summer of 1859 Major Johnson received a report that Bland had abducted two Native American men from Nome Cult. Johnson ordered the arrest of Bland and the seizure of any Native people he had with him. Several attempts were made to apprehend Bland over the course of the next few weeks. Johnson sent a corporal and a detachment of men to Bland's home. Seeing the troops approaching, Bland made his escape. At Bland's house the soldiers found only a lone Native woman.[90] According to Charles McLane, the "squaw" had been in Bland's home for two months. He also observed, "She was better looking than most . . . squaws." McLane seemed to believe she was with Bland voluntarily.[91] But evidence received by Johnson and Dillon stated that she had been taken by force, the woman herself telling the soldiers and Indian agents that she had no desire to return to Bland's house. Several nights later Bland appeared armed on the reservation and abducted the woman again. She resisted him and escaped into the mountains. Less than two months later, sometime in late September or early October 1859, Bland was dead.[92] Two scenarios must have seemed possible to Dillon. One possibility was that the Native woman, making her escape, returned to her people, who took vengeance upon Bland. Another possibility was that the Native American man whipped by Bland for theft had done much the same thing, with the same result. In either case, in the eyes of the two officers justice had been served. Perhaps they even felt Bland's death might serve as a lesson to citizens in the region terrorizing the reservations, frightening off the Indigenous population situated there.

Given the unsecured nature of the reservation, it is no wonder that Native Americans often fled from Nome Cult. The world they fled into, though, was now patrolled by the Eel River Rangers and troops under Dillon. Each man struggled to accomplish his aims in the face of opposition by the other. Most in the community around Nome Cult clearly sided with Jarboe, and despite the contempt many must have felt for Bland, approved of the retribution exacted on Native peoples. In fact local newspapers carried Bland's killing without comment on his earlier activities. Instead they published accounts of the finding of his burned remains, which one newspaper described as the product of his being burned at the stake.[93] This is not surprising; the newspapers of the region never sided with Native Americans and had already criticized Dillon and Johnson several times. The most recent occasion had been in the *Red Bluff Beacon*. In a reprinted letter criticizing Johnson and Dillon for insisting on evidence of guilt before killing Native Americans, an anonymous man called for the community to get behind the Eel River Rangers. The correspondent wrote from Nome Cult and was apparently one of the squatters living on the reservation illegally. His suggested course of action jibed well with his choice of residence: the gallantry and efficiency of Jarboe's Eel River Rangers should be exercised in destroying the Native American threat.[94] Jarboe and his Rangers did take the field in a campaign of several months throughout the region. During the campaign, Jarboe appealed to Lieutenant Dillon for assistance in capturing or killing local Indigenous people. Dillon refused him twice.[95] After the second refusal, Jarboe warned Dillon to keep all the Nome Cult Native people safely on the reserve, because all others they found were fair game, to be killed indiscriminately.[96] Events soon transpired to tip the balance further in the favor of Jarboe and his supporters.

The army closed posts in regions of northern California where Native Americans needed protection, including some within Major Johnson's area of responsibility. Johnson, disheartened by this, requested an extended leave. He left California and did not return. Johnson's second in command, Lt. William Carlin, took over. If locals had sighed with relief that the unsympathetic Johnson was gone, their relief was short-lived. If anything, Carlin was even more vociferous in his condemnation of white civilians in the region. He and Dillon continued to operate as Johnson had. Carlin arrested a white man for taking a Native woman by force from the reservation. But the new reservation agent not only reversed Carlin's order, he also let the man take the woman. Angry, Carlin kept a close watch on the agent and soon discovered that the agent was using government property to run a whiskey trade. The liquor was apparently being sold by another federal employee out of the local post office.[97]

Following the inauguration of Governor John Downey, citizens in

Round Valley bombarded the new governor with tales of woe blamed on hostile Native Americans and apathetic federal forces. Downey responded to his petitioners by demanding an explanation of the army high command in California. Dillon was called in by his superiors to help respond to Downey's queries. He contradicted local citizens by reporting that only one white had been killed in the past year, trying to kidnap a Native woman, and no stock was unaccounted for. Dillon argued that the settlers were attempting to obtain the rest of the Native American land in the region through the extermination of the Indigenous population. Carlin supported Dillon's opinions in his own message to Downey, and added new criticisms of the reservation agents. In addition to the liquor trade being run from the reservations, agents were using the reservation to provide brothel services to locals and also allowed squatters to occupy federal lands reserved for Native Americans.[98] But the complaints lodged by the two army officers—again, clear evidence of genocide offered to the government by its own agents—fell on deaf ears. Carlin departed California in the spring of 1860, disgusted as Johnson had been. Lieutenant Dillon was now in command.

Not long after assuming command, Dillon countered more wild claims by settlers of the Round Valley region. After settlers claimed in petitions that they had lost $100,000 in property to Indian depredations, Dillon researched the claims and concluded that losses were less than one-third that amount. Settlers then made complaints against the army officers, especially Dillon. One settler claimed that Dillon was rooting for the Native Americans, even helping them.[99] New developments in 1860 gave citizens opposed to Dillon something to be pleased about. Following the accidental death of the Mendocino reservation agent, Dillon was made temporary Indian agent of Mendocino Reservation while a replacement was being sought. He was forced to leave Round Valley while serving as temporary agent, leaving the Yukis unprotected. He believed that slaughter would ensue if Nome Cult and the local Yuki people were left unprotected.[100] The new posting as Indian agent, in conjunction with his military powers, gave him the authority to make important changes at the Mendocino reserve. Nome Cult's loss was Mendocino's gain. Dillon quickly fired most of the reservation employees, including the doctor, who was believed to be doing Native Americans harm rather than good. Dillon also took advantage of his temporary position as a member of the bureaucracy of the Interior Department and sent a detailed report of problems at the reservations in the region to the commissioner of Indian affairs.[101]

Dillon was in a position many army officers wished to be in during the second half of the nineteenth century. Most army officers involved in Native-white conflict after 1849 believed that civilians appointed to act as Indian agents were self-interested, corrupt, inefficient, inconsistent, and the source of tensions with Native Americans. However, the Board of Indian Commissioners opposed attempts to move control back to the military, successfully resisting all attempts to make permanent the postings of military men as Indian agents.[102] White citizens typically used their rights and voice in a democratic society to further their cause over Native Americans. Some officers believed this was particularly true in outlying regions. Capt. James Lovell called the settlers who falsely claimed affronts to them by Native Americans "the buckskin gentry." Lovell believed that much of the trouble between whites and Native Americans stemmed from this practice. But Dillon was unable to stop much of the trouble, including the most heinous practice of all, child abduction. When armed expeditions and combat between the army and Native Americans did happen, Dillon noted that civilians swept in behind them to gather up orphaned children. In 1861 he reported that he knew of at least fifty instances when Native children were kidnapped and sold to local settlers. This crime against Native Americans further damaged Native-white relations.[103] And it is clear evidence of a facet of genocide: stealing children to effect cultural and group destruction. In California it was a ubiquitous practice, especially where Native American adults were being killed in great numbers by disease, violence, exposure, or starvation. Since 1857, some local residents estimated, as many as five hundred Native Americans had been killed in Round Valley alone.[104]

Despite this grim statistic, the army outpost in Round Valley was closed in June 1861. A new commander deemed it an inefficient placement of troops, situated far from resupply. Dillon left the U.S. Army in spring 1861 and went east to join the Confederate Army.[105] The *Red Bluff Beacon* noted Dillon's departure with glee in an article on July 18, 1861:

Glad to Hear It—We notice among our eastern items that Lieut. Dillon's name has been stricken from the army list. . . . This brave officer, was the Lieutenant in charge of a small detachment of soldiers sent out to Round Valley two years ago, to protect the citizens of that section from the incursions of Indians; but instead of carrying out his instructions he protected the Indians, and took sides with them whenever they murdered or robbed the settlers in Mendocino county. Instead of chastising the red devils, he encouraged them in all their lawless acts, and used his authority to harass the settlers. We are glad he has been dismissed. He was a disgrace to the army.

The Yukis and other Native Americans housed in Round Valley were left completely at the mercy of the Indian agent and the local settlers. And Indian agents were certainly no guarantee of safety.

Many of the men employed by the United States to run Indian reservations quickly left their posts. They had few incentives to stay. One common factor in the departure of several agents was the acquisition of land near reservations. Agents such as Vincent Geiger, Thomas Henley, Edward Beale, and Edward Stevenson found their pay low, their problems many, but their opportunities great. Edward A. Stevenson surrendered his post as Indian agent in order to develop his land in Tehama County. As the *Red Bluff Beacon* asked rhetorically, "What is six thousand dollars a year among savages compared with the comforts of a home like the Colonel's, with his family around him?"[106] Of course what the *Beacon* did not mention was that he was still surrounded by Native Americans. Stevenson brought Native people from the reservation to work his land. But working for one of these men at their private home was no guarantee of safety. One Native American boy, tired of abusive treatment by Stevenson, attempted to burn down his house. The boy was caught and taken for trial in Red Bluff, where a mob of Stevenson's neighbors seized the ten-year-old and lynched him. The newspaper in Red Bluff criticized the mob, not for hanging the boy, but for not letting the court order the hanging.[107] Beale, Geiger, and Henley, like Stevenson, all obtained land near reservations and used Native Americans as unpaid labor to make their fortunes. In their time as reservation agents they had allowed whites to indenture Native Americans. Only when citizens took Native Americans without permission or for potentially nefarious purposes did they object. Still Indian agents, much more than army officers, were willing to give civilians what they wanted as regarded Indian affairs, though in some instances soldiers could be obliging enough.

What many white settlers wanted were federal troops willing to slaughter Native Americans on their behalf. Officers such as Lt. George Crook epitomized the ideal held by Californians in the late 1850s. Crook, whom William Tecumseh Sherman later called the greatest Indian fighter since Andrew Jackson, was posted to California fresh out of West Point.[108] Crook typified the strange duality that inhabits many soldiers: the ability to sympathize with those one is otherwise engaged in killing. The paradox likely stemmed from the belief of many officers that force was the foundation of successful relations with Native Americans. Savage Indians had to know the risk of disobedience for policies to be effective. Other officers, like most Euro-Americans, believed Native Americans were a dying race of people. In this line of thinking, killing an Indian was possibly a shortcut to a certainty. Some soldiers believed Native people fought out of instinctive savagery; others believed quite the opposite. This came from the type of experience soldiers gained in California. Over the course of his service, George Crook came to realize that Native Americans "fought . . . in order to stem American aggression, lust, or greed rather than to provide outlets to aimless savagery."[109] Crook's experience produced a strong positive sentiment later in his life for the capacities of Native Americans, despite his fame for killing them. At no time was this irony clearer than during a commencement address at West Point in 1884, where Crook, the nation's greatest living Indian fighter, said, "With all his faults, and he has many, the American Indian is not half so black as he has been painted. He is cruel in war, treacherous at times, and not overly cleanly. But so were our forefathers. His nature, however, is responsive to a treatment which assures him that it is based upon justice, truth, honesty, and common sense; it is not impossible that with a fair and square system of dealing with him the American Indian would make a better citizen than many who neglect the duties and abuse the privileges of that proud title."[110] Thirty-two years in the field, including a tour as a junior officer fighting Native Americans in California, informed Crook's viewpoint.

Crook had never seen a Native American before coming to California in 1852. He met Wiyot people on his first expedition to the Humboldt Bay region, describing them as living in several small groups around the periphery of the bay and as "poor, harmless, scrofuletic, and miserable creatures who lived principally on fish."[111] They were harmless people and friendly to whites in the region. The nearby Bald Mountain band, however, were dangerous killers. According to Crook, "The Americans became so incensed at the outrages committed by these Indians that some thought that those in the bay were in collusion with those in the mountains, so one night a lot of citizens assembled and massacred a number of these poor defenseless beings, who thought, doubtless, that their very condition would be their safeguard." The massacre was applauded by local newspapers. Meanwhile Crook's unit went on an expedition against the Bald Mountain Indians, but they could not be found. Crook lamented the wanton killing of innocent Native Americans, connecting the desire of the population to exterminate Native Americans with the mineral wealth being extracted in the Trinity River region.[112]

In 1853 Crook was stationed at Fort Jones, near Yreka. He was jittery enough about Native Americans to think that an owl he had startled and that had clawed him from behind as it flew off was an Indian scalping him. He soon learned that Native Americans were an unlikely source of trouble in the region. Shasta people inhabited the area around the post, and Crook found them, like the Wiyots, "well disposed" toward whites. Also like the Wiyots, the Shastas faced the constant depredations of settlers and ranchers in the region. In 1852, for instance, a group of white outlaws disguised as Native Americans were committing crimes in the Shasta region. Following some attacks on miners fooled by the disguises, citizens had hunted down a local Shasta man and lynched him in retaliation. Only later were the real culprits discovered.[113] Much of northern California, caught up in the lust for gold, was suffering through similar episodes. Crook recalled, "The country was over-run by people from all nations in search of the mighty dollar. Greed was almost unrestrained, and from the nature of our government there was little or no law that these people were bound to respect. . . . It was no unfrequent occurrence for an Indian to be shot down in cold blood, or a squaw to be raped by some brute. Such a thing as a white man being punished for outraging an Indian was unheard of. It was the fable of the wolf and lamb every time." With the civilian population Crook was supposed to protect causing most of the problems in the region, little chance existed for Native Americans to live in peace. Crook concluded, in a statement reminiscent of affairs all over California, "The consequence was that there was scarcely ever a time that there was not one or more wars with the Indians somewhere on the Pacific Coast."[114] As was the case to the south, in Round Valley, for Johnson, Dillon, and Carlin, so it was in far northern California for Crook: settlers beat, raped, abducted, and murdered Native peoples and then called for help when Native Americans defended their communities.

But unlike the orders received by Carlin and Dillon from Johnson, Crook would be ordered to exterminate every Native American he came across. Historically, military training and discipline have been effective tools in helping soldiers involved in genocide overcome compunction about killing unarmed or innocent civilians.[115] Whether training and discipline played a role in the genocidal events that followed, one cannot know for certain, especially as some of the members of the troop likely did not consider Native Americans human beings or hated them as many of their countrymen did, making training and discipline unnecessary. Crook, like a good officer, followed his orders to the best of his ability, though he did not like the orders or his commanding officer very much.

Crook also despised the volunteer companies he encountered. He noted that most of the volunteers out hunting Native Americans were drunk. This was little different than the state of his own men when encamped with his commanding officer. Drunkenness too has historically played a role in genocide, as men have used alcohol to help overcome compunctions about butchering the innocent or unarmed.[116] Crook's commanding officer was an alcoholic, and a difficult one at that. Crook liked nothing better than to be out on his own, away from the drunken excesses of camp life. In the winter of 1856–57 reports indicated that the Pitt River tribes were at war with settlers in the Pitt River Valley. The emergency provided a chance for Crook to lead his company into the field. Native Americans had reportedly killed all the whites and destroyed their property in the valley, and settlers were demanding retribution. Because the area was nearly one hundred miles distant and blocked by mountains covered with snow, news was slow to reach Fort Jones, but when the news arrived, it also reached nearby Yreka, where citizens convened a town meeting and voted to form a volunteer company in March 1857 to help exact revenge on the Native peoples near the Pitt River. The volunteer company returned in April claiming they had skirmished with Indians to no result. Meanwhile the army, including Crook and sixty-four other soldiers out of Fort Jones, went on an expedition in mid-May to investigate. Unfortunately for Crook, his drunken commanding officer was in command of the unit. The soldiers found the snow nearly impassable, even though it was springtime. The going was even slower because drunken enlisted men and officers often fell out, too drunk to march. Finally reaching the valley, the soldiers learned that not all settlers in the valley had been killed, as had been reported.[117]

Instead the soldiers found that the local citizenry were already kill-ing Native Americans in vengeance. The brother of one of the men killed admitted that "he had already killed several" and was intent upon "killing all the Indians he saw." Worse for Crook, though, was the drunkenness. Drunkenness in the ranks was a problem. The command-ing officer was constantly drunk, and was incompetent as a military man. Crook felt uncertain about their effectiveness in combat. The experienced Native peoples of the region easily evaded the clumsy attempts of the two companies to find them. Crook, however, was allowed to take a detachment of men away from the main body. This allowed him to discipline his men, prevent them from getting drunk, and engage in effective movement and operations against the Pitt River Native population. He moved at night in order to surprise Native camps. In this way, Crook emulated the strategy employed by the doz-ens of volunteer companies that had operated in California. By sneak-ing up on villages in the night, laying in wait until daybreak, one could achieve surprise against many Native groups, who traditionally did not operate at night. Crook reported that not one soldier was killed in the greater Yreka theater of operations thanks to this strategy. His first combat occurred in daylight. Native Americans had become aware of Crook and his men, and at least one group abandoned their village to avoid capture. Crook and his men spread out and hunted the refugees, finding them in daylight, in the open. The Native Americans attempted to parley with Crook, but instead he went to gather his forces. The villagers fled again, but two days later Crook caught them again and attacked them without provocation. In fact the Native Americans were running away from Crook, who was by himself scouting at the time, when he sighted them. He shot and wounded a Native man with his rifle and then killed the wounded man with a pistol. He was nearly killed by a large group of Native Americans who came suddenly upon the scene. Only by fleeing and rejoining his men did Crook survive. When he attempted to press the attack, he could find only "one old squaw who was lying beside the dead buck." He recalled, "This was my first Indian."[118]

Crook and his men set about what can only be called terrorizing the Native Americans of the Pitt River Valley. On June 10, 1857, Crook and ten of his men attacked a different group of Native Americans camped along the river. Crook shot a "buck" trying to flee by swimming the river. On an expedition in late June, he and his men killed two more Native Americans. No reason was given; presumably that they were Indians was reason enough. On July 2, 1857, Crook and his men attacked another village. The massacre began with the murder of a Native man who had surrendered, a sentinel who was perhaps trying to peacefully resolve the situation. As the soldiers attacked, men, women, and children tried to flee in every direction, screaming and yelling in terror as the soldiers fired into their homes. Crook recalled, "We killed a great many, and after the main fight was over, we hunted some reserved ground that we knew had Indians hidden. By deploying as skirmishers, and shooting them as they broke cover, we got them. One or two faced us, and made a manly fight, while others would attempt to run. There was but one squaw killed." He believed that the Native Americans were guilty of stock theft because *after* the fight they found beef in the village. Whether or not Crook knew it, Native Americans both owned cattle in California and also received cattle in trade or payment, sometimes from Indian agents. He released the captured women and children into the wilderness; apparently every man in the village was killed.[119]

The massacre produced little in the way of revulsion among Crook and his men. Crook noticed that the men were in the mood to kill Indians on the Fourth of July but found only one "buck" who had simply strayed across their path. On July 27 Crook and his men found a village of about five hundred persons. When the soldiers were spotted, the Native Americans fled and the soldiers began killing them at long range with rifles and at closer range by pursuit on mules and horses. Crook recalled the glory of it all in his memoirs: one Native American "singing his death song" as he fought; another with a broken back willing himself to fight half paralyzed, bringing down a soldier's mule with five arrow shots. Crook finished him with a pistol shot. Many of the villagers escaped, so Crook destroyed their provisions, including preparations of winter stores.[120] Presumably, he counted on winter or starvation to claim those who had escaped. Crook judged his campaign a success: the soldiers' actions put an end to the Indians' depredations, and whites moved freely in the region. He continued to kill any Native Americans he ran across, though.

During the summer Crook and his men continued to patrol the valley. One day they found the village of the Natives who had killed the whites earlier in the year. The villagers were away, and Crook found photographs and other objects that probably belonged to the men killed. All of the many men, women, and children Crook and his men had killed over the previous two months were in all likelihood proven innocent in this moment. But the realization did not stop Crook from exacting punishment on the real culprits. With the village currently vacant while the inhabitants were out gathering grass seed and swimming, Crook needed intelligence on the numbers he faced. To get information on the group, he captured a Native woman and her infant and forced her at gunpoint to return to his camp. That night Crook and his men returned to set up a surprise attack on the village. They took the woman and her three-week-old infant with them. But the Indians had moved their village to the opposite side of the deep river, preventing attack. Crook and his men searched in vain for a ford over the river to get to the rancheria to set up the trap. Though they failed to find a ford, they did find a damaged canoe, full of water and half sunk. The woman set down her child, and using a basket hat, she bailed out the canoe. Thinking that perhaps the canoe was serviceable and that she was willing to help, Crook and his men looked on, put off their guard by her seemingly willing aid. Suddenly the woman dove under the water and out of sight. Soon after, the Native village on the opposite bank doused all fires and fled. The woman had given up her baby to save her people.[121]

While Crook was profoundly impressed with the woman's resolve, he implied that instinctive savagery had something to do with her actions. He soon showed himself as the real savage. Crook and his men hung the "papoose" up in a tree when the baby began to cry incessantly.

The soldiers backed off into the brush, hoping to use the baby as a new trap, but the Native people either did not hear or did not dare to come. The fate of the still-nursing newborn was never mentioned, but Crook was days from camp and in a valley where there were likely no women and nobody with the ability to help the infant survive. Whether or not Crook included the infant in his casualty figures cannot be known.[122]

Indiscriminate warfare was brought to an end in the fall of 1857, when Pitt River tribes agreed to relocate around an army post and under the supervision of the soldiers. When Crook and his men were summoned to the Klamath region in October 1857, they departed as "heroes" in Yreka. The fort at Pitt River was named Fort Crook in honor of the chief hero.[123] The press, like the miners and settlers, praised Crook as "the true grit" and a man "determined to thrash [the Indians]."[124] Crook knew how to deal with Native Americans, delivering the type of peace that the citizenry liked, a peace achieved by arms.[125] Like Dillon, Crook went east in 1861 for the Civil War. He later returned as the general in command of operations against Native Americans in the West, and California newspapers published many articles praising Lieutenant Crook of old for his gallant actions of the 1850s.

Meanwhile federal Indian policy was collapsing in terms of effectiveness and its ability to control Native American populations. Much of this was due to the cumulative effects of years of corruption and mismanagement by Henley and others. Congress responded by punishing California's Indigenous population for the failures of its agents, failures complicated by the problems largely created by the white citizenry. In 1859 only $50,000 was authorized for Indian affairs in California.[126] Henley was forced out, as Beale had been. Following the change of authority in 1860, the seven reserves were either reduced or closed altogether. Congress acted to split control of California Indian affairs in two, creating a northern and a southern superintendency. Funding, however, was limited to $57,500 for the entire state. The act also limited the number of subagents and employees for each reservation. In 1864 Congress returned Indian affairs to the control of one superintendent and empowered the president to create four reservations in California, which could include existing ones or new ones. The reservations had to be as far from white population centers as possible. Worst of all, any lands previously reserved but not renewed by the president were to be made available to the public.[127] Federal policy had reached a new apathetic low. Not that this was enough to please many whites in California or the West. By 1868 some Californians had become further incensed by the lack of funds for Indian affairs compared to the Reconstruction efforts linked to the freedmen taking place in the South. However, they wanted funding not to relieve the plight of Indigenous people in California and the West, but to exterminate them. One newspaper editor argued:

It is time that the policies of the Government were changed. The negroes have been pampered at the expense of Americans long enough. The latter have some right to the protection of the Government. Their lives and property are quite as dear to them as are those of the colored people and they will begin to conclude pretty soon that the discrimination in favor of the negro is not exactly fair. They will protest against being left to the tender mercy of the savages, simply because their skins are unfortunately American, which is no fault of theirs.... [Without such change,] the people of the West are left to shift for themselves.[128]

What the editor failed to realize was that much of the apathy of federal agents and officers stemmed from the actions of whites in California over the previous two decades. In many instances, federal authorities had looked to preserve the interests of Native peoples over whites when it came to Native-white relations in California. Although the federal government had failed to protect Native Americans in California, acting rather as impotent bystanders to the power of the state and its white citizenry to shape events, they were determined about one thing to do with Indian affairs in California: they were not about to keep paying for the effort.

8

Advertising Genocide

Now that general Indian hostilities have commenced, we hope that
the Government will render such aid as will enable the citizens of
the North to carry on a war of extermination until the last red skin of
these tribes has been killed. Then, and not until then, are our lives and
property safe. Extermination is no longer even a question of time—the
time has already arrived, the work has been commenced, and let the
first white man who says treaty or peace be regarded as a traitor and
coward.

Marysville Daily Evening Herald (1853)

With the advent of the second, titanic wave of the Gold Rush, California became inundated not only with forty-niners but also with newspapers. Beginning in 1849, California offered newspaper publishers
an instant audience of tens of thousands of white readers hungry for
local and national news. As commercial enterprises situated in local
communities, many newspapers clearly reflected the views of the local white populace in their reporting. During the first thirty years of
statehood newspapers were deeply, sometimes consciously involved
in promoting the genocide of Indigenous people; Native American
genocide was what much of their readership wanted, especially in areas
near Native-white conflict. Newspapers also contributed to the genocide in subtle ways, such as by publishing stories about the wealth and
resources contained on lands occupied by Native peoples. Reporting of
this nature led to a host of crimes against Native peoples, from grave
robbing to forced removals to reservations. Newspapers also ran racist

stories that perpetuated established stereotypes of Native Americans and promulgated new ones. Typically it was only when white communities were empty of Native people that newspapers changed their editorial slant from supporting Native American genocide.[1]

Newspapers in areas near the center of Native-white conflict often implicitly and explicitly acted as proponents of genocide. By publishing stories that reinforced existing notions of the inferiority of Indigenous peoples based on race, religion, and culture, publishers helped to perpetuate the vision of an inevitable, divinely ordained extinction. Throughout the United States "Indians were explained in the press ethnocentrically; that is, not by their own standards . . . but by those of the press and its readers." This helped to promote genocide, as whites and Native Americans came into conflict over the land and resources that Native peoples controlled and that Euro-Americans fairly lusted after. Newspapers helped shape Indian identities in the minds of whites as savage, dangerous, and "deviant."[2] Over time such stories helped to naturalize atrocity against Native peoples as acceptable and inevitable. Ideas about the inequity between races especially encouraged the belief that whites, as a superior race, had rights over inferior races.

A brief report in the *Chico Weekly Courant* of December 13, 1867, summed up what many white citizens considered to be the relationship between democracy, race, and religion in the nineteenth century. Following the visit of an allegedly notable scholar, Professor Nasby, the *Courant* delivered a summary of the salient points he made: "Professor Nasby suggests the amendment of the word 'white' to the Sacred Scriptures to make them 'truly' Democratic wherever it might be necessary." The paper included examples provided by the professor, such as, "So God created a *white* man in His own image." Statements of this kind, predicated on scholarly authority, were particularly damaging, as they suggested a legitimacy born of long study and research. Eight days later the *Plumas National* picked up the story from the *Courant* and reprinted it.[3] Newspapers in the nineteenth century were allowed to reprint the stories of other papers for free.[4] This helped stock newspapers with stories at a reduced expense, but also let unchecked stories

and wild rumor circulate far and wide. Stories with popular appeal
were likely to be reprinted elsewhere. Apparently Nasby's suggestions
appealed to a wider audience than just the people of Chico. Supposedly scholarly tripe of this variety joined more common racist fare in
the pages of California newspapers.

Especially in the postwar years of Radical Reconstruction, many
California newspapers commented on race and democratic representation and the fears that attended them. In 1868 the *Red Bluff Sentinel*
was horrified by the developments in the South, especially the appearance of black representatives and officials in government. In response,
the *Sentinel* attempted to do for history what Nasby was doing for
religion. "White men were those who discovered America," claimed the
Sentinel, and "white men were those for whose benefit the government
was established." The *Sentinel* wanted people to know "white is the
word," especially "while the niggers are raising such a decided rumpus
with the assistance of their miscegenation allies, and clamoring for
a hand in government."[5] On Independence Day, of all days, the editors wanted fellow white Californians to understand their supremacy
as a race and as a part of history. A long article in the *Quincy Union*
in 1866 provided an example of what happened to whites who failed
to protect their rightful place at the head of society. Discussing the
downfall of Mexico over the previous forty years, the *Union* argued
that the calamity had happened because Mexico gave up rule by whites
and allowed "Mongrels" to take over. These Mongrels—made up of
Indians, Negroes, and mulattoes—were "allowed an equal voice with
them [Caucasians] in ruling and selecting rulers for the people." According to the *Union*, nothing could have been worse, because equality
of representation soon produced an equality of social standing among
races. The result was interracial marriage and offspring. Using a mixture
of flawed history and pseudoscience, the *Union* claimed that the purity
of white blood had been destroyed. Before, in "their purity of blood,"
Caucasians in Mexico had been able to "preserve also their purity of
laws, manners and customs." However, "with the pollution" of their
blood came their downfall through the "pollution" of their laws and

culture.[6] In 1866 the *Union* and its white readership were afraid of such mixing to come in the postwar United States. As the genocide scholars Daniel Chirot and Clark McCauley have argued, a "fear of pollution" has been a key, recurring factor in episodes of genocide.[7] Such rhetoric was common to genocide in California, and it had a discernible presence in newspapers.

Racial essentialism, used to degrade Native Americans and others as nonwhites, was not simply ignorant but harmless rhetoric. Racism had harsh consequences for Indigenous and other nonwhite peoples. The *Quincy Union* carried a transcript and description of a political appearance by Henry Haight, Democratic candidate for governor of California in 1867, that demonstrates how racist sentiment supported the election of candidates devoted to promoting white supremacy. Haight campaigned on a platform that included racial exclusion of racially inferior peoples. The publishers of the *Quincy Union* found Haight much to their liking, as did the crowd Haight appeared before. He exclaimed, "We do not believe a republican government can exist based upon the suffrage of Chinese, Negroes, and Indians." The *Union* reported that tumultuous applause and cheering went up in response. Haight claimed that any attempt to add such people to the representative mixture would taint the whole. If elected governor, he promised to ensure there would be no contamination.[8] Such talk playing on fears of racial pollution has engaged popular support for political leaders in other cases of genocide. On December 5, 1867, Haight was inaugurated as California's tenth governor.

Haight reflected the views of not only the *Quincy Union*'s publishers and editors, but also many other white Californians. Aside from political coverage and support of candidates, many newspapers ran a section containing humor in every issue, much of it based on the mockery of peoples considered inferior. Racist humor was deployed in two ways: as racist quips commenting on real-life events and as racist jokes. In an example of the former, the *Plumas National* took the opportunity to attach what they considered a witticism to the death of a Native person: "Another Good Indian—One of the Central Pacific freight cars smashed another Indian on Friday last, and started his soul on its journey to the 'home of fat grasshoppers.'"[9] Years later another death, this time of a deformed child, was their subject. In an article titled "Gone to Hell," the *National* described the visit of two white men gone out to see a deformed Native American boy as an entertainment, only to find him dead. The newspaper took it as an opportunity to generate laughs among their readership: "Sadly we chronicle it—tearfully we enter upon the painful subject—but the mournful story must be told—the Plumas County Bear Indian is no more. . . . The Society for the 'Prevention of Cruelty to Animals,' at San Francisco, can now sleep quietly. The Bear Boy will no longer enliven that village with his presence. His growl will never again be heard on Montgomery street. He has eaten his last acorn, folded himself in his robe, passed in his checks—'Gone to Hell.'"[10] Another favorite was to make fun of Native Americans wearing Euro-American clothing, especially Native women. Quips about "Digger fashion" and Native men and women dressed above their station were typical.[11]

In the quest to entertain readers, editors often included jokes that used racial stereotypes common to nineteenth-century Euro-Americans. Race, as defined in the nineteenth century, did not depend on pigmentation as evidence of whiteness or lack thereof. Rather, different ethnic groups were rendered down to recognizable stereotypes; racist sentiments against Irish American, Native American, and African American peoples could be delivered in a single "joke."[12] The pidgin English of Native people was a favorite target, so much so that some people today believe this is the idiom of Indigenous peoples. Native American speech was rendered in this way by the *Yreka Journal* in 1868: "No! white man gib Injin too much whisky. Injin big drunk last night; Injin sick; bye-bye Injin puke: den Injin get well again, ugh!"[13] According to the anthropologist Robert F. Heizer, a study of nineteenth-century newspapers in California that make Native Americans the target of humor have an important characteristic in common: only in areas where direct conflict with Native Americans had ceased, and where now only small groups of survivors remained, were Native Americans treated "as comic characters."[14] Until eradicated or neutralized, the character of the ruthless, savage Indian enemy had to be maintained in order to bring about his destruction. Native Americans, though, were just some of the enemies of whiteness in California.

Racist thinking often grouped different ethnicities together in strange ways. In a subtle instance, Chinese "copper colored heathens" who dared to fight a white man in the street were believed to be on the "warpath."[15] A more obvious example appeared in the story of two Native men shot dead and left unburied to rot for days. Once the news reached San Francisco, the *San Francisco Tribune* called on local white people to bury them. The *Quincy Union* suggested instead that the Indian corpses be made up in blackface, the better to attract the "negro-worshipping" editor of the *Tribune* to come do it himself.[16] Newspapers informed and organized the thinking of California's white majority as they set about securing the fruits of the young state for themselves.

In areas where California's Indigenous people were nearing demographic collapse, fears of armed conflict abated. Some newspapers began to deploy new arguments against remaining Native populations, many of them housed on reservations created by executive order. In one misguided and self-serving example, the *Plumas National* printed an exposé of Native American communism as a blight on Euro-American capitalism. The *National* argued that keeping California's Indigenous population alive on reservations was foolish. The paper criticized the policy using racist analogies. Should whites prop up other inferior races as well? Why not next create Irish reservations, stocked with "whiskey and blankets," or perhaps lodge the Chinese on reserves supplied with "stale fish and opium"? Certainly not, concluded the *National*. Inferior peoples either aspired to the benefits of white civilization or perished. Non-Natives who did not work either starved or were forced into workhouses. Native Americans, however, were kept at leisure by payments drawn from taxes to keep "lazy, drunken Indians" alive on valuable public lands. The paper called for an end to the "Red Republic" of Native American communism. Should the Native Americans, "thrown upon their own resources," fail, they could perish in defiance of "God's plan" of proper "human government."[17] What these resources might be, once reservations were dissolved, the *National* failed to mention.

In areas where Native Americans held on by raiding and armed resistance, however, newspapers shone as beacons for democratic genocide. Newspapers were the rallying points for the formation of local volunteer companies and open advocates of genocide. Some, such as the *Marysville Daily Evening Herald*, published open calls for Native American genocide: "Extermination is no longer even a question of time—the time has already arrived, the work has been commenced, and let the first white man who says treaty or peace be regarded as a traitor and coward." After reading the notice in the *Herald*, which demanded the murder of every "last red skin," one need not doubt that the crime of genocide in the twenty-first century was the same crime back in the nineteenth century.[18] Areas cursed with intense Native-white conflict were hotbeds of genocide. Papers frequently and vociferously called for extermination as a solution to the intolerable presence of Native Americans. The *Marysville Daily Evening Herald* was but one voice in a cacophony of Euro-American voices shouting for Native American genocide.

Hearing of a conflict between Indigenous peoples at Big Meadows and Mill Creek, the *Chico Weekly Courant* suggested that the citizens of Butte and Tehama counties join forces with the Big Meadows people to "exterminate the Mill Creeks."[19] The following month, the *Courant* suggested that the community "exterminate the fiends."[20] Even when Indian affairs in distant Trinity County came up, the *Courant* proposed its usual solution of genocide. Following the failure of a reservation in Trinity County to fully contain Native peoples in the region, the *Courant* called for an end to the present reservation system and the implementation of a new one: "There is only one effective reservation to send these red devils to, and that is the 'happy hunting grounds.'"[21] The editors commented that this solution was already well known in Chico, and undoubtedly would soon be known in Trinity once enough "lives were lost" to Indians.

In one particularly nasty statement by the *Chico Weekly Courant*, it was suggested that smallpox be introduced among the Indigenous populations as the most effective way of dealing with them: "A Hint—The small pox has killed more Indians in the Humboldt Valley this season, than General Sherman's troops. . . . Let us take the hint and promote Gen. Small Pox to the head of the Indian Bureau."[22] According to the *Daily Alta California*, whites in 1853 had already attempted to infect Native Americans with small pox to exterminate them.[23] But this was not the first time the *Courant* had proposed poisoning Indigenous populations; the previous year, the editors had complained that a "great fuss over the poisoning of two or three Diggers" was going on in the press in San Francisco. Instead of wasting time lamenting the deaths of worthless Indians, the *Courant* suggested that spreading strychnine-laced watermelons "promiscuously all over the Pacific Coast" might be time better spent.[24] The *Sacramento Daily Union*, disturbed by the poisoning of Native Americans in the Pitt River region, inadvertently educated settlers and ranchers on how to accomplish the feat effectively: "mix a considerable quantity of strychnine with flour" and leave it so as to be found by "starving Indians."[25] The *California Farmer* did much the same thing when it described one miner's trick for stopping Native Americans from taking some of his sugar while away prospecting. The miner would take an ounce of strychnine and mix it in with sugar in a bowl, which he would leave out in the open when he left. The man reportedly killed ten Native Americans in this manner, as well as putting an even greater number through agonizing pain before they recovered.[26] How many whites adopted these successful recipes for Native American genocide, one cannot know.

Poison and biological warfare, however, were not common measures proposed for dealing with Indigenous populations. Rather newspapers all over California published calls for democratic meetings, resolutions to organize volunteer companies, and requests for the men necessary to exterminate local Native American peoples. These companies were not for the defense that citizens proposed in petitions to the governor, however. California newspapers helped to define the actual intent of volunteer companies much more clearly than the official petitions sent to governors. One paper summarized the goals of a volunteer company: "When the people resolve upon exterminating these fiends, and put their resolution into effect by starting out a company of picked citizens to avenge the murders perpetrated, with a resolve to take no prisoners, there will be a cessation of these atrocities, and not till then."[27] Newspapers performed what editors no doubt thought was their civic duty: to inform the citizenry so that they might properly fulfill their functions as cogs in a democracy. Keeping citizens aware of upcoming meetings and the resolutions that followed was important in this regard.

Articles and notices related to settlers' conventions, town meetings, and meetings specifically to discuss Indian difficulties were commonplace in California newspapers in the 1850s and 1860s.[28] Curiously most calls for citizens' meetings seemed to state the outcome of the meeting before it had occurred. "We are requested to state," wrote one paper, "that a meeting of citizens will be held . . . to organize an independent company, according to law."[29] Newspapers also issued calls to other communities to meet and organize. "The people of Cottonwood and Deer Creek" were encouraged by newspaper editors in Red Bluff to "cooperate with the people of the Antelope [District] in providing means of mutual defense, and as a preliminary step, it is recommended that they hold similar meetings."[30] Resolutions to petition the governor and form volunteer companies were characteristic results, and these were also published. Newspapers also pressed federal authorities for assistance in genocide on behalf of their customers. The *Red Bluff Sentinel*, for example, called for the army to bring about a "total annihilation of the Indians" in the absence of any other means of bringing them to heel.[31] The people of Chico shared much the same sentiment, also calling for the government to exterminate Native Americans—the genocidal intent of the community baldly stated. "The man who takes a prisoner," suggested the *Chico Weekly Courant*, "should himself be shot." The *Courant* argued that the time for negotiation had passed, and encouraged the government to adopt the most effective treaty of all, "cold lead."[32] Newspapers kept local communities apprised of these and other efforts to organize against Native Americans.[33]

Resolutions, including the formation of volunteer companies and the election of officers, were carried in the pages of newspapers. Some demanded the censure of local officials by the community, warnings to citizens with Native American servants to keep them indoors when companies were out, and threats to whites cohabiting with Native women.[34] Communities also voted to pass resolutions making laws in their area. In the region surrounding Big Meadows, citizens met and voted to ban Native Americans altogether. Any found in or around the community would be shot on sight.[35] Citizens in Orleans Bar, Humboldt County, were a bit more discerning: only Native Americans seen in possession of firearms would be shot on sight.[36] The citizens of Long Valley went a step further, banning Native Americans from the entire county: "No Indian is now allowed under any pretext whatever to come into the county."[37] These local laws were technically unconstitutional and illegal under state and federal laws. However, being democratically arrived at and openly published in the press, they had an air of legitimacy. And as the state and federal government behaved typically as bystanders to the genocide, little censure was forthcoming in forms capable of contradicting the will of white citizens. Moreover citizens made sure to elect likeminded candidates to local, county, and state offices in order to protect their interests, adding a layer of legitimization and protection to their goals.

Resolutions were made to support political candidates and officeholders based on their willingness "to use [their] intelligence to promote the interests of the settler so far as is consistent with law and justice."[38] Declarations of this nature were the epitome of Euro-American representative democracy in the nineteenth century; officeholders were expected to be the tools of the white majority. The mention of "law and justice," in concert, represented the assumption by Euro-Americans that people other than whites need not be considered. Whites perhaps felt vindicated in their actions against Native people because they were achieved democratically, in writing, within the law, and with the consent of their elected officials. According to the *Daily Alta California*, the "foundation of all law is necessity."[39] The necessity of removing or killing Native Americans drove the democratic process in California, leading to the passing of laws and the approval of citizens' petitions. Bystanders relied on the legality of Native American genocide as a salve to their conscience for watching fellow citizens commit murder. Perpetrators were shielded legally to participate in the murder of Indigenous populations without threat of prosecution. By publishing and lauding the process, the press was another organ of legitimacy for white populations committing genocide. This public acceptance was part of the cognitive dissonance necessary for one human being to kill another. With stories and articles discussing extermination as acceptable, necessary, and even commendable, newspapers were a key support to the naturalized atrocity of genocide.[40]

When it came time to gather volunteers or offer incentives to kill Native Americans, newspapers were the logical choice to disseminate information to the community. Scalp bounties and subscriptions, discussed in a previous chapter, were unashamedly publicized. Newspapers kept communities abreast of the progress of volunteers. For communities financing genocide privately through subscriptions, newspapers such as the *Red Bluff Beacon* relayed messages from the company in the field. In this way the newspaper kept the citizenry updated so that they could "see if . . . [their] money [was] well invested."[41] When state militia commanders were dispatched by the governor, officers sometimes advertised for volunteers in local newspapers. Calling for men "experienced with the use of a rifle," advertisers left little doubt about the genocidal nature of expeditions against Native Americans.[42] Not only did newspapers advertise for killers; they also advertised for thieves.

Newspapers in California not only promoted Native American genocide directly by calling for the extermination of Native Americans; they also contributed to the main impetus behind genocide: the Euro-American desire to possess Native American land and resources. Some calls were general in nature, such as when the *Daily Alta California* demanded that the U.S. Congress make provisions for opening additional public land—land occupied by Native people, though this was not mentioned.[43] The *Alta's* argument was that if Congress did not legalize possession of the lands, Euro-American squatters would take it anyway, creating costly legal issues in the future. Newspapers specifically advertised Native resources. The predictable result was a stampede of Euro-Americans to lay claim to Native lands or demands for the immediate removal of Indigenous populations from such sites so that whites might safely move in. In the Pitt River region, Native peoples were subjected to a miniature gold rush following the widespread publication of gold's discovery. The *Yreka Daily Appeal* added to the misery of local Native peoples by spreading the conjecture that all the connected ranges and valleys were possessed of gold. The fact that Native peoples lived in the area described did not discourage the *Appeal* in the slightest. Instead the editors claimed, "We believe this unexplored region may prove [to be] one of the most valuable mining districts yet found on this coast."[44] Had they been more circumspect in their research, they might have known that the Native people of Pitt River had been almost wiped out eight years before by U.S. forces and volunteer companies, including a group of men calling themselves the Pitt River Rangers.[45] Even when Native peoples were a considerable presence, newspapers continued to advertise areas for settlement. According to the *Red Bluff Beacon*, it would take only "thirty white men [to] whip all the Indians" in the rich Carson Valley and get possession of the land and resources.[46] Federal reservations established by executive order were not immune to the press's habit of advertising the wealth to be found on Native American land.

The press coverage of the troubled reservations of Nome Lackee and Nome Cult Farm were examples of how newspapers helped to derail federal efforts to establish safe Native American reservations by making them attractive sites for Euro-Americans. In 1857 the *Red Bluff Beacon* published an article on the fecundity of the reservation and the coming crop of fifteen thousand bushels of wheat.[47] As the harvest came in and preparations were made for winter at Nome Lackee, the *Beacon* published a follow-up report with the final wheat harvest tally of twelve thousand bushels.[48] The same year, the *Beacon* advertised the resources of Nome Cult Farm as well, including the cattle and wheat contained there.[49] In 1858 the *Beacon* published an article describing a rich coal strike at the reservation. An unidentified person had brought the publishers a sample of the coal, which the publishers deemed of fantastic quality.[50] The following month, one W. S. Knott was back at the *Beacon*, this time with two sacks of the fine quality coal. Again the publishers fairly gushed over the quality of the coal.[51] By 1862 one might call the *Red Bluff Beacon* guilty of acting as real estate agents for the area in and around the reservation. In an article titled "A Beautiful Country," the paper reported on the profusion of water, timber, and "feed for every kind of stock in apparently inexhaustible profusion."[52] It is little wonder that settlers trespassed upon, and eventually overwhelmed, the Nome Lackee Reservation.

The *Red Bluff Beacon* also published articles describing the heinous acts of white men robbing Native American graves, in which they briefly listed the treasures one might find.[53] Similarly damaging was the description of cattle being sent to Nome Cult Indian Farm published on June 10, 1857: "Neat Cattle for Nome Cult—Mr. Storms the efficient superintendent of the above reservation . . . is preparing to drive 600 head of cattle to Nome Cult." Settlers and ranchers, particularly those who had lost animals in stock raids, were tempted by a new, easily accessible source for replacement animals. Worse still, the human resources represented by Native people, especially women and children, made Nome Cult and Nome Lackee popular places to obtain low-cost laborers, slaves, and women to rape. Community interest in connecting Red Bluff to Nome Lackee was so strong that the *Red Bluff Beacon* was part of an ongoing effort to build a road leading to the reservation. According to the editors of the *Beacon* in 1858, their goal of building a road from Red Bluff to Nome Lackee was soon to be realized with the help of "the friends of the enterprise at the other end," meaning reservation employees.[54] A reservation employee at Nome Cult Farm, Mr. Farr, was similarly engaged in destroying the chances of the reserve's operating for the benefit of Native peoples. The *Beacon* reported that Farr believed "gold might be found in considerable quantities" in the region of the reservation.[55] The

Beacon was fostering the necessary synergy between the citizens of Red Bluff and white reservation employees, an action that helped destroy Nome Lackee by the early 1860s. In fact, as is clear in the *Beacon* of June 24, 1857, the editor was a direct participant in Native American genocide. An assistant editor reported that the *Beacon*'s editor in chief was "away from home on an Indian hunt" lasting five days. But not all newspaper editors were interested in profiting on the misery of Native peoples.

The story of Francis Bret Harte provides an example of a newspaper situated near an Indigenous population attacking the actions of whites. Unfortunately, the story of Harte became a warning example to other California newspaper editors who might have considered speaking out against atrocities perpetrated on Indigenous populations in a region where campaigns were carried out. While serving as the guest editor of the *Northern Californian Union* in 1860, Harte did the unthinkable: he published a firsthand account of what he had witnessed following the attack of a volunteer company on an Native American village located at Humboldt Bay.[56] Perhaps because Harte was caught up in the invincibility of youth—he was only twenty-four at the time—he decided, while left in charge by the regular editor, to publish a report on the massacre. He made the mistake of believing that truth was what newspapers were to publish. At least where Native Americans were concerned, however, truth was often a one-sided affair in California. Most newspapers focused on the white side of Native-white relations, and frequently on the conflict and violence caused by savage Indians.[57] California was no exception; even in San Francisco and Sacramento sentiments sometimes changed. The *Daily Alta California*, perhaps the most sympathetic news organ in California as regards Indian affairs in the United States, lost faith at times: "Harsh and cruel as the policy of extermination may seem to be—inhuman, indeed, *if* we may please to call it so—there is no other way."[58] Articles with a Native American perspective were rare, especially when Native people were victims of white retaliation. Harte committed the sin of not ascribing the fate of the Wiyot population at Humboldt to their own savage nature. Instead he described the whites as savages.

On February 29, 1860, Harte published a long article with the head-line "Indiscriminate Massacre of Indians, Women and Children Butch-ered" describing what came to be known as the Indian Island Massacre. The story pulled no punches about what had happened or what Harte felt about the people who had done it. He asked what crimes existed that only a "babe's blood can atone for," and he had no answer that he would accept. "Perhaps," wrote Harte, "we do not rightly understand the doctrine of 'extermination.'" Harte was talking about genocide as we conceive of it today. He believed that perhaps "future moralists" would make some sense of the needless slaughter.[59]

The slaughter of the Wiyots of Indian Island was especially needless. The Wiyots were known as a friendly people, with a long-standing friendship with whites in the Humboldt Bay region. At the time of the massacre only Wiyot women and children were on the island; the men had gone off for a hunt. When the white men attacked Indian Island, they found no "bucks" and no resistance. Since the women and children were unarmed, the volunteers mostly saved their ammunition, instead hacking them to death with axes and knives. Harte did not leave what this meant to his reader's imagination:

> Little children and old women were mercilessly stabbed and their skulls crushed with axes. . . . Old Women wrinkled and decrepit lay weltering in blood, their brains dashed out and dabbled with their long grey hair. Infants scarce a span long, with their faces cloven with hatchets and their bodies ghastly with wounds. . . . No resistance was made, it is said, to the butchers who did the work, but as they ran or huddled together for protection like sheep, they were struck down with hatchets. Very little shooting was done, most of the bodies having wounds about the head.[60]

Harte reported on what was just one of four simultaneous massacres committed on February 26, 1860. Three days after the massacres, it was not generally known who the murderers were or how many had par-ticipated. Nobody came forward with names, and Harte refrained from speculation in an atmosphere not altogether hostile to the massacres.[61] It was not that Harte or anyone else in Union, Eureka, or Arcata could not make an educated guess. Capt. Seamen Wright and his unauthorized Humboldt Volunteers were in the field, even after having been denied approval by the governor. But the volunteers were only the weapon wielded by democracy to kill Wiyot people. The real culprits were the citizens of Humboldt County, who at a citizens' meeting had recently taken up a subscription to fund the company. Everyone in the area knew this; it was in the newspaper.[62]

Most people objected to the publicity and the frank descriptions of what had happened. Harte's report had the undesirable effect for bystanders of dragging their heads up out of the sand, if only for a moment. The attacks by these unauthorized volunteer companies claimed the lives of 188 men, women, and children. According to the report of a local army commander, Maj. Gabriel J. Raines, the massacre was a sickening, unprovoked slaughter. Despite denials about the character of the massacre in other papers, Harte's version was corroborated by Raines. Most of the 188 dead were women and children. Raines believed the perpetrators were men from the Eel River region, out without the consent of the governor. Raines's description echoed the story Harte published:

I was informed that these men, Volunteers, calling themselves such, from Eel River, had employed the earlier part of the day in murdering all the women and children of the above [Indian] Island and I repaired to the place, but villains—some 5 in number had gone—and midst the bitter grief of parents and fathers— many of whom had returned—I beheld a spectacle of horror, of unexampled description—babes, with brains oozing out of their skulls, cut and hacked with axes, and squaws exhibiting the most frightful wounds in death which imagination can paint—and this done . . . without cause, otherwise, as far as I can learn, as I have not heard of any of them losing life or cattle by the Indians. Certainly not these Indians, for they lived on an Island and nobody accuses them.[63]

Shocked as were some of the people of the Humboldt Bay region, others were not. Whites had years before precipitated trouble with Native Americans in the region and exterminated many, including women and children, in other massacres.[64] Perhaps this explained the way the massacres were reported in other area newspapers.

The editorial slant of the *Marysville Evening Herald* was typical: "Extermination is no longer even a question of time—the time has already arrived, the work has been commenced, and let the first white man who says treaty or peace be regarded as a traitor and coward."[65] The *Plumas National* was even more succinct. The *National*'s banner motto, included at the head of every issue, was "The right is always expedient."[66] Considering the difference between such views and Harte's, press and public reaction to his frank exposé was predictable. As he tried to demonstrate the monstrosity of Euro-American actions, Harte seemed to local people to be a traitor to his own race. The editor of *Humboldt Times* claimed that people who lamented the massacre and "shed crocodile tears over the 'poor Indians'" were fools.[67] Sheriff Van Ness of Humboldt County published articles in area newspapers filled with "thinly veiled justification[s]" for the massacres.[68] Local editors called the massacre an expression of what Native Americans deserved rather than an outrage. In March Harte was forced to flee from Union to avoid angry citizens and a lynch mob.[69] A grand jury was convened to investigate the matter, but its proceedings closed without results. No evidence existed, the jurors claimed, to bring charges.[70] Meanwhile, unlike most killings of Native Americans, the massacre at Indian Island was not widely reported outside of the newspapers in San Francisco.[71] Undoubtedly the true story would not sell in much of California: it was not to the tastes of those who wholeheartedly approved of Native American genocide, or at least those who wished to remain ostrich-like bystanders.

Many whites in the Humboldt Bay area were plainly interested in continuing the bloody work begun on Indian Island. A wave of attacks of Native American peoples followed in the region, receiving coverage in the press.[72] The Wiyots were forced to accept the dubious protection of the U.S. Army and relocation to the Klamath Reservation in the face of a white community that seemed determined to finish the genocidal job.[73] The motives of the community were made conspicuous by the fact that as the Native Americans were removed, their lands were immediately occupied by whites. A man named Robert Gunther cashed in on the misery of the Indian Island Wiyots; he purchased the entire island, after buying out other Euro-Americans snapping up pieces of it. Gunther made these transactions after returning a two-year-old Wiyot baby to the island to die; with a broken back or spine, the child who had survived the massacre was dying in slow misery, the doctor unable to do anything.[74] One cannot know if the babe were a boy or a girl, as Gunther called the baby "it." The dehumanized violence of Euro-Americans radiated outward for three more years, continuing in a series of one-sided conflicts euphemistically known as the Humboldt War.

The pages of many newspapers proved that whites had not lost their taste for blood. The *Humboldt Times* published numerous articles praising the efforts of volunteers. Headlines like "A Good Haul of Diggers—Band Exterminated" were typical.[75] The *Times* argued that those Native Americans unwilling to be removed were rightfully destined for extermination.[76] While the wanton murders of 188 innocent people seemed to make no lasting impression on whites in the Humboldt Bay region, Native peoples determined to go to war in hopes of expelling the whites. As one resolute Native man commented, white men had wiped out his family, and having nothing else to live for, he determined to live out the rest of his life in the mountains fighting against white incursion.[77]

Two years later, in April 1862, settlers in the region held a citizens' meeting to discuss recent fighting between whites and Native Americans, in which white communities had been destroyed and citizens driven from the region. According to the *Humboldt Times*, "[The citizens] resolved, that patience with us, with these Indians, and with everything except that which is manly, practical, and fully adequate to the immediate removal of the various tribes from our midst, has ceased to be a virtue, the trials of 12 years, and the gloom by barbarous murders being more than we can bear."⁷⁸ The resolution contained the answer to Harte's question: one could kill babies if one were willing to be a masculine, pragmatic white citizen willing to do what was necessary and expedient to bring about the will of the people. In fact according to the *Humboldt Times*, distinctions of guilt and innocence had lost all meaning. Plainly, the idea of killing indiscriminately, such as had been done at Indian Island, did little to sour Euro-Americans against spilling innocent blood. The *Times* reported, "Tribes will be held responsible for crimes and no special pain will be taken to find the individual perpetrators. . . . [Instead] any ten will be taken and hung if the guilty are not brought forward."⁷⁹

Harte was part of a small group of people ahead of their time in California. But even Harte never again made what he had seen in California a focus of his writing, and rarely ever spoke of the matter.⁸⁰ Not until the 1880s was there much interest in ameliorating the lot of Native peoples, and even then such efforts were often terribly misguided, even themselves genocidal. Scholars, anthropologists in particular, wanted to preserve Native American cultures and languages but not necessarily the people themselves.⁸¹ Hobbyists interested in the recovery of a Native American past to inform their own Euro-American identities sought to emulate Native Americans in the wake of their perceived disappearance.⁸² Even works of fiction, such as Helen Hunt Jackson's *Ramona*, attempted to reshape Euro-American thinking about Native Americans.⁸³ Jackson failed because her Native American characters were too far outside the popular conception of Indians as ignorant, lazy savages.⁸⁴ Writers of popular literature, for the most part, exhibited one of two diametrically opposed views on the destruction of Native Americans. Created in the context of Manifest Destiny, western expansion, and triumphal interpretations of America's historical past, "the Indian could be figured as a noble hero, tragic in defeat."⁸⁵ In California, though, Native Americans bore little resemblance to the characters of James Fenimore Cooper or even Jackson. California newspapers helped the white population to understand that the real Indigenous population was long gone, or perhaps had never been in California. Other writers, such as Mark Twain, scoffed at the idea of the noble savage, characterizing Native Americans in a manner typical of most California newspapers.[86] Voices like Twain's were commonplace in nineteenth-century literature discussing the frontier and Native Americans.[87]

Some inside and outside of California gave Harte a sympathetic hearing, but this was the exception rather than the rule. More commonly news about Native Americans in California confirmed the tropes Euro-Americans had carried with them into California since the 1840s, connecting ideas of national destiny to the destiny of Native people as a race. Some newspapers lamented the brutality but recognized that it was a necessary brutality. If Euro-Americans were to fulfill their national Manifest Destiny it would be necessary to remove all obstacles in their way, in the most expedient and efficient ways possible. Some newspapers went so far as to catalogue Native peoples and cultures in anticipation of their demise, in effect eulogizing a living people. The *Los Angeles Star*, for example, ran a multipart series on the Native Americans of Los Angeles County in 1852. The *Star*'s correspondent presupposed the loss of local Native Americans at some approaching date, and so catalogued a living people doomed to die. In fact attendant to his views on local Native peoples was that the missions had taken some of what was truly admirable from them and corrupted them. The Native Americans found in the Los Angeles area were not as they had been.[88] They were not authentic. Similar articles appeared in other papers.[89] Perhaps the greatest journalistic undertaking to preserve information about California's Native Americans was made in 1860–61 by the *California Farmer*. Published in San Francisco, the *Farmer* billed itself as a "journal of useful science." According to the editors, their two multipart articles on Native people was to preserve the "Indianology of California" in anticipation of Native American extinction.[90]

Newspapers helped reinforce the notions of Indian savagery, depravity, and ultimately the doomed nature of the race. Coverage of the animalized nature of Native peoples in California was represented by a letter to the editor of the *Knoxville Whig* of Tennessee, sent by James Brownlow. In the short letter, Brownlow used a recent appellation assigned to Native Americans, "Lo." So many times had "Lo! The poor Indian" appeared in print that cynics like Brownlow had shortened it simply to "Lo." His letter, which achieved approbation in California by its reprinting in the *Lassen Sage Brush*, attempted to educate readers in Tennessee about "Lo": "I think I have become pretty well acquainted with that poor Indian generally known as Lo. I think if J. Fennimore [*sic*] Cooper could spend two or three weeks with me in the Sacramento Mountains he would cease writing the life of Lo in the shape of cheap novels, or, if he could only see his 'lovely Indian maid' wading through the entrails of a coyote or lizard as long as one's arm, and winding up with a glandered horse head for dessert, he would come to the conclusion that there was more hyena than romance in her nature."[91] Brownlow's message was clear: Why lament the passage of such filthy animals? And passing they were.

Euro-Americans had long believed Indians were a dying race. It was a most convenient "fact" when one considered that white settlers desired the lands these dying people lived upon. In California the perception of the inevitable fate of Native Americans was publicized in newspapers. "The red men of California," announced the *Northern Journal*, "are fast passing away and if left to roam at will around and in the settlements, but a few more years will suffice to exterminate the race." Undoubtedly, given the evidence of how many Californians felt about Native Americans, most readers probably nodded and said, "Good." As the editors of the *Journal* well knew, it was their countrymen who were doing the exterminating. The *Journal* argued that the choice left to Native Americans was either to remain free and earn a bullet or succumb to disease in payment for their indolence, improvidence, and dishonest nature, or accept reservation life for their own protection.[92] Whether or not the editors knew that reservations were places of rape, murder, and disease, one cannot know. They were at least of two minds when it came to the fate of Native Americans; some apparent room for their physical survival was allowable, if they could manage to succumb to cultural genocide on a reservation. The *Chico Weekly Courant* was more unified in its beliefs about the inevitable fate of Native Americans in California. "Nothing but extermination" would solve the problem of Native-white relations, according to the *Courant*. Reservations and humane treatment were foolishness. The pragmatic solution was "a crusade" to exterminate every last Indian, "leaving not a root or branch of them" alive.[93] Some whites worked hard to bring an end to Native American existence, and many California newspapers were there to publicize, promote, and aggrandize the effort.

Even in 1890, when Native-white difficulties had nearly ceased in California, newspapers continued to exert a negative influence on the lives of Native Americans. When a case of smallpox was discovered in the vicinity of Greenville, the *Greenville Bulletin* called on the white citizenry to deal with the outbreak democratically: "The people of the valleys should at once hold meetings and adopt and enforce an effective quarantine of the present case and any others that may occur." This was particularly necessary because, as the *Bulletin* noted, the whites of the region still employed numerous Native people as servants in their homes, and the threat posed by contact was real. The paper proposed that Native Americans be made to stay away from towns and homes, while whites should be vaccinated against the disease; there was no consideration of vaccinating the Native Americans, though. The paper made no mention of any concern for the Native American community. Rather, the editors worried that the spread of the disease would hurt business in the region.[94] Such was American sentiment in Greenville, California, on Christmas Eve in 1890.

Conclusion
At a Crossroads in the Genocide

For every one of those miserable blankets furnished by the agents,
Government will have to pay dearly in money and the lifeblood of
her soldiers. For all the evil acts of those men invested with authority,
imposed upon the helpless Indians, Government is responsible.
Months and years may drag on before this outbreak of a handful of
desperate men will be quelled, which need never have been. There
seems now no course open for a final settlement of this war except
complete extermination of the unhappy tribe. Instead of appointing
men whose protestations the Indians could believe in, their worst
enemies are appointed as a "Peace Commission." That is, of a verity, like
that of a once renowned King of Egypt to another oppressed people.
Daily Alta California (1873)

When the *Daily Alta California*, one of the rare California newspapers
sometimes sympathetic to the Native American perspective, reported
on the coming peace talks between the Modocs and a peace commission led by Gen. Edward S. Canby, it could not have known that
less than two months later, Canby and other members of the commission would be assassinated by the Modocs and a no-holds-barred
war would commence between them and the United States. Why the
Modocs would choose this course was clear in the article: decades of
broken promises and treaties, lies and double-dealing, theft of land,
and numerous attempts to exterminate them by policy and by violence.
Indeed the *Alta* predicted that "no possible good" could come of the

conference.[1] And no good did come. In 1873, as Modoc warriors fought bloody engagements against soldiers of the U.S. Army in the bleak landscape of the Modoc Plateau in northeastern California, genocide in California was at a crossroads. In the years to come, the effort to exterminate Native Americans would shift from overt attempts at physical genocide of the previous twenty-five years to subtle, sometimes transparent attempts to destroy Native peoples by neglecting them into quiet starvation or wiping out their identity as sovereign peoples, as unique cultures, as cohesive groups. By the late 1860s much of the furor over Native-white relations was dying down in California. The Indigenous population had suffered massive decline due to murder, disease, and starvation, on and off reservations. As the 1870s dawned, California's Native Americans entered a new era in their relationship with whites. By 1870 Indigenous peoples of California numbered perhaps thirty thousand, a decline of 80 percent in twenty-four years. Whites began a final push toward exterminating Native Americans with a combination of war, allotment, and assimilation. In these last decades of the nineteenth century, whites would come as close as they ever would to the complete eradication of Indigenous people, as census data taken in 1900 revealed that California's Native population had dropped to a level of approximately fifteen thousand, 90 percent less than when white Americans began flowing into California a little over fifty years before.

In many ways the Transcontinental Railroad, which linked California to the transportation infrastructure of the United States beginning in 1869, signaled this new era. As California was connected to the Midwest and East, it became connected to the Native-white conflict raging in other parts of the United States during the years immediately following the Civil War. The white citizenry in the eastern half of the United States would come to understand California's Indian affairs mainly in their postwar incarnation, as a massively depleted Native American population divested of most of its land base, struggling against federal Indian agents and soldiers. The story was much the same for Native populations everywhere in North America at the time. The era of popular, democratically conceived, and government-subsidized death squads had passed, the bloodiest work mostly completed, to be followed by a new era characterized by reservations incapable of much more than well-meaning neglect. As was true since colonial times, treaties between whites and Native people were seldom honored in the long term, and the annuities, benefits, and protections promised were seldom afforded. This was even more true in California because of the failure to ratify the eighteen federal treaties.

The Native American experience in California in the 1840s–1860s was already being silenced in the national memory of the United States by virtue of this new connectivity between East and West. When white citizens heard of California Indian affairs in the 1870s and later, it was a familiar tale that jibed with the story of Native-white relations elsewhere in the United States. Early in the 1870s nationally publicized events surrounding the Modoc War in northeastern California helped whites in the East contextualize Native-white relations not in terms of the past two decades of California history, but in the context of the present state of Indian affairs in the United States: U.S. soldiers rooting out the final armed resistance of Native peoples and the forced removal of these groups onto isolated, desolate reservations.

The slow march toward the Modoc War of 1873 began in 1851, when miners founded the town of Yreka, west of the Modocs' land on the west side of Tule Lake in northeastern California. Troubles began between whites and the Modocs almost immediately. Ben Wright led a party of whites to massacre an entire Modoc village in 1852, as well as commit several other murders of Modoc people in the 1850s. The Modocs and other Indigenous peoples of the region responded in kind. Wright was so successful as a killer of Native Americans, and such a hero to the local whites, that he was made the Indian agent for the region following the massacre.[2] Hostilities continued until 1864, when the federal government agreed to remove the Modocs to Oregon.[3] They were relocated to the Klamath Reservation, already home to the Klamath people, who were traditional enemies of the Modocs.[4] Meanwhile white settlers flowed onto Modoc land in their absence. When a Modoc leader named Kenitpoos determined to lead members of his people back to the Lost River area of the Tule Lake region in 1865, they found whites settled there.[5] Kenitpoos's father had been among those murdered back in 1852, during the massacres led by Ben Wright to exterminate the Indigenous population.[6] Four years of tense relations followed, with the white settlers clamoring for permanent removal of Kenitpoos and his people. In 1869 the federal government acquiesced. The Modocs at Lost River were convinced by federal officials to move back to the Klamath Reservation; if they did not, the officials argued, local whites would exterminate them. The Modocs under Kenitpoos returned to the reservation for a second time.

In the spring of 1870 Kenitpoos and some of his people left again, to return home to the Lost River region. In 1872 the federal government again relented to pressure from white citizens to remove the Modocs at Lost River. This time, though, elements of the U.S. Army, commanded by Gen. Edward S. Canby, were dispatched to force the Modocs back to the Klamath Reservation. In the fall of 1872 this attempt at forced removal triggered war between the United States and the Modocs. More than four hundred U.S. soldiers with artillery support fought the Modocs on the lava fields of the Modoc Plateau. The Modocs, using the natural rocky cover and an intimate knowledge of their country, resisted for months, despite being outnumbered four to one by soldiers equipped with repeating rifles and modern artillery.

In the spring of 1873 the Modocs, under the leadership of Kenitpoos, entered into peace negotiations with General Canby and the former superintendent of Indian affairs for Oregon, A. B. Meacham. Earlier in the year Meacham had suggested that the Modocs be given their own reservation at Lost River, but his successor disagreed.[7] This unwillingness would cost the United States dearly. According to Lt. Harry De Witt Moore, serving in the 21st U.S. Infantry during the Modoc War, army intelligence reports indicated that Kenitpoos believed defeat was inevitable, and his only choice seemed to be to give in or give up his life in the war. The soldiers felt sure that he would choose the former. Moore stated that Canby had the power to offer the Modocs a reservation at Lost River, although the implication was that he would not offer one if possible.[8] Presumably the reason to hold back this option was the fury it would create among whites in the area. Under pressure from his people and other Modoc leaders, Kenitpoos chose a drastically different path of resistance: he and his men assassinated Canby at a peace conference on April 11, 1873. This triggered massive public outrage among whites and calls for Indian extermination, and hostilities were renewed between the United States and the Modocs.[9]

The ferocity of the fighting that ensued stunned young Lieutenant Moore. "I want no more of Indian fighting of this kind," he wrote, referring to the horror of the lava beds and being under constant threat of Modoc attack. He preferred fights in places such as Arizona, where "a troop of Cavalry can surprise an Indian camp, kill fifty or sixty and not lose a man. In fighting there the danger is not much above deer hunting." There were no easy kills in the lava fields around the lake. Moore and his men were pinned down among the rocks and in constant fear for their lives. He noted that the Modocs had been allowed to visit the army's camp many times, and they were now paying for it. Among other problems, they knew the officers by sight, and knew to kill them first, so Moore and other officers began dressing as enlisted men.[10] Despite the attrition of U.S. forces, the soldiers' ammunition, food, and reinforcements arrived with regularity. Throughout the remainder of April and into May, the Modocs' resources and numbers declined, even as they exacted a terrible toll on the army.

In June 1873, unable to hold out any longer, the Modocs surrendered. Kenitpoos and the other participants in the assassination were tried and sentenced to death by a military tribunal. In the fall of 1873 he and three other Modocs were hanged, their bodies, and their severed heads sent to the Army Medical Museum.[11] The survivors of Kenitpoos's band were forcibly removed to faraway Indian Territory. They remained there in exile until 1909, when they were allowed to return to the Klamath River Reservation, but not their homes.[12] For the those who had remained on the reservation and not participated in the war, the resistance of the Lost River Modocs produced tangible benefits. In 1879 a government report noted that the usual state of affairs for

Native Americans on reservations had developed at the Klamath River Reservation by the late 1870s: whites were squatting on parts of the reservation and claiming the lands as their own. But the government agreed to grant other land to the settlers rather than attempt to issue them title to the reservation lands. The reasoning was clear: the Modoc War was one of the most expensive Indian wars ever fought by the United States, in lives and money. The government feared that the Modocs, Klamaths, and other Native peoples housed on the reservation would launch a violent resistance that might make the earlier war pale by comparison.[13] Whites were ordered off the reservation, although the government made plans to shrink the reservation as the number of Native peoples housed there dwindled as early as the following year.[14]

Concurrent with the hope generated for some Native peoples through the active resistance of Kenitpoos and the Modocs was the Ghost Dance religion that sprang up in California in the 1870s.[15] Emanating from Paiute and Shoshone people in western Nevada and eastern California, the Ghost Dance provided a spiritual rallying point for resistance, using a syncretic blend of Native American beliefs and Christianity. Wodziwob and Tavivo spread the Ghost Dance among Indian peoples in California, Oregon, and Nevada in the 1870s. Native peoples in California began to sing, dance, and pray for the end of the world, when the Creator would return and set the world aright. Whites would be removed from Native American lands, and the people would return to their proper homes. Groups of northern and central California Indian peoples participated. Pomo, Achomawi, Yana, Wintu, Modoc, Wintun, Patwin, Maidu, Kato, Wappo, Shasta, Yurok, and Miwok peoples, among others, began to dance and sing.[16] Groups in the southern portion of the Central Valley also participated.[17] According to the anthropologist Cora Du Bois, Kenitpoos and the Modocs who participated in the Modoc War were all practitioners of the Ghost Dance, and some whites, including A. B. Meacham, believed the dance played a role in starting the war. However, Du Bois notes that no evidence exists that such a connection existed, especially as no examples of the dance being practiced by the Modocs during the war are to be found.[18]

Despite their ardent attempts to hasten the end of the world, the end did not come. The Ghost Dance receded, but did not disappear, into the spiritual background. Many other groups in California rejected the dance outright, and in some groups the people were divided in its use.[19] It was revived by Wovoka, son of Tavivo, in the 1880s.[20] Wovoka preached that both whites and Native peoples would be renewed by the Ghost Dance, and following the renewal of the world by the Creator, whites and Native Americans would be reborn to live separately. The Dance as proposed by Wovoka was to be peaceful and for the mutual benefit of both races. By 1890 the Ghost Dance had spread across the North American continent, offering Indian peoples hope and striking fear into the hearts of whites, who interpreted the movement as violent. Indeed some scholars argue that the press willfully misrepresented the nature of the Ghost Dance in order to purposefully strike terror into the hearts of their readers, hoping to sell newspapers to a fearful public hungry for news.[21] Ironically, in California the dance excited little attention and none of the widespread, exaggerated panic that would characterize it elsewhere in the United States. According to the *Greenville Bulletin*, the Ghost Dance had been an annual occurrence in the region for some time, with hundreds of dancers, and whites attended the dances with interest.[22] To the east, though, whites became fearful with the help of the popular press. As a result, it was popularly resolved to eradicate the Ghost Dance, and any Native peoples who refused to end its practice. In 1890 this idea of kill or be killed had its most terrible manifestation at the Wounded Knee Massacre in South Dakota.

Reservations and Indian schools also began to take new shapes during the 1870s and after. The organization of reservations for California's Indigenous populations was a jerrybuilt system, owing to the U.S. Senate's decision not to ratify the eighteen proposed treaties. Instead the federal government set up a system established piecemeal by executive order, which set aside lands to move Native peoples to but did not otherwise establish a coherent system.[23] Indeed much of the land went unsurveyed and unused. The federal government continued its policy of neglect even in the face of clear reports of problems from its agents and a small but vocal group of concerned white citizens.[24] Reports of problems among Indians ostensibly living under the care of the federal government were essentially the same throughout California during the second half of the nineteenth century. Edward Beale's reports of the 1850s, which acquainted his superiors with the problems of Native-white relations, mirror those of later officials. In 1862, for example, William Dole, serving as commissioner for Indian affairs, issued a report calling attention to the plight of Native Americans living on federal reserves. Without the protection of official treaties, Dole claimed, California's Native populations were reduced to a "steal or starve" strategy for survival, owing to the fact that whites claimed any lands that they might derive a living from, and in general did not tolerate the presence of Indians in or around their communities. The tragic effect was to plant a sense of insecurity and injustice in Native people in the face of encroachment by white civilization. This engendered distrust and proved an obstacle to Native-white relations, even when legitimate and thoughtful attempts to aid Native Americans were made. Dole believed only a unilateral decision on the part of the U.S. government to provide support and justice could reverse the situation.[25]

Eleven years later Reverend John G. Ames, acting as a special agent for the Office of Indian Affairs, issued a report on the state of former Mission Indian bands in southern California. They had been shunted onto small pieces of their former land base, unable to get legal title even to these plots. This was despite the fact that Mission Indians were providing the majority of the farm labor in the region that would become parts of San Diego, Riverside, and San Bernardino counties. Native leaders implored Ames to aid them in establishing the legal right to inhabit their lands. The Cahuilla leader Cabezon, for instance, asked Ames to secure the rights for his people to live on their lands as his dying wish. Ames reaffirmed Dole's position, suggesting that without federal intervention Native peoples in California were doomed to live at the whim of white settlers. The acting secretary of the interior, Gen. B. R. Cowan, and the commissioner of Indian affairs, E. P. Smith, concurred with this position. Cowan asked the House Committee on

Appropriations to fund reservations for the five thousand Indigenous people in the region who had had their lands, homes, and once-prospering civilization destroyed by white settlers.[26] But, in practice, even funding was no guarantee of success.

In 1870 J. V. Farwell, a special agent sent to northern California Indian reservations by the Office of Indian Affairs, found the reservations overrun by whites, mismanaged, and breeding grounds for diseases. Rotten food, white men forcing Native women into prostitution, and epidemic disease were the norms. Farwell found that more than three-quarters of the population on the reservation at Hoopa were suffering from disease, some afflicted by multiple types. The only way a Native person might survive would be to flee.[27] Of course, in some areas a Native American found off the reservation risked outright murder and would find few protections under the laws of California. A year later Farwell reported that matters had only become worse.[28]

In 1875 Charles A. Wetmore issued a report to Congress detailing the state of affairs for former Mission Indians in California, with echoes of Dole, Ames, and Farwell: "The Indians have been forced by superior power to trade their patrimony and their liberties for civilized bubbles blown by the breath of political insincerity; trading by compulsion from bad to worse until they have, as the Mission Indians of California, simply the right to beg. They beg bread of their white neighbors on whose land they are trespassers; on roads where they are vagrants, and in the jails which are their only asylums. They have begged in vain for legal rights. Their right to petition Congress has been ignored."[29] Clearly the earlier efforts undertaken by the United States on behalf on Indigenous peoples in southern California had not borne fruit by 1875. The tone of Wetmore's and earlier reports suggests why this was. The tone is paternalistic and representative of officials and government convinced that Indians were inferior, "totally unfit for citizenship," and likely disappearing as a race.[30]

In 1877 the federal government established the Mission Indian Agency at San Bernardino and the people were placed under the care of the Reverend S. S. Lawson. But the presence of Lawson did little to secure a stable future for the Indigenous population of southern California. According to the scholars Lowell Bean and Harry Lawton, not until 1879 did Lawson establish a working agency, and then only for Native peoples on his roll. It would take until 1882 for Lawson to begin the distribution and use of agricultural implements and programs to aid agency enrolled Native Americans.[31] In 1880 the Cahuilla leader Cabezon died, his last wish unfulfilled. By the time Helen Hunt Jackson's "Report on the Conditions and Needs of the Mission Indians" was submitted in 1883, and even before her *Century of Dishonor* was published in 1881, thousands more of California's Indigenous population had perished through starvation, murder, and neglect in the face of a justice system that paid more attention to them as criminals to be prosecuted than victims to be defended, a state and federal government that put the interests of white citizens first, and non-Native populations generally unconcerned with the unavoidable fate of the "vanishing race" of Indians. In 1891 the "Indian question" was no longer an open one. Many white Californians believed the destruction of the Indigenous population of North America was a fait accompli. This included the publishers of the *Greenville Bulletin*, who reprinted the words of Gen. Nelson A. Miles: "Indians are practically a doomed race, and none realize it better than themselves."[32] Not only were Native people "vanishing" on reservations through neglect, disease, and apathy, but so too were the hopes for recovery of future generations of Native peoples. Far from convincing white officials of the ineffectiveness of attempting to enforce reservation policies, the practice continued into the twentieth century with the attendant problems intact.[33] The U.S. government had decades of evidence that life on reservations endangered the health and welfare of Native people. But the only alternative to enforcing their captivity would be to limit the freedom of movement and actions of white citizens, their constituency. The indirect, painfully slow genocidal policies and conditions in California on and off reservations were allowed to proceed rather than restrain the liberty of white citizens. Other genocidal programs were also being carried out, both on and off reservations. In particular, Native American children were being taken from parents, with a genocidal goal in mind.

Beginning in 1879 at Carlisle Barracks in Pennsylvania, Indian boarding schools became part of the assault on Native American identity and existence. Education, in conjunction with allotment, became the primary focus of federal Indian policy in the late nineteenth century. In 1891 Congress enacted a law that Native children attend some type of supervised schooling, either on reservation in day schools or off reservation at boarding schools. This led to attempts by Native people to hide their children and prevent their removal to boarding schools where reservation programs were not available. It led too to military forces being used to separate parents from their children. According to the historian Roger Nichols, when Native American families successfully resisted the taking of their children to white schools, federal agents responded by cutting "weekly food rations to uncooperative families."[34] Families retained their children but suffered the threat of starvation. According to a congressional report in 1891, such was often the sad case. Some Native American families who did send their children to school saw it as a way to maintain the favor of the reservation and Indian agents.[35] There were 148 Indian boarding schools and 225 Indian day schools with an enrollment of twenty thousand children in the United States by the beginning of the twentieth century.[36]

Sherman Indian Institute and Fort Yuma were the primary boarding school facilities for southern California. In northern California there were boarding schools at Fort Bidwell, Greenville, Round Valley, and Hoopa. In 1911 there were perhaps 1,100 students in boarding schools, approximately half of them housed at the Sherman Institute in Riverside, California. Another thousand students may have attended Indian day schools at one of the twenty-two locations spread between northern and southern California.[37] Curricula were genocidal; they focused on assimilating Indian children to Western ideals of behavior, morality, and civilization. Classes also included instruction in vocations. At Greenville, for example, agriculture was emphasized. At Fort Bidwell, instruction was gendered: domestic work for girls and agriculture for boys.[38] But the primary aim was to take the Indianness out of Indians.

Indian schools made no secret of their genocidal intent. In the words of the first superintendant of the Carlisle Indian School, Richard Henry Pratt, these institutions were to "kill the Indian, save the man."[39] Removing children from their parents' care, banning Native American culture and language, and indoctrinating students in Western culture and white civilization, were the key strategies employed. These schools were engaged in a subset of genocide, often termed ethnocide or culturicide.[40] Native American children were exposed to diseases, and many perished in these schools or were sent home to their families to die.[41] The key point made by one official at the Greenville boarding school in his 1903 annual report was not to increase funding for education at the school, but to build a hospital at the school due to the number of ill children.[42] Still, the greatest threat to the health of Native children was local whites, who often attacked without provocation. In one instance in 1896, two Native American boys were shot in the face at short range with a shotgun for fishing on a white man's property. One boy received fifty-five pellets in his face. The paper noted that the boy was likely to die.[43] Creating stable relations with Native people was difficult, if not impossible with occurrences such as these. As the nineteenth century wore on, new policies sought to take Indian affairs in new directions.

In the 1870s many white Americans began to question the utility and sustainability of the treaty system and the associated system of reservations. In California this discussion may have been influenced by the declining importance of Native labor in some parts of the state during the 1870s. As the United States was gripped by one of the worst depressions of the nineteenth century, the Panic of 1873, white Californians responded with an aggressive wave of nativism. Attacks and punitive legislation were directed against Chinese immigrants, and whites called on state and federal government to aid white labor in a time of crisis. Measures such as the state's new constitution of 1879 and the federal Chinese Exclusion Act of 1882 demonstrated the responsiveness of government to its citizenry's demands. According to the scholar Richard Thomas, by 1880 "the Indian had practically been removed from the labor market."[44] By the mid-1880s the federal government declared that Indian reservations were not the property of Native peoples, but of the United States. Native peoples were allowed to reside upon these lands at the pleasure of the United States. Collectively, then, Native Americans owned nothing when it came to reservation lands. Indeed the government and reformers claiming to have Native people's best interests in mind began to sponsor the idea that Indian ownership was not impossible for an individual. If Native peoples were willing to adopt white conceptions of property ownership, then they might possess land of their own and have it protected, as any white might have property protected under state and federal laws.

Senator Henry L. Dawes of Massachusetts, chairman of the Senate Committee on Indian Affairs, codified this proposed new relationship between Native Americans and the land in the overtly genocidal General Allotment Act, or Dawes Act, in 1887. Indigenous peoples were to be allotted parcels of land up to 160 acres in size from existing lands reserved for Native American occupancy. The idea behind the law was to destroy the ties of community and culture bound up in the way Native peoples traditionally used and occupied their lands. Land not allotted would be purchased by the government, the price paid not to Native peoples but to the Office of Indian Affairs to fund other culturally erosive assimilation programs. These lands were then sold to individuals or corporations for private development. Native Americans in the United States lost over 100 million acres of land in this manner, and untold billions of dollars in the value of resources extracted from these lands. In California, however, where Native people had been prevented almost completely from obtaining legal titles under U.S. law and whites lived illegally on many reservations, the Dawes Act did little to make matters any worse. None of the reservations extant in California was fully allotted, and in fact most Native Americans in California resisted allotment. In some cases, such as at Round Valley, whites interfered with the process, complicating matters.[45] Those who accepted allotment often found that the lands conferred were in areas so poor and isolated as to be unviable as economic units for self-sufficiency.[46] Allotment, then, did little to change the state of Indian affairs in California, despite the Dawes Act's genocidal intent of forcing

Native Americans to abandon traditional, communal landownership and subsistence practices in favor of individual ownership.[47]

Many Native people in California entered the twentieth century living in viable communities still bound together by tradition and culture, despite the tenuous nature of their land claims and relationships with non-Native neighbors, the state, and the U.S. government. And this despite decades of overt attempts to bring about a bloody, physical genocide by the white citizens of the state. The earliest of these attempts involved a two-decade-long direct assault on Native Americans by armed citizen-soldiers operating under the cover of the law, and sometimes not, resulting in the murder, maiming, kidnapping, and general terrorizing of generations of Native people. These efforts to exterminate the Indigenous population physically or culturally drew on the support of local, state, and federal government to authorize, to fund, and to augment with troops the popular campaigns. These grim endeavors were catalogued by the popular press, which celebrated them frequently, condemned them rarely, and ultimately did their only truly positive service to Native Americans in the production of a historical record that has survived to condemn the perpetrators, who failed to fully execute their intended genocide of California's Indigenous peoples, despite some success in exterminating their actions from popular memory, the national consciousness, and not a few history books.

Epilogue
Forgetting and Remembering Genocide

The end of the Mill Creek "war" was unusual and to some extent tragic. A party of armed whites, acting without other authority than resentment and inborn savagery, surprised the [Mill Creek Yahi] tribe on the upper waters of Mill Creek in 1865. Their effort was apparently to wipe out this Indian group on the spot. On the admission of men who took part in the action, fire was opened on the defenseless Indians in the early morning, and an uncertain number of them, men, women, and children, shot down. A few, not more than three or four, perhaps, escaped into the brush and got clear. The Mill Creek tribe as a tribe disappeared from history at this time.

T. T. Waterman, "The Last Wild Tribe of California" (1915)

According to one progressive reformer in 1911, more than half of California's Native population were living on lands to which they technically had no legal claim and were in danger of having their bare subsistence level of life stripped from them at any moment. Such was the case for one unidentified band of Native Americans in Healdsburg, who were evicted from their homes without warning in 1910. The group was forced to live under a bridge until the federal government could step in and remove them.[1] Unfortunately, to many whites in California, the sad state of California's Indigenous peoples was acceptable. Aside from progressive reform groups, such as the Northern California Indian Association, many whites considered Native Americans still present in California as essentially no longer authentic Native peoples. A type of nostalgia for what was Indian developed. In 1905, for instance, burial sites of Native people only recently deceased were being treated as curiosities and the sources of decor for the homes of whites.[2] Others attempted to re-create Indianness by dressing up or emulating Native Americans by living in the wilderness for brief periods.[3] At the same time, Native peoples were often dispersed and no longer living in ways that whites imagined as recognizably Indian. A man known as Ishi demonstrates this misconception, and also shows how white Californians had already effectively silenced the truth of Native-white relations in nineteenth-century California and replaced reality with an aggrandized tale of a noble pioneer tradition. Barely into the twentieth century, the genocide was already nearly forgotten.

In 1911 a Yahi Indian man who came to be known as Ishi walked out of the rugged mountains and foothills of northern California, near death from starvation and exhaustion.[4] Ishi and several other Yahi people, whom whites referred to as the Mill Creek Indians, had been in hiding from whites for more than forty years. Ishi was the last remaining member of the group and the last of the Yahi people; indeed Ishi and his Yahi people are the most famous example of a total physical genocide in California history.[5] He was the last man on Earth who spoke the Yahi language. For many whites, Ishi embodied a living vessel of Yahi culture, beliefs, and history. And in 1911 they were fascinated by him when he appeared, unlooked for, in the midst of a civilization well along in forgetting about the genocidal history of nineteenth-century California. While whites wished to forget such horrors, they were interested in celebrating the men who had "won" California. Ishi's story would appear in newspapers also publishing stories celebrating men like Robert Anderson and Hi Good, the heroes of the relatively recent slaughter of Indian peoples, but without any sense of irony at the time, despite the fact that Anderson and Good were among those who exterminated most of the Yahi.[6] The appearance of Ishi yielded the perfect opportunity to celebrate the best memories of how California had been tamed.

Ishi wandered, near death, into a butcher's slaughterhouse near Oroville, California.[7] Despite his being barely able to move due to hunger and exhaustion, some local papers described him as a thief, caught by a white man who called the local sheriff.[8] The sheriff took Ishi to jail and locked him up. There Ishi waited until the Bureau of Indian Affairs could decide on his disposition. Even as Ishi sat in jail, there was much ado about him. Many, especially the press, considered the strange, "wild" Indian to be the last real Indian in the country. Ishi became an instant curiosity, described and celebrated as a living relic. Newspapers ran headlines such as "Least Civilized Man Tells His Tales by Sign," "Last Lost Indian Finally Captured," and "Lost Language Revived."[9] Newspaper editors and correspondents included what they thought were humorous imitations of Indian speech, as papers of the previous century had been wont to do. Authorities held "pow wows" and Ishi uttered made-up phrases such as "ow wow gullabulub."[10] Such headlines and articles painted Ishi as a survivor of "lost" peoples, not exterminated ones. Even though some of the murderers yet lived, history had already silenced much about the genocide. Indeed part of the excitement surrounding Ishi flowed from the genocide committed on Native peoples in nineteenth-century California. In 1911 the state had only about 10 percent of the Indigenous population it had sixty years before.

In much of California, Native Americans were a rarity. Many whites may have never seen a California Native American, although many seemed unaware of the depth of atrocity resorted to by nineteenth-century Americans. In 1911 there were barely sixteen thousand Native Americans living in California, and many of them were hanging on to a bare existence in a state of abject poverty in out-of-the-way places. Perhaps these Native people were the lucky ones; they had moved far enough away from whites to live free, had created strategies to subsist and preserve their cultures, and had not died from one of the many Euro-American diseases that had helped genocide along in the state. Only 10 percent of the California Indian population of 1848 remained, though this is a misleading figure as it fails to describe the aggregate loss of life in the intervening years, being a simple comparison of totals. Few whites had direct experience of Native peoples in California in the early twentieth century; Ishi represented an opportunity to glimpse a bygone era that was largely forgotten by whites, even though it lay in the recent past. For scholars such as the anthropologist Alfred Kroeber, recovering the past and preserving it for future generations was a mission made omnipresent by the appearance of Ishi. Kroeber, the first professor of anthropology at the University of California, Berkeley, instantly grasped the wealth of information that Ishi surely possessed. He believed Ishi was the only untainted specimen of a wild Indian left in California, unaffected by years of Euro-American contact. In this, Kroeber was wrong.

In 1908 surveyors had stumbled upon Ishi and his small band. Led by a trail guide, Merle Apperson, a surveying party of white men burst into the Yahi camp and caused all but one to flee. The one remaining behind, an old Yahi woman too sick and feeble to move, was wrapped in a blanket. Finding her sick and near death, the party left her, but took many of the possessions of the group, including fur robes, fishing gear, bows and arrows, and all the supplies that the Yahi needed to survive the upcoming winter.[11] Three years later, only Ishi remained; the woman, who turned out to be Ishi's mother, and all the others died that winter following the surveyors' thefts. Even had this been the only contact Ishi had with whites, Kroeber's claim that Ishi was unaffected by whites flew in the face of reason. Ishi and his people, like other Indigenous populations in California, were constantly under white American assault from 1846 onward. Direct assaults in his lifetime had killed his father and sister, as well as hundreds of other Yahi people. The Yahi culture centered on community, and the destruction of that community changed much about the way Ishi and the survivors lived in exile. Indirectly, depopulation of game species, destruction of native plants used for food and medicine, and the seizure of the Yahis' land base all had lasting, deleterious consequences for the survivors. The Yahis living in exile hid from the outside world, no longer engaged in trade, and could not sustain their community in the absence of Yahi women. Kroeber's claim that Ishi was a pure example of unchanged Yahi culture was a deeply flawed conclusion.

When Ishi came out of the mountains near death, he underwent a new round of assaults and adjustments. After some discussion, the Bureau of Indian Affairs allowed Kroeber to take Ishi as a specimen for study. Here lay the manifestation of Kroeber's thinking that Ishi was an example of a real, "wild" Indian. Nothing could exemplify the way a social scientist thought about culture in 1911 better. For Kroeber and other scholars, the excitement centered on Ishi was associated with their belief that "inferior" cultures were mutable and destroyed by contact with "superior" cultures. Ishi represented purity. However, such scholars were limited in their conception of culture. Ideas about cultural hybridity, the mutability of all cultures, and the constant change, adaptation, and metamorphosis of culture exhibited by peoples of all races around the world were as yet unexplored. Rather Kroeber and others thought of Western civilization as the epitome of civilization, by which all other cultures were to be measured and improved by contact. Once contact was made, however, a process introducing impurities began. In this way, whites in 1911 believed Ishi was a real Indian, the last one, while other living Native Americans in the state were not, by virtue of prolonged exposure to Euro-American civilization. As Ishi experienced California in 1911, he made adaptations to his culture. He was no less Yahi because he wore the dress of white men or ate their food. Newspapers seized on these instances as mimicry, not adaptation. According to the *San Francisco Call*, Ishi was "awed by the white man's life."[12]

Despite Kroeber's excitement to find such a "pure" subject for study, he knew nothing of the Yahi. Finding out more became his focus. Even learning the "last wild Indian in North America's" name was impossible. Eventually Kroeber decided to call him Ishi, a word meaning "man" in Yana.[13] Kroeber housed Ishi in a museum, in a room that contained some of the stolen goods from the surveyors' raid. Kroeber and his associates attempted to bring in another Native man, a member of the Northern Yana people, who had lived near the Yahi and had contact with them in the previous century, but the man could not communicate with Ishi effectively. Yana was a related but separate dialect.

The men studying Ishi could not fully understand even what little the Yana man was able to tell them about Ishi. In their interviews, Ishi was reluctant to give his name or describe the recent events of his life. He sang stories about his past, including a six-hour story of "the loves of T-Tut-Ne, the Wood Duck."[14] Ishi would sing many more songs to the scholars in the years ahead.

Kroeber and his colleagues did much the same things Euro-Americans had done to the Native population in the nineteenth century. Kroeber put Ishi to work to further his own ends. He had Ishi dress up in some of the museum collection clothing and pose for cameras and reporters. The photographers captured what they believed to be a glimpse of prehistoric Native Americans. Most of the stories in California newspapers portrayed Ishi the way earlier newspapers had portrayed Indians, as a dying man from an already dead people. Ishi was a survivor only because he had been "lost." Little mention was made of the way Ishi became "lost."

Perhaps Ishi's greatest shock was the number of white people living in and around San Francisco.[15] At its peak, there were about forty people in his band. In the 1840s, before Ishi's birth, perhaps four hundred Yahis lived in the vicinity of Deer Creek and Mill Creek. The story of the Yahis was the story shared by many of California's Indigenous population. White settlers coming in the 1840s began to occupy Indian lands and disrupt traditional subsistence patterns by hunting game and introducing domestic herd animals that crowded out native species. Hunting Native Americans became commonplace. Near the Yahis, white communities made such hunting legal through the introduction by county governments of bounties that paid rewards for Native American heads and scalps. The state government created laws that made it very difficult for Native people to seek redress through state courts or justices of the peace. When Native people resisted by stock raiding or violence, the state responded by legalizing and funding paramilitary volunteer companies to exterminate them and enslave the survivors. Kroeber, wanting to know what had happened to Ishi's people, but with Ishi unwilling to speak of the dead, began to research published accounts of white-Yahi conflicts of the past century. He learned of several brutal massacres, including those that had killed women and children indiscriminately. Kroeber found that between 1865 and 1871, five massacres by whites killed nearly two hundred Yahis.[16] Kroeber had little trouble researching the events, as the press had covered them. Indian genocide, he found, was hidden in plain sight. Hiding murder was easy when the perpetrators and the bystanders were of a like mind, as were their governments and laws.

The state of California petitioned the federal government for assistance in sponsoring genocide, the call for which was loudly supported in the press. When the federal government responded, it was with both troops and money. The federal government eventually reimbursed the state millions of dollars spent on volunteer companies engaged in bringing about genocide in California. White citizens in California supported these measures with letters and petitions, with their tax dollars, with their service, and with their silence about the rape, murder, and enslavement used to deliver the object of the genocidal exercise: land.

Part of the reason Native Americans in California were so hard hit by violence was the effusion of hate and apathy toward them by the Euro-Americans flooding into California. California's Indigenous population was considered completely uncivilized, animal-like, perhaps with an intensity beyond anywhere else in the United States. Their consumption of insects and wild roots in particular were mentioned as signs of their savagery. According to one observer of the animal nature of California Indians, "The men and boys, especially, look more like orangutans than human beings." Their groups, another observer claimed, were like "passels of snakes."[17] Others, as early as the 1860s, were applying tainted versions of Darwin's theories to Native Americans in California, likening them to the "connecting link" between man and beast.[18] But by 1911 the fear of animal-like Indian "depredations" had vanished in California and much of the United States. The widespread genocide had delivered whites the spoils they sought and temporarily taxed the ability of Native people to mount an effective resistance. Given these preconceptions about Native people, it is not surprising that Kroeber decided to put Ishi on display.

Ishi was made an exhibit at the Phoebe A. Hearst Museum of Anthropology at the University of California, Berkeley, in 1911. Thousands of people eventually came to see him.[19] As these thousands came into contact with Ishi, he developed a serious case of pneumonia, a disease that he had no natural immunity to. Despite his grave condition, Kroeber forced Ishi to continue to work. Ishi was also made to work with a linguist in order that Yahi speech might be preserved for study. Ishi aided Kroeber and the linguist Edward Sapir in their attempts to understand the Yahi language. Ishi made several hundred recordings for them. He also used language and song to help people in a nearby hospital, as he sang songs to the sick. Following Ishi's recovery from pneumonia, Kroeber persuaded Ishi to take him to the hiding place of the Yahi survivors.

In the spring of 1914 Kroeber took Ishi on an expedition to his former hiding place. Kroeber hired the guide that had led the surveying party that raided his camp, Merle Apperson. Although Apperson claimed not to have looted the Yahi camp years before, evidence retained by Apperson himself proved otherwise.[20] Apperson still had some of the items he had stolen, and after some haggling was willing to sell the artifacts to Kroeber.[21] Ishi demonstrated hunting and fishing techniques, including the cultural rituals that accompanied subsistence practices. Kroeber had his treasure trove of knowledge, which was lucky for him, as Ishi soon became ill again.

In August 1915 Ishi became ill with tuberculosis. One newspaper claimed that Kroeber was taking Ishi back into the wilderness for his health, suggesting perhaps that wild animals do best in their natural habitat.[22] But Ishi died in March 1916. His brain was removed and sent to a museum, and after dissection his body was cremated and the remains buried in a local cemetery.[23] Clearly the rights afforded to whites in death had not been afforded to Ishi. This was likely due to the fact that many, even in 1916, might have yet felt that Native Americans were more animal than human. The powerful stereotypes and tropes created to explain differences between whites and Native Americans, and more important, to justify their killing and dispossession, were alive and well in the twentieth century. Even T. T. Waterman, Kroeber's assistant and a man who considered Ishi a friend, said, "He was bound to go this way, sooner or later."[24] Despite over forty years of hiding and survival, Ishi was still a member of a dying race, even to his friends. It is not surprising that many people seemed little moved by Ishi's passing. One newspaper described his death in a manner still typical of white attitudes of the previous century:

> "Ishi," the primeval man is dead. He could not stand the rigors of civilization, and tuberculosis, that arch-enemy of those who live in the simplicity of nature and then abandon that life, claimed him. . . . Doubtless much of ancient Indian lore was learned from him, but we do not believe he was the marvel that the professors would have the public believe. He was just a starved-out Indian from the wilds of Deer Creek who, by hiding in its fastness, was long able to escape the white man's pursuit. And the white man with his food and clothing and shelter killed the Indian just as effectually as he would have killed him with a rifle.[25]

One might as well have said that Native Americans would be claimed, one way or another, by white civilization, and that there was neither need nor desire to help it. Ishi represented the end of an inevitable, natural process. Indeed many whites familiar with Ishi judged that with his passing, passed California Indians; the remaining California Indians, on reservations or living as part of multiethnic communities throughout California were judged un-Indian because they had adapted certain elements of Euro-American culture to suit their own needs. Nothing could be further from the truth.

As the historian Jack Forbes has remarked, "Indian people have survived as Indians. They have resisted every form of attack, short of physical annihilation, successfully. In spite of the efforts of Spaniards, Mexicans, and Anglo-Americans to cause them to disappear they have sustained their Indianness, although at times by a slender thread." In the years since the passing of Ishi, California's Native peoples have made a remarkable recovery with little assistance from people outside their communities. Beginning around 1910, Native Americans began to harness the organs of democracy that had been used against them in the preceding six decades. Native people formed organizations, such as the Mission Indian Federation, in order to formulate and deploy strategies to increase their level of representation in local, state, and national government. Sometimes they cooperated with non-Natives; sometimes they worked alone and unaided. They also began "to appeal to white public opinion to improve conditions."[26] They also appealed to other Native peoples, individually and as groups. Some published memoirs for other Native Americans to read and relate to their situations.[27] Native people also passed on the stories, techniques, and beliefs vital to the survival of their culture. Many bands today use revenue derived from Indian gaming or other economic engines to reestablish sovereignty and promote cultural revival movements. In this process, one battle that Native people still wage is against history, and the way many in academia and society conceive of the history of Native-white relations as something other than genocidal in nature. After the evidence presented in this work, one hopes that this may be surprising and disturbing to the reader.

The words of the Holocaust scholar Steven Katz help one understand the current thinking of some scholars about Native American genocide as an event that never happened, at least as they would define it: "Contra the misconceived genocidal school of historical interpreters, it is here relevant to recognize the salient fact—not forgetting particular massacres perpetrated by American military forces, indeed, precisely in light of them—that once the U.S. Army had subdued the great western tribes on the field of battle, it could have slaughtered all the remaining tribal members had genocide been its determinate purpose. It was not and it did not."[28]

As Katz argues, so do others. Katz seems to suggest that the genocide of Native Americans was driven by the U.S. military or the federal government, rather than the acquisitive white citizenry of the United

States. He also misconstrues the presence of survivors for evidence of intent to bring about something other than genocide, rather than the unwillingness of soldiers to fully carry out citizens' wishes or as a reflection of the high costs of actually bringing about total Native American annihilation due to the fiscal impossibility of funding such a campaign. One could more easily and cheaply let people die by starvation, disease, and neglect, particularly if one placed Native Americans out of sight and mind on sometimes arid, isolated reservations. Given the oblique and peripherally organized ways genocide was attempted in the nineteenth century in California, historians outside the field of Native American history have often been reticent to classify the treatment of Native Americans by the United States as genocidal.[29] Much of this is attributable to elements of the debate, especially disputes over the definition of genocide, the role of disease in Native American genocide, and the role of the government in planning and executing genocide, to name but a few.

As this study has argued, genocide in the state of California in the nineteenth century was "planned" by white settlers, miners, and ranchers who used extermination, either physical or cultural, to obtain Indian land and resources. By legalizing, funding, and generally assisting citizens in the commission of genocide, the state and federal governments created a new definition of state-assisted genocide. The free press in California, as well as the many letters, diaries, and petitions created by the perpetrators and bystanders, have come down to us over a century later because, first and foremost, there was no shame in killing savage Indians, and not a little glory. The way Euro-Americans naturalized atrocity as the way to relate to Native peoples allowed the evidence to be preserved rather than destroyed, an ironic silver lining in an otherwise dark history of the attempts to eradicate Indians in California or at least do nothing to prevent such horrors. Hopefully this study is sufficient to generate shame and outrage, today at least, and help in the process of revitalizing, rebuilding, and remunerating Native communities by educating all Americans of the genocidal past of the shared place that Native and non-Native persons now call home.

Notes

The epigraph is from Record 363, Military Department, Office of the Adjutant General, Indian War Papers, 1850–1880, California State Archives, Sacramento (hereafter cited as Indian War Papers). Throughout this work I have corrected spelling errors in source quotations. Spelling in the nineteenth century, even for the formally educated, was often a creative enterprise, with writers frequently spelling the same word differently within the space of a few sentences. Rather than repetitively inserting [sic], I have used the modern spelling. I have preserved grammatical structure as originally written.

1. Throughout this work I have avoided employing the flawed term "Indian" to describe the Native American population of California, except when expressing and analyzing the views of the historical actors using the term. I have also avoided the term "American" as potentially misleading, instead employing the term "Euro-American" so as to not suggest that the white U.S. citizens the term typically refers to are somehow the only "true" Americans. For excellent discussions of the problematic nature of the terms "American" and "Indian" that have shaped my view, see the work of Forbes: *The Indian in America's Past*, 1–5; *Native Americans of California and Nevada*, 122–44; and especially "The Name Is Half the Game: The Theft of 'America' and Indigenous Claims of Sovereignty," in M. Moore, *Eating Fire*, 32–51.

2. Here one must note that while scholars prior to 1945 researched California's Indigenous population and their history—A. L. Kroeber and Stephen Powers notable among them—that work was typically ethnographic or anthropological in its focus, and the histories collected were often incidental to the process of attempting to recover or preserve cultural elements and artifacts. Important work has been done on genocide or elements of genocide in the era preceding the U.S. conquest of California, during the Mexican and

Spanish periods of California history, by scholars such as Edward D. Castillo, Albert Hurtado, Rupert Costo, George Harwood Phillips, and others. These studies have been important in understanding the larger history of genocide in California.

3. Cook's early work has been collected or reprinted in *The Conflict* and *The Population*.

4. For an appraisal of Cook's work and the challenges of Native American demography in California, see Hurtado, "California Indian Demography," 323–43. Some scholars have disputed Cook's findings at length. For an example of such refutation, see Guest, "An Examination," 1–77. For Cook and California placed in the context of Native North American demography, see Lenore A. Stiffarm and Phil Lane Jr., "The Demography of Native North America: A Question of American Indian Survival," in Jaimes, *The State of Native America*, 23–53.

5. Forbes, *Native Americans of California and Nevada*, 53.

6. See also Heizer and Almquist, *The Other Californians*.

7. Phillips's later works are *The Enduring Struggle*; *Indians and Intruders*; *Indians and Indian Agents*; *"Bringing Them under Subjection."*

8. Coffer, "Genocide," 11.

9. The most recent example is Benjamin Madley in his 2009 PhD dissertation at Yale University, "American Genocide: The California Indian Catastrophe, 1846–1873." As of this writing, the dissertation is not available on DAI or via interlibrary loan, but according to his abstract, he too utilizes the Convention.

10. For a compendium of Jack Norton's thoughts in the thirty years following the publication of his seminal work, see Norton, *Centering in Two Worlds*.

11. One must note that despite the title, Beard and Carranco do not discuss the forms and structures of genocide.

12. Baumgardner, *Killing for Land*, 11. Baumgardner seems to suggest that what happened in Round Valley was not genocide. But it is important to note that his work is not a refutation of the claim of genocide; indeed, to be fair, his comments are quite brief on the matter and perhaps do not express his ideas fully, one way or the other.

13. Other important contributions by Hurtado are "Controlling California's Indian Labor Force," 217–38; "'Hardly a Farm House,'" 245–70.

14. W. Churchill, *A Little Matter of Genocide*.

15. Hauptman, *Tribes and Tribulations*.

16. Chalk and Jonassohn, *The History and Sociology of Genocide*; Chirot and McCauley, *Why Not Kill Them All?*; Wilshire, *Get 'Em All!*

17. Other scholars have seen this year as the key juncture; for example, see Rawls, *Indians of California*, 205–6.

18. Faragher, *Women and Men on the Overland Trail.*

19. Raphael Lemkin, "Genocide," in Hinton, *Genocide*, 27.

20. Lemkin, "Genocide," 28.

21. Lemkin, "Genocide," 27.

22. Horowitz, "Many Genocides," 74–89.

23. While I do not engage in a comparative study of genocide in this work, some examples including California Native populations do exist, and manage to do so by comparing the case of California with examples other than the Jewish Holocaust. See Sousa, "'They Will Be Hunted Down,'" 193–209; Madley, "Patterns of Frontier Genocide," 167–92.

24. Lemkin, "Genocide," 27.

25. Lemkin, "Genocide," 29–35.

26. In the Nazi case, although genocide began with relocation and ghettoization, expanded to include slave labor, and eventually focused on actual extermination following the notorious Wansee Conference in 1942, in all of these phases the intent was genocidal. Each phase sought to isolate and then remove or destroy targeted groups from German-controlled territory. Decisions flowed mainly from the Nazi hierarchy, although German industry certainly helped dictate some of the slave-labor measures employed, and average Germans acted as agents, enablers, or, as Daniel Goldhagen has called them, "Hitler's willing executioners." For more on the support for the Holocaust by ordinary German citizens, see Goldhagen, *Hitler's Willing Executioners.*

27. United Nations Treaty Series no. 1021, vol. 78 (1951), 277.

28. United Nations Treaty Series no. 1021, vol. 78 (1951), 277. The original resolution was Resolution 96 (I), made on December 11, 1946.

29. United Nations Treaty Series no. 1021, vol. 78 (1951), 277.

30. Norton, *When Our Worlds Cried*, 137–38.

31. This is David Wallace Adams's evocative phrasing of the aims of Euro-American systems of education for Indians; see *Education for Extinction.*

32. Chirot and McCauley, *Why Not Kill Them All?*, 19–44.

33. Chirot and McCauley, *Why Not Kill Them All?*, 19–22.

34. Chirot and McCauley, *Why Not Kill Them All?*, 25–29.

35. Chirot and McCauley, *Why Not Kill Them All?*, 29.

36. Chirot and McCauley, *Why Not Kill Them All?*, 29.

37. Chirot and McCauley, *Why Not Kill Them All?*, 31–32.

38. Chirot and McCauley, *Why Not Kill Them All?*, 36–44.

39. Chirot and McCauley, *Why Not Kill Them All?*, 44.

40. Vetlesen, "Genocide," 520.

41. It should be noted that the role of bystanders can also be played by other states on the international stage. For example, see Stohl, "Outside of a Small Circle of Friends," 151–66.

42. Vetlesen, "Genocide," 520.

43. Vetlesen, "Genocide," 520–21.

44. Vetlesen, "Genocide," 521.

45. Chalk and Jonassohn, *History and Sociology of Genocide*, 203. The authors identify the United States as not only directly responsible for perpetrating genocidal massacres with its armed forces, but also as "accessories to genocide" in cases such as that of the Yukis being massacred in Round Valley as a result of inaction in protecting them from settlers.

46. Tate, *Indians and Emigrants*. Tate focuses on the immediate encounters of emigrants and Indians on the trail and does not much discuss the indirect assault that emigrants made on Indians by interfering with game trails, intertribal commerce and relations, and freedom of movement, as well as the environmental and epidemiological impacts of their presence.

47. This is not to suggest that California's Indigenous population had been free of such trouble in the past. Under the rule of Spain and then Mexico such dispossession and degradation had occurred. Nor is it my intention to suggest that other minority groups were not subject to such assaults at the hands of emigrants from the United States. In particular the Californios, who had not long before taken lands from Native peoples, found themselves dispossessed by settlers and miners from the United States despite their status as citizens by virtue of the Treaty of Guadalupe Hidalgo. However, as these incidents exist outside of the purview of this study, I will leave them aside, except in cases where they intersect with the story of California's Native peoples.

48. The pertinent statute is section 394 of California's Civil Practice Act. For an example, see the case of the *People v. Hall* (1854), which involved the overturning of the murder conviction of a white murderer, George W. Hall, on the grounds that the witnesses who helped convict him were nonwhite. Hall's appeal was successful under section 394, which stipulated that nonwhite testimony was not admissible if any party in the case was a white person. In

this case the witnesses were Chinese, who were considered to be racially related to Indians. See Heizer, "Civil Rights," 129–37.

49. *Chico Courant,* July 28, 1866, quoted in Trafzer and Hyer, *"Exterminate
Them!,"* 1.

50. California newspapers in the 1850s to 1870s obtained stories mainly by
hearsay or by reprinting the stories of other newspapers that came to hand,
either from the East or other portions of California. They did not have corps
of professional reporters.

PART I INTRODUCTION

1. Staub, "The Psychology of Perpetrators and Bystanders," 65.
2. Horowitz, *Genocide and State Power,* 189–90.
3. Staub, "Psychology of Perpetrators and Bystanders," 63.
4. Rubenstein, *The Cunning of History,* 91.
5. John H. Bodley, "Victims of Progress," in Hinton, *Genocide,* 137.
6. Staub, "Psychology of Perpetrators and Bystanders," 69.
7. Staub, "Psychology of Perpetrators and Bystanders," 66.
8. Staub, "Genocide and Mass Killing," 369–72. Staub is discussing these
ideas in both an abstract sense and in historical cases drawn from Europe and
Africa, not in reference to California Indians.
9. Duster, "Conditions for Guilt-Free Massacre," 27.

I. THE CORE VALUES OF GENOCIDE

1. I make the pre–Gold Rush distinction here because of the noticeable
change in motives following the discovery of gold.
2. For a fuller discussion of how thought about the frontier can be revealed
through an analysis of language, see Babcock, "The Social Significance of the
Language of the American Frontier," 256–63.
3. Stohl, "Outside of a Small Circle of Friends," 152–53. To be clear, Stohl's
article deals with state-sponsored genocide, not popularly sponsored genocide, although I believe the processes that abrogate guilt, redirect feelings of
responsibility, and harness dehumanization appear closely related by their
similar uses.
4. For an extended study of Euro-American attitudes toward Native
Americans in the process of western expansion, see Drinnon, *Facing West.*
5. One of the finest studies available is Coward, *The Newspaper Indian.*
Coward explores many aspects of the portrayal of Native peoples in the press

and the role this played in shaping the Euro-American consciousness as regards Indian-white relations.

6. For examples of the work of popular historians of the mid-nineteenth
century, see Bancroft, *History of the United States*; Bartlett, *History of the
United States*.

7. Bancroft, *History of the United States* (1854–60), 1:4.

8. Genesis 1:28.

9. Leavitt's "[grape] vine and fig tree" were just two of the nonnative plant
species that Europeans brought to the New World. For the consequences of
such importation, see Crosby, *The Columbian Exchange*.

10. Bancroft, *History of the United States* (1854–60), 1:3–4; Locke, *The Second
Treatise*, 19–21.

11. Bancroft, *History of the United States* (1854–60), 1:3–4.

12. For a sampling of the many-decades-long historiography on this topic
in California history, see Goodrich, "The Legal Status of the California
Indian," 83–100; Fernandez, "Except a California Indian," 161–75; Gunther,
"Indians," 26–34.

13. Stohl, "Outside of a Small Circle of Friends," 159. I am departing from
Stohl's focus on genocidal actions of a state and the decision by individuals to
ignore it. As I will argue later, in nineteenth-century California it is the state
and federal government often acting as bystanders to genocide being committed by citizens.

14. Bancroft, *History of the United States* (1854–60), 1:4.

15. This righteous indignation can often be found whenever Euro-Americans made treaties with Native peoples. Typically whites scorned what was
"given" to uncivilized Indians as too much, too generous, too acute a waste of
resources. Rather than attempt to discuss the history of treaty making and
breaking in this brief historical review, I will concern myself in chapter 7 with
a discussion of treaties made and broken in California, including the attitudes
of Euro-Americans to these agreements.

16. Nash, *Red, White, and Black*, 110–15.

17. Bancroft, *History of the United States* (1854–60), 1:450–80.

18. Nash, *Red, White, and Black*, 248–69.

19. Bancroft, *History of the United States* (1854–60), 1:558–65.

20. Nugent, *Habits of Empire*, 234–35.

21. Merk, *Manifest Destiny*.

22. Texas was annexed during the Tyler administration, prior to Polk's inauguration but following his election.

23. Thomas R. Hietala, "'This Splendid Juggernaut': Westward a Nation and Its People," in Haynes and Morris, *Manifest Destiny*, 48–51. Hietala uses artist George Catlin as an emblematic example of a voice of protest "drowned out" by presidents, senators, congressmen, and others.

24. Quoted in John M. Belohlavek, "Race, Progress, and Destiny: Caleb Cushing and the Quest for American Empire," in Haynes and Morris, *Manifest Destiny*, 25. A native of Massachusetts, Cushing was a state representative and senator, a representative to the U.S. Congress, and the attorney general of the United States for the Pierce administration.

25. Belohlavek, "Race, Progress, and Destiny," 25–26. See also John H. Bodley, "Victims of Progress," in Hinton, *Genocide*, 137–63.

26. Bartlett, *History of the United States*, 3:511.

27. Bancroft, *History of the United States* (1885), 1:3.

28. Much of my thinking about race as a social construction has been informed by Barbara J. Field, "Ideology and Race in American History," in Kousser and McPherson, *Region, Race, and Reconstruction*, 145–77.

29. For another way some Americans viewed Native Americans during the nineteenth century, see Sheehan, *Seeds of Extinction*. Sheehan argues that some, like Thomas Jefferson, believed that Native Americans were capable of equality with whites as their savagery disappeared through the process of civilization.

30. Bancroft, *History of the United States* (1885), 2:108–10.

31. Bancroft, *History of the United States* (1885), 2:124–28.

32. Bancroft, *History of the United States* (1885), 2:124–28.

33. Bartlett, *History of the United States*, 3:511–12.

34. Bartlett, *History of the United States*, 3:715.

35. As Sherburne Cook points out, this widely believed idea was based almost solely on fiction; in fact, despite the many very real and documented instances of white male sexual violence to Indian women, Indian men almost never subjected white women to similar treatment, even in retribution. For more, see Cook, *The Conflict*.

36. Dippie, "'His Visage Wild,'" 114–15.

37. Chirot and McCauley, *Why Not Kill Them All?*, 19–20.

38. Chirot and McCauley, *Why Not Kill Them All?*, 31.

39. Chirot and McCauley, *Why Not Kill Them All?*, 31–32.

40. Stohl, "Outside of a Small Circle of Friends," 160.

41. W. C. Bryant and Gay, *A Popular History*, 610–11.

42. The rejection of Turner is a key element of the New Western History. Historians of the West have long rejected Turner's thesis, although many continue to employ him as a foil to the new narratives; for examples, see Limerick, *Legacy of Conquest*; White, *It's Your Misfortune*.

43. Turner, *The Frontier*, 1.

44. Turner, *The Frontier*, 263–64.

45. Turner, *The Frontier*, 264.

46. This portion of Turner's book first appeared as "Contributions of the West to American Democracy," *Atlantic Monthly*, January 1903.

47. Turner, *The Frontier*, 266.

48. Turner, *The Frontier*, 266–68.

49. Limerick, *Legacy*, 20.

50. For an example, see Lamar, *The Far Southwest*.

51. Turner, *Frontier*, 13. Turner implied that much of the slowdown was from the guns that were put in Indian hands, rather than the spirit and will of Native peoples to resist.

52. Bartlett, *History of the United States*, 3:719. Bartlett notes that any victories by Indians in combat with whites serve only to "mark them for destruction."

53. Coward, *Newspaper Indian*, 14.

54. Coward, *Newspaper Indian*, 14.

55. *Arkansas Gazette*, October 27, 1845.

56. *Arkansas Gazette*, October 27, 1845. The notice suggested as the number one necessity for all emigrants "a rifle or heavy shot gun, 16 lbs. of shot or lead, [and] 4 lbs. of powder."

57. Slotkin, *The Fatal Environment*, xiv.

58. For a multifaceted discussion of the complexities of Manifest Destiny, including comment on the historiography developing since Frederick Merk's *Manifest Destiny and Mission*, see Haynes and Morris, *Manifest Destiny*.

59. *New York Morning News*, December 27, 1845.

60. For some of the relatively recent scholarship on Manifest Destiny, see Brown, *Agents of Manifest Destiny*; Haynes, *James K. Polk*; Haynes and Morris, *Manifest Destiny*; Hietala, *Manifest Design*; Horsman, *Race and Manifest Destiny*; Nugent, *Habits of Empire*.

61. For a thorough study of the importance of the concept of the "vanishing Indian" trope of the nineteenth century, see Dippie, *The Vanishing American*.

62. Dippie, *The Vanishing American*, 30.
63. Dippie, *The Vanishing American*, 241–42.
64. Dippie, "This Bold but Wasting Race," 5.
65. *Northern Journal* (Yreka CA), February 2, 1860.
66. Chirot and McCauley, *Why Not Kill Them All?*, 81–82.
67. For a study of the changing ways white society viewed Native peoples, see Pearce, *Savagism and Civilization*.
68. Several explanations exist as to how the term "digger" came to be applied to California Indians. See, for example, the letter of Bidwell to Miller in 1894 explaining its earliest origins in the words of a man contemporary to the event (John Bidwell to Miss Miller, December 28, 1894, "Indian Manuscript Material," box 32, Annie E. K. Bidwell Collection, California State Library, Sacramento). For a scholarly explanation, see Rawls, *Indians of California*, 49–51.
69. *Arkansas Gazette*, October 27, 1845.
70. "The Indians of California," *Parley's Magazine*, January 1843, 292.
71. *Christian Inquirer*, February 23, 1850.
72. *National Era* (Washington DC), March 13, 1851.
73. *Chico (ca) Weekly Courant*, November 18, 1865.
74. Hirsch, *Genocide*, 3.

2. EMIGRANT GUIDES

1. Foundational works include Faragher, *Women and Men on the Overland Trail*; Unruh, *The Plains Across*.
2. The most important and convincing recent study is Tate, *Indians and Emigrants*.
3. Lewis, "Argonauts," 285–305.
4. Unruh, *Plains Across*, 408.
5. Lewis, "Argonauts," 293.
6. This average time is based on a departure from Independence, Missouri.
7. Lewis, "Argonauts," 293. Lewis points out that the overall death rate (from any cause) on the trail between 1842 and 1859 was between 4 and 6 percent; the death rate in the United States was 2.5 percent in the mid-nineteenth century.
8. There are but few biographies of Dana, all of them dated. For examples, see Shapiro, *Richard Henry Dana*; Gale, *Richard Henry Dana*; C. F. Adams, *Richard Henry Dana*.

9. Dana, *Two Years*, 124, 175, 176–78.

10. Dana, *Two Years*, 179.

11. Rawls, *Indians of California*, 43, 64–65. Rawls also points out that "prophetic patterns" of denigrating California Indians began with first contact and perpetuated from then on (see pages 25–43).

12. Dana, *Two Years*, 119–79.

13. Here I am thinking of prominent men from Massachusetts living in California before and after Dana's visit, like Abel Stearns, John Marsh, and Thomas O. Larkin. For a fuller discussion of the earliest Americans coming into California and their influential correspondence and literary productions, see Rawls, *Indians of California*, 44–65.

14. Dana, *Two Years*, 179.

15. Robinson, *Land in California*, 65–67.

16. The best recent work on Bidwell is Gillis and Magliari, *John Bidwell and California*.

17. They were not, however, the first settlers from the United States in California. Settlement by Americans traveling over the ocean had begun in the 1820s. It should also be noted that they were not the first travelers from the United States to go west over the Rockies and the Sierra Nevada; this distinction belongs to mountain men and trappers engaged in trade, trapping, and horse thievery.

18. Bidwell, *Echoes of the Past*, 13–14, 14.

19. Bidwell, *Echoes of the Past*, 14–15.

20. Marsh had a formal college education and read enough medical books to convince many people that he was a physician.

21. Bidwell, *Echoes of the Past*, 15.

22. Bidwell, *Echoes of the Past*, 20–22.

23. Bidwell, *Echoes of the Past*, 5–8, 9, 11–12. To Bidwell's credit, one must acknowledge that he was naturalized as a Mexican citizen as part of getting title to his land. But one must also note that he was part of the Bear Flag Revolt, seeking to overthrow the Mexican government in California.

24. Robinson, *Land in California*, 111.

25. John Bidwell, "Dictation from John Bidwell: An autobiography," 9, C-D 802, Bancroft Library, University of California, Berkeley.

26. Bidwell, *Echoes of the Past*, 41, 46, 47, 48, 57. Carson Lake is in present-day Nevada. The parties of Bartleson and Bidwell remained separate after this meeting.

27. Bidwell, *Echoes of the Past,* 22.

28. Bidwell, *Echoes of the Past,* 23, 53.

29. Bidwell, *Echoes of the Past,* 28–29, 29.

30. P. B. Reading to his brother, Monterey, California, January 2, 1844, 72/66c, P. B. Reading Family Papers, Bancroft Library, University of California, Berkeley. Like Bidwell, Reading was considered one of the Founders of American California.

31. Unruh, *Plains Across,* 408.

32. Bidwell, *Echoes of the Past,* 48, 49.

33. Bidwell, *Echoes of the Past,* xix.

34. For recent biographical works on Frémont, see Rolle, *John Charles Frémont;* Roberts, *A Newer World;* Chaffin, *Pathfinder.*

35. This is not to say that all such men were dishonest, as some openly acknowledged Frémont as their primary source. For the most notable example, see Ware, *Emigrant's Guide.* According to the historian John Caughey, who provided an introduction and notes, the guide produced by Ware was perfectly poised to become a popular resource among gold-seekers by virtue of its publication date. Ironically Ware died on the trail to California using his own book, which was based heavily on Frémont's and Hastings's narratives.

36. For more on the influential nature of Frémont's reports to the government, see Weiss, "The John C. Frémont 1842, 1843–'44 Report and Map," 297–313.

37. For viewpoints on the role played by Kit Carson in shaping relations with Native peoples, see Gordon-McCutchan, *Kit Carson;* Dunlay, *Kit Carson and the Indians;* Trafzer, *The Kit Carson Campaign.*

38. Frémont, *Report,* 12–13.

39. Frémont, *Report,* 25, 31.

40. Frémont, *Report,* 51.

41. For some additional examples, see Frémont, *Report,* 57–58, 60.

42. Frémont, *Report,* 63, 64. In another example, just prior to the completion of their second expedition, Frémont and his men were caught in the open by two hundred Arapahos and twenty Sioux, "painted and armed for war." Through another parley and exchange of gifts, trouble was avoided (see Frémont, *Report,* 387–88).

43. For some of the dozens of examples, see Frémont, *Report,* 67–68, 106, 123, 125, 161, 173, 198–99, 212–13, 215, 237, 240, 244, 268, 289, 294–95, 300–301.

44. For a few of the many examples, see Frémont, *Report,* 122–23, 143–44,

147, 199, 326. I have not attempted to be exhaustive here, but suffice it to say that Frémont's expedition ate its way to the Pacific mostly on local foods. Some of these foods they obtained in regions with scarce resources but never acknowledged the strain this put on the subsistence of local Native peoples.

45. Frémont, *Report*, 155, 263, 18, 29.

46. Frémont, *Report*, 23, 145–46, 156.

47. Frémont, *Report*, 125, 149.

48. Frémont, *Report*, 171–72, 181, 191, 221. "Snake" is a dysphemism used to describe Shoshone people.

49. Frémont, *Report*, 255.

50. Frémont, *Report*, 212–13, 285.

51. Frémont, *Report*, 323–24, 328.

52. Frémont, *Report*, 266, 266–67, 267.

53. Frémont, *Report*, 267, 270.

54. Frémont, *Report*, 279, 291.

55. Frémont, *Report*, 305, 309.

56. Frémont, *Report*, 290, 296, 331. They lost several more on the return trip, including some to Native groups.

57. Frémont, *Report*, 352–53, 354, 356.

58. Frémont, *Report*, 357, 357–58, 360, emphasis added. Frémont noted that the women had been captured, not killed as the two men were.

59. Frémont, *Report*, 365–66, 368.

60. Lewis, "Argonauts," 294.

61. Bidwell, *Echoes of the Past*, 37.

62. Rutledge, *Casualties on the California Trail*, 39–46.

63. Hastings, *Emigrant's Guide*, 5.

64. Lewis, "Argonauts," 298–303. Lewis argues that these democracies often failed, were ineffective, or were abandoned altogether.

65. Hastings, *Emigrant's Guide*, 5.

66. Hastings, *Emigrant's Guide*, 6. Hastings says only that the whole company voted, giving no other details; one must assume that he meant men but likely not women and certainly not children.

67. Hastings, *Emigrant's Guide*, 6.

68. Hastings, *Emigrant's Guide*, 6, 6–7, 7.

69. Hastings, *Emigrant's Guide*, 10, 13.

70. Hastings, *Emigrant's Guide*, 263–64.

71. Lewis, "Argonauts," 302–3. In Lewis's study of forty-four emigrant companies, 88 percent adopted some form of "democratic social organization."

72. Ware, *Emigrant's Guide*, 43–44.

73. Hastings, *Emigrant's Guide*, 109–10.

74. One should also note that, like Dana, Hastings thought that Mexicans were not much above Native Americans on the racial ladder. For an example, see Hastings, *Emigrant's Guide*, 180–83, 196.

75. Hastings, *Emigrant's Guide*, 102, 103, 116, 101.

76. Hastings, *Emigrant's Guide*, 196–97.

77. Hastings, *Emigrant's Guide*, 259–60, 260.

78. To my knowledge, no first-person account exists of Native Americans using animal disguises to attack emigrants.

79. Hastings, *Emigrant's Guide*, 110, 112–13, 11, 13.

80. Other than one death due to illness, a close call with a buffalo herd, and the accidental death just described, the emigrants completed the trip unscathed. Indeed Hastings never mentions even the sight of a Native American, let alone a meeting, for the remainder of the narrative.

81. The Bartleson-Bidwell Party was practicing this strategy several years before Hastings's guide was published. See Bidwell, *Echoes of the Past*, 28.

82. Hastings, *Emigrant's Guide*, 256–62.

83. Lewis, "Argonauts," 292. Many thousands of dead stock animals lined the overland trails, where they fell from dehydration, malnourishment, and overwork.

84. Hastings, *Emigrant's Guide*, 261, 249–50.

85. Hastings, *Emigrant's Guide*, 255, 247–48. The assertion that Native people knew nothing of money or its value seems a gross generalization.

3. THE OVERLAND TRAIL EXPERIENCE

The epigraph is from "Indian Manuscript Material," box 32, Annie E. K. Bidwell Collection. Reproduced courtesy of the California History Room, California State Library, Sacramento.

1. Ezra M. Hamilton, "'Story of the lost Children': Reminiscences of Ezra M. Hamilton," 96–114, box 213, folder 3, Ezra M. Hamilton Collection, California State Library, Sacramento.

2. Chirot and McCauley, *Why Not Kill Them All?*, 61.

3. Riley, "The Specter of a Savage," 427–44.

4. Hamilton, "'Story of the lost Children,'" 104–5.

5. Chirot and McCauley, *Why Not Kill Them All?*, 64–65.

6. Unruh, "Against the Grain," 74, 75, 75–79. Unruh provides several estimates from sources in the 1850s of west-to-east travel figures. They range from perhaps as few as "several hundred" to 1,200 persons per year.

7. Hamilton, "'Story of the lost Children,'" 130.

8. What indirect damage to Native people was done by thousands of emigrants passing year after year through hunting, fishing, and trading zones—or even the type of cultural damage being done by people like Hamilton in the disruption of spiritual and funerary practices—is more difficult to gauge.

9. Hamilton, "'Story of the lost Children,'" 106. All one can deduce about the group in question is that Hamilton was just short of Fort Laramie when he encountered the site.

10. Hamilton, "'Story of the lost Children,'" 106, 158–59, 165.

11. Hamilton, "'Story of the lost Children,'" 152.

12. When I say "unsuspecting," I mean this literally. California Native Americans living outside of the mission system, which was the majority of the population, likely had no knowledge of metalworking or the properties of metal when heated. Of course, over time Native people in California adopted the use of metal into their cultures. This incident, however, comes from an encounter with Native people of the Sierra foothills in the early 1850s.

13. Pritchard, *Journal*, 46.

14. Tate, *Indians and Emigrants*, 100.

15. Quoted in Tate, *Indians and Emigrants*, 100.

16. For more on the role of fear as it relates to genocide, see Chirot and McCauley, *Why Not Kill Them All?*, 61–65.

17. Harter, *Wagon Tracks*, 26.

18. Frémont, *Report*, 290.

19. Pratt, *Journals*, 340–42. The company of men was a remnant of the Mormon Battalion that had entered California near the end of the Mexican War.

20. Pratt, *Journals*, 343–44.

21. Pratt, *Journals*, 345.

22. Gould, *The Oregon and California Trail Diary*, 53.

23. Harter, *Wagon Tracks*, 28.

24. Pratt, *Journals*, 345.

25. Pratt, *Journals*, 346.

26. Pratt, *Journals*, 376–410.

27. Many other scholars agree. For examples, see Tate, *Indians and Emigrants*; Unruh, *Plains Across*.

28. Gilbert, "Pioneers," 46.

29. Europeans came as well, and used emigrant guides too. For an example of an Irish guide using Frémont's and others' reports, see *Notes of Travel in California*. For a German version published in Germany and Great Britain, see Schmölder, *The Emigrant's Guide to California*.

30. "The Frazier River Gold-Fields," *Harper's Weekly*, July 24, 1858. *Harper's Weekly* was one of the most widely circulated magazines of the nineteenth century.

PART 2 INTRODUCTION

1. Many studies of the Gold Rush are available. Two of the best are Holliday, *The World Rushed In*, and Johnson, *Roaring Camp*.

2. Admittedly, much debate exists on the California Indian population. For an overview of some of the many positions, see Hurtado, "California Indian Demography," 323–43.

3. Rawls and Bean, *California*, III. This is not to suggest the distribution of wealth was even: some struck it extremely rich, and others made little, all depending on where one chose to look.

4. Robinson, *Land in California*, 185–90, 167.

5. "Nov 1846–Jun 1847," C-B 796, Naglee Family Collection, Bancroft Library, University of California, Berkeley; "Military papers: Re: Bounty land, etc.," box 388, folder 23, Ephraim Morse Papers, California State Library, Sacramento.

6. Hornbeck, "Land Tenure and Rancho Expansion," 373, 388. Based on the grants submitted to the U.S. land commissioners, perhaps 809 grants were made under Mexican rule.

7. For a discussion of the role of convenience and practical necessity in genocide, see Chirot and McCauley, *Why Not Kill Them All?*, 20–25.

8. This motive has been prevalent in other cases of genocide; see Chirot and McCauley, *Why Not Kill Them All?*, 31–36.

9. Chirot and McCauley, *Why Not Kill Them All?*, 25–31.

10. Chirot and McCauley, *Why Not Kill Them All?*, 52, 52–54.

4. THE ECONOMICS OF GENOCIDE

1. For the purposes of this work, southern California is everything south of the Tejón Pass in the Tehachapi Mountains.

2. The Quechans, famously, had resisted all attempts by the Spanish to sub-

due them or incorporate them into mission systems. Until the massive influx of Euro-Americans, they had remained free of Spanish or Mexican control. For a recent study, see Santiago, *Massacre at the Yuma Crossing*.

3. Hyer, *"We Are Not Savages,"* 57.

4. Trafzer, *Yuma*, 74.

5. E. C. Smith, "Massacre on the Colorado River," 10. For a later example of a scare associated with a potential war with the Chemehuevi people along the Colorado River, see Walker, "An Indian Scare"; Roth, "The Calloway Affair."

6. Forbes, *Warriors*, 311.

7. E. C. Smith, "Massacre on the Colorado River," 10.

8. E. C. Smith, "Massacre on the Colorado River," 14; Trafzer, *Yuma*, 75.

9. Forbes, *Warriors*, 312.

10. Hyer, *"We Are Not Savages,"* 57.

11. Benjamin Hayes to Governor Peter H. Burnett, April 27, 1850, Record 1, Indian War Papers.

12. Forbes, *Warriors*, 312–13.

13. Hyer, *"We Are Not Savages,"* 57.

14. Forbes, *Warriors*, 313; Hyer, *"We Are Not Savages,"* 57.

15. Forbes, *Warriors*, 314.

16. E. C. Smith, "Massacre on the Colorado River," 16, 17.

17. Lt. William T. Sherman to Colonel Stevenson, May 8, 1848, Record Group 98, M210 Reel 1, Letters Received, 1848, Records of Continental Commands, 10th Military Department, U.S. Army, National Archives and Records Administration.

18. E. C. Smith, "Massacre on the Colorado River," 18.

19. Governor Peter H. Burnett to Maj. Gen. J. H. Bean, June 1, 1850, Record 2, Indian War Papers.

20. Governor Peter H. Burnett to Sheriff William Rogers, October 25, 1850, Record 9, Indian War Papers.

21. Burnett to Bean, June 1, 1850.

22. Governor Peter H. Burnett to Maj. Gen. J. H. Bean, June 4, 1850, Record 3, Indian War Papers.

23. For more on the monetary costs involved, see chapter 6.

24. Maj. Gen. J. H. Bean to Brig. Gen. J. C. Morehead, July 11, 1850, Record 6, Indian War Papers.

25. Phillips, *Chiefs and Challengers*, 73.

26. Governor Peter H. Burnett to Maj. Gen. J. H. Bean, September 4, 1850, Record 7, Indian War Papers.

27. Phillips, *Chiefs and Challengers*, 73.

28. Hyer, *"We Are Not Savages,"* 58.

29. Trafzer, *As Long as the Grass Shall Grow*, 192. For a similar contemporary episode, see the story of John Irving, another former Texas Ranger engaged in criminal action. When Irving was killed by Cahuillas under the leadership of Juan Antonio, the people of Los Angeles were incensed that Indians had dared raise their hands against white men. The fullest account is Hanks, "Vicissitudes of Justice."

30. Members of the California State Legislature to Governor John Bigler, January 8, 1852, Record 145, Indian War Papers.

31. *Daily Alta California*, December 27, 1851.

32. Pitt, *The Decline of the Californios*, 140.

33. Hurtado, "Controlling California's Indian Labor Force," 219.

34. For the most recent comprehensive work on Native Americans as *vaqueros* in southern California's economy, see Phillips, *Vineyards and Vaqueros*.

35. There are various definitions of "Californio." I am using Californio in the sense of a group of men, mostly born in California and Spanish-speaking, who considered themselves an elite, landowning clique. Their personal and political identities focused on California rather than Mexico. Some Euro-Americans were considered Californios as well (e.g., the aforementioned Warner, Don Tomás Larkin, Don Abel Stearns, and Don Benito Wilson), although not all accepted Mexican citizenship (e.g., Larkin). Their power emanated from huge Mexican land grants, the Native American labor they exploited to run the ranching economy of California, and, for some, their status and responsibilities as *alcaldes* (local leaders empowered with elements of executive, legislative, and judicial powers).

36. This is not to say that such systems in the United States were truly democratic, as the system excluded many (e.g., nonwhites, white males under a certain age, and women).

37. For an extended discussion of the political fortunes of the Californios in the early 1850s, see Pitt, *Decline of the Californios*, 130–47.

38. Rawls, *Indians of California*, 144–45.

39. Quoted in Rawls, *Indians of California*, 145.

40. Magliari, "Free Soil," 349–52, 351–52.

41. California's Native Americans were subject to a different set of legal

standards than others in California. For recent divergent views on the subject, see Gunther, *Ambiguous Justice*. For a critical review of Gunther's work, see Magliari, review of *Ambiguous Justice*. My view is that both—Gunther's views in concert with Magliari's critical corrections—are of value. For a review of laws targeting Native people in California, see Fernandez, "Except a California Indian."

42. Carrico, *Strangers*, 53.

43. Maj. Gen. J. H. Bean to Governor John McDougal, February 9, 1851, Record 117, Indian War Papers. Major General Bean was commander of the 4th Division of the state militia, one of four divisions existing at the time.

44. Bean to McDougal, February 9, 1851.

45. Citizens of Los Angeles County to Maj. Gen. J. H. Bean, March 1, 1851, Record 119, Indian War Papers.

46. Governor John McDougal to Maj. Gen. J. H. Bean, March 1, 1851, Record 120, Indian War Papers.

47. Governor John McDougal to the People of Los Angeles County, March 6, 1851, Record 121, Indian War Papers.

48. *San Diego Herald*, October 7, 1853.

49. *San Diego Herald*, December 13, 1856.

50. Carrico, *Strangers*, 23–25.

51. Bell, *Reminiscences*, 34–35.

52. *California Statutes*, 1850, chapter 133.

53. *Los Angeles Star*, September 17, 1853.

54. Bell, *Reminiscences*, 2, 35, 35–36.

55. Hurtado, "'Hardly a Farm House,'" 252–53.

56. Bell, *Reminiscences*, 36.

57. *Los Angeles Star*, July 17, 1852.

58. Carrico, *Strangers*, 15.

59. Hurtado, "California Indians and the Workaday West," 5–6.

60. Chandler and Quinn, "Emma Is a Good Girl," 34–37.

61. Andrew Chase to Ephraim Morse, September 2, 1857, quoted in Chandler and Quinn, "Emma Is a Good Girl," 35.

62. See "Bi-Annual Reports of the Superintendent of Public Education," *Appendix to the Journals of the Senate and Assembly of the State of California*, 1860–1890, for an enumeration of Native children living in white households. This subject is also discussed in chapter 6.

63. Magliari, "Free Soil, Unfree Labor," 353. Magliari is using Robert Heizer's estimate.

64. For a discussion of the deleterious effects of labor systems on birthrates in southern California, see Hurtado, "'Hardly a Farm House,'" 255.

65. Hyer, *"We Are Not Savages,"* 51, 63.

66. Hyer, *"We Are Not Savages,"* 62, 61–65.

67. Maj. Gen. J. H. Bean to Governor John McDougal, March 17, 1851, Record 123, Indian War Papers.

68. George H. Davis to Governor John McDougal, November 24, 1851, Record 139, Indian War Papers. George H. Davis was the secretary appointed by the citizens to convey their actions to the governor.

69. Fitzgerald was eventually replaced as commander by Cave Johnson Couts, who apparently found no conflict in being a federal Indian agent and leading a company of men to destroy Indians. Such was the case with other Indian agents in California as well (e.g., B. D. Wilson, T. J. Henley).

70. Maj. Gen. J. H. Bean to Governor John McDougal, November 30, 1851, Record 140, Indian War Papers.

71. Bean to McDougal, November 30, 1851.

72. Governor John McDougal to Maj. Gen. J. H. Bean, December 9, 1851, Record 142, Indian War Papers.

73. Governor John McDougal to Gen. E. A. Hitchcock, December 4, 1851, Record 141, Indian War Papers.

74. Governor John McDougal, February 14, 1854, Record 172, Indian War Papers. This record is McDougal's endorsement of a petition by the disbanded Bay Area volunteers for compensation for the time and expense of preparing to head to southern California.

75. Maj. Gen. J. H. Bean to Governor John McDougal, January 1, 1852, Record 144, Indian War Papers.

76. *Los Angeles Star*, October 16, 1852.

77. Hyer, *"We Are Not Savages,"* 73.

78. Pitt, *Decline of the Californios*, 124.

79. Carrico, *Strangers*, 50.

80. Senator William Gwin, quoted in *Los Angeles Star*, October 30, 1852.

81. *Los Angeles Star*, May 7, 1853.

82. *Daily Alta California*, March 31, 1853.

83. *Los Angeles Star*, May 7, 1853.

84. Hyer, *"We Are Not Savages,"* 72–73.

85. Hurtado, *John Sutter*, 22–23, 76–77; Broadbent, "Conflict at Monterey," 86–101.

86. *Los Angeles Star*, May 7, 1853.

87. *Los Angeles Star*, April 2, 1853.

88. C. B. Churchill, "Benjamin Davis Wilson," 31–35.

89. *Los Angeles Star*, May 7, 1853.

90. *Los Angeles Star*, July 16, 1853.

91. *Daily Alta California*, March 31, 1853.

92. C. B. Churchill, "Benjamin Davis Wilson," 32.

93. *Daily Alta California*, March 31, 1853.

94. *Los Angeles Star*, June 14, 1851.

95. *Daily Alta California*, June 3, 1851; June 17, 1851. See also Hanks, "Vicissitudes of Justice."

96. *California Statutes*, 1850, chapter 133. See chapter 6 in this book for a fuller discussion of the extralegal system set up for Indian peoples in California. In 1855 the prohibition against Native American testimony as covered under the act was repealed by the state legislature; see Magliari, review of *Ambiguous Justice*, 321–22.

97. *Daily Alta California*, March 31, 1853.

98. Stohl, "Outside of a Small Circle of Friends," 159.

99. Oral interview, Clifford E. Trafzer with Katherine Saubel, 1997.

100. Carrico, *Strangers*, 56, 52, 54.

101. Antonio Garra, for instance, was respected by some Americans because he fought.

102. Carrico, *Strangers*, 56.

103. Inyo County Board of Supervisors, *Inyo*, 5–6.

104. Inyo County Board of Supervisors, *Inyo*, 9.

105. Most records indicate that the Indians in question were Paiutes, but there are some indications that Shoshones may also have been involved as well.

106. Inyo County Board of Supervisors, *Inyo*, 5, 15.

107. Chalfant, *The Story of Inyo*, 148–49, 149–50.

108. Quoted in Chalfant, *The Story of Inyo*, 178.

109. James Allen to Governor Leland Stanford, July 21, 1862, Record 606, Indian War Papers.

110. Allen to Stanford, July 21, 1862.

111. For a fuller discussion of this argument, see Limerick, *Legacy of Conquest*.

112. Inyo County Board of Supervisors, *Inyo*, 16–17.

113. Chalfant, *The Story of Inyo*, 219–24.

114. *Sacramento Daily Union*, March 12, 1866.

115. Worster argues, however, that California eventually "developed anti-democratic, centralized forms of power" that controlled water and irrigation rights by the twentieth century, abandoning the "early promise" of democracy ("Irrigation and Democracy in California," 30, 31).

116. Hyer, *"We Are Not Savages,"* 73.

117. Shipek, "A Strategy for Change."

5. DEMOCRATIC DEATH SQUADS

1. In Hall's estimation, Eden Valley was about thirty square miles.

2. Heizer and Whipple, *The California Indians*, 25, 35, 49, 367–68, 459.

3. *Mount Shasta Herald*, November 20, 1888.

4. Knyphausen Geer, "Captain Knyphausen Geer: His Life and Memoirs," 10–11, 69/9c, Bancroft Library, University of California, Berkeley.

5. Geer, "Captain Knyphausen Geer," 11–13.

6. Wilshire, *Get 'Em All!*, 15–17. Wilshire covers California's Native American genocide as part of his study; see pages 15–32 in particular.

7. *Red Bluff Beacon*, October 30, 1862.

8. For example, see the diatribe directed at squirrels and their destruction of crops in the Santa Clara Valley in *Sacramento Union*, May 13, 1861.

9. For the story of the destruction of the ecology of California in the nineteenth and twentieth centuries, see Mike Davis, "Maneaters of the Sierra Madre," in *Ecology of Fear*, 197–271.

10. For a specific discussion of this in Round Valley, see Bauer, "'We Were All Migrant Workers Here.'" Bauer argues convincingly that even as Native Americans resisted these exploitive labor systems, they participated as a survival strategy.

11. Pierson B. Reading to his brother, February 7, 1844, 72/66c, P. B. Reading Family Papers, Bancroft Library, University of California, Berkeley.

12. Heizer and Almquist, *The Other Californians*, 27.

13. For some examples, see *Red Bluff Beacon*, October 28, 1857; December 23, 1857; and July 4, 1861.

14. Heizer and Almquist, *Other Californians*, 27.

15. Deposition of H. L. Hall, February 26, 1860, Record 449, Indian War Papers.

16. Deposition of H. L. Hall.

17. Quoted in Heizer and Almquist, *Other Californians*, 25.

18. "Buck" was the derogatory, animalized term used to described male Native Americans; it was the masculine counterpart to the equally racist term for women, "squaw." Native people living outside of reservations or white communities were typically called "wild Indians," while those living within these areas were called "tame Indians" or "domesticated Indians."

19. *Red Bluff Beacon*, August 5, 1857.

20. *Daily Alta California*, May 22, 1858.

21. *Butte Democrat*, September 17, 1859.

22. For examples of diseases afflicting horses and cattle, see *Yreka Journal*, February 28, 1868; *Red Bluff Beacon*, February 27, 1861; *Daily Alta California*, October 25, 1857.

23. *Red Bluff Sentinel*, July 4, 1868.

24. *Butte Democrat*, November 19, 1859.

25. *Lassen Advocate*, March 4, 1874.

26. For examples of Euro-American horse thieves, see *Butte Democrat*, October 1, 1859; *Plumas Standard*, June 7, 1862; June 14, 1862.

27. *Yreka Journal*, November 8, 1867; *Lassen Sage Brush*, August 29, 1868.

28. *Daily Alta California*, December 31, 1851.

29. *Yreka Union*, quoted in *Red Bluff Beacon*, April 1, 1857.

30. See also *Quincy Union*, February 18, 1865; June 10, 1865; October 27, 1866; *Yreka Journal*, October 30, 1868.

31. *Red Bluff Beacon*, May 25, 1859.

32. *Red Bluff Beacon*, July 21, 1858.

33. For two examples of Americans attempting to pass crimes off on Native Americans, see *Daily Alta California*, December 5, 1851; *Sacramento Union*, August 9, 1865.

34. For an example of an accident judged as such, see *Red Bluff Beacon*, May 8, 1862.

35. *Daily Alta California*, October 25, 1857.

36. Deposition of H. L. Hall.

37. *Lassen Sage Brush*, May 2, 1868.

38. Secrest, *When the Great Spirit Died*, 259.

39. Carranco and Beard, *Genocide and Vendetta*, 169, 171–73, 40, 61, 48.

40. Secrest, "Jarboe's War," 17.

41. Elijah Renshaw Potter, "Reminiscences of the Early History of Northern California," c-d 5136:2, California State Library, Sacramento.

42. Secrest, "Jarboe's War," 17.

43. Deposition of Isaac W. Shannon, February 28, 1860, Record 467, Indian War Papers.

44. Deposition of H. L. Hall.

45. Deposition of H. L. Hall.

46. Secrest, "Jarboe's War," 18.

47. Carranco and Beard, *Genocide and Vendetta*, 109.

48. Deposition of H. L. Hall.

49. Lt. Edward Dillon to Maj. W. W. Mackall, May 16, 1860, quoted in Heizer, *The Destruction of California Indians*, 296.

50. See chapter 6 for a fuller discussion of the support California laws supplied to genocide.

51. Deposition of H. L. Hall.

52. Deposition of H. L. Hall.

53. See Records 342, 343, 344, 345, 346, 347, 348, 354, 360, 361, 369, 370, 371, 372, 375, 386, and 387, Indian War Papers, for examples of petitions sent to the governor by individuals and communities demanding action against Native Americans in and around Tehama County in 1859.

54. Petition of the Citizens of Tehama County, May 29, 1859, Record 348, Indian War Papers.

55. S. C. Hastings to Governor John B. Weller, May 4, 1859, Record 363, Indian War Papers. Robertson, for example, had gone "shares" with Hastings on 240 head of cattle and, later, over 800 more. In all, Robertson was watching in excess of one thousand animals for the judge.

56. Deposition of William Robertson, February 21, 1860, Record 433, Indian War Papers.

57. Deposition of H. L. Hall.

58. Minutes of the Meeting of the Citizens of Tehama County, May 27, 1859, Record 347, Indian War Papers.

59. Chirot and McCauley, *Why Not Kill Them All?*, 20–25.

60. Minutes of the Meeting of the Citizens of Tehama County.

61. William Bull Meek, "Reminiscences of William Bull Meek of Camptonville, California," 73/130c, Bancroft Library, University of California, Berkeley.

62. Chirot and McCauley, *Why Not Kill Them All?*, 31–36.

63. Meek, "Reminiscences of William Bull Meek" (emphasis added).

64. Deposition of H. L. Hall.

65. Governor John B. Weller to the Citizens of Tehama County, June 2, 1859, Record 349, Indian War Papers.

66. *Red Bluff Beacon*, June 8, 1859.

67. For hundreds of examples of reimbursement and back pay claims filed by Californians, see Indian War Papers.

68. For example, see the petition of thirty-six citizens of Klamath County attempting to get compensation for Edward H. Burns, a representative they sent to ask the governor for a volunteer company. "To the California State Legislature: Petition for the settlement of the Claim of Edward H. Burns," 1–2, January 1857, c-a 123, Bancroft Library, University of California, Berkeley.

69. Deposition of Dryden Lacock, February 25, 1860, Record 441, Indian War Papers.

70. Deposition of H. H. Buckles, February 23, 1860, Record 438, Indian War Papers.

71. Secrest, "Jarboe's War," 18.

72. Deposition of H. L. Hall.

73. Deposition of H. L. Hall.

74. *California Statutes*, 1850, chapter 133, section 6, 11–13, 16–17.

75. Deposition of H. L. Hall.

76. Deposition of H. L. Hall.

77. Deposition of H. L. Hall.

78. Deposition of Isaac Shannon.

79. For an example of the former, see Deposition of Chesley Vaughn, February 28, 1860, Record 463, Indian War Papers; for an example of the latter, see Deposition of H. L. Hall.

80. Deposition of Isaac Shannon.

81. Chirot and McCauley, *Why Not Kill Them All?*, 53, 147.

82. Based on Walter Jarboe to Governor John B. Weller, September 16, 1859, Record 383, Indian War Papers. Figures are for the operating period July 31–September 2, 1859.

83. Governor John B. Weller to W. S. Jarboe, September 8, 1859, Record 382, Indian War Papers.

84. W. S. Jarboe to Governor John B. Weller, September 16, 1859, Record 385, Indian War Papers.

85. W. S. Jarboe to Governor John B. Weller, October 1, 1859, Record 388, Indian War Papers.

86. W. S. Jarboe to S. C. Hastings, October 7, 1859, Record 392, Indian War Papers.

87. W. S. Jarboe to Governor John B. Weller, October 16, 1859, Record 398, Indian War Papers. For more on the killing of John Bland, see chapter 7.

88. Governor John B. Weller to W. S. Jarboe, October 23, 1859, Record 399, Indian War Papers.

89. W. S. Jarboe to Governor John B. Weller, October 28, 1859, Record 400, Indian War Papers.

90. Browne, *Crusoe's Island*, 290–91

91. W. S. Jarboe to Governor John B. Weller, December 3, 1859, Record 402, Indian War Papers. The total includes a Native American girl who froze to death while hiding from the Rangers, although Jarboe indicated that it was the girl's fault, not his. I have interpreted his use of the word "several" in one account of the number of "bucks" killed to mean five.

92. Petition of the Residents of Round Valley, undated [ca. December 1859], Record 407, Indian War Papers.

93. Governor John B. Weller to W. S. Jarboe, January 3, 1860, Record 409, Indian War Papers.

94. Petition of Residents of Mendocino County, January 15, 1860, Record 413, Indian War Papers.

95. Apparently more than one man was discharged for rape, even though Jarboe reported only one incident.

96. Petition of the Eel River Rangers, January 15, 1860, Record 414, Indian War Papers.

97. Second Petition of the Eel River Rangers, January 25, 1860, Record 420, Indian War Papers.

98. Deposition of H. H. Buckles.

99. Deposition of B. Newman, February 23, 1860, Record 440, Indian War Papers.

100. Edward Dillon to Headquarters, Department of California, January 27, 1860, Record 423, Indian War Papers. This report was forwarded to Governor John G. Downey; see N. A. Clarke to John G. Downey, February 1, 1860, Record 424, Indian War Papers.

101. *Marysville Weekly Express*, April 16, 1859.

102. *Humboldt Times*, quoted in *Red Bluff Beacon*, September 29, 1858.

103. *Red Bluff Beacon*, June 15, 1859.

104. *Chico Weekly Courant*, November 18, 1862.

105. *Red Bluff Beacon*, June 22, 1859.

106. *Red Bluff Beacon*, June 29, 1859.

107. For additional examples drawn from the period under discussion, see Greene to Kibbe, January 31, 1860, Record 425, Indian War Papers; Deposition of William J. Hildreth, February 24, 1860, Record 443, Indian War Papers.

108. Rawls, *Indians of California*, 185.

109. Rice, Bullough, and Orsi, *Elusive Eden*, 199.

110. *Shasta Herald*, May 11, 1861.

111. *Sacramento Union*, morning ed., May 13, 1861.

112. *Quincy Union*, October 27, 1866.

113. *Lassen Sage Brush*, May 16, 1868.

114. Heizer, *The Destruction of the California Indians*, 268.

115. Quoted in Heizer, *The Destruction of the California Indians*, 247.

116. Quoted in Heizer, *The Destruction of the California Indians*, 248.

117. Chirot and McCauley, *Why Not Kill Them All?*, 37–38, 51–57.

118. Deposition of Jackson Farley, February 26, 1860, Record 448, Indian War Papers.

119. Deposition of William Frazier, February 22, 1860, Record 436, Indian War Papers.

120. Deposition of William Frazier. Frazier called these Indian people Cayapomos.

121. Deposition of Jackson Farley.

122. Deposition of William Frazier.

123. Deposition of Jackson Farley.

124. G. H. Woodman to Governor Milton S. Latham, undated [ca. December 1859], Record 354, Indian War Papers.

125. Deposition of William Frazier.

126. Deposition of William Frazier.

127. Deposition of Jackson Farley.

128. *Lassen Sage Brush*, May 23, 1868.

129. Deposition of William Frazier.

130. This conclusion is based on the collective lack of evidence gathered from Farley, Frazier, and the community petitions of the residents of Long Valley.

131. Hill, "The Early Mining Camp," 295–96.

132. Quoted in Hill, "The Early Mining Camp," 296–97. This excerpt is from the preamble of the district regulations for Gold Hill (Nevada).

133. Rawls, "Gold Diggers," 28, 30, 37.

134. Heizer and Almquist, *Other Californians*, 28.

135. Royce, *California*, 220. Royce does not suggest that relations were always orderly or harmonious in a mining camp, but in the case of how miners dealt with Native Americans, one finds no evidence of disagreement about the solutions to "Indian problems" in Royce's or others' accounts.

136. James Mason Hutchings to Mr. Armfield, April 14, 1851, 69/80c, J. M. Hutchings Diaries, Bancroft Library, University of California, Berkeley.

137. *Sacramento Union*, September 18, 1859.

138. Royce, *California*, 286.

139. Interview with Alexander Hamilton Willard, 71/249c, "Interviews with the Inhabitants of Trinity County," Bancroft Library, University of California, Berkeley.

140. "Indians (General): Clippings; correspondence 1905–08; 1924; 1926–27; 1929–30," box 802, folder 1, George W. Stewart Collection, California State Library, Sacramento. The story appeared in an unidentified newspaper in an article dated December 13, 1929.

141. Meek, "Reminiscences of William Bull Meek."

142. Some scholars believe that a form of syphilis was present in California before contact. However, given the massively debilitating effects to Native populations from syphilis in the nineteenth century, it would seem that, even if these scholars are correct, it was a newly introduced strain of the disease since Indian peoples seemed to have no resistance whatsoever. For an example of a scholar arguing that a strain of syphilis was already in California before Euro-American contact, see Hackel, *Children of Coyote*, 22. An author claiming that syphilis was an imported contagion is Cook, *The Conflict between Indians and White Civilization*.

143. For a discussion of the epidemiological aspects of contact between Old World and New, see Diamond, *Guns, Germs, and Steel*; Crosby, *The Columbian Exchange*; and Crosby, *Ecological Imperialism*.

PART 3 INTRODUCTION

1. See table 1 for a review of the changing population figures.

2. For short biographies of California governors, see www.californiagovernors.ca.gov.

3. Constitution of the State of California, 1849, Article II, section 1.

4. "An Act for the Government and Protection of Indians," *California Statutes*, 1850, chapter 133, was an omnibus bill that dealt with myriad aspects of Indian-white relations in California. Much of it operated throughout the remainder of the nineteenth century.

5. *California Statutes*, 1850, chapter 133.

6. Michno, *Encyclopedia of Indian Wars*, 1, 367. Although Michno's coverage of California is incomplete, his evidence shows at least 1,600 casualties in documented encounters between soldiers (including militia but excluding volunteer companies) and Native peoples.

7. The most important example was the *Daily Alta California*. This San Francisco daily was the official newspaper of the California State Legislature. Few Native Americans lived in San Francisco, and by the late 1850s the paper began to be increasingly critical of the atrocities being perpetrated on Indigenous populations. Although no less racist than other papers, the *Alta* took a more cynical view of what was going on between settlers and Native Americans elsewhere in California. As Native communities disappeared from other localities, papers in these places took an editorial line similar to the *Alta*'s.

8. Tocqueville, *Democracy in America*, 320–21.

6. THE MURDER STATE

1. "Address to the Legislature," *Journal of the Senate of the State of California*, 3rd session, 1852, 714.

2. Governor John Bigler to Gen. E. Hitchcock, April 8, 1852, quoted in Heizer and Almquist, *The Other Californians*, 26, emphasis added.

3. "Majority and Minority Reports of the Special Joint Committee on the Mendocino War," *Appendix to the Journal of the Senate of the State of California*, 11th session, 1860.

4. See examples discussed in the previous chapter, including the early actions of Hall and Jarboe.

5. "Majority Report of the Special Joint Committee on the Mendocino War," *Appendix to the Journal of the Senate of the State of California*, 11th session, 1860, 4, 3.

6. "Majority Report," 6, 4, 4–5.

7. "Majority Report," 6.

8. Nome Cult Farm was a temporary federal Indian reservation. See the following chapter for additional details.

9. "Minority Report of the Special Joint Committee on the Mendocino War," *Appendix to the Journal of the Senate of the State of California*, 11th session, 1860, 9, 9–10.

10. "Minority Report," 11.

11. *California Statutes*, 1850, chapter 133.

12. "Report of the Commissioners of California War Debt," *Appendix to the Journal of the Senate of the State of California*, 11th session, 1860, 3, 8–10.

13. The state legislature made a joint resolution calling on the federal government to repay the expenses incurred fighting Indians. See "In relation to the War Debt," Joint Resolution of the California Senate and Assembly, approved March 1, 1853, *California Statutes*, 1853.

14. "Report of the Comptroller of the State of California," *Journals of the Senate and Assembly of the State of California*, 2nd session, 1851, 544–46.

15. "Requesting our Senators and Representatives in Congress to use their best efforts to obtain certain Arms from the General Government," Joint Resolution of the California Senate and Assembly, approved March 6, 1852, *California Statutes*, 1852.

16. "An Act Authorizing the Governor of this State to transmit to the Secretary of War at Washington City a statement in relation to 'War Debt' in California," *California Statutes*, 1855, chapter 54.

17. "Concurrent Resolution relative to the Removal of Indians," number 24, passed April 19, 1858, *California Statutes*, 1858.

18. "Concurrent Resolution Relative to the Indian Reserves in this State," number 37, passed April 16, 1860, *California Statutes*, 1860.

19. "Concurrent Resolution," number 13, adopted March 28, 1862, *California Statutes*, 1862.

20. "Concurrent Resolution," number 13, 545. The commutation tax was $2 per annum. The legislature took Houston's suggestion in 1855, dropping the tax to 25 cents per annum. For California's Militia Law, see "An Act concerning the Organization of the Militia," *California Statures*, 1850, chapter 76, section 28. For changes in the law in the 1850s, see *California Statutes*, 1852, chapter 40; 1855, chapter 115; 1856, chapter 74; 1860, chapter 331; 1863, chapter 309.

21. "An Act concerning Volunteer or Independent Companies," *California Statutes*, 1850, chapter 54.

22. "An Act prescribing the Amount of Compensation and Mode of Payment to Persons who have Performed Military Services for the State of California, and Expenses incurred therein," *California Statutes*, 1851, chapter 125.

23. Brigadier General Winn to Governor Peter Burnett, November 11, 1850, Record 24, Indian War Papers.

24. "Address to the Legislature," *Journal of the Senate of the State of California*, 3rd session, 1852, 714.

25. Winn to Burnett, November 11, 1850.

26. Examples include both unauthorized and authorized musters of more than one hundred men. Fitzgerald mustered well over one hundred men to fight Antonio Garra's forces (see chapter 4), and over two hundred men fought the Tulares under Sheriff James Burney and Maj. James Savage in 1851.

27. Governor John McDougal to Sheriff James Burney, January 13, 1851, Record 50, Indian War Papers.

28. Governor John McDougal to the California State Legislature, January 20, 1851, Record 52, Indian War Papers.

29. State and county taxes during this era included a tax on personal property. Cattle, horses, and other stock were part of the valuation of individual tax liability. Animals that were taken by Native people in raids were assets citizens were paying property taxes on each year. Undoubtedly this forced the issue of taxation and representation to the forefront of the minds of aggrieved parties suffering stock losses. See "An Act Prescribing the Mode of Assessing and Collecting Public Revenue," *California Statutes*, 1850, chapter 52.

30. Forbes, "The Native American Experience in California History," 236.

31. Heizer and Almquist, *The Other Californians*, 195–203.

32. "An Act Concerning Crimes and Punishments," *California Statutes*, 1850, chapter 99, section 14.

33. *Marysville Daily Evening Herald*, August 12, 1853.

34. *Sacramento Union*, December 14, December 15, 1859.

35. *Quincy Union*, June 23, July 14, October 6, 1866.

36. *Sacramento Union*, November 14, 1851.

37. *Los Angeles Star*, January 11, 1855.

38. *Los Angeles Star*, February 21, 1852.

39. *Los Angeles Star*, June 18, 1853.

40. *Los Angeles Star*, April 3, 1852.

41. *Daily Alta California*, January 22, 1853.

42. *Sacramento Daily Union*, June 11, 1863.

43. *Red Bluff Sentinel*, January 29, 1870.

44. *Quincy Union*, October 3, 1868.

45. *San Francisco Bulletin*, May 12, 1859.

46. *Marysville Herald*, February 14, 1851.

47. Lt. Col. A. D. Nelson to Office of the Adjutant General, Department of California, September 22, 1873, Record 666, Indian War Papers.

48. *Los Angles Star*, March 31, 1855. In Los Angeles County, for example, convicts who were non-Natives did not usually receive public work gang sentences, whereas Native Americans did.

49. *Los Angeles Star*, November 8, 1851. In 1855 this was changed to allow Native American testimony.

50. *Los Angeles Star*, March 31, 1855.

51. For example, see *Los Angeles Star*, March 31, 1855.

52. *Quincy Union*, October 13, 1866.

53. *Quincy Union*, October 20, 1866.

54. *Los Angeles Star*, January 4, 1855.

55. *Los Angeles Star*, December 3, 1853.

56. According to Gunther, Indians were paid one-third of their auction price as wages, "a price which was often paid in alcohol" ("Ambiguous Justice," 56).

57. *Los Angeles Star*, January 4, 1855.

58. Monroy, *Thrown among Strangers*, 190.

59. Gunther, "Ambiguous Justice," 56.

60. The historian Albert Hurtado argues that the military occupation of California by the United States during the Mexican War "adumbrates the federal method for making Indian policy for California during the 1850s." See Hurtado, "Controlling California's Indian Labor Force."

61. *California Statutes*, 1850, chapter 133, section 20.

62. See in particular sections 1, 3, 5, 9, and 11 of *California Statutes*, 1850, chapter 133.

63. Secrest, "Jarboe's War," 22.

64. *Marysville Weekly Express*, March 5, 1859.

65. Bauer, "'We Were All Migrant Workers Here,'" 43–63.

66. *California Statutes*, 1850, chapter 133, section 3.

67. *California Statutes*, 1850, chapter 133, section 7.

68. Rawls, *Indians of California*, 94–106, 103.

69. *Humboldt Times*, May 5, 1855.

70. *San Francisco Bulletin*, March 2, 1861.

71. *Sacramento Daily Union*, May 8, 1857; *Sacramento Union*, March 13, 1863.

72. *Sacramento Daily Union*, May 20, 1857.

73. Harmon A. Good to Governor Leland Stanford, August 8, 1862, Record 608, Indian War Papers.

74. Good to Stanford, August 8, 1862.

75. *Humboldt Times*, May 5, 1855.

76. *Marysville Appeal*, October 17, 1861.

77. *Marysville Appeal*, October 18, 1861.

78. *Marysville Appeal*, October 19, 1861.

79. *Marysville Appeal*, October 24, 1861.

80. *Notes on California and the Placers* (1850), quoted in Heizer and Almquist, *The Other Californians*, 20.

81. *California Statutes*, 1860, chapter 231.

82. Gunther, "Ambiguous Justice," 31n.

83. *California Statutes*, 1850, chapter 133, section 3. The apprentice might also be transferred to a new master.

84. Heizer, *The Destruction of the California Indians*, 219.

85. "Recommendation on Federal Assistance for California Indians," November 22, 1852, quoted in Heizer, *Federal Concerns*, 2–3.

86. Monroy, *Thrown among Strangers*, 180–81.

87. The Rangers were composed of infantry and cavalry companies. The City Guard was an infantry company. Both groups trained sporadically, threw dances for the town, and were the subject of much adulation in Los Angeles and much derision in the northern California press, who accused them of bloodthirstiness and a shoot-first policy.

88. Woolsey, "Crime and Punishment," 83, 91.

89. *California Star*, December 11, 1847, quoted in Rawls, *Indians of California*, 83.

90. Edward F. Beale to Luke Lea, quoted in Heizer, *Federal Concerns*, 4–5.

91. "Report of Special Agent John G. Ames on the Condition of the Mission Indians, 1874," quoted in Heizer, *Federal Concerns*, 59–60, 60.

92. "Report of Special Agent John G. Ames," 63.

93. Rawls, *Indians of California*, 104.

94. *Red Bluff Beacon*, June 22, 1859.

95. *Los Angeles Star*, October 30 1852.

96. Monroy, *Thrown among Strangers*, 185.

97. "An Act Concerning Hogs found running at large, in the Counties of Colusa, Tehama, Butte, Sonoma, and Napa," *California Statutes*, 1857, chapter 102. Acts such as Chapter 102 spread to other counties in later years.

98. For examples, see "An Act Restricting the Herding of Sheep to Certain Pastures in the Counties of Sonoma and Marin," *California Statutes*, 1857, chapter 194.

99. "An Act for the protection of Game," *California Statutes*, 1852, chapter 61. For later modifications, see *California Statutes*, 1854, chapter 50; 1869–70, chapter 557.

100. "An Act to Prevent the Sale of Fire-arms and Ammunition to Indians in this State," *California Statutes*, 1854, chapter 12.

101. "An Act to prohibit the erection of Weirs, or other obstructions, to the run of Salmon," *California Statutes*, 1852, chapter 62. The following year, the act was modified to exclude application to Native people, but in later years it would be put back into place. See "An Act to amend the Seventh Section of 'an Act to prohibit the erection of Weirs, or other obstructions, to the run of Salmon,' approved April twelfth, one thousand eight hundred and fifty-two," *California Statutes*, 1853, chapter 38. Later modifications include "An Act to amend an Act entitled 'An Act to prohibit the erection of Weirs, or other obstructions, to the run of Salmon,'" *California Statutes*, 1854, chapter 70.

102. Burnett, *Recollections*, 367, 367–68.

103. This was not true of Native peoples of far southern and southeastern California, where corn along the Colorado River and mesquite pods were staples. Pine nuts were a staple throughout the state.

104. "An Act Concerning Lawful Fences, and Animals Trespassing on Premises Lawfully Inclosed," *California Statutes*, 1850, chapter 49. Violators were subject to the cost of damage done by their stock; multiple offenders were subject to double the cost of damage.

105. "Concurrent Resolution," number 17, adopted February 15, 1864, *California Statutes*, 1864.

106. "Joint Resolution, relative to Mendocino Indian Reservation," number 37, approved March 19, 1868, *California Statutes*, 1867–68.

107. Other than the story of Emma contained in chapter 4, I am unaware of any records left regarding children raised in white households in this era, despite the fact that records clearly indicate thousands of children fell into this category.

108. "An Act to provide for a System of Common Schools," *California Statutes*, 1865–66, chapter 52, sections 57–58.

109. Lydia B. Lascy to Governor Newton Booth, September 13, 1873, Record 665, Indian War Papers.

110. Lascy to Booth, September 13, 1873.

7. FEDERAL BYSTANDERS TO AND AGENTS OF GENOCIDE

1. The military governors of California, however, left much of the governing to local *alcaldes*, some left over from the Mexican era as well as ones newly appointed. For a full discussion of the period, see Grivas, *Military Governments in California*.

2. Legal interpretations by U.S. courts and the laws and policies of the United States made Native American sovereignty something less than sovereign. Over time the limits of sovereignty shifted as well. Since the Supreme Court decision in *Cherokee Nation v. Georgia* (1831) Native nations have been categorized as "domestic dependent nations," with sovereignty secondary to that of the United States. For a full discussion, see Wilkins, *American Indian Sovereignty*.

3. Under the Treaty of Guadalupe Hidalgo, all lands not the legal property of Mexican land grant holders became the property of the United States. The California Land Act of 1851 regulated the transfer of titles from one government to the next. For more on this tendentious process, see Hornbeck, "The Patenting of California's Private Land Claims," 434–48.

4. V. Deloria, *Behind the Trail of Broken Treaties*.

5. For a time, Catalina Island was proposed as a home for California Indians. Serious consideration was given to the proposal in the early 1860s, but land claims on the island by white Americans made the prospect overcomplicated.

6. Ball, "By Right of Conquest," 8–16.

7. Heizer, *Eighteen Unratified Treaties*, 3.

8. R. B. Dixon and A. L. Kroeber, "Linguistic Families of California," in Heizer and Whipple, *The California Indians*, 105–11; A. L. Kroeber, "The Tribe in California," in Heizer and Whipple, *The California Indians*, 367–74.

9. Heizer, *Eighteen Unratified Treaties*, 4–5, 3.

10. Phillips, *Indians and Indian Agents*, 187–89.

11. Hoopes, *Domesticate or Exterminate*, 90–91, 93.

12. *Congressional Globe*, 32nd Congress, 1st session, 213.

13. Hoopes, *Domesticate or Exterminate*, 65–66.

14. Ball, "By Right of Conquest," 12.

15. Ellison, "The Federal Indian Policy in California," 57.

16. Hoopes, *Domesticate or Exterminate*, 102–3, 105–6.

17. Phillips, *"Bringing Them under Subjection,"* 106–7.

18. Some Native Americans were able to remain in place for extended periods because until land was surveyed and put up for sale by the federal government, they were not required to move.

19. M. T. Smith, "The History of Indian Citizenship," 25–35. Not until 1924 were all Native Americans residing in the United States granted citizenship. Before this, there had been only sporadic cases.

20. On the creation of California's early reservations, see Phillips, *Indians and Indian Agents*, especially 183–90.

21. Hoopes, *Domesticate or Exterminate*, 109–10.

22. Superintendent Edward F. Beale to Commissioner of Indian Affairs Luke Lea, May 11, 1852, quoted in Heizer, *Eighteen Unratified Treaties*, 19–26.

23. Ellison, "Federal Indian Policy," 59.

24. Senator John B. Weller, August 11, 1852, quoted in Hoopes, *Domesticate or Exterminate*, 110–13.

25. Phillips, *Indians and Indian Agents*, 49–54, 78–91.

26. Superintendent Edward F. Beale, quoted in Heizer, *Federal Concerns*, 2–3.

27. Ellison, "Federal Indian Policy," 61.

28. The reservation was usually called the Tejón reservation. For information on the creation and purpose of the reserve, see Phillips, *"Bringing Them under Subjection,"* 106–8, 131–34.

29. John R. Grice to George Manypenny, commissioner of Indian affairs, November 15, 1855, M234, roll 35, ser. no. 32–36, Office of Indian Affairs, Letters Received, California Superintendency, 1849–80 (hereafter cited as Office of Indian Affairs), National Archives and Records Administration, Pacific Branch, San Bruno, California (hereafter cited as NARA). Grice was an employee at Tejón and was writing in defense of Henley, laying blame on Beale for the problems at the reservation.

30. Ellison, "Federal Indian Policy," 63.

31. For a look into Henley's corruption having a negative impact on the reservation system, see Secrest, "The Rise and Fall of Thomas J. Henley," 23–29.

32. Ellison, "Federal Indian Policy," 64–65.

33. Browne, *J. Ross Browne*, 182. Browne did similar work in Oregon and Washington. For serviceable biographies of Browne, see Dillon, *J. Ross Browne*; Goodman, *A Western Panorama*.

34. John Ross Browne to commissioner of Indian affairs, April 19, 1858, M234, roll 36, ser. no. 33–46, Office of Indian Affairs, NARA.

35. Henley and other Indian agents made no secret of the presence of many whites living on reservations in the form of employees they had taken on to work the reservation as farmers, physicians, carpenters, laborers, and numerous other categories of employment found on reservation reports. They did not list the sometimes considerable number of white squatters they were

allowing to occupy the reservations. For an example of a quarterly census of reservation personnel, see Thomas J. Henley's Quarterly Report of the California Superintendency, M234, roll 35, ser. no. 180–93, Office of Indian Affairs, NARA.

36. John Ross Browne to commissioner of Indian affairs, April 19, 1858, M234, roll 36, ser. no. 33–46, Office of Indian Affairs, NARA. Browne notes that Indian employees of the mill were promised pay at a rate of 50 cents per day, but that these wages "had never yet been paid." White employees, by comparison, made about $3 per day, more for specialized positions.

37. John Ross Browne to commissioner of Indian affairs, July 2, 1858, M234, roll 37, ser. no. 79–85, Office of Indian Affairs, NARA.

38. John Ross Browne to J. W. Denver, commissioner of Indian affairs, January 18, 1859, M234, roll 37, ser. no. 14–21, Office of Indian Affairs, NARA.

39. Petition of the Settlers of Shasta County, California, September 1867, M234, roll 42, ser. no. 235–42, Office of Indian Affairs, NARA.

40. Petition of the Citizens of Fresno and Tulare to Judge M. B. Lewis, Indian subagent, November 14, 1858, M234, roll 37, ser. no. 953–54, Office of Indian Affairs, NARA. There were six petitioners.

41. Thomas J. Henley, superintendent of Indian affairs, to Charles E. Mix, commissioner of Indian affairs, December 4, 1858, M234, roll 37, ser. no. 944–45, Office of Indian Affairs, NARA.

42. For perhaps his most widely seen articles, see Browne, *The Coast Rangers*, especially chapter 2. Browne originally published this work as a serial in *Harper's New Monthly Magazine* 23–34 (1861–62).

43. Chalk and Jonassohn, *The History and Sociology of Genocide*, 203. Here I have substituted some of the dietary staples of various Native peoples of California inspired by the example and genocidal results described by Chalk and Jonassohn in reference to the extermination of the buffalo.

44. Browne, *The Coast Rangers*, 41.

45. Wild, *J. Ross Browne*, 11–12. In fact this talent may have been what lost Browne his posting and later made it difficult for him to get or keep appointed posts in the federal government.

46. Browne, *J. Ross Browne*, 191, 298–99, 315.

47. Ellison, "Federal Indian Policy," 66.

48. Hitchcock, *Fifty Years in Camp and Field*, iii, 71, 221, 228, 395.

49. The quote as well as the entire exchange of letters from November to December 1855 can be found in M234, roll 35, ser. no. 114–23, Office of Indian Affairs, NARA.

50. S. G. Whipple, Indian agent, to Thomas J. Henley, California superintendent of Indian affairs, June 11, 1856, M234, roll 35, ser. no. 451–53, Office of Indian Affairs, NARA.

51. Strobridge, *Regulars in the Redwoods*, 177–78.

52. Strobridge, *Regulars in the Redwoods*, 183–84.

53. Strobridge, *Regulars in the Redwoods*, 185.

54. Strobridge, *Regulars in the Redwoods*, 186.

55. Lt. Edward Dillon to Maj. Edward Johnson, March 23, 1859, Record 356, Indian War Papers.

56. Strobridge, *Regulars in the Redwoods*, 187.

57. Strobridge, *Regulars in the Redwoods*, 187–88, 189.

58. For an example persisting into the late 1860s, see J. B. McIntosh, superintendent of Indian affairs, to Gen. E. O. C. Ord, commanding officer, Department of California, August 14, 1869, M234, roll 43, ser. no. 166–67, Office of Indian Affairs, NARA. This case concerned an outbreak of measles at the Tule River Reservation.

59. For an example in the 1850s, see John Ross Browne to commissioner of Indian affairs, April 19, 1858, M234, roll 36, ser. no. 33–46, Office of Indian Affairs, NARA. For one drawn from the 1860s, see H. J. Hart, Indian agent, to General Parker, commissioner of Indian affairs, June 20, 1869, M234, roll 43, ser. no. 21–23, Office of Indian Affairs, NARA.

60. Strobridge, *Regulars in the Redwoods*, 190.

61. Dillon to Johnson, March 23, 1859.

62. Strobridge, *Regulars in the Redwoods*, 189–90.

63. Deposition of Charles Eberle, February 22, 1860, Record 434, Indian War Papers.

64. In many documents, John Bland is also identified as John Blan.

65. Deposition of Charles Eberle.

66. See chapter 4.

67. Deposition of James Wilsey, February 28, 1860, Record 442, Indian War Papers.

68. Deposition of Charles Eberle.

69. Deposition of James Wilsey.

70. Deposition of George Rees, February 27, 1860, Record 455, Indian War Papers.

71. Deposition of Charles Eberle.

72. Deposition of William J. Hildreath, February 24, 1860, Record 443, Indian War Papers.

73. Deposition of George Rees.

74. *Sacramento Union*, August 19, 1865. A search of subsequent issues indicates that Hildreath was never brought to trial.

75. Deposition of William Hildreath.

76. Deposition of William Hildreath.

77. Second Deposition of Lt. Edward Dillon, February 27, 1860, Record 451, Indian War Papers.

78. Deposition of George Rees.

79. *Humboldt Times*, May 5, 1855.

80. Deposition of George Rees.

81. Deposition of George W. Henley, February 27, 1860, Record 459, Indian War Papers.

82. Deposition of Simon P. Storms, February 28, 1860, Record 461, Indian War Papers.

83. *Greenville Bulletin*, April 25, 1881.

84. Chirot and McCauley, *Why Not Kill Them All?*, 80–81, 139–40.

85. *Red Bluff Beacon*, December 30, 1857.

86. *Red Bluff Beacon*, May 19, 1858.

87. *Red Bluff Beacon*, undated (ca. August 1859), copy in author's possession.

88. *Chico Weekly Courant*, September 8, 1866.

89. *Red Bluff Beacon*, May 5, 1858.

90. Second Deposition of Lt. Edward Dillon.

91. Deposition of Charles McLane, February 28, 1860, Record 465, Indian War Papers.

92. First deposition of Lt. Edward Dillon, undated (1860), Record 357, Indian War Papers.

93. *Red Bluff Beacon*, November 19, 1859.

94. *Red Bluff Beacon*, August 24, 1859.

95. For the exchange, see Records 393, 394, 396, and 397, Indian War Papers.

96. Walter S. Jarboe to Lt. Edward Dillon, December 21, 1859, Record 406, Indian War Papers.

97. Strobridge, *Regulars in the Redwoods*, 193–94, 195–97. Johnson was gone when Bland's body was discovered.

98. Strobridge, *Regulars in the Redwoods*, 197–98, 199.

99. Affidavit of Simon P. Storms, January 20, 1860, Record 417, Indian War Papers.

100. Lt. Edward Dillon to Maj. W. W. Mackall, January 14, 1860, Record 412, Indian War Papers.

101. Strobridge, *Regulars in the Redwoods*, 200–201.

102. S. L. Smith, *The View from Officers' Row*, 98.

103. Strobridge, *Regulars in the Redwoods*, 239, 241–42.

104. Deposition of Simon P. Storms, February 26, 1860, Record 447, Indian War Papers.

105. Strobridge, *Regulars in the Redwoods*, 244.

106. *Red Bluff Beacon*, December 30, 1857.

107. *San Francisco Bulletin*, May 31, 1859, quoted in Heizer, *"They Were Only Diggers,"* 37.

108. Crook, *General George Crook*, xv.

109. S. L. Smith, *View from Officer's Row*, 92, 102, 106, 126.

110. Crook, *General George Crook*, xvi.

111. Crook, *General George Crook*, 11. Scrofula is a type of tuberculosis.

112. Crook, *General George Crook*, 13–14.

113. Strobridge, *Regulars in the Redwoods*, 32.

114. Crook, *General George Crook*, 15–16, 16.

115. Chirot and McCauley, *Why Not Kill Them All?*, 54.

116. Chirot and McCauley, *Why Not Kill Them All?*, 53, 147.

117. Crook, *General George Crook*, 16–33, 34–35.

118. Crook, *General George Crook*, 35, 36–38, 38, 53, 39.

119. Crook, *General George Crook*, 40–42, 43, 44, 45, 45–46.

120. Crook, *General George Crook*, 46–48.

121. Crook, *General George Crook*, 49–50.

122. Crook, *General George Crook*, 51.

123. Crook, *General George Crook*, 51–53.

124. *Red Bluff Beacon*, June 17, 1857.

125. *Red Bluff Beacon*, September 1, 1857.

126. Ellison, "Federal Indian Policy," 66.

127. Norton, *When Our Worlds Cried*, 153.

128. *Red Bluff Sentinel*, June 10, 1868.

8. ADVERTISING GENOCIDE

1. Rawls, *Indians of California*, 183.

2. Coward, *The Newspaper Indian*, 10, 10–11.

3. *Plumas National*, December 21, 1867.

4. Coward, *Newspaper Indian*, 14–15.

5. *Red Bluff Sentinel*, July 4, 1868.

6. *Quincy Union*, August 11, 1866.

7. Chirot and McCauley, *Why Not Kill Them All?*, 36–44.

8. *Quincy Union*, July 13, 1867.

9. *Plumas National*, June 22, 1872.

10. *Plumas National*, November 24, 1878.

11. For examples, see *Sacramento Union*, September 6, 1863; *San Francisco Bulletin*, August 10, 1863.

12. *Chico Weekly Courant*, December 12, 1868.

13. *Yreka Journal*, February 21, 1868. For other examples of pigeon English, see *Chico Weekly Courant*, December 12, 1868; *Quincy Union*, February 20, 1864; *Marysville Appeal*, March 27, 1864.

14. Heizer, *The Destruction of the California Indians*, 309.

15. *Weekly Mercury*, February 21, 1879.

16. *Quincy Union*, August 4, 1866.

17. *Plumas National*, September 13, 1873.

18. *Marysville Daily Evening Herald*, August 12, 1853. For the full text, see the epigraph to this chapter.

19. *Chico Weekly Courant*, August 11, 1866.

20. *Chico Weekly Courant*, September 8, 1866.

21. *Chico Weekly Courant*, October 6, 1866.

22. *Chico Weekly Courant*, December 13, 1867.

23. *Daily Alta California*, March 6, 1853.

24. *Chico Weekly Courant*, September 15, 1866.

25. *Sacramento Daily Union*, March 18, 1857.

26. *California Farmer*, March 27, 1861.

27. *Chico Weekly Courant*, June 19, 1868.

28. For examples drawn from the particularly active community of Red Bluff, see *Red Bluff Beacon*, July 15, 1857; May 26, June 2, June 9, June 16, August 11, 1858; June 8, August 10, 1859; October 23, 1862.

29. *Red Bluff Beacon*, August 11, 1858.

30. *Red Bluff Beacon*, May 26, 1858.

31. *Red Bluff Sentinel*, June 20, 1868.

32. *Chico Weekly Courant*, July 28, 1866.

33. Not surprisingly, many Americans' greatest fear was that Indians would do what they themselves were doing: organize on a large scale and launch a war of extermination. For example, see *Red Bluff Beacon*, July 17, 1862.

34. *Red Bluff Beacon*, May 26, 1858.

35. *Quincy Union*, June 16, 1865.

36. *Humboldt Times*, January 27, 1855.

37. *Lassen Sage Brush*, May 23, 1868.

38. *Red Bluff Beacon*, July 15, 1857.

39. *Daily Alta California*, May 29, 1856.

40. For further discussion of dissonance theory and the way dissonance can be achieved, see Chirot and McCauley, *Why Not Kill Them All?*, 52–57.

41. *Red Bluff Beacon*, July 31, 1862.

42. *Red Bluff Beacon*, August 10, 1859.

43. *Daily Alta California*, December 15, 1851.

44. *Yreka Daily Appeal*, May 17, 1867.

45. *Sacramento Daily Union*, December 12, 1859.

46. *Red Bluff Beacon*, April 22, 1857.

47. *Red Bluff Beacon*, June 24, 1857.

48. *Red Bluff Beacon*, September 30, 1857.

49. *Red Bluff Beacon*, May 6, 1857.

50. *Red Bluff Beacon*, April 14, 1858.

51. *Red Bluff Beacon*, May 26, 1858.

52. *Red Bluff Beacon*, November 6, 1862.

53. *Red Bluff Beacon*, March 17, 1858. Even in the twentieth century, newspapers continued to publish the location and contents of Indian burial sites. For instance, see *Chico Post*, November 9, 1905.

54. *Red Bluff Beacon*, April 21, 1858.

55. *Red Bluff Beacon*, May 6, 1857.

56. Rawls, *Indians of California*, 183.

57. Coward, *Newspaper Indian*, 232–33.

58. *Daily Alta California*, June 10, 1858.

59. *Northern Californian*, February 29, 1860. The massacre is also sometimes called the Gunther Island Massacre.

60. *Northern Californian*, February 29, 1860.

61. Carranco, "Bret Harte in Union," 109.

62. *Humboldt Times*, unknown date (ca. 1860), quoted in Norton, *When Our Worlds Cried*, 85.

63. Maj. G. J. Raines to assistant adjutant general, March 10, 1860, quoted in Heizer and Almquist, *The Other Californians*, 30.

64. For examples of trouble in the region, see *Humboldt Times*, January 20, January 27, February 3, May 5, May 26, August 11, 1855; October 4, 1856; October 30, 1858.

65. *Marysville Daily Evening Herald*, August 12, 1853.

66. *Plumas National*, November 10, 1866.

67. *Humboldt Times*, March 3, 1860.

68. Secrest, *When the Great Spirit Died*, 332.

69. Carranco, "Bret Harte in Union," 109–10.

70. Norton, *When Our Worlds Cried*, 85.

71. *San Francisco Bulletin*, June 18, 1860; *California Farmer*, March 27, 1861.

72. *San Francisco Bulletin*, February 28, March 2, May 24, 1860.

73. Heizer, *Destruction of the California Indians*, 154–61.

74. Norton, *When Our Worlds Cried*, 86–88.

75. *Humboldt Times*, January 17, 1863.

76. *Humboldt Times*, May 23, 1863.

77. *San Francisco Bulletin*, February 28, 1860.

78. *Humboldt Times*, quoted in *Marysville Appeal*, April 16, 1862, quoted in Trafzer and Hyer, *"Exterminate Them!,"* 131.

79. *Humboldt Times*, April 9, 1862.

80. Carranco, "Bret Harte in Union," 99.

81. S. L. Smith, *Reimagining Indians*, 4–7.

82. P. J. Deloria, *Playing Indian*.

83. Mathes, "I Am Going to Write an Indian Novel," 109–13.

84. Jackson made several important efforts to assist Native people, in California and throughout the United States. See Jackson, *A Century of Dishonor* and *Ramona*; Mathes, *The Indian Reform Letters*. For a discussion of Jackson's legacy, see C. C. Davis and Alderson, *The True Story of "Ramona"*; DeLyser, *Ramona Memories*; Mathes, *Helen Hunt Jackson*.

85. Sundquist, *Empire and Slavery*, 71.

86. For a discussion of Twain's pejorative characterization of Indians, see Harris, "Mark Twain's Response"; Coulombe, "Mark Twain's Native Americans."

87. Goodwyn, "The Frontier in American Fiction," 356–69.

88. See *Los Angeles Star* issues from February through July 1852 for the twenty installments.

89. *Butte Democrat*, September 17, 1859.

90. See *California Farmer* issues from February 22 through June 29, 1860, and from October 26, 1860, through March 29, 1861, for all installments of both parts.

91. *Lassen Sage Brush*, June 13, 1868.

92. *Northern Journal*, February 2, 1860.
93. *Chico Weekly Courant*, November 18, 1865.
94. *Greenville Bulletin*, December 24, 1890.

CONCLUSION

1. *Daily Alta California*, February 22, 1873.
2. E. N. Thompson, *Modoc War*, vii–xii. For a report on the Modoc response, see Senate Miscellaneous Document 59, 36th Congress, 1st session, 1860.
3. Further details of army operations preceding the Modoc War in northeastern California can be found in Brodhead, "'This Indian Gibraltar.'"
4. The commissioner of Indian affairs had high hopes for this new arrangement in 1864. In a report to Congress he noted that the Modocs were excellent marksmen and capable of defending themselves effectively. See "Annual Report of the Commissioner of Indian Affairs, 1864," House Executive Document 1, 38th Congress, 2nd session, 1864.
5. Kenitpoos was also known as Captain Jack, especially among whites. His name is sometimes spelled Kientipoos or Keintpoos.
6. E. N. Thompson, *Modoc War*, xi, 5.
7. Senate Executive Document 29, 42nd Congress, 3rd session, 1873.
8. H. D. Moore, "A Modoc War Letter," 1–7. This is a published transcription of part of a letter from Moore to an unidentified recipient. The letter was written April 29, 1873, at Tule Lake.
9. Even the *Daily Alta California* carried such calls. For examples, see *Daily Alta California*, April 16, 1873; *Sacramento Daily Union*, April 14, 1873.
10. H. D. Moore, "A Modoc War Letter," 7.
11. E. N. Thompson, *Modoc War*, 125–26.
12. For more on the Modoc War, see Dillon, *Burnt Out Fires*; Murray, *The Modocs and Their War*. Government documents associated with the war are contained in "Message on the Modoc War," House Executive Document 122, 43rd Congress, 1st session, 1874.
13. Senate Report 731, 45th Congress, 3rd session, 1879; House Report 75, 45th Congress, 3rd session, 1879.
14. House Report 1354, 46th Congress, 2nd session, 1880.
15. The Ghost Dance is the name given by whites to the dance performed by a variety of Native American peoples in the United States. Interpretations of the dance, how it was named, and its meaning varied among Native peoples.

16. Though originally published in 1946 and containing much cultural bias, the best work on the 1870 Ghost Dance in California is still probably Du Bois, "The 1870 Ghost Dance."

17. Gayton, "The Ghost Dance."

18. Du Bois, "The 1870 Ghost Dance," 11.

19. Du Bois, "The 1870 Ghost Dance," 138.

20. Wovoka was known among whites as Jack Wilson.

21. Hoyer, "Prophecy in a New West," 235–56. Hoyer is restating the argument of L. G. Moses regarding the role of the press.

22. *Greenville Bulletin*, January 7, 1891.

23. The best scholarship on California's reservation system in the nineteenth century has come from George Harwood Phillips. In particular, see *Indians and Indian Agents* and *"Bringing Them under Subjection."*

24. For coverage of federal Indian policy since the 1880s, see Cadwalader and Deloria, *The Aggressions of Civilization.*

25. Quoted in Heizer and Almquist, *The Other Californians*, 90, 89–90. Dole's original report was titled "Report on the Mission Indians in California, 1875."

26. "Letter from the Secretary of the Interior," House Executive Document 91, 43rd Congress, 1st session, 1874. This document contains letters from the secretary of the interior, the commissioner for Indian affairs, and the 1873 report on the Mission Indians of southern California prepared by the Reverend John G. Ames.

27. "Annual Report of the Commissioner of Indian Affairs, 1870," House Executive Document 1, 41st Congress, 3rd session, 1870.

28. "Annual Report of the Commissioner of Indian Affairs, 1871," House Executive Document 1, 42nd Congress, 2nd session, 1871.

29. Quoted in Heizer and Almquist, *The Other Californians*, 90.

30. Wetmore, "Report on the Mission Indians in California," 8–9, 12.

31. Bean and Lawton, *The Cahuilla Indians*, 2, 3.

32. *Greenville Bulletin*, January 7, 1891.

33. In 1909, for example, 77 percent of the Native people at Hoopa tested positive for tuberculosis. See "Annual Report of the Commissioner of Indian Affairs, 1909," House Document 107, 61st Congress, 2nd session, 1910.

34. Nichols, *American Indians in U.S. History*, 155.

35. "Annual report of the Commissioner of Indian Affairs," House Executive Document 1, 52nd Congress, 1st session, 1891.

36. Trafzer, *As Long as the Grass Shall Grow*, 291.

37. Taber, *California and Her Indian Children*, iv.

38. "Annual report of the Commissioner of Indian Affairs, 1902," House Document 5, 57th Congress, 2nd session, 1903.

39. For studies of boarding schools as genocidal, see D. W. Adams, *Education for Extinction*; W. Churchill, *Kill the Indian*.

40. For an extended discussion of culturicide, see Fenelon, *Culturicide, Resistance, and Survival of the Lakota*, especially chapter 2, "Culturicide Processes over Native Nations."

41. For more on the experience of Native American children at the Sherman Institute, see Keller, *Boarding School Blues*. For the broader context of the genocidal efforts to exterminate Indianness, see D. W. Adams, *Education for Extinction*.

42. "Annual Report of the Commissioner of Indian Affairs, 1903," House Document 5, 58th Congress, 2nd session, 1904.

43. *Oroville Register*, October 1, 1896.

44. Thomas, "The Mission Indians," 54.

45. House Executive Document 21, 49th Congress, 1st session, 1886.

46. Thomas, "The Mission Indians," 65. According to Thomas, only "ten out of thirty-three" of the reservations were allotted, and those only partially.

47. The seminal work on the Dawes Act and its purposes is Washburn, *The Assault on Tribalism*.

EPILOGUE

The epigraph is from T. T. Waterman, "The Last Wild Tribe of California," Popular Science Monthly *(March 1915), quoted in Heizer and Kroeber,* Ishi, the Last Yahi, *126.*

1. Taber, *California and Her Indian Children*, 9.

2. *Chico Post*, November 9, 1905.

3. For an investigation of whites "playing Indian," see P. J. Deloria, *Playing Indian*. For the "Nature Men" inspired by public interest in Ishi, see Sackman, *Wild Men*, 208–13.

4. The story and interpretation of the Yahi man called "Ishi" has generated much scholarship, including Heizer and Kroeber, *Ishi, the Last Yahi*; Kroeber, *Ishi in Two Worlds*; Sackman, *Wild Men*; Starn, *Ishi's Brain*.

5. For a recent discussion of the Yahis in the context of genocide, see Sackman, *Wild Men*, especially 16–43.

6. For examples of paeans to Good and Anderson, see *Plumas National Bulletin*, February 27, 1913; March 4, 1915.

7. *Chico Record*, August 29, 1911.

8. *Plumas National*, August 30, 1911.

9. Kroeber, *Ishi in Two Worlds*, 5.

10. *Plumas National*, September 7, 1911; *Redding Searchlight*, September 19, 1911.

11. Kroeber, *Ishi in Two Worlds*, 110–11.

12. *San Francisco Call*, September 16, 1911.

13. Kroeber, *Ishi in Two Worlds*, 10, 129. Yana is the language of the people living adjacent to the Yahis. Kroeber engaged a Yana man, Sam Botwi, to facilitate communication with Ishi. They had only limited success.

14. *San Francisco Examiner*, September 7, 1911.

15. *San Francisco Call*, October 8, 1911.

16. "Ishi: The Last Yahi."

17. Quoted in "Ishi: The Last Yahi."

18. Rawls, *Indians of California*, 200.

19. Kroeber, *Ishi in Two Worlds*, 150–83.

20. Kroeber, *Ishi in Two Worlds*, 111.

21. "Ishi: The Last Yahi."

22. *San Francisco Examiner*, October 8, 1915.

23. For the story of Ishi as told through one scholar's hunt for his remains, see Starn, *Ishi's Brain*. Ishi's brain was recovered from a chemical tank at the Smithsonian Museum of Natural History, reunited with his ashes, and the whole was reburied in northeastern California in 2000. For an anthropologist's reflections on the subject of Native remains, see Scheper-Hughes, "Ishi's Brain, Ishi's Ashes."

24. *San Francisco Examiner*, October 8, 1915.

25. *Chico Record*, March 28, 1916.

26. Forbes, "The Native American Experience," 241.

27. For an early example, see the book of memories by Lucy Thompson, a Yurok woman, published in 1916: *To the American Indian*.

28. Steven T. Katz, "The Uniqueness of the Holocaust: The Historical Dimension," in Rosenbaum, *Is the Holocaust Unique?*, 27.

29. Katz, "The Uniqueness of the Holocaust," 27.

Bibliography

ARCHIVAL SOURCES

Bidwell, Annie E. K., Collection. California State Library, Sacramento.

Bidwell, John. "Dictation from John Bidwell: An autobiography." Bancroft Library, University of California, Berkeley.

Geer, Knyphausen. "Captain Knyphausen Geer: His Life and Memoirs." Bancroft Library, University of California, Berkeley.

Hamilton, Ezra M. "'Story of the lost Children': Reminiscences of Ezra M. Hamilton." Ezra M. Hamilton Collection. California State Library, Sacramento.

Hutchings, J. M., Diaries. Bancroft Library, University of California, Berkeley.

"Interviews with the Inhabitants of Trinity County." Bancroft Library, University of California, Berkeley.

Meek, William Bull. "Reminiscences of William Bull Meek of Camptonville, California." Bancroft Library, University of California, Berkeley.

Military Department. Office of the Adjutant General. Indian War Papers, 1850–1880. California State Archives, Sacramento.

Morse, Ephraim, Papers. California State Library, Sacramento.

Naglee Family Collection. Bancroft Library, University of California, Berkeley.

Office of Indian Affairs, Letters Received. California Superintendency, 1849–80. National Archives and Records Administration.

Reading, P. B., Family Papers. Bancroft Library, University of California, Berkeley.

Records of Continental Commands, Department of the Pacific, U.S. Army. National Archives and Records Administration.

Records of Continental Commands, 10th Military Department, U.S. Army. National Archives and Records Administration.

Stewart, George W., Collection. California State Library, Sacramento.

"To the California State Legislature: Petition for the settlement of the Claim of Edward H. Burns." Bancroft Library, University of California, Berkeley.

PUBLISHED SOURCES

Abbott, Carlisle S. *Recollections of a California Pioneer*. New York: Neale, 1917.

Adams, Charles Francis. *Richard Henry Dana: A Biography*. Reprint, Detroit: Gale Research Group, 1968.

Adams, David Wallace. *Education for Extinction: American Indians and the Boarding School Experience, 1875–1928*. Lawrence: University Press of Kansas, 1995.

Anderson, Robert A. *Fighting the Mill Creeks: Being a Personal Account of the Campaigns against Indians of the Northern Sierras*. Chico CA, 1909.

Ansted, David T. *The Gold-Seeker's Manual*. New York: D. Appleton, 1849.

Babcock, C. Merton. "The Social Significance of the Language of the American Frontier." *American Speech* 24, no. 4 (1949): 256–63.

Ball, Durwood. "By Right of Conquest: Military Government in New Mexico and California, 1846–1851." *Journal of the West* 41, no. 3 (2002): 8–16.

Bancroft, George. *The History of the United States of America, from the Discovery of the Continent*. 6 vols. New York: Little, Brown, 1854–60.

———. *The History of the United States of America, from the Discovery of the Continent*. Author's final revision. 6 vols. 1885. Reprint, Port Washington NY: Kennikat Press, 1967.

Bandel, Eugene. *Frontier Life in the Army, 1854–1861*. Translated by Olga Bandel and Richard Jente. Edited by Ralph A. Bieber. Glendale CA: Arthur H. Clarke, 1932.

Bartlett, William Henry. *The History of the United States of North America; from the Discovery of the Western World to the Present Day*. 3 vols. New York: George Virtue, 1856.

Bauer, William J. "'We Were All Migrant Workers Here': Round Valley Indian Labor in Northern California, 1850–1929." *Western Historical Quarterly* 37, no. 1 (2003): 43–63.

Baumgardner, Frank H. *Killing for Land in Early California: Indian Blood at Round Valley, 1856–1863*. New York: Algora, 2006.

Bean, Lowell, and Harry Lawton. *The Cahuilla Indians of Southern California*. Banning CA: Malki Museum Press, 1965.

Bell, Horace. *Reminiscences of a Ranger: Early Times in Southern California*. Introduction by John Bossenecker. Norman: University of Oklahoma Press, 1999.

Benson, Todd. "The Consequences of Reservation Life." *Pacific Historical Review* 60 (1991): 221–44.

Bidwell, John. *Echoes of the Past about California: An Account of the First Emigrant Train to California, Fremont in Conquest of California, the Discovery of Gold and Early Reminiscences.* Edited by Milo Milton Quaife. Chicago: Lakeside Press, 1928.

Bledsoe, Anthony Jennings. *Indian Wars of the Northwest: A California Sketch.* Foreword by Joseph A. Sullivan. Oakland CA: Biobooks, 1956.

Blew, Robert W. "Vigilantism in Los Angeles, 1835–1874." *Southern California Quarterly* 54 (Spring 1972): 11–30.

Brewer, William H. *Up and Down California in 1860–1864: The Journal of William H. Brewer.* 4th ed., with maps. Edited by Francis P. Farquhar. Foreword by William Bright. Berkeley: University of California Press, 2003.

Broadbent, Sylvia M. "Conflict at Monterey: Indian Horse Raiding, 1820–1850." *Journal of California Anthropology* 1, no. 1 (1974): 86–101.

Brodhead, Michael. "'This Indian Gibraltar': The Battle of the Infernal Caverns and Other Incidents of George Crook's Campaign of 1866–1868." *Journal of America's Military Past* 29, no. 3 (2003): 60–87.

Brown, Charles H. *Agents of Manifest Destiny: The Lives and Times of the Filibusters.* Chapel Hill: University of North Carolina Press, 1980.

Browne, J. Ross. *The Coast Rangers: A Chronicle of Adventures in California.* Balboa Island CA: Paisano Press, 1959.

———. *Crusoe's Island.* New York: Harper Brothers, 1867.

———. *J. Ross Browne, His Letters, Journals, and Writings.* Edited with introduction and commentary by Lina Fergusson Browne. Albuquerque: University of New Mexico Press, 1969.

———. *Report of the Debates in the Convention of California.* 1850.

Bryant, Edwin. *What I Saw in California.* Introduction by Thomas D. Clark. 1848. Reprint, Lincoln: University of Nebraska Press, 1985.

Bryant, William Cullen, and Sydney Howard Gay. *A Popular History of the United States, from the First Discovery of the Western Hemisphere by the Northmen, to the End of the First Century of the Union of the United States.* Vol. 3. New York: Charles Scribner's Sons, 1879.

Burnett, Peter H. *Recollections and Opinions of an Old Pioneer.* New York: Da Capo Press, 1969.

Burns, John F., and Richard J. Orsi, eds. *Taming the Elephant: Politics, Government, and Law in Pioneer California.* Berkeley: University of California Press, 2003.

Cadwalader, Sandra D., and Vine Deloria, eds. *The Aggressions of Civilization: Federal Indian Policy Since the 1880s.* Philadelphia: Temple University Press, 1984.

California State Board of Education. "Model Curriculum for Human Rights and Genocide." California Department of Education, 2000.

Carranco, Lynwood. "Bret Harte in Union (1857–1860)." *California Historical Society Quarterly* 45, no. 2 (1966): 99–112.

Carranco, Lynwood, and Estle Beard. *Genocide and Vendetta: The Round Valley Wars of Northern California.* Norman: University of Oklahoma Press, 1981.

Carrico, Richard L. *Strangers in a Stolen Land: American Indians in San Diego, 1850–1880.* Sacramento: Sierra Oaks, 1987.

Carter, Robert W. "Sometimes When I Hear the Winds Sigh." *California History* 74 (Summer 1995): 146–61.

Castillo, Edward D. "An Indian Account of the Decline and Collapse of Mexico's Hegemony over the Missionized Indians of California." *American Indian Quarterly* 13, no. 4 (Autumn 1989): 391–408.

Caughey, John W., ed. *The Indians of Southern California in 1852.* San Marino CA: Huntington Library, 1952.

Chaffin, Tom. *Pathfinder: John Charles Frémont and the Course of American Empire.* New York: Hill and Wang, 2002.

Chalfant, W. A. *The Story of Inyo.* Bishop CA: Piñon Book Store, 1933.

Chalk, Frank, and Kurt Jonassohn. *The History and Sociology of Genocide: Analyses and Case Studies.* New Haven CT: Yale University Press, 1990.

Chandler, Robert J. "The Failure of Reform: White Attitudes and Indian Response in California during the Civil War Era." *Pacific Historian* 24, no. 3 (1980): 284–94.

Chandler, Robert J., and Ronald J. Quinn. "Emma Is a Good Girl." *Californians* 8, no. 5 (1991): 34–37.

Chirot, Daniel, and Clark McCauley. *Why Not Kill Them All? The Logic and Prevention of Mass Political Murder.* Princeton NJ: Princeton University Press, 2006.

Churchill, Charles B. "Benjamin Davis Wilson, Man in the Middle." *Californians* 10, no. 3 (1992): 31–35.

Churchill, Ward. *Kill the Indian, Save the Man: The Genocidal Impact of American Indian Residential Schools.* San Francisco: City Lights, 2004.

———. *A Little Matter of Genocide: Holocaust and Denial in the Americas 1492 to the Present.* San Francisco: City Lights, 1997.

Clapp, John T. *A Journal of Travels to and from California*. 1851. Reprint, Kalamazoo MI: Kalamazoo Public Museum, 1977.

Coffer, William E. "Genocide of the California Indians, with a Comparative Study of Other Minorities." *Indian Historian* 10, no. 2 (1977): 8–15.

Colton, Walter. *Three Years in California*. Cincinnati OH: H. W. Derby, 1850.

Cook, Sherburne F. *The Conflict between the California Indian and White Civilization*. Berkeley: University of California Press, 1976.

———. *The Population of the California Indians, 1769–1970*. Foreword by Woodrow Borah and Robert F. Heizer. Berkeley: University of California Press, 1966.

Costo, Rupert, and Jeanette Henry Costo, eds. *The Missions of California: A Legacy of Genocide*. San Francisco: Indian Historian Press, 1987.

Coulombe, Joseph L. "Mark Twain's Native Americans and the Repeated Racial Pattern in *Adventures of Huckleberry Finn*." *American Literary Realism* 33, no. 3 (2001): 261–79.

Coward, John M. *The Newspaper Indian: Native American Identity in the Press, 1820–1890*. Chicago: University of Illinois Press, 1999.

Cozzens, Peter. *Eyewitness to the Indian Wars, 1865–1890*. Vol. 5, *The Army and the Indian*. Mechanicsburg PA: Stackpole Books, 2005.

Crook, George. *General George Crook: His Autobiography*. Edited and annotated by Martin F. Schmitt. Norman: University of Oklahoma Press, 1960.

Crosby, Alfred W. *The Columbian Exchange: Biological and Cultural Consequences of 1492*. Westport CT: Greenwood, 1972.

———. *Ecological Imperialism: The Biological Expansion of Europe, 900–1900*. Cambridge, UK: Cambridge University Press, 1986.

Dana, Richard Henry. *Two Years before the Mast*. Garden City NY: Dolphin Books, n.d.

Davis, Carlyle Channing, and William A. Alderson. *The True Story of "Ramona."* New York: Dodge, 1914.

Davis, Mike. *Ecology of Fear: Los Angeles and the Imagination of Disaster*. New York: Vintage Books, 1998.

Deloria, Philip J. *Playing Indian*. New Haven CT: Yale University Press, 1998.

Deloria, Vine, Jr. *Behind the Trail of Broken Treaties: An Indian Declaration of Independence*. Austin: University of Texas Press, 1974.

DeLyser, Dydia. *Ramona Memories: Tourism and the Shaping of Southern California*. Minneapolis: University of Minnesota Press, 2005.

Diamond, Jared. *Guns, Germs, and Steel: The Fates of Human Societies*. New York: Norton, 1999.

Dillon, Richard H. *Burnt Out Fires.* Englewood Cliffs NJ: Prentice-Hall, 1973.

————. *J. Ross Browne: Confidential Agent in Old California.* Norman: University of Oklahoma Press, 1965.

Dippie, Brian W. "'His Visage Wild; His Form Exotick': Indian Themes and Cultural Guilt in John Barth's *The Sot-Weed Factor.*" *American Quarterly* 21, no. 1 (1969): 113–21.

————. "This Bold but Wasting Race: Stereotypes and American Indian Policy." *Montana* 23, no. 1 (1973): 2–13.

————. *The Vanishing American: White Attitudes and U.S. Indian Policy.* Middletown CT: Wesleyan University Press, 1982.

Drinnon, Richard. *Facing West: The Metaphysics of Indian Hating and Empire Building.* New introduction by the author. New York: Schocken Books, 1990.

Du Bois, Cora. "The 1870 Ghost Dance." *University of California Publications in Anthropological Records* 3, no. 1 (1946): 1–152.

Duchell, Margaret. "Bret Harte and the Indians of Northern California." *Huntington Library Quarterly* 18 (November 1954): 59–63.

Dunlay, Tom. *Kit Carson and the Indians.* Lincoln: University of Nebraska Press, 2000.

Duster, Troy. "Conditions for Guilt-Free Massacre." In Sanford and Comstock, *Sanctions for Evil,* 25–36.

Eccleston, Robert. *The Mariposa Indian War, 1850–1851: Diaries of Robert Eccleston.* Edited by C. Gregory Crampton. Salt Lake City: University of Utah Press, 1950.

Ellison, William H. "The Federal Indian Policy in California, 1846–1860." *Mississippi Valley Historical Review* 9, no. 1 (1922): 37–67.

Faragher, John Mack. "The Social Fabric of the American West." *Historian* 66, no. 3 (2004): 442–54.

————. *Women and Men on the Overland Trail.* New Haven CT: Yale University Press, 1979.

Fenelon, James V. *Culturicide, Resistance, and Survival of the Lakota.* New York: Garland, 1998.

Fernandez, Ferdinand F. "Except a California Indian: A Study in Legal Discrimination." *Southern California Quarterly* 50, no. 2 (1968): 161–75.

Flynn, Michael, and Charles B. Strozier, eds. *Genocide, War, and Human Survival.* Lanham MD: Rowman & Littlefield, 1996.

Foner, Eric. *The New American History.* Revised and expanded edition. Philadelphia: Temple University Press, 1997.

Forbes, Jack D. *The Indian in America's Past*. Edgewood Cliffs NJ: Prentice-Hall, 1964.

———. "The Native American Experience in California History." *California Historical Quarterly* 50, no. 3 (1971): 234–42.

———. *Native Americans of California and Nevada*. Healdsburg CA: Naturegraph, 1969.

———. *Warriors of the Colorado*. Norman: University of Oklahoma Press, 1965.

Freeman, Michael. "Genocide, Civilization, and Modernity." *British Journal of Sociology* 46, no. 2 (1995): 207–23.

———. "Puritans and Pequots: The Question of Genocide." *New England Quarterly* 68, no. 2 (1995): 278–93.

Frémont, John C. *Report of the Exploring Expedition to the Rocky Mountains in the Year 1842, and to Oregon and North California in the Years 1843–44*. 1845. Reprint, Santa Barbara CA: Narrative Press, 2002.

Frey, Robert S., ed. *The Genocidal Temptation: Auschwitz, Hiroshima, Rwanda, and Beyond*. Lanham MD: University Press of America, 2004.

Gale, Robert L. *Richard Henry Dana, Jr.* New York: Twayne, 1969.

Gayton, Anna Hadwick. "The Ghost Dance of 1870 in South-Central California." *University of California Publications in American Archaeology and Ethnology* 28, no. 3 (1930).

Gilbert, Bill. "Pioneers Made a Lasting Impression on Their Way." *Smithsonian* 25, no. 2 (1994): 40–49.

Gillis, Michael J., and Michael F. Magliari, eds. *John Bidwell and California: The Life and Writings of a Pioneer, 1841–1900*. Spokane WA: Arthur H. Clarke, 2003.

Goldhagen, Daniel J. *Hitler's Willing Executioners: Ordinary Germans and the Holocaust*. New York: Knopf, 1996.

Goodman, David Michael. *A Western Panorama, 1849–1875: The Travels, Writings and Influence of J. Ross Browne on the Pacific Coast, and in Texas, Nevada, Arizona and Baja California, as the First Mining Commissioner, and Minister to China*. Glendale CA: Arthur H. Clark, 1966.

Goodrich, Chauncey S. "The Legal Status of the California Indian." *California Law Review* 14, no. 2 (1926): 83–100.

Goodwyn, Frank. "The Frontier in American Fiction." *Inter-American Review of Bibliography* 10, no. 4 (1960): 356–69.

Gordon-McCutchan, R. C., ed. *Kit Carson: Indian Fighter or Indian Killer?* Niwot: University Press of Colorado, 1996.

Gould, Jane. *The Oregon and California Trail Diary of Jane Gould in 1862*. Introduction and contemporary comments by Bert Webber. Medford OR: Webb Research Group, 1987.

Grivas, Theodore. *Military Governments in California, 1846–1850*. Glendale CA: A. H. Clark, 1963.

Guest, Francis F. "An Examination of the Thesis of S. F. Cook on the Forced Conversion of Indians in the California Missions." *Southern California Quarterly* 61, no. 1 (1979): 1–77.

Gunther, Vanessa Ann. *Ambiguous Justice: Native Americans and the Law in Southern California, 1848–1890*. East Lansing: Michigan State University Press, 2006.

———. "Ambiguous Justice: Native Americans and the Legal System in Southern California, 1848–1890." PhD diss., University of California, Riverside, 2001.

———. "Indians and the Criminal Justice System in San Bernardino and San Diego Counties, 1850–1900." *Journal of the West* 39, no. 4 (2000): 26–34.

Hackel, Steven W. *Children of Coyote, Missionaries of Saint Francis: Indian-Spanish Relations in Colonial California*. Chapel Hill: University of North Carolina Press, 2005.

Hague, Harlan, and David J. Langum. *Thomas O. Larkin: A Life of Patriotism and Profit in Old California*. Norman: University of Oklahoma Press, 1990.

Hamilton, Wynette L. "The Correlation between Societal Attitudes and Those of American Authors in the Depiction of American Indians, 1607–1860." *American Indian Quarterly* 1, no. 1 (1974): 1–26.

Hanks, Richard B. "Vicissitudes of Justice: Massacre at San Timoteo Canyon." *Southern California Quarterly* 82, no. 3 (2000): 233–56.

Hansen, Woodrow James. *The Search for Authority in California*. Oakland CA: Biobooks, 1960.

Harris, Helen L. "Mark Twain's Response to the Native American." *American Literature* 46, no. 4 (1975): 495–505.

Harter, George. *Wagon Tracks: George Harter's 1864 Journey to California*. Edited by Robert D. Harter. Tucson AZ: Patrice Press, 2003.

Hastings, Lansford W. *The Emigrant's Guide to Oregon and California in 1845*. Santa Barbara CA: Narrative Press, 2001.

Hauptman, Laurence M. *Tribes and Tribulations: Misconceptions about American Indians and Their Histories*. Albuquerque: University of New Mexico Press, 1995.

Haynes, Sam W. *James K. Polk and the Expansionist Impulse*. New York: Longman, 1997.

Haynes, Sam W., and Christopher Morris, eds. *Manifest Destiny and Empire: American Antebellum Expansionism*. College Station: Texas A&M University Press, 1997.

Heizer, Robert F. "Civil Rights in California in the 1850s: A Case History." *Kroeber Anthropological Society Papers* 31 (1964): 129–37.

———, ed. *The Destruction of California Indians*. Introduction by Albert L. Hurtado. Lincoln: University of Nebraska Press, 1993.

———. *The Eighteen Unratified Treaties of 1851–1852 between the California Indians and the United States Government*. Berkeley: Archaeological Research Facility of the Department of Anthropology, 1972.

———. *Federal Concerns about Conditions of California Indians 1853–1913: Eight Documents*. Socorro NM: Ballena Press, 1979.

———. *"They Were Only Diggers": A Collection of Articles from California Newspapers, 1851–1866, on Indian and White Relations*. Socorro NM: Ballena Press, 1974.

Heizer, Robert F., and Alan J. Almquist. *The Other Californians: Prejudice and Discrimination under Spain, Mexico, and the United States to 1920*. Berkeley: University of California Press, 1971.

Heizer, Robert F., and M. A. Whipple, eds. *The California Indians: A Source Book*. 2nd ed. Berkeley: University of California Press, 1971.

Heizer, Robert F., and Theodora Kroeber, eds. *Ishi, the Last Yahi: A Documentary History*. Berkeley: University of California Press, 1979.

Hietala, Thomas R. *Manifest Design: Anxious Aggrandizement in Late Jacksonian America*. Ithaca NY: Cornell University Press, 1985.

Hill, Jim Dan. "The Early Mining Camp in American Life." *Pacific Historical Review* 1 (1932): 295–311.

Hinton, Alexander Laban, ed. *Genocide: An Anthropological Reader*. Malden MA: Blackwell, 2002.

Hirsch, Herbert. *Genocide and the Politics of Memory: Studying Death to Preserve Life*. Chapel Hill: University of North Carolina Press, 1995.

Hitchcock, E. A. *Fifty Years in Camp and Field: Diary of Major-General Ethan Allen Hitchcock, U.S.A.* Freeport NY: Books for Libraries Press, 1971.

Holliday, J. S. *The World Rushed In: The California Gold Rush Experience*. New York: Simon and Schuster, 1981.

Hoopes, Chad L. *Domesticate or Exterminate: California Indian Treaties Un-*

ratified and Made Secret in 1852. San Francisco: Redwood Coast Publications, 1975.

Hornbeck, David. "Land Tenure and Rancho Expansion in Alta California, 1784–1846." *Journal of Historical Geography* 4, no. 4 (1978): 371–90.

———. "The Patenting of California's Private Land Claims, 1851–1885." *Geographical Review* 69, no. 4 (1979): 434–48.

Horowitz, Irving L. *Genocide: State Power and Mass Murder*. New Brunswick NJ: Transaction Books, 1976.

———. "Many Genocides, One Holocaust? The Limits of the Rights of States and the Obligations of Individuals." *Modern Judaism* 1, no. 1 (1981): 74–89.

Horsman, Reginald. *Race and Manifest Destiny: The Origins of American Racial Anglo-Saxonism*. Cambridge MA: Harvard University Press, 1981.

Hoyer, Mark T. "Prophecy in a New West: Mary Austin and the Ghost Dance Religion." *Western American Literature* 30, no. 3 (1995): 235–56.

Hughes, John T. *Doniphan's Expedition*. 1848. Reprint, Chicago: Rio Grande Press, 1962.

Hundley, Norris. *The Great Thirst: Californians and Water, a History*. Rev. ed. Berkley: University of California Press, 2001.

Hurtado, Albert L. "California Indian Demography, Sherburne F. Cook, and the Revision of American History." *Pacific Historical Review* 58 (1989): 323–43.

———. "California Indians and the Workaday West: Labor, Assimilation, and Survival." *California History* 69, no. 1 (1990): 2–11.

———. "Controlling California's Indian Labor Force: Federal Administration of California Indian Affairs during the Mexican War." *Southern California Quarterly* 61, no. 3 (1979): 217–38.

———. "'Hardly a Farm House—A Kitchen without Them': Indian and White Households on the California Borderland Frontier in 1860." *Western Historical Quarterly* 13, no. 3 (1982): 245–70.

———. *Indian Survival on the California Frontier*. New Haven CT: Yale University Press, 1988.

———. *John Sutter: A Life on the North American Frontier*. Norman: University of Oklahoma Press, 2006.

Hutchings, James Mason. *Scenes of Wonder and Curiosity in California*. New York: A. Roman, 1876.

Hyer, Joel R. *"We Are Not Savages": Native Americans in Southern California and the Pala Reservation, 1840–1920*. East Lansing: Michigan State University Press, 2001.

Hyslop, Richard S., and Crane S, Miller. *California: The Geography of Diversity*. Mountain View CA: Mayfield, 1983.

Inyo County Board of Supervisors. *Inyo, 1866–1966*. Inyo CA: Inyo County Board of Supervisors, 1966.

"Ishi: The Last Yahi." *American Experience*. DVD. Produced and directed by Jed Riffe and Pamela Roberts. Originally aired 1992. Shanachie Entertainment Corporation, 2001.

Jackson, Helen Hunt. *A Century of Dishonor: A Sketch of the United States Government's Dealings with Some of the Indian Tribes*. Foreword by Valerie Sherer Mathes. Norman: University of Oklahoma Press, 1994.

———. *Ramona: A Story*. Boston: Little, Brown, 1901.

Jaimes, Annette, ed. *The State of Native America: Genocide, Colonization, and Resistance*. Boston: South End Press, 1992.

Johnson, Susan Lee. *Roaring Camp: The Social World of the California Gold Rush*. New York: Norton, 2000.

Johnston-Dodds, Kimberly. *Early California Laws and Policies Related to California Indians*. Sacramento: California Research Bureau of the California State Library, CRB-02-014, 2002.

Katz, Steven T. "Pequots and the Question of Genocide: A Reply to Michael Freeman." *New England Quarterly* 68, no. 4 (1995): 641–49.

Keller, Jean. *Boarding School Blues: Revisiting American Indian Educational Experiences*. Lincoln: University of Nebraska Press, 2006.

Kelsey, Harry. "The California Indian Treaty Myth." *Southern California Quarterly* 55 (1973): 225–35.

Kemble, Edward C. *A History of California Newspapers, 1846–1858*. Edited by Helen Harding Bretnor. 1858. Reprint, Los Gatos CA: Talisman Press, 1962.

Kousser, Morgan, and James M. McPherson, eds. *Region, Race, and Reconstruction: Essays in Honor of C. Vann Woodward*. New York: Oxford University Press, 1982.

Kroeber, Clifton B. "The Mohave as Nationalist, 1859–1874." *Proceedings of the American Philosophical Society* 109, no. 3 (1965): 173–80.

Kroeber, Theodora. *Ishi in Two Worlds: A Biography of the Last Wild Indian in North America*. Berkeley: University of California Press, 1976.

Lamar, Howard R. *The Far Southwest, 1846–1912*. New Haven CT: Yale University Press, 1966.

Lang, Julian, ed. and trans. *Ararapikva: Creation Stories of the People: Traditional Karuk Indian Literature from Northwestern California*. Berkeley CA: Heyday Books, 1994.

Larkin, Thomas O. *The Larkin Papers*. Edited by George P. Hammond. 10 vols. Berkeley: University of California Press, 1951–64.

Lewis, David Rich. "Argonauts and the Overland Trail Experience: Method and Theory." *Western Historical Quarterly* 16 (July 1985): 285–306.

Lewy, Guenter. "The First Genocide of the 20th Century?" *Commentary* 120, no. 5 (2005): 47–52.

———. "Were American Indians the Victims of Genocide?" *Commentary* 118, no. 2 (2004): 55–63.

Limerick, Patricia Nelson. *The Legacy of Conquest: The Unbroken Past of the American West*. New York: Norton, 1987.

Locke, John. *The Second Treatise on Civil Government*. New York: Prometheus Books, 1986.

Lovett, W. E. *Report of W. E. Lovett, Special Indian Agent to Austin Wiley, Superintendent of Indian Affairs in California*. San Francisco: Mining and Scientific Affairs, 1865.

Maddox, Robert James. *Annual Editions: American History*. Vol. 1, *Colonial through Reconstruction*. 19th ed. Dubuque IA: McGraw-Hill Contemporary Learning Series, 2007.

Madley, Benjamin. "California's Yuki Indians: Defining Genocide in Native American History." *Western Historical Quarterly* 39, no. 3 (2008): 303–32.

———. "Patterns of Frontier Genocide 1803–1910: The Aboriginal Tasmanians, the Yuki of California, and the Herero of Namibia." *Journal of Genocide Research* 6, no. 2 (2004): 167–92.

Magliari, Michael. "Free Soil, Unfree Labor: Cave Johnson Couts and the Binding of Indian Workers in California, 1850–1867." *Pacific Historical Review* 73, no. 3 (2004): 349–89.

———. Review of *Ambiguous Justice: Native Americans and the Law in Southern California, 1848–1890*, by Vanessa Ann Gunther. *Pacific Historical Review* 77, no. 2 (2008): 321–22.

Margolin, Malcolm, ed. *The Way We Lived: California Indian Stories, Songs, and Reminiscences*. Berkeley CA: Heyday Books, 1993.

Mathes, Valerie Sherer. *Helen Hunt Jackson and Her Indian Reform Legacy*. Austin: University of Texas Press, 1990.

———. "I Am Going to Write an Indian Novel, the Scene Laid in California." *San Diego History* 42, no. 2 (1996): 109–13.

———. "Indian Philanthropy in California." *Arizona and the West* 25 (Summer 1983): 153–66.

———, ed. *The Indian Reform Letters of Helen Hunt Jackson, 1879–1885*. Norman: University of Oklahoma Press, 1998.

McDowell, Steve. "Images across Boundaries: Photographing the American Indian." *El Palacio* 99, no. 1 (1994): 38–78.

Meister, Cary W. "Demographic Consequences of Euro-American Contact on Selected American Indian Populations and Their Relationship to the Demographic Transition." *Ethnohistory* 23, no. 2 (1976): 161–72.

Merk, Frederick. *Manifest Destiny and Mission in American History, a Reinterpretation*. New York: Knopf, 1963.

Michno, Gregory F. *Encyclopedia of Indian Wars: Western Battles and Skirmishes, 1850–1890*. Missoula MT: Mountain Press, 2003.

Monroy, Douglas. *Thrown among Strangers: The Making of Mexican Culture in Frontier California*. Berkley: University of California Press, 1990.

Moore, Harry De Witt. "A Modoc War Letter." *Journal of the Shaw Historical Library* 14 (2000): 1–7.

Moore, MariJo, ed. *Eating Fire, Tasting Blood: An Anthology of the American Indian Holocaust*. New York: Thunder's Mouth Press, 2006.

Murray, Keith A. *The Modocs and Their War*. Norman: University of Oklahoma Press, 1958.

Nash, Gary B. *Red, White, and Black: The Peoples of Early North America*. Upper Saddle River NJ: Prentice Hall, 2000.

Nichols, Roger L. *American Indians in U.S. History*. Norman: University of Oklahoma Press, 2003.

Norton, Jack. *Centering in Two Worlds: Essays on Native Northwestern California History, Culture and Spirituality*. Gallup NM: Center for the Affirmation of Responsible Education, 2007.

———. *When Our Worlds Cried: Genocide in Northwestern California*. San Francisco: Indian Historian Press, 1979.

Notes of Travel in California. Dublin, Ireland: James M'Glashan, 1849.

Nugent, Walter. *Habits of Empire: A History of American Expansion*. New York: Vintage Books, 2008.

Palmquist, Peter. "The California Indian in Three-Dimensional Photography." *Journal of California and Great Basin Anthropology* 1, no. 1 (1979): 89–116.

———. *Carleton E. Watkins: Photographer of the American West*. Albuquerque: University of New Mexico Press, 1983.

Pearce, Roy Harvey. *Savagism and Civilization: A Study of the Indian and the American Mind*. Berkeley: University of California Press, 1988.

Peterson, Richard H. "Anti-Mexican Nativism in California, 1848–1853." *Southern California Quarterly* 62 (Winter 1980): 309–28.

Phillips, George Harwood. *"Bringing Them under Subjection": California's Tejón Indian Reservation and Beyond, 1852–1864*. Lincoln: University of Nebraska Press, 2004.

———. *Chiefs and Challengers: Indian Resistance and Cooperation in Southern California*. Berkley: University of California Press, 1975.

———. *The Enduring Struggle: Indians in California History*. San Francisco: Boyd and Fraser, 1981.

———. *Indians and Indian Agents: The Origins of the Reservation System in California, 1849–1852*. Norman: University of Oklahoma Press, 1997.

———. *Indians and Intruders in Central California, 1769–1849*. Norman: University of Oklahoma Press, 1993.

———. *Vineyards and Vaqueros: Indian Labor and the Economic Expansion of Southern California, 1771–1877*. Spokane WA: Arthur H. Clark, 2010.

Pitt, Leonard. *The Decline of the Californios: A Social History of the Spanish-Speaking Californians, 1846–1890*. Foreword by Ramón A. Gutiérrez. Berkeley: University of California Press, 1998.

Platt, P. L., and A. M. Slater. *Traveler's Guide across the Plains upon the Overland Route to California*. Introduction by Dale Morgan. 1852. Reprint, San Francisco: John Howell Books, 1963.

Pratt, Addison. *The Journals of Addison Pratt: Being a Narrative of Yankee Whaling in the Eighteen Twenties, a Mormon Mission to the Society Islands, and of Early California and Utah in the Eighteen Forties and Fifties*. Edited with introduction and notes by S. George Ellsworth. Salt Lake City: University of Utah Press, 1990.

Pritchard, William Fowler. *Journal of William Fowler Pritchard: Indiana to California 1850, Return via Nicaragua, 1852*. Edited by Earl H. and Phil Pritchard. Fairfield WA: Ye Galleon Press, 1995.

Rawls, James J. "Gold Diggers: Indian Miners in the California Gold Rush." *California Historical Quarterly* 55 (Spring 1976): 28–45.

———. *Indians of California: The Changing Image*. Norman: University of Oklahoma Press, 1984.

Rawls, James J., and Walton Bean. *California: An Interpretive History*. New York: McGraw-Hill, 2003.

Reid, Bernard J. *Overland to California with the Pioneer Line: The Gold Rush Diary of Bernard J. Reid.* Edited by Mary McDougall Gordon. Chicago: University of Illinois Press, 1987.

Rice, Richard B., William A. Bullough, and Richard J. Orsi. *Elusive Eden: A New History of California.* Boston: McGraw Hill, 1996.

Rice, William B. *The Los Angeles Star, 1851–1864.* Berkeley: University of California Press, 1947.

Riley, Glenda. "The Specter of a Savage: Rumors and Alarmism on the Overland Trail." *Western Historical Quarterly* 15, no. 4 (1984): 427–44.

Roberts, David. *A Newer World: Kit Carson, John C. Frémont, and the Claiming of the West.* New York: Simon and Schuster, 2000.

Robinson, W. W. *Land in California: The Story of Mission Lands, Ranchos, Squatters, Mining Claims, Railroad Grants, Land Scrip, Homesteads.* Berkeley: University of California Press, 1997.

Rolle, Andrew. *John Charles Frémont: Character as Destiny.* Norman: University of Oklahoma Press, 1991.

Rosenbaum, Alan S., ed. *Is the Holocaust Unique? Perspectives on Comparative Genocide.* Introduction by Alan S. Rosenbaum. Foreword by Israel W. Charny. Boulder CO: Westview Press, 1996.

Roth, George. "The Calloway Affair of 1880." *Journal of California Anthropology* 4, no. 2 (1977): 273–86.

Royce, Josiah. *California: A Study of American Character.* Foreword by Ronald A. Wells. Berkeley CA: Heyday Books, 2002.

Rubenstein, Richard L. *The Cunning of History: The Holocaust and the American Future.* New York: Harper & Row, 1975.

Rutledge, Harry E., ed. *Casualties on the California Trail: Some Forty-niner Diary Accounts.* Tokyo: Sheridan A. Sims, 1996.

Sackman, Douglas Cazaux. *Wild Men: Ishi and Kroeber in the Wilderness of Modern America.* New York: Oxford University Press, 2010.

Sanford, Nevitt, and Craig Comstock, eds. *Sanctions for Evil.* San Francisco: Jossey-Bass Behavioral Science Series, 1971.

Santiago, Mark. *Massacre at the Yuma Crossing: Spanish Relations with the Quechans, 1779–1882.* Tucson: University of Arizona Press, 1998.

Scheper-Hughes, Nancy. "Ishi's Brain, Ishi's Ashes: Anthropology and Genocide." *Anthropology Today* 17, no. 1 (2001): 12–18.

Schmölder, B. *The Emigrant's Guide to California.* London: Pelham Richardson, 1849.

Secrest, William B. "Jarboe's War." *Californians* 6, no. 6 (1988): 16–22.

———. "The Rise and Fall of Thomas J. Henley in California." *Californians* 6, no. 6 (1988): 23–29.

———. *When the Great Spirit Died: The Destruction of the California Indians, 1850–1860.* Sanger CA: Word Dancer Press, 2003.

Shapiro, Samuel. *Richard Henry Dana, Jr., 1815–1882.* East Lansing: Michigan State University Press, 1961.

Sheehan, Bernard W. *Seeds of Extinction: Jeffersonian Philanthropy and the American Indian.* New York: Norton, 1974.

Shipek, Florence Connolly. "A Strategy for Change: The Luiseno of Southern California." PhD diss., University of Hawaii, 1977.

Shipley, William, ed. and trans. *The Maidu Indian Myths and Stories of Hanc'ibyjim.* Foreword by Gary Snyder. Berkeley CA: Heyday Books, 1991.

Slotkin, Richard. *The Fatal Environment.* New York: Harper Perennial, 1994.

Smith, Edgar C. "Massacre on the Colorado River." *Overland Journal* 21, no. 1 (2003): 10–21.

Smith, Michael T. "The History of Indian Citizenship." *Great Plains Journal* 10, no. 1 (1970): 25–35.

Smith, Shawn Michelle. *American Archives: Gender, Race, and Class in Visual Culture.* Princeton NJ: Princeton University Press, 1999.

Smith, Sherry L. *Reimagining Indians: Native Americans through Anglo Eyes, 1880–1940.* New York: Oxford University Press, 2000.

———. *The View from Officers' Row: Army Perceptions of Western Indians.* Tucson: University of Arizona Press, 1990.

Sousa, Ashley Riley. "'They Will Be Hunted Down Like Wild Beasts and Destroyed!' A Comparative Study of Genocide in California and Tasmania." *Journal of Genocide Research* 6, no. 2 (2004): 193–209.

Starn, Orin. *Ishi's Brain: In Search of the Last "Wild" Indian.* New York: Norton, 2004.

Starr, Kevin J. *Americans and the California Dream, 1850–1915.* New York: Oxford University Press, 1973.

Starr, Kevin J., and Richard J. Orsi, eds. *Rooted in Barbarous Soil.* Berkeley: University of California Press, 2000.

Staub, Ervin. "Genocide and Mass Killing: Origins, Prevention, Healing and Reconciliation." *Political Psychology* 21, no. 2 (2000): 367–82.

———. "The Psychology of Perpetrators and Bystanders." *Political Psychology* 6, no. 1 (1985): 61–85.

Steele, John. *In Camp and Cabin.* Edited by Milo Milton Quaife. Chicago: Lakeside Press, 1928.

Stewart, George R. *The California Trail.* New York: McGraw-Hill, 1962.

Stohl, Michael. "Outside of a Small Circle of Friends: States, Genocide, Mass Killing and the Role of Bystanders." *Journal of Peace Research* 24, no. 2 (1987): 151–66.

Strobridge, William F. *Regulars in the Redwoods: The U.S. Army in Northern California, 1852–1861.* Spokane WA: Arthur H. Clarke, 1994.

Stuart, Paul. *Nations within a Nation: Historical Statistics of American Indians.* New York: Greenwood Press, 1987.

Sundquist, Eric J. *Empire and Slavery in American Literature, 1820–1865.* Jackson: University Press of Mississippi, 2006.

Taber, Cornelia. *California and Her Indian Children.* San Jose CA: Northern Indian Association, 1911.

Tate, Michael L. *Indians and Emigrants: Encounters on the Overland Trails.* Norman: University of Oklahoma Press, 2005.

Thomas, Richard M. "The Mission Indians: A Study of Leadership and Cultural Change." PhD diss., University of California, Los Angeles, 1964.

Thompson, Erwin N. *Modoc War: Its Military History and Topography.* Preface by Keith A. Murray. Sacramento: Argus Books, 1971.

Thompson, Gerald. *Edward F. Beale and the American West.* Albuquerque: University of New Mexico Press, 1983.

Thompson, Lucy. *To the American Indian: Reminiscences of a Yurok Woman.* Foreword by Peter E. Palmquist. Introduction by Julian Lang. Berkeley CA: Heyday Books, 1991.

Thornton, Russell. *American Indian Holocaust and Survival: A Population History Since 1492.* Norman: University of Oklahoma Press, 1987.

Tocqueville, Alexis de. *Democracy in America.* Translated, edited, and with an introduction by Harvey C. Mansfield and Debra Winthrop. Chicago: University of Chicago Press, 2000.

Townsend, E. D. *The California Diary of E. D. Townsend.* Edited by Malcolm Edwards. New York: Ward Ritchie Press, 1970.

Trafzer, Clifford E. *As Long as the Grass Shall Grow and Rivers Flow: A History of Native Americans.* Belmont CA: Thomson Wadsworth, 2000.

———. *The Kit Carson Campaign: The Last Great Navajo War.* Norman: University of Oklahoma Press, 1982.

———. *Yuma: Frontier Crossing of the Colorado.* Wichita KS: Western Heritage Books, 1980.

Trafzer, Clifford E., and Joel R. Hyer, eds. *"Exterminate Them!" Written Accounts of the Murder, Rape, and Enslavement of Native Americans during the California Gold Rush.* Foreword by Edward D. Castillo. East Lansing: University of Michigan Press, 1999.

Turner, Frederick Jackson. *The Frontier in American History.* 1920. Reprint, New York: Dover, 1996.

Unruh, John D., Jr. "Against the Grain: West to East on the Overland Trail." *Kansas Quarterly* 5, no. 2 (1973): 72–84.

———. *The Plains Across: The Overland Immigrants and the Trans-Mississippi West, 1848–1860.* Urbana: University of Illinois Press, 1979.

Utley, Robert M. *Frontier Regulars: The United States Army and the Indian, 1866–1891.* Lincoln: University of Nebraska Press, 1973.

Vartanian, Nicole Elise. "When History Hurts: An Analysis of the Influences upon the Teaching of Genocide in U.S. Public Schools." PhD diss., Columbia University, 2000.

Vetlesen, Arne Johan. "Genocide: A Case for the Responsibility of the Bystander." *Journal of Peace Research* 37, no. 4 (2000): 519–32.

Walker, Henry P. "An Indian Scare on the Colorado River in 1880: The Letters of Lieutenant John M. Hyde." *Arizona and the West* 26, no. 2 (1984): 153–66.

Ware, Joseph E. *The Emigrant's Guide to California, 1849.* Introduction and notes by John W. Caughey. Princeton NJ: Princeton University Press, 1932.

Washburn, Wilcomb E. *The Assault on Tribalism: The General Allotment Law (Dawes Act) of 1887.* Edited by Harold M. Hyman. Philadelphia: J. B. Lippincott, 1975.

Weiss, Stephen Craig. "The John C. Frémont 1842, 1843–'44 Report and Map." *Journal of Government Information* 26, no. 3 (1999): 297–313.

Wetmore, Charles A. "Report on the Mission Indians in California." Washington DC: Government Printing Office, 1875.

White, Richard. *It's Your Misfortune and None of My Own: A History of the American West.* Norman: University of Oklahoma Press, 1991.

Wild, Peter. *J. Ross Browne.* Boise ID: Boise State University Press, 2003.

Wilke, Philip J., and Harry W. Lawton, eds. *The Expedition of J. W. Davidson from Fort Tejon to the Owens Valley in 1859.* Socorro NM: Ballena Press, 1976.

Wilkins, David E. *American Indian Sovereignty and the U.S. Supreme Court: The Masking of Justice.* Austin: University of Texas Press, 1999.

Wilshire, Bruce. *Get 'Em All! Kill 'Em! Genocide, Terrorism, Righteous Communities.* Lanham MD: Lexington Books, 2005.

Woolsey, Ronald C. "Crime and Punishment: Los Angeles County, 1850–1856." *Southern California Quarterly* 61, no. 1 (1979): 79–98.

Worster, Donald E. "Irrigation and Democracy in California: The Early Promise." *Pacific Historian* 27, no. 1 (1983): 30–35.

Index

Achomawis, 340

Adobe Meadows, 175–76

Agua Caliente, 147, 159

Allen, James, 173–74

Ames, John G., 260–62, 342

"An Act for the Government and Protection of Indians." *See* Chapter 133

Anderson, Robert, 214, 350

Antelope Creek, 255

Antelope Mill, 298

Antonio, Juan, 145, 156, 160, 166, 169, 377n29

Apaches, 137–38

Apperson, Merle, 352, 356

Arapahos, 86, 90

Arcata, 328

Arizona, 339

Arkansas Gazette, 43, 47, 63, 66

Army Medical Museum, 339

Asbill brothers, 191

Bacilio (nation unknown), 246

Bacon's Rebellion, 50–51

Bailey, Godard, 285, 290

Bald Mountain Indians, 305

Bancroft, George, 37, 47–49, 51–52, 55–57, 60, 62–63, 366n6; *The History of the United States of America*, 47

Barbour, George, 272

Bartleson, John, 78, 83–84

Bartleson-Bidwell Party, 76, 78–84, 98, 370n26, 373n81

Bartlett, William Henry, 47, 55–57, 60, 62, 366n6

Bauer, William, 252, 381n10

Baumgardner, Frank H., 6

Beale, Edward, 258–62, 278–79, 281, 303–4, 311, 342

Bean, Joshua H., 141–43, 148–51, 157–61, 167, 169

Bean, Lowell, 344

Beard, Estle, 5–6

Bear Flag Revolt, 104

Bear River, 182

Bell, Horace, 152–54

Belohlavek, John, 55

Bidwell, John, 74, 76–84, 105, 107–9, 112, 148, 212, 370n16, 370n23, 370n26

Bigler, John, 144, 231–32

Bishop (town), 171

Bishop, Samuel Addison, 171

Bland, John, 205, 292–94, 298–99

Board of Indian Commissioners, 302

Bodley, John H., 37
Booth, Newton, 268–70
Brown, Elam, 147
Browne, John Ross, 206, 282–85, 291
Brownlow, James, 333
Bryant, William Cullen: *A Popular History of the United States*, 59
Bureau of Indian Affairs, 351, 353
Burnett, Peter H., 140–43, 159, 231, 233, 240–41, 265
Burney, James, 241
Butte Democrat, 187

Cabezon (Cahuilla), 342, 344
Cahtos. *See* Katos
Cahuillas, 145, 156, 166–69, 342
Cajón Pass, 120, 163
California Civil Practice Act, 364n48
California Constitution (1849), 245
California Farmer, 320, 332
California Land Act, 394n3
Californian, 271
California Star, 259
California State Assembly, 144, 149, 194, 226–27, 232, 238, 266
California State Senate, 144, 149, 194, 226–27, 232, 238, 266
California State Supreme Court, 227
Californios, 129, 131, 146, 152, 162, 278, 377n35
Canby, Edward S., 335, 338, 339
Carlin, William, 288, 300–301, 306
Carlisle Barracks, 345
Carlisle Indian School, 346
Carranco, Lynwood, 5–6
Carson, Kit, 85–87, 89, 94, 97–98, 371n37

Carson Lake, 81
Carson Valley, 324
Catlin, George, 366n23
Caughey, John W., 371n35
Central Valley, 340
Century Magazine, 84
A Century of Dishonor (H. Jackson), 344
Chalk, Frank, 8, 284, 364n45
Chapter 133, 147, 152–56, 168, 202, 236, 244–46, 248–54, 257–58, 261–62, 267–68
Chase, Andrew, 155
Chemehuevis, 163
Cherokee Nation v. Georgia (1831), 394n2
Cherokee Removal, 18, 276
Cherokees, 137
Cheyennes, 82–83, 90
Chico Advertiser, 84
Chico Weekly Courant, 67, 210–11, 298, 314, 319–21, 334
Chinese, 318, 364n48
Chinese Exclusion Act, 346
Chino, 120, 160–61
Chirot, Daniel, 8, 17–19, 22–23, 132, 316
Churchill, Ward, 8
Civil War, 29, 170
Clear Lake, 248
Coffer, William, 5
Colonization Act, 76
Colorado River, 136–37, 141–44, 157, 159
commutation tax, 239
Cook, Sherburne F., 3, 367n35, 387n142

Cooper, James Fennimore, 331, 333
Couts, Cave Johnson, 157–58, 177, 379n69
Cowan, B. R., 342
Coward, John M., 365n5
Crook, George, 304–10
Crosby, Alfred W., 387n143
Crows, 88
Cupeños, 147, 156, 248
Cushing, Caleb, 54–55, 57, 367n24

Daily Alta California, 145, 165, 179, 188, 320, 322–24, 326, 335
Daley, William, 206, 208
Dana, Richard Henry, 103, 122, 369n8; *Two Years before the Mast*, 74–76, 84
Dawes, Henry L., 347
Dawes Act, 347
Dawson, Cheyenne, 80, 82–83
Deloria, Vine, 273
Diamond, Jared, 387n143
Digueños, 155
Dillon, Edward, 193–98, 204–5, 209, 288–89, 291, 294, 296–97, 299, 300–303, 306, 311
Dippie, Brian, 65, 368n61
Dole, William, 342
Doll, J. G., 196
Donner Party, 73
Downey, John, 208, 300
Du Bois, Cora, 340
Duster, Troy, 35, 40

Eberle, Charles H., 291–93
Eden Valley, 1, 180, 184, 190, 192–93, 195–96, 201–4, 206, 209, 214

Eel River, 180, 182, 195, 203, 328
Eel River Rangers, 201–8, 216, 251, 292, 294–95, 299–300
El Dorado County, 165
The Emigrant's Guide to California (Ware), 103–4, 371n35
The Emigrant's Guide to Oregon and California (L. Hastings), 70–71, 73–74, 99, 100–108
Emma (Kumeyaay or Digueño), 155
Emory, William, 154
Eureka, 210, 328

Farley, Jackson, 214–17
Farr, Mr. (reservation employee), 325
Farrell, W. C., 157
Farwell, J. V., 343
Fillmore, Millard, 274
Fitzgerald, E. H., 157–58, 379n69
Fitzgerald's Volunteers, 158
Flint, F. F., 197–98, 200
Forbes, Jack D., 3–4, 357, 361n1
Fort Bidwell, 345
Fort Bragg, 288
Fort Crook, 186
Fort Jones Indian Reserve, 287, 305, 307
Fort Laramie, 102, 111, 113
Fort Tejón, 171, 173
Fort Yuma, 143–44, 345
4th Division California State Militia, 141
Francisco (Luiseño), 170
Frazier, William, 214–17
Frémont, John C., 74, 84–99, 104, 107–8, 127, 275; *Report of the Exploring Expedition to the Rocky Mountains*, 116–17

Frémont expeditions, 74, 84–98, 107–8, 116–17

French and Indian War. *See* Seven Years' War

Fresno Indian Farm, 281, 283

Garra, Antonio, 156, 158, 160–61, 169

Garra Revolt, 148, 156–61, 166

Gay, Sydney Howard: *A Popular History of the United States*, 59

Geer, Knyphausen, 181–82

Geiger, Vincent, 254, 297, 303–4

General Allotment Act. *See* Dawes Act

George, Captain (Paiute), 172

Ghost Dance, 340–41, 403n15

Gibson, Isaac, 115

Gibson, J. Watt, 115

Gila River, 142

Gila River Trail, 131, 137

Glanton, John, 137–41, 143–44, 157, 161, 163

Goldhagen, Daniel, 363n26

Good, Harmon "Hi," 214, 254–55, 350

Gould, Jane, 119

Greenville, 345–46

Greenville Bulletin, 334, 341, 344

Grice, John R., 280, 395n29

Guadalupe Hidalgo, Treaty of, 28, 64, 129, 146, 217, 273, 277, 364n47, 394n3

Gunther, Robert, 330

Gunther, Vanessa Ann, 377n41, 391n56

Gwin, William M., 162, 275, 277

Hackel, Steven W., 387n142

Haight, Henry, 316

Hall, George W., 364n48

Hall, H. L., 180, 184–85, 190, 192–96, 199–203

Hamilton, Ezra M., 109–16

Hanks, Henry, 172–73

Harper's Monthly, 284

Harper's Weekly, 122

Hart, H. J., 397n59

Harte, Francis Bret, 326–29, 331–32

Harter, George, 116, 119

Hastings, Lansford, 99–109, 127, 217; *The Emigrant's Guide to Oregon and California*, 70–71, 73–74, 99, 100–108

Hastings, Serranus C., 1, 17, 30, 180, 184–85, 190, 192, 195–96, 201–2, 205, 209, 227, 243

Hauptman, Laurence, 8

Hayes, Benjamin, 138

Healdsburg, 349

Heintzelman, Samuel, 157, 161

Heizer, Robert F., 3, 4, 184, 213, 258, 317

Henley, Thomas J., 170, 184–85, 201–2, 238, 254–57, 281–82, 285, 288–91, 296–97, 303–4, 311, 395n29, 395n35

Hicks, Charles, 181–82

Hilan, James, 245–46

Hildreath, William, 294–95

Hirsch, Herbert, 68

The History of the United States of America (Bancroft), 47

Hitchcock, Ethan Allen, 213, 286–87

Holocaust, 12, 363n26

Hoopa Reservation, 5, 343, 345, 404n33

Hoopes, Chad L., 5

Horowitz, Irving, 12, 36

House Committee on Appropriations, 342–43
Houston, John, 237, 239
Humboldt Bay, 305, 326–27, 329
Humboldt County, 181–82, 186, 210, 283, 322, 328–29
Humboldt Times, 254, 329–31
Humboldt Volunteers, 328
Humboldt War, 330
Hupas, 5
Hurtado, Albert, 7, 375n2, 391n60
Hutchings, James Mason, 219
Hyer, Joel, 7, 143

Indian Island Massacre, 327–31
Indian Territory, 339
Indian Valley, 199
Indian War Bonds, 237
Irving, John, 377n29
Ishi (Yahi), 350–54, 356–58, 406n23

Jack, Captain. *See* Kenitpoos (Modoc)
Jackson, Andrew, 304
Jackson, Helen Hunt, 21; *A Century of Dishonor*, 344; *Ramona*, 331; "Report on the Conditions and Needs of the Mission Indians," 344
Jarboe, Walter S., 201–9, 216, 251, 290–91, 294, 299–300
Jefferson, Thomas, 53–54, 367n29
Johnson, Edward, 190, 192, 196, 204, 288–91, 293, 298–99, 300–301, 306
Jonassohn, Kurt, 8, 284, 364n45
Judah, H. M., 287–88

Kaipomos. *See* Katos
Katos, 340

Katz, Steven T., 358
Kenitpoos (Modoc), 337–40, 403n5
King, William, 277
King's River Reserve, 281
Klamath County, 384n68
Klamath Reservation, 281, 330, 337–40
Klamath River, 218
Klamaths, 93–94, 189, 340
Knott, W. S., 325
Knoxville Whig, 333
Kroeber, Alfred, 352–57, 361n2
Kumeyaays, 155–56

Lacock, Dryden, 200–201
Lamar, J. B., 235–36
Lane, George, 298
Larkin, Thomas O., 370n13, 377n35
Lascy, Lydia B., 268–70
Lassen, 187
Lassen Sage Brush, 190, 212, 333
Latham, Milton, 208
Lawton, Harry, 344
Lea, Luke, 218
Leavitt, D. G. W., 43, 47–48, 63
Lemkin, Raphael, 11–14, 17, 22–23
Lewis and Clark Expedition, 53
Limerick, Patricia, 61
Lincoln, Abel, 137–39
Locke, John, 48
Lone Pine, 171
Long Valley, 180, 205–7, 214–17, 294, 322
Los Angeles (city and county), 136, 138–41, 145, 148–54, 158–62, 164, 166–69, 249–50, 252, 258–59, 261, 332

Los Angeles City Guard, 259
Los Angeles Rangers, 152, 259
Los Angeles Star, 135–36, 153, 161, 163–64, 166–68, 250, 262, 332
Lost River, 338
Louisiana Purchase, 53
Lovell, James, 302
Luiseños, 156, 170, 177

Madley, Benjamin, 6, 362n9
Magliari, Michael, 377n41
Maidus, 218, 340
Manifest Destiny, 22–23, 25, 37–38, 52, 54–55, 63–65, 67, 71, 74, 102–3, 122–23, 231, 233, 244, 331–32, 368n58, 368n60
Manifest Destiny and Mission (Merk), 53
Mantle, William, 192, 292
Manypenny, George, 280
Mariposa War, 171, 240–43, 370n13
Marsh, John, 77–78, 84
Marysville, 247, 256–57
Marysville Appeal, 256
Marysville Daily Evening Herald, 319
Marysville Evening Herald, 329
Marysville Weekly Express, 209–10
McCauley, Clark, 8, 17, 18, 19, 22, 23, 132, 316
McDaniel, John, 192, 292
McDougal, John, 148, 150–51, 157–60, 241–43
McKee, Redick, 191, 218, 272
McLane, Charles, 299
Meacham, A. B., 338
Meek, William Bull, 199
Mendocino County, 180, 184, 207–8, 233

Mendocino Reservation, 216, 266, 281, 283, 288, 295, 301–2
Merk, Frederick: *Manifest Destiny and Mission*, 53
Mexican-American War, 85, 130–31
Miles, Nelson A., 344
Militia Law, 195, 200, 202, 239–40, 243
Mill Creek Indians, 212. *See also* Yahis
Mission Indian Agency, 343
Mission Indian Federation, 358
Mission Indians, 260
Miwoks, 218, 340
Moak, Jake, 214
Moak, Sim, 214
Modoc Plateau, 336, 338
Modocs, 335–40
Modoc War, 10, 337, 340, 403nn3–4
Mohaves, 96–97
Mono Lake, 172–75
Monroy, Douglas, 263
Moore, Harry De Witt, 338–39
Morehead, J. C., 142–44
Mormon Battalion, 374n19
Mormons, 117, 120

Nasby, Professor, 314
Nash, Gary, 50
Nazi Third Reich, 12, 14. *See also* Holocaust; Wansee Conference
Negro Alley, 250
Nichols, Roger L., 345
Nissenans, 218
Nome Cult Farm, 191, 202, 266, 281, 284, 288–90, 292, 295–302, 324–25, 388n8

Nome Lackee Reservation, 191, 266, 281–82, 287–88, 324–26
Northern California Indian Association, 349
Northern Californian Union, 326
Northern Journal, 65–66, 333
Norton, Jack, 5, 14, 362n10
Nugent, Walter, 53

Office of Indian Affairs, 279, 342–43, 347
Old Spanish Trail, 131
Oregon-California Trail, 10, 131
Orleans Bar, 322
Oroville, 350
O'Sullivan, Stephen L., 37, 63–65
Owens Valley, 163–64, 170, 172–75

Paiutes, 91, 97, 163–66, 170–71, 173, 175, 340
Panic of 1873, 346
Paris, Treaty of (1763), 51
Parley's Magazine, 67
Patwins, 340
Paul, Ransom, 246
Pawnees, 86
Pello, Caballo en, 139
People v. Hall (1854), 364n48
Phillips, George Harwood, 4, 404n23
Pitt River, 307–9, 311, 320, 324
Pitt River Indians. *See* Achomawis
Pitt River Rangers, 324
Plumas National, 314, 316–18, 329
Polk, James K., 54, 122
Pomos, 215–17, 340
A Popular History of the United States (Bryant and Gay), 59

Powers, Stephen, 361n2
Powhatan Confederation, 50
Pratt, Addison, 117–20
Pratt, Richard Henry, 346
Proclamation Line, 51

Quechans, 136–44, 156–57, 163
Quechan War. *See* Quechans
Quincy Union, 315–16, 318

Radical Reconstruction, 315
Raines, Gabriel J., 328
Ramona (H. Jackson), 331
Rancho del Chino. *See* Chino
Rawls, James J., 6, 261
Reading, Pierson Barton, 83, 183
Red Bluff, 186, 197, 210
Red Bluff Beacon, 188–89, 200, 298, 300, 303, 323–26
Red Bluff Sentinel, 315, 321
Rees, George, 292–94, 296
Report of the Exploring Expedition to the Rocky Mountains (Frémont), 116–17
"Report on the Conditions and Needs of the Mission Indians" (H. Jackson), 344
Riley, Bennett, 140
Riverside, 342
Robinson, W. W., 79
Rodgers, William, 240–41
Ross, John, 214
Round Valley, 5, 6, 180, 185, 187, 190–93, 195–96, 200, 203–9, 214, 216, 235–36, 238, 252, 281, 288–91, 294–95, 301–3, 306, 345
Round Valley Reservation, 207–8,

Round Valley Reservation (*cont.*) 235–36, 238, 281–82, 306, 345. *See also* Nome Lackee Reservation

Royce, Josiah, 127, 219

Rubidoux, Joseph, 77–78

Sacramento, 140

Sacramento Daily Union, 320

Sacramento Mountains, 333

Sacramento Union, 212–13

Sacred Expedition, 221

Salt Lake City, 117, 120

Salt River Indians, 181–82

San Bernardino, 166, 169, 260, 342–43

San Diego (city and county), 139–41, 145, 152, 156–62, 342

San Diego Herald, 152

San Francisco, 117, 160, 165, 247

San Francisco Call, 353

San Francisco Tribune, 318

San Gabriel, 247

San Gorgonio, 160, 166

San Joaquin Valley, 163

Santa Barbara, 138, 245–46

Santa Fe Trail, 10

Sapir, Edward, 356

school land warrants, 129–30, 196

Sebastian Military Reserve, 280, 395n29

Seven Years' War, 51

Shannon, Isaac, 192

Shasta (region), 188, 306

Shasta City, 211

Shasta Herald, 212

Shastas, 306, 340

Sheehan, Bernard, 367n29

Sherman, William Tecumseh, 140, 304

Sherman Indian Institute, 345

Shipek, Florence, 177

Shoshones, 81–82, 90, 91–92, 94, 164, 340

Simmons, Edward, 245

Sioux, 87, 115

6th U.S. Infantry, 288

Slotkin, Richard, 63

Smith, E. P., 342

Smith, Persifor, 140

Social Darwinism, 20, 56

Sonora (Mexico), 131

South Dakota, 341

Special Joint Committee on the Mendocino War, 232–36

"squaw men," 297–98

Stanford, Leland, Sr., 173–74, 254

Staub, Irving, 38, 365n8

Stearns, Abel, 370n13, 377n35

Stevenson, Edward, 303–4

St. Francis Ranch, Treaty of, 172, 174

Stohl, Michael, 48, 365n3

Storms, Simon P., 186, 191, 297, 325

Susanville, 247

Sutter, John, 78, 117

Sutter's Fort, 117

Tabeau, Baptiste, 98

Tate, Michael, 364n46

Tavivo (Paiute), 340–41

Tehachapi, 280

Tehama County, 179, 183–84, 196–200, 210–11, 292, 383n53

Tejón, 280, 281

Tejón Pass, 163–64, 166

Tejón Reservation. *See* Sebastian Military Reserve

Temecula, Treaty of, 167
Tenaya, Chief. *See* Yosemite, Chief (Ahwahnechee)
Texas Rangers, 137, 377n29
Thomas, Richard, 346
Thompson, Al, 172
Thompson, Lucy, 406n27
Tocqueville, Alexis de, 225, 229
Trafzer, Clifford, 7
Transcontinental Railroad, 336
Trinity River, 305
Tulare, 283
Tule Lake, 337–38
Turner, Frederick Jackson, 59–62, 367n42
Twain, Mark, 332, 402n86
21st U.S. Infantry, 338
Two Years before the Mast (Dana), 74–76, 84

Union, 328–29
Uniontown, 210
United Nations Convention on the Prevention and Punishment of the Crime of Genocide, 5, 14–17, 22–23
unratified treaties, 273–77
Unruh, John, Jr., 72, 111, 374n6
U.S. Army, 278, 286, 330, 336, 338. *See also* 6th U.S. Infantry; 21st U.S. Infantry
U.S. Department of the Interior, 272, 278, 289, 302
U.S. Department of War, 272, 289
U.S. Land Commission, 147, 375n6
U.S. Senate Committee on Indian Affairs, 347

Utah Territory, 120
Utes, 164

Vallejo, Mariano, 148
Van Ness, Sheriff, 329
Vetlesen, Arne, 20

Wailakis, 180
Walker, Joseph Redford, 91
Wansee Conference, 363n26
Wappos, 340
Ware, Joseph: *The Emigrant's Guide to California*, 103–4, 371n35
Warner, J. J., 144–48, 154, 156, 158, 161, 248, 377n35
Warner Springs, 156
Washoe, 254
Waterman, T. T., 357
Weaver, D. G., 166–67
Weller, John B., 1, 196–200, 204–7, 275–77, 279
Western Emigration Society, 77–78
Wetmore, Charles A., 343
Whipple, S. G., 288
White, Robert, 282
Wild, Peter, 285
Willard, Alexander Hamilton, 220
Wilsey, James, 293, 296
Wilshire, Bruce, 8, 183
Wilson, Benjamin, 161, 164–66, 377n35
Wilson, Jack. *See* Wovoka (Paiute)
Winn, A. M., 240–41
Wintuns, 340
Wintus, 180, 340
Wiyots, 274, 305–6, 326–30
Wodziwob (Paiute), 340

Woodman, G. H., 205, 215
Woolsey, Ronald, 259
Workman-Rowland Party, 85
Worster, Donald, 176
Wounded Knee Massacre, 341
Wovoka (Paiute), 341
Wozencraft, Oliver, 272
Wright, Benjamin, 213, 337–38

Yahis, 350, 352, 354–56
Yanas, 340

Yosemite, Chief (Ahwahnechee), 171
Yreka, 187–88, 213, 305, 307–8, 311, 337
Yreka Daily Appeal, 324
Yreka Journal, 317
Yukis, 6, 28–29, 180, 190–97, 199,
    201–2, 205, 216–17, 292, 294–96,
    298, 301, 303, 364n45
Yuma Crossing, 136, 143
Yumas. *See* Quechans
Yuroks, 340

CPSIA information can be obtained
at www.ICGtesting.com
Printed in the USA
LVHW042238110122
708276LV00001B/11

9 780803 269668